THE AENEID

Aeneas

THE AENEID
OF VIRGIL

A Verse Translation by
Allen Mandelbaum

With Thirteen Drawings by
Barry Moser

University of California Press

Berkeley   Los Angeles   London

University of California Press
Berkeley and Los Angeles, California
University of California Press, Ltd.
London, England
Copyright © 1971, 1981 by Allen Mandelbaum
First Paperback Printing 1982
ISBN 0-520-04550-5

Library of Congress Catalog Card Number: 80-53773
Printed in the United States of America

08 07 06 05
12 11 10 9

The paper used in this publication is both acid-free and totally
chlorine-free (TCF). It meets the minimum requirements of
ANSI/NISO Z39.48-1992 (R 1997) (Permanence of Paper). ∞

CONTENTS

This translation is inscribed to:

Giuseppe Ungaretti, for Aeneas,
lost Dido, pious Palinurus, and
the mind that moves across your *Promised Land;*
and Jonathan, my son, for a Dogon horseman
you hunted down one hot September noon,
that rider on the plains of Troy within us.

Rome · San Francisco · Orta S. Giulio · New York
May 1964 · May 1970

in memoriam
Giuseppe Ungaretti
February 8, 1888–June 1, 1970

PREFACE

On the fifth terrace of the Mountain of Purgatory, Dante and Virgil, ascending, meet Statius. Born in the century after Virgil's, Statius is the pagan poet whom Dante's scheme and passion redeem, proclaiming him a Christian. Before his is aware that he is speaking in the presence of Virgil, Statius declares that he had found the "mother" and "nurse" of his own poetry in the Aeneid, *whose "holy fire" provided "the sparks that warmed me, the seeds of my ardor." His* ardor *reaches for the almost-anagram* adore *(the word employed by the historical Statius at the end of the* Thebaid *to tell his love of "the divine* Aeneid*"). For he then exclaims that "to have lived on earth when Virgil lived—/ for that I would extend by one more year/ the time I owe before my exile's end." In sum, he would be willing to delay his entry to— and sacrifice one year of—Paradise, could he but set his eyes on Virgil. And when he learns from Dante that Dante's guide is indeed "that same Virgil from whom you have drawn/ the power to sing of men and of the gods," Statius bends to kiss the feet of his predecessor. Virgil's response is at once a caution against the deification of the human and a reminder that he and Statius are not bodies: "Brother, there's no need—/ you are a shade, a shade is what you see." Rising, Statius replies: "Now you can under-stand/ how much love burns in me for you, when I/ forget our insubstantiality,/ treating the shades as one treats solid things."*

Is translation but shade embracing shade—though with enough love to make one forget the emptiness of shades? Certainly, this new edition of my Aeneid *translation makes that forgetfulness more understandable, augmenting, as it does, the quantity of love with the added reach of Barry Moser's images. These images intersect and complement our long collaboration on the California Dante; they extend the lines of ascent, descent, allusion, evasion, metamorphosis, and willed and unwilled otherness that link the fictions of Virgil and Dante. In the mask that measures Aeneas's aloneness, reflecting the public weight of each private doubt; in Moser's metamorphosis of Raphael's and Baskin's Aeneas carrying Anchises, a gaunt reprise that fully enacts Delmore Schwartz's caption, "Child labor"; in the pathos of monstrosity outwitted in Polyphemus; in the blood of Dido, which trails across and beyond the superb formal web of her forensic rhetoric; in the un-Luciferian fall of the pious helmsman, Palinurus; in the brief sabbath amid wars and wanderings that is the glint of the golden bough; in the embrace of Venus and Vulcan, which incited Montaigne's most candid, cunning, disquieting yet strangely equanimous meanderings; in the frenzied war-horse of Book XI, an icon descended from the Dogon horse and rider my earlier preface had conjured, but now with the rider dead; and in the final weariness of Aeneas as killer in whom an unwilled fury rises from an unchartable, demonic grotto—in these images, lives that "have fled to Shades below" are re-embraced.*

For this edition, I am grateful to three tutelary presences: Stanley Holwitz, Toni Burbank, and Czeslaw Jan Grycz, tenacious editors, colleagues, co-makers.

A.M.

January, 1981

INTRODUCTION

I was late come to a full encounter with the *Aeneid*. Three judgments stood in my way. One was a tag line of Mark Van Doren that echoed through my youth with tenacious resonance: "Homer is a world; Virgil, a style" (a late variant of Coleridge's: "If you take from Virgil his diction and metre, what do you leave him?"). The second was a passage in a book long since hallowed for me, Georg Lukács' *Die Theorie des Romans:* "The heroes of Virgil live the cool and limited existence of shadows, nourished by the blood of noble zeal, blood that has been sacrificed in the attempt to recall what has forever disappeared." The third was Concetto Marchesi's personal version of the traditional comparison between Homer and Virgil in the most lucid history of Latin literature we have, his *Storia della letteratura latina.* There he was so alert to every defect of the *Aeneid* that its virtues seemed secondary. Marchesi was so splendid on Lucretius, then central to me, that with an illogical extension of trust, I allowed his estimate of the *Aeneid* to usurp my own reading.

All three obstacles were variations on the theme of Homer versus Virgil, using the father to club the son, coupled at times with some variations on the theme of Dante versus Virgil, using the son to club the father. Whichever way one turned in the line of affiliation (Homer-Virgil-Dante) —toward parricide or filicide—the middleman Virgil lost. Nor did another son of that same line, Milton, the English poet who filled the largest space within me when I was growing up, clear the way to the *Aeneid.* Milton was too separate, too massive a mountain then for me to see what lay behind him.

Three ways led me across these obstacles. On one I walked alone; on two my guides were Dante and Giuseppe Ungaretti. Let me begin with Ungaretti, who died as this preface was being written, one of two to whom this translation is dedicated. In the season of his life, in the autumn of his life that followed *Sentimento del tempo* (*Sentiment of Time*), Ungaretti's meditations mingled with Virgilian evocations in *La Terra Promessa* (*The Promised Land*). This was published in "final" form in 1950 with the Dido choruses and Palinurus sestina; in 1960 his *Il taccuino del vecchio* (*The Old Man's Notebook*) appeared with an additional 27 "Final Choruses for the Promised Land." In the mid-50's I had translated and introduced the 1950 *Promised Land* in *Poetry* and then in a volume of Ungaretti's selected poems called *Life of a Man;* and the final stages of the revision of the *Aeneid* were completed even as I prepared for publication a much fuller *Selected Poems of Giuseppe Ungaretti*, which includes some of the 1960 choruses. In those mid-50's years, then, these words of Ungaretti were often with me:

Perennial beauty (but bound inexorably to perishing, to images, to earthly vicissitudes, to history, and thus but *illusively* perennial, as Palinurus will say) assumed in my mind the aspect of Aeneas. Aeneas is beauty, youth, ingenuousness ever in search of a promised land, where, in the contemplated, fleeting beauty, his own beauty smiles and enchants. But it is not the myth of Narcissus: it is the animating union of the life of memory, of fantasy and of speculation, of the life of the mind; and it is, too, the fecund union of the carnal life in the long succession of generations.

Dido came to represent the experience of one who, in late autumn, is about to pass beyond it; the hour in which living is about to become barren; the hour of one from whom the horrible, tremendous, final tremor of youth is about to depart. Dido is the experience of nature as against the moral experience (Palinurus).

. . . *La Terra Promessa*, in any case, was, and is still, to begin at the point at which, Aeneas having touched the promised land, the figurations of his former experience awaken to attest to him, in memory, how his present experience, and all that may follow, will end, until, the ages consumed, it is given to men to know the true promised land.

Even when allegorical readings were less in fashion than they are today, Ungaretti could have been seen not only as "using" Virgil but as seeing into him. Here Ungaretti's Virgil is seen both *from* the autumn of a civilization, across the long divides of memory, and *as* the autumnal voice of a civilization, just as he is in Ungaretti's strangely beautiful reading of the first canto of the *Inferno*. In the later 1960 choruses, the promised land of Virgil fuses with the promised land of the Bible and with the terminus of all desire. But the "true promised land" is never a certainty. Much recent criticism has seen the ache and bite of doubt in the *Aeneid*, ever less—as we read more—a triumphant poem in praise of the *imperium* of Caesar Augustus. But for me, it was chiefly through Ungaretti that I saw in the *Aeneid* the underground denial—by consciousness and longing—of the total claims of the state and history: the persistence in the mind of what is not there, of what is absent, as a measure of the present. The young Lukács who found Virgil too "utopian," that is, casting back for what is irretrievable, was himself, at the end of *Die Theorie des Romans,* to leave the way open for his own later castings ahead, his affirmations of utopia as nearer and perhaps here, in the same climate that allowed the absolute conviction of Trotsky's 1924 coda to *Literature and Revolution:* "The average human type will rise to the heights of an Aristotle, a Goethe, or a Marx. And above this ridge new peaks will rise." Virgil was never so utopian, he never so deified the present or the future, and, as we shall soon see, he understood better the dynamics of deifying the past.

Witness: Van Doren in *The Noble Voice,* following a brilliant suggestion of Jacob Klein, brings to bear a passage from Plato's *Statesman* on the section in Book VI where Anchises says, "But all the rest, when they have passed time's circle / for a millennium, are summoned by / the god to Lethe in a great assembly / that, free of memory, they may return / beneath the curve of the upper world, that they / may once again begin to wish for bodies." In citing the *Statesman,* Van Doren assumes that Virgil was geared to the lulling myth of cycles, that he hoped for peace by "miracle" and "magic," never coming to terms with the fact that civilization is "arduous." But the man who had written the *Georgics* knew what human labor was; as did the man who, born in 70 B.C., spent the last eleven years of his life, before his death in 19 B.C., at work on one poem—leaving it still incompletely revised. He was not wagering all on the gods or on the man-made god Augustus. Not only is the very myth Anchises posits framed by the terminus of Book VI, with the query raised by Clausen as to its meaning; another, less enigmatic passage, often neglected, reminds us of how complex was Virgil's vision of god-making. In Book IX, 243-246, Nisus, about to embark on a mission, asks his comrade Euryalus: "Euryalus, is it / the gods who put this fire in our minds, / or is it that each man's relentless longing / becomes a god to him?" And the god of Nisus and Euryalus plays them false.

Far from belief in miracle and magic, in the utopian leap, there is in Virgil a sense of the lost as truly irretrievable. He was indeed a celebrator of dominion, of the rule of law: "For other peoples will, I do not doubt, / still cast their bronze to breathe with softer features, / or draw out of the marble living lines, / plead causes better, trace the ways of heaven / with wands and tell the rising constellations; / but yours will be the rulership of nations, / remember, Roman, these will be your arts: / to teach the ways of peace to those you conquer, / to spare defeated peoples, tame the proud" (VI, 1129-1137). But he is able to look with longing not only at the rule of Saturn (the gods, too, have their vicissitudes: Saturn had been evicted by Jupiter) of which Evander speaks in Book VIII, where Saturn is represented as a giver of laws, but also at Latinus' description of his people as *"needing no laws"*: "Do not forget / the Latins are a race of Saturn, needing / no laws and no restraint for righteousness; / they hold themselves in check by their own will / and by the customs of their ancient god" (VII, 267-271). This is more than a pastoral backward glance: Aeneas and Jupiter are to defeat the people of Saturn; but Virgil knows the price that is paid by the victory of the order of positive law over natural law. He knows, too, that his "Saturn" may be the product of his own "relentless longing," and just as powerless as that longing.

This then was the way on which Ungaretti first led me. But Ungaretti was a true Petrarchan (there is no Dantesque tradition in Italy); his is not a percussive line, moving ahead relentlessly toward certainties, but a self-reflexive line, moving toward queries, shaped by consciousness aware of its fragility and the fragility of its images. The way to Dante's Virgil was different. It need only be sketched here in part. In these last two decades, no poetic text has been closer to me than that of the *Commedia;* and for about a decade, I had planned to translate the *Inferno* with a full commentary. That translation is now complete, but in 1964, two years before I began to work on the *Inferno,* certain aspects of Virgil that I had felt through Dante gave the *Aeneid* priority. One aspect of Dante's Virgil is not too distant from Tennyson's "Wielder of the stateliest measure ever moulded by the lips of man"; this is the Virgil of *"lo bello stile,"* "the beautiful style," in Canto I of the *Inferno.* But Dante was able to learn from Virgil not only *the* beautiful style, but the *styles* of Virgil. Virgil cannot compare with Dante in the range of his lexis, in the range of the real he comprehends. His words are fewer than Dante's; and he and Dante belong to separate classes in the two types of poets distinguished by Donald Davie in *Purity of Diction in English Verse:* "One feels that Hopkins could have found a place for every word in the language if only he could have written enough poems. One feels the same about Shakespeare. But there are other poets, I find, with whom I feel the other thing—that a selection has been made and is continually being made, that words are thrusting at the poem and being fended off from it, that however many poems these poets wrote certain words would never be allowed into the poems, except as a disastrous oversight." One knows that Dante belongs in the first class, Virgil in the second. But Dante was not always in that first class; the writer of the *Vita nuova* and the *Canzoniere,* with their relative homogeneity—the homogeneity of eros—only passed into another and more complex order, the order of politics and history, with the *Commedia.* Virgil had not only preceded him there; he had preceded him there with a style that was not only "stately" but, as Macrobius noted in the *Saturnalia,* was "now brief, now full, now dry, now rich . . . now easy, now impetuous." Also, beginning with a tercet that marked clause or sentence somewhat mechanistically, Dante was to learn from Virgil a freer relation of line and syntax, a richer play of enjambment, *rejet,* and *contre-rejet.* The instances belong elsewhere; the lesson of freedom and definition is what is important here. That freedom also reached an area that Dante, the fastest of poets, never fully realized: the rapid shifts of tense in Virgil, the sudden intrusions of past on present and present on past within the narrative sequence itself (though the double lands of the narrative past and the present of simile were fully explored by Dante). There is no uniform explanation for these shifts in Virgil; but each instance counts in its place and is motivated there.

I have tried to impress what Macrobius heard and Dante learned on this translation, to embody both the grave tread and the speed and angularity Virgil can summon, the asymmetrical thrust of a mind on the move. I have tried to annul what too many readers of Virgil in modern translations have taken to be his: the flat and unvarious, and the loss of shape and energy where the end of the line is inert—neither reinforced nor resisted—and the mass of sound becomes amorphous and anonymous. In the course of that attempt, a part of the self says with Dryden, as he did on VIII, 364-365 (478-480 in our English): "For my part, I am lost in the admiration of it: I contemn the world when I think of it, and my self when I translate it"; the other part of the self brings me to the last way, the unmediated one.

That way is the path that opens when the guides, for whom one has been grateful, fall away or say: "I crown and miter you over yourself." Time, with all its density, does not disappear; but it seems to heighten and not to muffle the words of the past addressing us. And place, which for me at least had always been the last mode through which I heard a poet, after twelve years lived in the landscapes of Virgil, finally began, even as I was leaving Italy, to reinforce the voice of Virgil. That happened to me at a time of much personal discontent. I had long contemned any use of the poetic word for purposes of consolation. But pride lessens with the years, and Virgil consoled. The years of my work on this translation have widened that personal discontent; this state (no longer, with the Vietnam war, that innocuous

word "society") has wrought the unthinkable, the abomina-
ble. Virgil is not free of the taint of the proconsular; but he
speaks from a time of peace achieved, and no man ever felt
more deeply the part of the defeated and the lost. Above all,
if T. S. Eliot celebrated a Virgil who is linked to Dante in
the continuity that "led Europe towards the Christian cul-
ture he could not know," there is the other Virgil who calls
to mind deep discontinuities between antiquity and our-
selves. Virgil does not have Plato's humor; but he does
have Platonic tolerance (and more compassion than Plato).
And if the relative weights of the Epicurean, the Stoic, the
Pythagorean in him are often hard to assess, his humanity
is constant—and vital, not lumbering, not marmoreal. And
not shrill; and when, with the goad of public despair, my
own poetic voice has had to struggle often with shrillness,
the work on this translation has been most welcome.

Past these three ways—Ungaretti, Dante, self—there lies
another mode of encounter, where Virgil may be defined
in relation to others, but then speaks only as himself. Yeats,
at a critical point in his own work, in 1909, noted that:
"Our modern poetry is imaginative. It is the poetry of the
young. The poetry of the greatest periods is a sustained ex-
pression of the appetites and habits. Hence we select where
they exhausted." Virgil does not swarm with the "appetites
and habits" that pack Homer and Dante and Shakespeare.
He is not as exhaustive as they are; his is *a* world, not *the*
world. He is more selective, less objective, more bent on the
color that feeling casts. He seems to lie on the near—not
far—side of Wordsworth's watershed for modern poetry:
"The feeling therein developed gives importance to the
action and situation, and not the action and situation to the
feeling." But he is "sustained," and is not "of the young"
(though *for* them, and for the aged, too, of Plato's *Laws*);
and none of his selection and imagination seems to involve
what I think of as premature stripping, where the other
world of poetry takes over *before* this world is known:
Virgil selects *after* his knowing this world. For this, he is
a name-giver whose letters and syllables seem to imitate not
what Lukács called "the cool and limited existence of
shadows" but "the real nature of each thing."

Any work that spans six years in the life of a man must come to seem a communal project in his mind. The partial record of my gratefulness to those who have written on Virgil is recorded in the bibliographical note at the end of this volume. Beyond that, I am indebted to many. Sears Jayne, once the best of colleagues and always *"l'amico mio, e non de la ventura"* (as glossed by M. Casella), read portions of this manuscript in the third draft with the kind of care that made the numberless final draft possible, as did Jane Cooper, who has been for me the poet-reader each poet needs: may all my work be worthy of them both. My editor, Toni Burbank, watched over, nurtured, welcomed; Mrs. Ruth Hein, my copy editor, was quarrelsome, scrupulous, a pleasure; Mrs. Ila Traldi helped in many binds of time and spirit. Mrs. Efrem Slabotzky worked on the first draft of the glossary. Mrs. Sybil Langer was prodigal with comments on the early drafts, and Helen McNeil read the manuscript in its middle stages. Seth Benardete, M. T. Grendi, and G. Lanata helped with urgent queries. Susan Hirshfeld was my graduate assistant for two years; during and beyond that span, she has been totally patient with all drafts, with me; for all deadlines, she has served as conscience. My indebtedness to the late Giuseppe Ungaretti is more fully indicated earlier in this foreword and in the dedication; the dedication to my son is an incomplete expression of what his help has meant in countless details. (The Dogon horseman he pointed out to me in the fall of 1966 is a wood statue in the Museum of Primitive Art, reproduced as Number 227 in the Metropolitan's 1969 catalogue, *Art of Oceania, Africa, and the Americas.*) Helaine Newstead and my other colleagues and the students at the Graduate Center have made it a place where to teach is to learn, a place that has sustained me in the work that follows, in all work. All who were patient with my distracted presence and my needed absence while this translation was under way, and especially Bruce Bassoff, Hilail Gildin, Paul Mariani, Joseph Moses, and Isaak Orleans, have been *"amigos a quien amo / sobre todo tesoro."*

Allen Mandelbaum

The Graduate Center
The City University of New York
June, 1970

THE AENEID

I·166

BOOK I

I SING OF arms and of a man: his fate
had made him fugitive; he was the first
to journey from the coasts of Troy as far
as Italy and the Lavinian shores.
Across the lands and waters he was battered   5
beneath the violence of High Ones, for
the savage Juno's unforgetting anger;
and many sufferings were his in war—
until he brought a city into being
and carried in his gods to Latium;   10
from this have come the Latin race, the lords
of Alba, and the ramparts of high Rome.

Tell me the reason, Muse: what was the wound
to her divinity, so hurting her
that she, the queen of gods, compelled a man   15
remarkable for goodness to endure
so many crises, meet so many trials?
Can such resentment hold the minds of gods?

There was an ancient city they called Carthage—
a colony of refugees from Tyre—   20
a city facing Italy, but far

away from Tiber's mouth: extremely rich
and, when it came to waging war, most fierce.
This land was Juno's favorite—it is said—
more dear than her own Samos; here she kept   25
her chariot and armor; even then
the goddess had this hope and tender plan:
for Carthage to become the capital
of nations, if the Fates would just consent.
But she had heard that, from the blood of Troy,   30
a race had come that some day would destroy
the citadels of Tyre; from it, a people
would spring, wide-ruling kings, men proud in battle
and destined to annihilate her Libya.
The Fates had so decreed. And Saturn's daughter—   35
in fear of this, remembering the old war
that she had long since carried on at Troy
for her beloved Argos (and, indeed,
the causes of her bitterness, her sharp
and savage hurt, had not yet left her spirit;   40
for deep within her mind lie stored the judgment
of Paris and the wrong done to her scorned
beauty, the breed she hated, and the honors
that had been given ravished Ganymede)—
was angered even more; for this, she kept   45
far off from Latium the Trojan remnant
left by the Greeks and pitiless Achilles.
For long years they were cast across all waters,
fate-driven, wandering from sea to sea.
It was so hard to found the race of Rome.   50

With Sicily scarce out of sight, the Trojans
had gladly spread their canvas on the sea,
turning the salt foam with their brazen prows,
when Juno, holding fast within her heart
the everlasting insult, asked herself: 55
"Am I, defeated, simply to stop trying,
unable to turn back the Trojan king
from Italy? No doubt, the Fates won't have it.
But Pallas—was she powerful enough
to set the Argive fleet on fire, to drown   60
the crewmen in the deep, for an outrage done
by only one infuriated man,
Ajax, Oileus' son? And she herself

could fling Jove's racing lightning from the clouds
and smash their galleys, sweep the sea with tempests.   65
Then Ajax' breath was flame from his pierced chest;
she caught him up within a whirlwind; she
impaled him on a pointed rock. But I,
the queen of gods, who stride along as both
the sister and the wife of Jove, have warred   70
so many years against a single nation.
For after this, will anyone adore
the majesty of Juno or, before
her altars, pay her honor, pray to her?"

Then—burning, pondering—the goddess reaches   75
Aeolia, the motherland of storms,
a womb that always teems with raving south winds.
In his enormous cave King Aeolus
restrains the wrestling winds, loud hurricanes;
he tames and sways them with his chains and prison.   80
They rage in indignation at their cages;
the mountain answers with a mighty roar.
Lord Aeolus sits in his high citadel;
he holds his scepter, and he soothes their souls
and calms their madness. Were it not for this,   85
then surely they would carry off the sea
and lands and steepest heaven, sweeping them
across the emptiness. But fearing that,
the all-able Father hid the winds within
dark caverns, heaping over them high mountains;   90
and he assigned to them a king who should,
by Jove's sure edict, understand just when
to jail and when, commanded, to set free.
Then Juno, suppliant, appealed to him:

"You, Aeolus—to whom the king of men   95
and father of the gods has given this:
to pacify the waves or, with the wind,
to incite them—over the Tyrrhenian
now sails my enemy, a race that carries
the beaten household gods of Ilium   100
to Italy. Hammer your winds to fury
and ruin their swamped ships, or scatter them
and fling their crews piecemeal across the seas.
I have twice-seven nymphs with splendid bodies;

the loveliest of them is Deiopea,   105
and I shall join her to you in sure marriage
and name her as your own, that she may spend
all of her years with you, to make you father
of fair sons. For such service, such return."

And Aeolus replied: "O Queen, your task   110
is to discover what you wish; and mine,
to act at your command. For you have won
this modest kingdom for me, and my scepter,
and Jove's goodwill. You gave me leave to lean
beside the banquets of the gods, and you   115
have made me lord of tempests and of clouds."

His words were done. He turned his lance head, struck
the hollow mountain on its side. The winds,
as in a column, hurry through the breach;
they blow across the earth in a tornado.   120
Together, Eurus, Notus, and—with tempest
on tempest—Africus attack the sea;
they churn the very bottom of the deep
and roll vast breakers toward the beaches; cries
of men, the creaking of the cables rise.   125
Then, suddenly, the cloud banks snatch away
the sky and daylight from the Trojans' eyes.
Black night hangs on the waters, heavens thunder,
and frequent lightning glitters in the air;
everything intends quick death to men.   130

At once Aeneas' limbs fall slack with chill.
He groans and stretches both hands to the stars.
He calls aloud: "O, three and four times blessed
were those who died before their fathers' eyes
beneath the walls of Troy. Strongest of all   135
the Danaans, o Diomedes, why
did your right hand not spill my lifeblood, why
did I not fall upon the Ilian fields,
there where ferocious Hector lies, pierced by
Achilles' javelin, where the enormous   140
Sarpedon now is still, and Simois
has seized and sweeps beneath its waves so many
helmets and shields and bodies of the brave!"

Aeneas hurled these words. The hurricane
is howling from the north; it hammers full   145
against his sails. The seas are heaved to heaven.
The oars are cracked; the prow sheers off; the waves
attack broadside; against his hull the swell
now shatters in a heap, mountainous, steep.
Some sailors hang upon a wave crest; others   150
stare out at gaping waters, land that lies
below the waters, surge that seethes with sand.
And then the south wind snatches up three ships
and spins their keels against the hidden rocks—
those rocks that, rising in midsea, are called   155
by the Italians "Altars"—like a monstrous
spine stretched along the surface of the sea.
Meanwhile the east wind wheels another three
off from the deep and, terrible to see,
against the shoals and shifting silt, against   160
the shallows, girding them with mounds of sand.

Before Aeneas' eyes a massive breaker
smashes upon its stern the ship that carries
the Lycian crewmen led by true Orontes.
The helmsman is beaten down; he is whirled headlong. 165
Three times at that same spot the waters twist
and wheel the ship around until a swift
whirlpool has swallowed it beneath the swell.
And here and there upon the wide abyss,
among the waves, are swimmers, weapons, planks,   170
and Trojan treasure. Now the tempest takes
the sturdy galleys of Ilioneus
and brave Achates, now the ships of Abas
and many-yeared Aletes; all receive
their enemy, the sea, through loosened joints   175
along their sides and through their gaping seams.

But Neptune felt the fracas and the frenzy;
and shaken by the unleashed winds, the wrenching
of the still currents from the deep seabed,
he raised his tranquil head above the surface.   180
And he can see the galleys of Aeneas
scattered across the waters, with the Trojans
dismembered by the waves and fallen heavens.
Her brother did not miss the craft and wrath

of Juno. Catching that, he calls up both   185
the east wind and the west. His words are these:

"Has pride of birth made you so insolent?
So, Winds, you dare to mingle sky and land,
heave high such masses, without my command?
Whom I——? But no, let me first calm the restless   190
swell; you shall yet atone—another time—
with different penalties for these your crimes.
But now be off, and tell your king these things:
that not to him, but me, has destiny
allotted the dominion of the sea   195
and my fierce trident. The enormous rocks
are his—your home, East Wind. Let Aeolus
be lord of all that lies within that hall
and rule in that pent prison of the winds."

So Neptune speaks and, quicker than his tongue,   200
brings quiet to the swollen waters, sets
the gathered clouds to flight, calls back the sun.
Together, then, Cymothoë and Triton,
thrusting, dislodge the ships from jagged crags.
But now the god himself takes up his trident   205
to lift the galleys, and he clears a channel
across the vast sandbank. He stills the sea
and glides along the waters on light wheels.
And just as, often, when a crowd of people
is rocked by a rebellion, and the rabble   210
rage in their minds, and firebrands and stones
fly fast—for fury finds its weapons—if,
by chance, they see a man remarkable
for righteousness and service, they are silent
and stand attentively; and he controls   215
their passion by his words and cools their spirits:
so all the clamor of the sea subsided
after the Father, gazing on the waters
and riding under cloudless skies, had guided
his horses, let his willing chariot run.   220

And now Aeneas' weary crewmen hurry
to find the nearest land along their way.
They turn toward Libya's coast. There is a cove
within a long, retiring bay; and there

an island's jutting arms have formed a harbor   225
where every breaker off the high sea shatters
and parts into the shoreline's winding shelters.
Along this side and that there towers, vast,
a line of cliffs, each ending in like crags;
beneath the ledges tranquil water lies   230
silent and wide; the backdrop—glistening
forests and, beetling from above, a black
grove, thick with bristling shadows. Underneath
the facing brow: a cave with hanging rocks,
sweet waters, seats of living stone, the home   235
of nymphs. And here no cable holds tired ships,
no anchor grips them fast with curving bit.

Aeneas shelters here with seven ships—
all he can muster, all the storm has left.
The Trojans, longing so to touch the land,   240
now disembark to gain the wished-for sands.
They stretch their salt-soaked limbs along the beach.
Achates was the first to strike a spark
from flint and catch the fire up with leaves.
He spread dry fuel about, and then he waved   245
the tinder into flame. Tired of their trials,
the Trojan crewmen carry out the tools
of Ceres and the sea-drenched corn of Ceres.
And they prepare to parch the salvaged grain
by fire and, next, to crush it under stone.   250

Meanwhile Aeneas climbs a crag to seek
a prospect far and wide across the deep,
if he can only make out anything
of Antheus and his Phrygian galleys, or
of Capys, or the armor of Caicus   255
on his high stern. There is no ship in sight;
all he can see are three stags wandering
along the shore, with whole herds following
behind, a long line grazing through the valley.
He halted, snatched his bow and racing arrows,   260
the weapons carried by the true Achates.
And first he lays the leaders low, their heads
held high with tree-like antlers; then he drives
the herds headlong into the leafy groves;
they panic, like a rabble, at his arrows.   265

He does not stay his hand until he stretches,
victoriously, seven giant bodies
along the ground, in number like his galleys.
This done, he seeks the harbor and divides
the meat among his comrades. And he shares   270
the wine that had been stowed by kind Acestes
in casks along the shores of Sicily:
the wine that, like a hero, the Sicilian
had given to the Trojans when they left.
Aeneas soothes their melancholy hearts: 275

"O comrades—surely we're not ignorant
of earlier disasters, we who have suffered
things heavier than this—our god will give
an end to this as well. You have neared the rage
of Scylla and her caves' resounding rocks;   280
and you have known the Cyclops' crags; call back
your courage, send away your grieving fear.
Perhaps one day you will remember even
these our adversities with pleasure. Through
so many crises and calamities   285
we make for Latium, where fates have promised
a peaceful settlement. It is decreed
that there the realm of Troy will rise again.
Hold out, and save yourselves for kinder days."

These are his words; though sick with heavy cares,   290
he counterfeits hope in his face; his pain
is held within, hidden. His men make ready
the game that is to be their feast; they flay
the deer hide off the ribs; the flesh lies naked.
Some slice off quivering strips and pierce them with   295
sharp spits, while on the beach the others set
caldrons of brass and tend the flame. With food
their strength comes back again. Along the grass
they stretch and fill their bellies full of fat
venison meat and well-aged wine. That done—   300
their hunger banished by their feasting and
the tables cleared—their talk is long, uncertain
between their hope and fear, as they ask after
their lost companions, wondering if their comrades
are still alive or if they have undergone   305
the final change and can no longer hear

when called upon. Especially the pious
Aeneas moans within himself the loss
now of the vigorous Orontes, now
of Amycus, the cruel end of Lycus,   310
the doom of brave Cloanthus, of brave Gyas.

Their food and talk were done when Jupiter,
while gazing from the peaks of upper air
across the waters winged with canvas and
low-lying lands and shores and widespread peoples,   315
stood high upon the pinnacle of heaven
until he set his sight on Libya's kingdom.
And as he ponders this, the saddened Venus,
her bright eyes dimmed and tearful, speaks to him:

"O you who, with eternal rule, command   320
and govern the events of gods and men,
and terrify them with your thunderbolt,
what great offense has my Aeneas given,
what is his crime, what have the Trojans done
that, having undergone so many deaths,   325
the circle of all lands is shut against them—
and just because of Italy? Surely
you have sworn that out of them, in time to come,
with turning years, the Romans will be born
and, from the resurrected blood of Teucer,   330
rise up as rulers over sea and land?
What motive, Father, made you change? That promise
was solace for Troy's fall and its sad ruin;
I weighed this fate against the adverse fates.
But now their former fortune still pursues   335
the Trojans driven by so many evils.
Great king, is there no end to this ordeal?
Antenor could escape the Argive army,
then make his way through the Illyrian bays,
the inner lands of the Liburnians,   340
and safely cross the source of the Timavus,
where, with a mighty mountain's roar, it rushes
through nine mouths, till its flood bursts, overwhelming
the fields beneath with its resounding waters.
Yet here he planted Padua, a town   345
and home for Teucrians, and gave his nation
a name and then hung up the arms of Troy;

and now, serene, he tastes tranquillity.
But we, your very children, we whom you
had promised heaven's heights, have lost our ships—   350
unspeakable! Just for the rage of one
we are betrayed, kept far from Italy.
Is this the way you give us back our scepter?"

But then he smiled upon her—Jupiter,
father of men and gods—just as he calms   355
the heavens and the storms. He lightly kissed
his daughter's lips; these were his words to Venus:
"My Cytherea, that's enough of fear;
your children's fate is firm; you'll surely see
the walls I promised you, Lavinum's city;   360
and you shall carry your great-hearted son,
Aeneas, high as heaven's stars. My will
is still the same; I have not changed. Your son
(I now speak out—I know this anxiousness
is gnawing at you; I unroll the secret   365
scroll of the Fates, awake its distant pages)
shall wage tremendous war in Italy
and crush ferocious nations and establish
a way of life and walls for his own people—
until the time of his third summer as   370
the king of Latium, until he has passed
three winters since he overcame the Latins.
But then the boy Ascanius, who now
is carrying Iülus as his surname (while
the state of Ilium held fast, he still   375
was known as Ilus), with his rule shall fill
the wheeling months of thirty mighty years.
He shall remove his kingdom from Lavinium
and, powerful, build Alba Longa's walls.
For full three hundred years, the capital   380
and rule of Hector's race shall be at Alba,
until a royal priestess, Ilia,
with child by Mars, has brought to birth twin sons.
And then, rejoicing in the tawny hide
of his nursemaid, the she-wolf, Romulus   385
shall take the rulership and build the walls
of Mars' own city. Romulus shall call
that people 'Romans,' after his own name.
I set no limits to their fortunes and

no time; I give them empire without end.   390
Then even bitter Juno shall be changed;
for she, who now harasses lands and heavens
with terror, then shall hold the Romans dear
together with me, cherishing the masters
of all things, and the race that wears the toga.   395
This is what I decree. An age shall come
along the way of gliding lustra when
the house born of Assaracus shall hold
both Phthia and illustrious Mycenae
and rule defeated Argos. Then a Trojan   400
Caesar shall rise out of that splendid line.
His empire's boundary shall be the Ocean;
the only border to his fame, the stars.
His name shall be derived from great Iülus,
and shall be Julius. In time to come,   405
no longer troubled, you shall welcome him
to heaven, weighted with the Orient's wealth;
he, too, shall be invoked with prayers. With battle
forgotten, savage generations shall
grow generous. And aged Faith and Vesta,   410
together with the brothers, Romulus
and Remus, shall make laws. The gruesome gates
of war, with tightly welded iron plates,
shall be shut fast. Within, unholy Rage
shall sit on his ferocious weapons, bound   415
behind his back by a hundred knots of brass;
he shall groan horribly with bloody lips."

The words of Jupiter are done. He sends
the son of Maia down from heaven that
the newfound lands and fortresses of Carthage   420
be opened wide in welcome to the Trojans;
that Dido, ignorant of destiny,
not drive away Aeneas from her boundaries.
He flies across the great air; using wings
as oars, he quickly lands on Libyan shores.   425
He does as he was told. And the Phoenicians
now set aside their savagery before
the will of god; and Dido, above all,
receives into her spirit kindliness,
a gracious mind to greet the Teucrians.   430

     ❂   ❂   ❂

But, nightlong, many cares have held the pious
Aeneas. And as soon as gracious daylight
is given to him, this is his decision:
to go out and explore this foreign country,
to learn what shores the wind has brought him to,   435
who lives upon this land—it is untilled—
are they wild beasts or men—and then to tell
his comrades what he has found. He hides his fleet
inside the narrows of the wooded cove,
beneath a hollow rock shut in by trees,   440
with bristling shades around. And he himself,
only Achates at his side, moves on;
he brandishes two shafts tipped with broad iron.

But in the middle of the wood, along
the way, his mother showed herself to him.   445
The face and dress she wore were like a maiden's,
her weapons like a girl's from Sparta or
those carried by Harpalyce of Thrace
when she tires out her horses, speeding faster
even than rapid Hebrus as she races.   450
For, as a huntress would, across her shoulder,
Venus had slung her bow in readiness;
her hair was free, disheveled by the wind;
her knees were bare; her tunic's flowing folds
were gathered in a knot. And she speaks first: 455
"Young men there! Can you tell me if by chance
you have seen one of my sisters pass—she wore
a quiver and a spotted lynx's hide—
while she was wandering here or, with her shouts,
chasing a foaming boar along its course?"   460

So Venus. Answering, her son began:
"I have not seen or heard your sister, maiden—
or by what name am I to call you, for
your voice is not like any human voice.
O goddess, you must be Apollo's sister   465
or else are to be numbered with the nymphs!
Whoever you may be, do help us, ease
our trials; do tell us underneath what skies,
upon what coasts of earth we have been cast;
we wander, ignorant of men and places,   470
and driven by the wind and the vast waves.

Before your altars many victims will
fall at our hands, as offerings to you."

Then Venus: "I can hardly claim such honor.
The girls of Tyre are used to wearing quivers   475
and bind their calves with scarlet hunting boots.
You see a Punic country, men of Tyre,
the city of Agenor; but at the border
the Libyans lie—a tribe that swears by war.
Our ruler here is Dido, she who left   480
her city when she had to flee her brother.
The tale of wrong is intricate and long,
but I s'hall trace its chief events in order.

"Her husband was Sychaeus: wealthiest
landowner in Phoenicia. For her father   485
had given her, a virgin, to Sychaeus
and joined them with the omens of first marriage.
Unhappy Dido loved him with much passion.
Pygmalion, her brother, held the kingdom
of Tyre; beyond all men he was a monster   490
in crime. Between Sychaeus and her brother
dividing fury came. Pygmalion—
unholy, blind with lust for gold—in secret
now catches Dido's husband off his guard
and cuts him down by sword before the altars,   495
heedless of his own sister's love. For long
he kept this hidden and, insidious,
invented many stories to mock Dido—
she is sick and longing—with an empty hope.
But in her sleep, to Dido came the very   500
image of her unburied husband; he
lifted his pallid face—amazingly—
and laid bare to his wife the cruel altars,
his breast impaled upon the blade, revealing
to her the hidden horror of the house.   505
He urges her to speed her flight, to leave
her homeland; and to help her journey, he
discloses ancient treasure in the earth,
a hoard of gold and silver known to none.
And Dido, moved by this, prepared her flight   510
and her companions. Now there come together
both those who felt fierce hatred for the tyrant

and those who felt harsh fear. They seize the ships
that happen to be ready, loading them
with gold. The wealth of covetous Pygmalion   515
is carried overseas. A woman leads.
They landed at the place where now you see
the citadel and high walls of new Carthage
rising; and then they bought the land called Byrsa,
'The Hide,' after the name of that transaction   520
(they got what they were able to enclose
inside a bull's skin). But who, then, are you?
From what coasts have you come? Where are you going?"
To these her questions he replied with sighs;
he drew his words from deep within his breast: 525

"O goddess, if I tracked my story back
until its first beginning, were there time
to hear the annals of our trials, then
the evening would have shut Olympus' gates
and gathered in the day before I ended.   530
But we were sailing out from ancient Troy—
if Troy means anything to you—across
strange seas when, as it willed, a tempest drove us
upon the coasts of Libya. I am pious
Aeneas, and I carry in my ships   535
my household gods together with me, rescued
from Argive enemies; my fame is known
beyond the sky. I seek out Italy,
my country, my ancestors born of Jove.
When I set out upon the Phrygian sea,   540
I had twice-ten ships, and my goddess-mother
showed me the way; I followed my firm fates.
Now I am left with scarcely seven galleys,
ships shattered by the waves and the east wind;
and I myself, a needy stranger, roam   545
across the wilderness of Libya; I
am driven out of Europe, out of Asia."
But Venus had enough of his complaints,
and so she interrupted his lament:

"Whoever you may be, I hardly think   550
the heaven-dwellers hold a grudge against you:
the breath of life is yours, and you are near
a Tyrian city. Only make your way
until you reach the palace of the queen.

For I can tell you truthfully: your comrades   555
are given back to you, your fleet is saved
and driven toward sure waters by the winds
that shifted to the north—unless my parents
have taught me augury to no good end.
Look there, where you can make out twice-six swans   560
that gladly file along, whom once the bird
of Jupiter had scattered, swooping down
from upper air into the open sky.
And now, in long array, they either seem
to settle down or else to hover, waiting   565
and watching those that have already landed;
and just as they, returning, play with rustling
wings, as they wheel about the sky in crews,
and give themselves to song—not otherwise
your ships and youths are either in the harbor   570
or near its mouth with swelling sails. Only
move on and follow where this pathway leads."

These were the words of Venus. When she turned,
her neck was glittering with a rose brightness;
her hair anointed with ambrosia,   575
her head gave all a fragrance of the gods;
her gown was long and to the ground; even
her walk was sign enough she was a goddess.

And when Aeneas recognized his mother,
he followed her with these words as she fled: 580
"Why do you mock your son—so often and
so cruelly—with these lying apparitions?
Why can't I ever join you, hand to hand,
to hear, to answer you with honest words?"

So he reproaches her, then takes the road   585
to Carthage. But as goddess, Venus cloaks
Aeneas and Achates in dark mist;
she wraps them in a cape of cloud so thick
that none can see or touch them or delay
their way or ask why they had come. And she   590
herself glides through the skies to Paphos, gladly
revisiting her home, her temple and
her hundred altars fragrant with fresh garlands
and warm with their Sabaean frankincense.
    ❁   ❁   ❁

Meanwhile Aeneas and the true Achates   595
press forward on their path. They climb a hill
that overhangs the city, looking down
upon the facing towers. Aeneas marvels
at the enormous buildings, once mere huts,
and at the gates and tumult and paved streets.   600
The eager men of Tyre work steadily:
some build the city walls or citadel—
they roll up stones by hand; and some select
the place for a new dwelling, marking out
its limits with a furrow; some make laws,   605
establish judges and a sacred senate;
some excavate a harbor; others lay
the deep foundations for a theater,
hewing tremendous pillars from the rocks,
high decorations for the stage to come.   610
Just as the bees in early summer, busy
beneath the sunlight through the flowered meadows,
when some lead on their full-grown young and others
press out the flowing honey, pack the cells
with sweet nectar, or gather in the burdens   615
of those returning; some, in columns, drive
the drones, a lazy herd, out of the hives;
the work is fervent, and the fragrant honey
is sweet with thyme. "How fortunate are those
whose walls already rise!" Aeneas cries   620
while gazing at the rooftops of the city.
Then, sheltered by a mist, astoundingly,
he enters in among the crowd, mingling
together with the Tyrians. No one sees him.

Just at the center of the city stood   625
a thickly shaded wood; this was the place
where, when they landed, the Phoenicians first—
hurled there by whirlwind and by wave—dug up
an omen that Queen Juno had pointed out:
the head of a fierce stallion. This had meant   630
the nation's easy wealth and fame in war
throughout the ages. Here Sidonian Dido
was building a stupendous shrine for Juno,
enriched with gifts and with the goddess' statue,
where flights of steps led up to brazen thresholds;   635
the architraves were set on posts of brass;

the grating hinges of the doors were brass.
Within this grove, the sights—so strange to him—
have, for the first time, stilled Aeneas' fear;
here he first dared to hope he had found shelter,   640
to trust more surely in his shattered fortunes.
For while he waited for the queen, he studied
everything in that huge sanctuary,
marveling at a city rich enough
for such a temple, at the handiwork   645
of rival artists, at their skillful tasks.
He sees the wars of Troy set out in order:
the battles famous now through all the world,
the sons of Atreus and of Priam, and
Achilles, savage enemy to both.   650
He halted. As he wept, he cried: "Achates,
where on this earth is there a land, a place
that does not know our sorrows? Look! There is Priam!
Here, too, the honorable finds its due
and there are tears for passing things; here, too,   655
things mortal touch the mind. Forget your fears;
this fame will bring you some deliverance."
He speaks. With many tears and sighs he feeds
his soul on what is nothing but a picture.

He watched the warriors circling Pergamus: 660
here routed Greeks were chased by Trojan fighters
and here the Phrygian troops pursued by plumed
Achilles in his chariot. Nearby,
sobbing, he recognized the snow-white canvas
tents of King Rhesus—with his men betrayed,   665
while still in their first sleep, and then laid waste,
with many dead, by bloody Diomedes,
who carried off their fiery war horses
before they had a chance to taste the pastures
of Troy, or drink the waters of the Xanthus.   670

Elsewhere young Troilus, the unhappy boy—
he is matched unequally against Achilles—
runs off, his weapons lost. He is fallen flat;
his horses drag him on as he still clings
fast to his empty chariot, clasping   675
the reins. His neck, his hair trail on the ground,
and his inverted spear inscribes the dust.

Meanwhile the Trojan women near the temple
of Pallas, the unkindly; hair disheveled,
sad, beating at their breasts, as suppliants,   680
they bear the robe of offering. The goddess
averts her face, her eyes fast to the ground.

Three times Achilles had dragged Hector round
the walls of Troy, selling his lifeless body
for gold. And then, indeed, Aeneas groans   685
within the great pit of his chest, deeply;
for he can see the spoils, the chariot,
the very body of his friend, and Priam
pleading for Hector with defenseless hands.
He also recognized himself in combat   690
with the Achaean chiefs, then saw the Eastern
battalions and the weapons of black Memnon.
Penthesilea in her fury leads
the ranks of crescent-shielded Amazons.
She flashes through her thousands; underneath   695
her naked breast, a golden girdle; soldier-
virgin and queen, daring to war with men.

But while the Dardan watched these scenes in wonder,
while he was fastened in a stare, astonished,
the lovely-bodied Dido neared the temple,   700
a crowding company of youths around her.
And just as, on the banks of the Eurotas
or though the heights of Cynthus, when Diana
incites her dancers, and her followers,
a thousand mountain-nymphs, press in behind her,   705
she wears a quiver slung across her shoulder;
and as she makes her way, she towers over
all other goddesses; gladness excites
Latona's silent breast: even so, Dido;
so, in her joy, she moved among the throng   710
as she urged on the work of her coming kingdom.

And then below the temple's central dome—
facing the doorway of the goddess, guarded
by arms—she took her place on a high throne.
Dido was dealing judgments to her people   715
and giving laws, apportioning the work
of each with fairness or by drawing lots;

when suddenly Aeneas sees, as they
press forward through that mighty multitude,
Sergestus, Antheus, and the brave Cloanthus,   720
and other Trojans whom the black whirlwind
had scattered on the waters, driven far
to other coasts. Aeneas is astounded;
both joy and fear have overcome Achates.
They burned to join right hands with their companions, 725
but this strange happening confuses them.
They stay in hiding, screened by folds of fog,
and wait to see what fortune found their friends,
on what beach they have left the fleet, and why
they come; for these were men who had been chosen   730
from all the ships to ask for grace, who now
made for the temple door with loud outcries.

When they had entered and received their leave
to speak in Dido's presence, then the eldest,
Ilioneus, calmly began: "O Queen,   735
whom Jupiter has granted this: to bring
to being a new city, curbing haughty
nations by justice—we, unhappy Trojans,
men carried by the winds across all seas,
beg you to keep the terror of fire from   740
our fleet, to spare a pious race, to look
on with us kindliness. We do not come
to devastate your homes and with the sword
to loot the household gods of Libya or
to drive down stolen booty toward the beaches.   745
That violence is not within our minds;
such arrogance is not for the defeated.
There is a place the Greeks have named Hesperia,
an ancient land with strong arms and fat soil.
Its colonists were the Oenotrians.   750
Now rumor runs that their descendants call
that nation 'Italy,' after their leader.
Our prows were pointed there when suddenly,
rising upon the surge, stormy Orion
drove us against blind shoals; and insolent   755
south winds then scattered us, undone by brine,
across the crushing sea, the pathless rocks.
A few of us have drifted to your shores.
What kind of men are these? Or is your country

so barbarous that it permits this custom?   760
We are denied the shelter of the beach;
they goad us into war; they will not let us
set foot upon the border of their land.
If you despise the human race and mortal
weapons, then still consider that the gods   765
remember right and wrong. We had a king,
Aeneas, none more just, no one more pious,
no man his better in the arts of war.
If fate has saved this man, if he still feeds
upon the upper air, if he is not   770
laid low to rest among the cruel Shades,
then we are not afraid and you will not
repent if you compete with him in kindness.
Within Sicilian territory, too,
are fields and cities and the famed Acestes,   775
born of the blood of Troy. Let us haul up
our fleet, smashed by the winds, along your beaches
and fit out timber from your forests, trim
our oars; and if we find our king and comrades
and are allowed to turn toward Italy   780
and Latium, then let us sail out gladly.
But if our shelter there has been denied us,
and you, the finest father of the Trojans,
were swallowed by the sea of Libya, and
no hope is left us now for Iülus, then   785
at least let us seek out again the straits
of Sicily, the land from which we sailed.
There houses wait for us, and King Acestes."
So spoke Ilioneus. The other sons
of Dardanus approved his words with shouts.   790

Then Dido softly, briefly answers him:
"O Teucrians, enough of fear, cast out
your cares. My kingdom is new; hard circumstances
have forced me to such measures for our safety,
to post guards far and wide along our boundaries.   795
But who is ignorant of Aeneas' men?
Who has not heard of Troy, its acts and heroes,
the flames of that tremendous war? We Tyrians
do not have minds so dull, and we are not
beyond the circuit of the sun's yoked horses.   800
Whatever you may choose—Hesperia and

the fields of Saturn, or the land of Eryx
and King Acestes—I shall send you safe
with escort, I shall help you with my wealth.
And should you want to settle in this kingdom   805
on equal terms with me, then all the city
I am building now is yours. Draw up your ships.
I shall allow no difference between
the Tyrian and the Trojan. Would your king,
Aeneas, too, were present, driven here   810
by that same south wind. I, in fact, shall send
my trusted riders out along the shores,
to comb the farthest coasts of Libya and
to see if, cast out of the waters, he
is wandering through the forests or the cities."   815

The words of Dido stir the brave Achates
and father Aeneas; long since, both of them
had burned to break free from their cloud. Achates
speaks first to his companion: "Goddess-born,
what counsel rises in your spirit now?   820
You see that everything is safe, our ships
and sailors saved. And only one is missing,
whom we ourselves saw sink among the waves.
All else is as your mother said it would be."

Yet he was hardly done when suddenly   825
the cloud that circled them is torn; it clears
away to open air. And there Aeneas
stood, glittering in that bright light, his face
and shoulders like a god's. Indeed, his mother
had breathed upon her son becoming hair,   830
the glow of a young man, and in his eyes,
glad handsomeness: such grace as art can add
to ivory, or such as Parian marble
or silver shows when set in yellow gold.

But then, surprising all, he tells the queen: 835
"The man you seek is here. I stand before you,
Trojan Aeneas, torn from Libyan waves.
O you who were alone in taking pity
on the unutterable trials of Troy,
who welcome us as allies to your city   840
and home—a remnant left by Greeks, harassed

by all disasters known on land and sea,
in need of everything—we cannot, Dido,
repay you, then, with gratitude enough
to match your merits, neither we nor any   845
Dardans scattered over this great world.
May gods confer on you your due rewards,
if deities regard the good, if justice
and mind aware of right count anywhere.
What happy centuries gave birth to you?   850
What splendid parents brought you into being?
While rivers run into the sea and shadows
still sweep the mountain slopes and stars still pasture
upon the sky, your name and praise and honor
shall last, whatever be the lands that call me."   855
This said, he gives his right hand to his friend
Ilioneus; his left he gives Serestus;
then turns to brave Cloanthus and brave Gyas.

First at the very sight of him, and then
at all he had endured, Sidonian Dido   860
was startled. And she told the Trojan this:
"You, goddess-born, what fortune hunts you down
through such tremendous trials? What violence
has forced you onto these ferocious shores?
Are you that same Aeneas, son of Dardan   865
Anchises, whom the gracious Venus bore
beside the banks of Phrygian Simois?
Indeed, I still remember banished Teucer,
a Greek who came to Sidon from his native
kingdom, when with the help of Belus he   870
was seeking out new realms (my father Belus
was plundering then, as victor, wealthy Cyprus).
And even then I learned of Troy's disaster,
and of your name and of the kings of Greece.
And though he was the Trojans' enemy,   875
Teucer would often praise the Teucrians
and boast that he was born of their old race.
Thus, young men, you are welcome to our halls.
My destiny, like yours, has willed that I,
a veteran of hardships, halt at last   880
in this country. Not ignorant of trials,
I now can learn to help the miserable."
    ❋   ❋   ❋

So Dido speaks. At once she leads Aeneas
into the royal palace and announces
her offerings in the temples of the gods.   885
But meanwhile she does not neglect his comrades.
She sends down to the beaches twenty bullocks,
a hundred fat lambs with their ewes, and Bacchus'
glad gift of wine. Within the palace gleam
the furnishings of royal luxury;   890
the feast is readied in the atrium.
And there are draperies of noble purple
woven with art; and plate of massive silver
upon the tables; and, engraved in gold,
the sturdy deeds of Dido's ancestors,   895
a long, long line of happenings and heroes
traced from the first beginnings of her race.

Aeneas (for his father's love could not
permit his mind to rest) now quickly sends
Achates to the Trojan ships, to carry   900
these tidings to Ascanius, to lead
Aeneas' son up to the walls of Carthage:
all his paternal love and care are for
Ascanius. He also tells Achates
to bring back gifts snatched from the wreck of Troy: 905
a tunic stiff with images of gold,
and then a veil whose fringes were of saffron
acanthus—these once worn by Argive Helen,
who had borne them off to Troy and her unlawful
wedding when she had fled Mycenae—splendid   910
gifts of her mother Leda; and besides,
the scepter that had once been carried by
Ilione, eldest of Priam's daughters,
a necklace set with pearls, and then a crown
that had twin circles set with jewels and gold.   915
And hurrying to do all he was told,
Achates made his way down to the boats.

But in her breast the Cytherean ponders
new stratagems, new guile: that Cupid, changed
in form and feature, come instead of sweet   920
Ascanius and, with his gifts, inflame
the queen to madness and insinuate

a fire in Dido's very bones. For Venus
is much afraid of that deceptive house
and of the Tyrians with their double tongues.   925
The thought of savage Juno burns; by night
her care returns. Her words are for winged Love:

"Son, you are my only strength, my only power;
son, you who scorn the shafts of the great Father's
Typhoean thunderbolts, I flee to you   930
for refuge; suppliant, I call upon
the force within your godhead. For you know
how, through the hatred of resentful Juno,
across the sea and every shore your brother
Aeneas has been hunted down; and often   935
you have sorrowed with my sorrow. Now Phoenician
Dido has hold of him; with sweet words she
would make him stay. The hospitality
of Juno—and where it may lead—makes me
afraid; at such a turn I know she'll not   940
be idle. So, before she has a chance,
I plan to catch the queen by craftiness,
to girdle Dido with a flame, so that
no god can turn her back; I'll hold her fast
with great love for Aeneas. Hear me now;   945
I need your help to carry out this plot.
Ascanius, my dearest care, is ready
to go along to the Sidonian city,
called by his loving father, carrying
gifts saved from Troy in flames and from the sea.   950
But I shall lull the royal boy to sleep
on high Cythera or Idalium
and hide him in my holy house, so that
he cannot know—or interrupt—our trap.
And you will need—for one night and no more—   955
to counterfeit his features; as a boy,
to wear that boy's familiar face, and so
when Dido, joyful, draws you close during
the feasting and the flowing wine, when she
embraces you, and kisses tenderly,   960
your breath can fill her with a hidden flame,
your poison penetrate, deceivingly."

Love does what his dear mother asks. He sheds
his wings and gladly tries the walk of Iülus.
But Venus pours upon Ascanius   965
a gentle rest. She takes him to her breast
caressingly; and as a goddess can,
she carries him to her Idalium
where, in high groves, mild marjoram enfolds him
in flowers and the breath of its sweet shade.   970

Now Cupid's on his way, as he was told.
Gladly—Achates is his guide—he brings
the Tyrians royal gifts. As he arrives,
he finds the banqueting begun, the queen
already settled on her couch of gold   975
beneath resplendent awnings, at the center.
Father Aeneas and the Trojan warriors
now gather; they recline on purple covers.
The servants pour out water for their hands
and promptly offer bread from baskets and   980
bring towels smooth in texture for the guests.
Inside are fifty handmaids at their stations—
their care to stock the storerooms and to honor
the household gods with fire—and a hundred
more women, and as many male attendants   985
of equal age with them, to load the tables
with food and place the cups. The Tyrians, too,
have gathered, crowding through the happy halls—
all these invited to brocaded couches.
They marvel at Aeneas' gifts, at Iülus—   990
the god's bright face and his fictitious words—
and at the cloak, the veil adorned with saffron
acanthus borders. And above all, luckless
Dido—doomed to face catastrophe—
can't sate her soul, inflamed by what she sees;   995
the boy, the gifts excite her equally.
And he pretends to satisfy a father's
great love by hanging on Aeneas' neck
in an embrace. Then he seeks out the queen.
Her eyes cling fast to him, and all her heart;   1000
at times she fondles him upon her lap—
for Dido does not know how great a god
is taking hold of her poor self. But Cupid,

remembering his mother, Venus, slowly
begins to mist the memory of Sychaeus   1005
and with a living love tries to surprise
her longings gone to sleep, her unused heart.

And at the first pause in the feast the tables
are cleared away. They fetch enormous bowls
and crown the wine with wreaths. The uproar grows;   1010
it swells through all the palace; voices roll
across the ample halls; the lamps are kindled—
they hang from ceilings rich with golden panels—
and flaming torches overcome the night.
And then the queen called for a golden cup,   1015
massive with jewels, that Belus once had used,
Belus and all the Tyrian line; she filled
that golden cup with wine. The hall fell still.

"O Jupiter, for they say you are author
of laws for host and guest, do grant that this   1020
may be a day of happiness for those
who come from Tyre and Troy, and may our sons
remember it. May Bacchus, gladness-giver,
and gracious Juno, too, be present here;
and favor, Tyrians, this feast with honor."   1025
Her words were done. She offered her libation,
pouring her wine upon the boards; and then
she was the first to take the cup, but only
touching her lips to it. She passed it next
to Bitias and spurred him to be quick.   1030
He drained the foaming cup with eagerness
and drenched himself in that gold flood; in turn
the other chieftains drank. Long-haired Iopas,
whom mighty Atlas once had taught, lifts up
his golden lyre, sounding through the hall.   1035
He sings the wandering moon; the labors of
the sun; the origins of men and beasts,
of water and of fire; and of Arcturus,
the stormy Hyades, and the twin Bears;
and why the winter suns so rush to plunge   1040
in Ocean; what holds back the lingering nights.
The Tyrians applaud again, again.
The Trojans follow. So the luckless Dido
drew out the night with varied talk. She drank

long love and asked Aeneas many questions: 1045
of Priam; Hector; how Aurora's son
was armed; and now, how strong were Diomedes'
horses; now, how tremendous was Achilles.

"No, come, my guest," she calls, "and tell us all
things from the first beginning: Grecian guile,   1050
your people's trials, and then your journeyings.
For now the seventh summer carries you,
a wanderer, across the lands and waters."

H·1082

BOOK II

A SUDDEN SILENCE fell on all of them;
their eyes were turned, intent on him. And father
Aeneas, from his high couch, then began:

"O Queen—too terrible for tongues the pain
you ask me to renew, the tale of how   5
the Danaans could destroy the wealth of Troy,
that kingdom of lament: for I myself
saw these sad things; I took large part in them.
What Myrmidon or what Dolopian,
what soldier even of the harsh Ulysses,   10
could keep from tears in telling such a story?
But now the damp night hurries from the sky
into the sea; the falling stars persuade
to sleep. But if you long so much to learn
our suffering, to hear in brief the final   15
calamity of Troy—although my mind,
remembering, recoils in grief, and trembles,
I shall try.

          "The captains of the Danaans,
now weak with war and beaten back by fate,
and with so many gliding years gone by,   20

are able to construct, through the divine
art of Minerva, a mountainous horse.
They weave its ribs with sawed-off beams of fir,
pretending that it is an offering
for safe return. At least, that is their story.   25
Then in the dark sides of the horse they hide
men chosen from the sturdiest among them;
they stuff their soldiers in its belly, deep
in that vast cavern: Greeks armed to the teeth.

"Before their eyes lies famous Tenedos,   30
an island prosperous and powerful
as long as Priam's kingdoms held their own,
but now only a bay, a treacherous
ships' anchorage. And here the Argives sail
to hide themselves along that lonely shore.   35
We thought that they had left, to seek Mycenae
before the wind. And all of Troy is free
of long lament. The gates are opened wide;
gladly we go to see the Doric camp,
deserted places, the abandoned sands.   40
For here a squadron of Dolopians,
here fierce Achilles once had pitched his tent;
and here their ships were anchored; here they fought.
Some wonder at the deadly gift to maiden
Minerva, marveling at the horse's bulk;   45
Thymoetes was the first of us to urge
that it be brought within the walls and set
inside the citadel. He so advised
either through treachery or else because
the fates of Troy had willed this course. But Capys   50
and those with sounder judgment counsel us
to cast the Greek device into the sea,
or to set fire to this suspicious gift,
or else to pierce and probe that hollow belly.
The doubting crowd is split into two factions.   55

"The lead is taken by Laocoön.
He hurries from the citadel's high point
excitedly; and with a mob around him,
from far off he calls out: 'Poor citizens,
what wild insanity is this? Do you   60
believe the enemy have sailed away?

Or think that any Grecian gifts are free
of craft? Is this the way Ulysses acts?
Either Achaeans hide, shut in this wood,
or else this is an engine built against   65
our walls to spy upon our houses or
to batter down our city from above;
some trickery is here. Trojans, do not
trust in the horse. Whatever it may be,
I fear the Greeks, even when they bring gifts.'   70
And as he spoke he hurled his massive shaft
with heavy force against the side, against
the rounded, jointed belly of the beast.
It quivered when it struck the hollow cavern,
which groaned and echoed. Had the outcome not   75
been fated by the gods, and had our minds
not wandered off, Laocoön would then
have made our sword points foul the Argive den;
and, Troy, you would be standing yet and you,
high fort of Priam, you would still survive.   80

"Meanwhile with many shouts some Dardan shepherds
were dragging to the king a youth they had found.
His hands were bound behind his back; he was
a stranger who had surrendered willingly,
that he might bring about this very thing   85
and open Troy to the Achaeans; he
was sure of spirit, set for either end:
to win through stratagems or meet his death.
From every side the young of Troy rush out,
all swarming in their eagerness to see him,   90
contending in their taunts against the captive.
Now listen to the treachery of the Danaans
and learn from one the wickedness of all.
For as he stood with every eye upon him,
uneasy and unarmed, and looked around   95
while taking in the Phrygian ranks—'What land,'
he cries, 'what seas can now receive me? What
awaits my misery? I have no place
among the Danaans; and in bitterness
the Trojans ask for vengeance, for my blood   100
as penalty.' His lamentation turned
our feelings. Every violence was checked.
We urge him on to speak, to tell us who

his family may be, what word he brings,
what is he hoping for as prisoner.   105
At last he lays aside his fear and speaks:

" 'O King, I shall hide nothing of the truth,
whatever comes of it for me. I'll not
deny that I am born an Argive; this
I first confess. For fortune made of Sinon   110
a miserable man but not a man
of faithlessness and falsehood. Now by chance
you may have heard men talk of Palamedes,
the son of Belus, famous, glorious;
though he was innocent, the Greeks condemned him   115
to death on lying evidence, false charges,
simply because he had opposed the war.
Now that his light is lost, his killers mourn him.
When I was young, my father—a poor man—
sent me to serve in arms as a companion   120
to Palamedes, our close relative.
And while my kinsman's realm was safe and sure
and while his word was strong in the kings' council,
I was respected and I shared his fame.
But after he had left these upper shores,   125
a victim of the sharp Ulysses' envy
(no man is ignorant of what I tell),
I dragged my bitter life through grief and darkness,
I raged within me at the doom of my
innocent friend. And in my madness I   130
did not keep silent, but I swore to act
as his avenger if I found the chance,
if ever I returned to my homeland
of Argos as a victor. With my words
I stirred up bitter hatred; and for this   135
I first was touched by threats; from that time, too,
Ulysses menaced me with fresh complaints;
the words he spread among the army were
ambiguous; aware of his own guilt,
he looked for weapons. And he did not stop   140
until, with Calchas as his tool—but why
do I tell over this unwelcome story,
this useless tale? Why do I hold you back?
If you consider all Achaeans one,
it is enough for you that I am Grecian.   145

Then take your overdue revenge at once:
for this is what the Ithacan would wish;
the sons of Atreus—they would pay for this.'

"But then indeed we burn to know, to ask
the reasons; we were far too ignorant   150
of so much wickedness, of Greek deception.
Trembling, he carries on. His words are false:

" 'The Greeks have often wanted to abandon
the plain of Troy, to slip away, to flee,
weary of this long war: would that they had!   155
But each time they were blocked by bitter tempests
across the waters, terrified because
the south wind beat against their sails. Above all,
when this high horse you see was ready, built
of maple beams, storm clouds droned through the
        heavens.   160
Bewildered, we send out Eurypylus
to ask the oracle of Phoebus; from
the shrine he brings back these grim words to us:
"By blood and by the slaying of a virgin,
Grecians, you stilled the winds when you first came   165
to Troy; by blood seek out your homeward way.
The only offering that is suitable:
an Argive life." And when the army heard
this oracle, they were amazed; within
the Grecians' deepest marrow cold fear shuddered.   170
For whom has fate prepared this end? Whose life
does Phoebus want? At this, with much fanfare
the Ithacan drags out the prophet Calchas
before the crowd and asks of him what are
the god's demands. And many now foretold   175
to me this schemer's ruthless villainy;
they saw—but unprotestingly—what was
to come. For twice-five days the seer is still,
secluded in his tent; his tongue refuses
to name a single Greek or to betray   180
death's victim. Finally, with difficulty
and driven by the Ithacan's loud urgings,
as they had planned, he breaks his silence and
assigns me to the altar. All approved;
what each feared for himself he now endured   185

when someone else was singled out for ruin.

" 'And now the day of horror was at hand;
the rites were being readied for me: cakes
of salt and garlands round my temples. I
confess, I snatched myself from death; I broke   190
my bonds; and in a muddy pond, unseen,
nightlong I hid among the rushes, waiting
for them to sail away—if only that
could be! And now there is no hope for me
to see my old country, my tender sons,   195
my longed-for father, on whom they may levy
the punishment for my escape, making
poor victims pay for my crime with their death.
I beg you, therefore, by the High Ones, by
the powers that know the truth, and by whatever   200
still uncontaminated trust is left
to mortals, pity my hard trials, pity
a soul that carries undeserved sorrows.'

"We grant life to his tears and, more, our mercy.
And Priam is the first to have the fetters   205
and tight chains taken off the fugitive;
he speaks to him with words of friendliness:
'Whoever you may be, from this time on
forget the Greeks you lost; you are one of us.
And answer truthfully the things I ask: 210
Why have they built this massive horse? Who was
its maker? And what are they after? What
religious gift is it? Or engine of war?'

"He stopped. The other, schooled in Grecian guile
and wiles, lifts his unfettered hands to heaven: 215
'You everlasting fires,' he cries, 'and your
inviolable power, be my witness;
you altars, savage swords that I escaped,
you garlands of the gods I wore as victim,
it now is right for me to break the holy   220
oath of my loyalty and right for me
to hate the Greeks, to bring all things to light,
whatever they conceal. I am no longer
bound to obey the laws of my own country.
But, Troy, you must hold fast what you have promised;   225

preserved, preserve your word to me, if now
I tell the truth and so repay you fully.

" 'The only hope and confidence the Danaans
had ever had in undertaking war
lay in the help of Pallas. But in fact,   230
since that time when the godless Diomedes,
the son of Tydeus, first went with Ulysses,
inventor of impieties, and tried
to tear down from its sacred shrine the fateful
Palladium, when they cut down the guardians   235
of that high citadel with ruthless hands,
daring to touch the virgin goddess' garlands—
since then the Danaans' hopes have ebbed away,
receding, falling back; their force is broken;
the mind of Pallas has not turned toward them.   240
The omens of her change were not uncertain.
No sooner was her image in the Grecian
camp site than salt sweat poured across its body
and quivering flames blazed from its staring eyes;
and then, amazingly, three times the goddess   245
herself sprang from the ground with trembling shaft
and shield. And straightway Calchas warns them that
they must try out the seas in flight, that Troy
could never be destroyed by Argive arms
unless fresh auspices were brought from Argos;   250
that would regain the favor of the gods
who first helped bring the curving keels from Greece.
Then with the wind they sought their native land,
Mycenae, to make ready gods and weapons
as their companions, to recross the seas,   255
to come back suddenly. For so had Calchas
interpreted the omens. And he warned them
to build this effigy as their atonement
for the Palladium, to serve as payment
for their outrage against the goddess' image,   260
to expiate so great a sacrilege.
But he instructed them to make this mass
of interwoven timbers so immense
and build it up so high to heaven that
it cannot pass the gate, can never be   265
received within Troy's walls, never protect
the people under its old sanctity.

For if your hands should harm Minerva's gift,
then vast destruction (may the gods turn this
their prophecy against the priest's own lips!)   270
would fall on Priam's kingdom and the Phrygians;
but if it climbed by your hands into Troy,
then Asia would repel the Greeks and, more,
advance in war as far as Pelops' walls;
this is the doom that waits for our descendants.'   275

"Such was the art of perjured Sinon, so
insidious, we trusted what he told.
So we were taken in by snares, forced tears—
yes, we, whom neither Diomedes nor
Achilles of Larissa could defeat,   280
nor ten long years, a thousand-galleyed fleet.

"Now yet another and more dreadful omen
is thrust at us, bewilders our blind hearts.
Laocoön, by lot named priest of Neptune,
was sacrificing then a giant bull   285
upon the customary altars, when
two snakes with endless coils, from Tenedos
strike out across the tranquil deep (I shudder
to tell what happened), resting on the waters,
advancing shoreward side by side; their breasts   290
erect among the waves, their blood-red crests
are higher than the breakers. And behind,
the rest of them skims on along the sea;
their mighty backs are curved in folds. The foaming
salt surge is roaring. Now they reach the fields.   295
Their eyes are drenched with blood and fire—they burn.
They lick their hissing jaws with quivering tongues.
We scatter at the sight, our blood is gone.
They strike a straight line toward Laocoön.
At first each snake entwines the tiny bodies   300
of his two sons in an embrace, then feasts
its fangs on their defenseless limbs. The pair
next seize upon Laocoön himself,
who nears to help his sons, carrying weapons.
They wind around his waist and twice around   305
his throat. They throttle him with scaly backs;
their heads and steep necks tower over him.
He struggles with his hands to rip their knots,

his headbands soaked in filth and in dark venom,
while he lifts high his hideous cries to heaven,   310
just like the bellows of a wounded bull
when it has fled the altar, shaking off
an unsure ax. But now the snakes escape:
twin dragons, gliding to the citadel
of cruel Pallas, her high shrines. They hide   315
beneath the goddess' feet, beneath her shield.

"At this, a stranger terror takes its way
through every trembling heart. Laocoön
has justly paid the penalty—they say—
for outrage, since his spearhead had profaned   320
the sacred oak, his cursed shaft been cast
against the horse's back. Their cry is that
the image must be taken to the temple,
the favor of the goddess must be sought.

"We break the walls and bare the battlements.   325
We set to work; beneath the horse's feet
we fasten sliding wheels; about its neck
we stretch out ropes of hemp. And fat with weapons,
the engine of our fate climbs up the rampart.
And boys and unwed girls surround it, singing   330
their sacred chants, so glad to touch the cable.
The horse glides, menacing, advancing toward
the center of the city. O my land,
o Ilium, the home of gods and Dardan
walls long renowned in war, four times it stalled   335
before the gateway, at the very threshold;
four times the arms clashed loud inside its belly.
Nevertheless, heedless, blinded by frenzy,
we press right on and set the inauspicious
monster inside the sacred fortress. Even   340
then can Cassandra chant of what will come
with lips the gods had doomed to disbelief
by Trojans. That day was our last—and yet,
helpless, we crown the altars of the gods
with festive branches all about the city.   345

"Meanwhile the heavens wheel, night hurries from
Ocean and clothes within its giant shadow
the earth, the sky, the snares of Myrmidons.

The silent Trojans lie within their city
as sleep embraces their exhausted bodies.　　　　350

"And now from Tenedos the Argive army
were moving in their marshaled ships, beneath
the friendly silence of the tranquil moon,
seeking familiar shores. The royal galley
has signaled with its beacon torches; Sinon,　　　　355
shielded by the unkindly destinies
of gods, can secretly set free the Danaans
out of the monster's womb, the pinewood prison.
The horse, thrown open, gives them back to air.
They exit gladly from the hollow timber:　　　　360
Thessandrus, Sthenelus, the captains; fierce
Ulysses, gliding down the lowered rope;
and Thoas, Acamas, and then the grandson
of Peleus, Neoptolemus; the chieftain
Machaon, Menelaus, then Epeos,　　　　365
the very maker of the stratagem.
They fall upon the city buried deep
in wine and sleep. The guards cut down, the gates
thrown open, they can welcome their companions
and gather the conspirators in one.　　　　370

"It was the hour when for troubled mortals
rest—sweetest gift of gods that glides to men—
has just begun. Within my sleep, before
my eyes there seemed to stand, in tears and sorrow,
Hector as once he was, dismembered by　　　　375
the dragging chariot, black with bloodied dust;
his swollen feet were pierced by thongs. Oh this
was Hector, and how different he was
from Hector back from battle, putting on
Achilles' spoils, or Hector when he flung　　　　380
his Phrygian firebrands at Dardan prows!
His beard unkempt, his hair was thick with blood,
he bore the many wounds he had received
around his homeland's walls. And I myself
seemed then to weep, to greet him with sad words:　　　　385
'O light of Troy, o Trojans' trusted hope!
What long delay has held you back? From what
seashores, awaited Hector, have you come?
For, weary with the many deaths of friends,

the sorrows of your men, your city, how   390
our eyes hold fast to you! What shameful cause
defaced your tranquil image? Why these wounds?'

"He wastes no words, no time on useless questions—
but drawing heavy sighs from deep within,
'Ah, goddess-born, take flight,' he cries, 'and snatch   395
yourself out of these flames. The enemy
has gained the walls; Troy falls from her high peak.
Our home, our Priam—these have had their due:
could Pergamus be saved by any prowess,
then my hand would have served. But Troy entrusts   400
her holy things and household gods to you;
take them away as comrades of your fortunes,
seek out for them the great walls that at last,
once you have crossed the sea, you will establish.'
So Hector speaks; then from the inner altars   405
he carries out the garlands and great Vesta
and, in his hands, the fire that never dies.

"Meanwhile the howls of war confound the city.
And more and more—although my father's house
was far, withdrawn, and screened by trees—the roar   410
is sharper, the dread clash of battle grows.
I start from sleep and climb the sloping roof
above the house. I stand, alerted: just
as when, with furious south winds, a fire
has fallen on a wheat field, or a torrent   415
that hurtles from a mountain stream lays low
the meadows, low the happy crops, and low
the labor of the oxen, dragging forests
headlong—and even then, bewildered and
unknowing, perched upon a rock, the shepherd   420
will listen to the clamor. Now indeed.
the truth is plain, the guile of Greece made clear.
The spacious palace of Deiphobus
has fallen, victim of the towering Vulcan.
And now Ucalegon's, his neighbor, burns;   425
and wide Sigeum's harbor gleams with fire.
The cries of men are high, the trumpets clang.

"Insane, I seize my weapons. There's no sense
in weapons, yet my spirit burns to gather

a band for battle, to rush out against   430
the citadel with my companions. Rage
and anger drive my mind. My only thought:
how fine a thing it is to die in arms.

"But Panthus, slipping past the Grecian swords—
Panthus, the son of Othrys, priest of Phoebus   435
within the citadel—now rushes toward
my threshold, madly; in his hand he carries
the holy vessels and defeated gods.
He drags his tiny grandson. 'Panthus, where's
the crucial struggle? Where are we to stand?'   440
My words are hardly done when, with a groan,
he answers: 'It has come—the final day
and Troy's inevitable time. We Trojans
were; Troy has been; gone is the giant glory
of Teucrians: ferocious Jupiter   445
has taken all to Argos. And the city
now burns beneath its Danaan overlords.
The horse stands high within the heart of Troy
and it pours out armed men. The mocking Sinon,
now he has won, is scattering firebrands.   450
Some crowd the open gates—as many thousands
as ever came from great Mycenae; others
have blocked the narrow streets with ready blades;
the sword edge stands, unsheathed, its gleaming point
is set for slaughter; at the forward line   455
the guards can scarcely stand; they battle blind.'

"The words of Panthus and the will of gods,
these carry me into the flames and weapons,
where bitter Fury, where the roar and cries
that climb the skies call out. And in the moonlight   460
I now am met by comrades: Epytus,
great warrior, and Ripheus come to join us;
to march beside us, Hypanis and Dymas
and then the young Coroebus, son of Mygdon.
For in those days he chanced to come to Troy,   465
insane with love for his Cassandra, bringing
his help, as son-in-law, to Priam and
the Phrygians—sad Coroebus, would he had
heeded the warnings of his frantic bride!
   *   *   *

"And when I saw them hot again for battle,   470
in tight ranks, I began: 'Young men, your hearts
are sturdy—but for nothing; if you want
to follow me into my last attempt,
you see what fortune watches us. For all
the gods on whom this kingdom stood have quit   475
our shrines and altars, gone away. The city ·
that you would help is now in flames. Then let
us rush to arms and die. The lost have only
this one deliverance: to hope for none.'

"So were these young men's spirits spurred to fury.   480
Then—just as plundering wolves in a black fog,
when driven blindly by their belly's endless
frenzy, for they have left behind their cubs
to wait with thirsty jaws—through enemies,
through swords we pass to certain death; we make   485
our way into the heart of Troy; around us
the black night hovers with its hollow shade.

"Who has the words to tell that night's disaster?
And who to tell the deaths? What tears could equal
our agony? An ancient city falls   490
that ruled for many years; through streets and houses
and on the sacred thresholds of the gods
so many silent bodies lie about.
Nor are the Teucrians the only ones
to pay the penalty of blood: at times   495
new courage comes to beaten hearts, and then
the Danaan victors die; and everywhere
are fear, harsh grief, and many shapes of slaughter.

"The first to face us is Androgeos,
surrounded by a mighty mob of Greeks.   500
In ignorance, he thinks us fellow troops
and welcomes us at once with friendly words:
'But hurry, men! What laziness has kept
you back? The others are at sack and plunder
in burning Pergamus. Have you just come   505
from your tall ships?' He spoke and knew at once—
for he received no sure reply from us—
that he was in the hands of enemies.

He drew back, dazed. He checked his step and voice.
Even as one who works his way along   510
the ground through tangled briers when, unawares,
he treads upon a serpent and recoils
in terror, suddenly, as it ignites
in anger, puffing up its azure neck:
just so, on seeing us, Androgeos trembled,   515
trying to make his quick escape. We rush
to ring the Greeks, our weapons thick; we kill
on every side. They do not know the ground
and panic overcomes them. Fortune smiles
on our first trial. And here Coroebus, glad   520
at our success and spirits, cries: 'My comrades,
where Fortune first points out the path of safety,
where first she shows herself auspicious, there
must be the way to follow: let us change
our shields, take Danaan armor for ourselves.   525
If that be guile or valor—who would ask
in war? Our enemies will give us weapons.'

"These were Coroebus' words. Then he puts on
Androgeos' crested helmet and his shield
with handsome emblem, fastening to his thigh   530
the Argive sword. So Dymas does and Ripheus
and the excited youths: each arms himself
with these new spoils. We move ahead, to mingle
with Argives under auspices not ours.
Through that long night we clash in many combats,   535
and we send many Danaans down to Orcus.
Some scatter to the ships, to seek the shore
of safety; some in their low fear climb back
to the familiar belly of the horse.

"But oh, it is not right for anyone   540
to trust reluctant gods! For there the virgin
Cassandra, Priam's daughter, hair disheveled,
was dragged out from the temple, from Minerva's
shrine, and her eyes were raised in vain to heaven—
her eyes, for chains held fast her gentle hands.   545
Coroebus, maddened, could not stand the sight.
He threw himself, about to die, against
the very center of the Grecian line.
We follow close behind him, charging thick.

Here, from the shrine's high roof, we are struck down   550
for the first time by our own Trojan weapons:
the image of our arms, the error of
our Danaan helmets, starts a wretched slaughter.
But then the Grecians groan with indignation
because the virgin is rescued. From all sides   555
they muster to attack us: Ajax most
ferociously, and both of Atreus' sons,
and all the army of Dolopians:
as, when a hurricane has burst, the crosswinds
will clash together—West and South and East,   560
exulting in his oriental steeds—
the woods are shrill, and foam-washed Nereus rages,
his trident stirs the seas up from their deeps.
And any whom our stratagems had driven
beneath the shades of dark night, whom we had chased 565
across the city, now appear; and first
they recognize our shields, our miming weapons,
then note our speech that does not sound like theirs.
Such numbers overcome us instantly.
Coroebus is the first to fall; he dies   570
beneath Peneleus' right hand, beside
the altar of the warrior goddess, Pallas.
Then Ripheus, too, has fallen—he was first
among the Teucrians for justice and
observing right; the gods thought otherwise.   575
Both Hypanis and Dymas perish, pierced
by their own comrades; neither your great goodness,
o Panthus, nor Apollo's garland could
protect you when you fell. O final flames
that take my people, ashes of my Ilium,   580
be you my witness that, in your disaster,
I did not shun the Danaan blades or battle:
if fate had willed my end, my hand had earned it.
Then we are forced apart. Along with me
go Iphitus and Pelias: one was   585
already slow with his long years, the other,
slow-footed through a wound got from Ulysses.
The clamor calls us on to Priam's palace.

"And here the fight is deadly, just as if
there were no battles elsewhere, just as if   590
no one were dying now throughout the city;

for here the god of war cannot be tamed.
The Danaans rush the roofs; they storm the threshold
with linked and lifted shields; their ladders hug
the walls—the rungs reach up the very doorposts.   595
Against the darts their left hands thrust their bucklers,
and with their right, they clutch the battlements.
In turn the Trojans tear down roofs and towers
to fling as missiles; they can see the end
is near, but even at death's point they still   600
prepare defense. They roll down gilded rafters,
our ancient fathers' splendors; while below,
the others block the gates with naked blades.
They guard in tight array. Made new again,
our spirits rush relief to Priam's palace,   605
help to our men, and fresh force to the beaten.

"There was an entry gate with secret doors:
a passageway that ran to Priam's rooms,
a postern at the palace rear; and there,
while Troy still stood, the sad Andromache ·   610
would often, unattended, come to see
her husband's parents; there she brought her boy
Astyanax to visit his grandfather.
That is the way I take to reach the ramparts
along the roof; from there the wretched Trojans   615
fling useless weapons with their hands. And from
the sheer edge of that roof a tower rose,
built starward; it had served as lookout over
all Troy, the Danaan ships, the Grecian camp.
And where the upper storeys show loose joints,   620
there we attack with iron to tug it free,
to wrench it from the top, to thrust it down.
It suddenly collapses; with a crash
it tumbles wide across the Danaan ranks;
its fall is ruinous. But fresh Greeks come;   625
the stones, the other missiles never stop.

"And then, before the very porch, along
the outer portal Pyrrhus leaps with pride;
his armor glitters with a brazen brilliance:
he is like a snake that, fed on poisonous plants   630
and swollen underground all winter, now,
his slough cast off, made new and bright with youth,

uncoils his slippery body to the light;
his breast erect, he towers toward the sun;
he flickers from his mouth a three-forked tongue.   635
With Pyrrhus are the giant Periphas
together with Automedon, Achilles'
charioteer and armor-bearer; all
the youths of Scyros now assault the palace;
they fling their firebrands up toward the roof.   640
Pyrrhus himself, among the first, takes up
a two-edged ax and cracks the stubborn gates.
He rips the bronze-bound portals off their hinges,
cuts through a beam, digs out tough oak: the breach
is vast, a gaping mouth. The inner house   645
is naked now, the long halls, open; naked,
the private rooms of Priam and the ancient
kings; and the Greeks can see the threshold guards.

"But deep within, confusion takes the palace,
anguish and sad commotion; and the vaulted   650
walls echo with the wail and woe of women,
lament that beats against the golden stars.
Across the huge apartments in their terror
the matrons wander, clutching at the doors,
embracing them, imprinting kisses. Pyrrhus,   655
his father's force within him, presses forward—
no barrier, and not the guards themselves,
can hold him off. The gate gives way before
the ram's repeated hammerings; the doors
are severed from their hinges, topple out.   660
Force cracks a breach; the Danaans storm and pour
across the passage, butchering the first
they meet; their soldiers stream across the palace—
less furious than these, the foaming river
when it has burst across resisting banks   665
and boundaries and overflows, its angry
flood piling in a mass along the plains
as it drags flocks and folds across the fields.
And I myself saw Neoptolemus,
insane with blood, and both of Atreus' sons   670
upon the threshold. I saw Hecuba
together with her hundred daughters, and
among the altars I could see King Priam,
polluting with his blood the fires he

himself had hallowed. And the fifty bridal   675
chambers that had such hopes of sons of sons,
the doors that once had stood so proud with booty
and with barbaric gold lie on the ground.
What fire cannot do, the Danaans can.

"Perhaps you now will ask the end of Priam.   680
When he has seen his beaten city ruined—
the wrenching of the gates, the enemy
among his sanctuaries—then in vain
the old man throws his armor, long unused,
across his shoulders, tottering with age;   685
and he girds on his useless sword; about
to die, he hurries toward the crowd of Greeks.

"Beneath the naked round of heaven, at
the center of the palace, stood a giant
shrine; at its side an ancient laurel leaned   690
across the altar stone, and it embraced
the household gods within its shadow. Here,
around that useless altar, Hecuba
together with her daughters—just like doves
when driven headlong by a dark storm—huddled;   695
and they held fast the statues of the gods.
But when she saw her Priam putting on
the armor he had worn when he was young,
she cried: 'Poor husband, what wild thought drives you
to wear these weapons now? Where would you rush?   700
This is no time for such defense and help,
not even were my Hector here himself.
Come near and pray: this altar shall yet save
us all, or you shall die together with us.'
When this was said she took the old man to her   705
and drew him down upon the sacred seat.

"But then Polites, one of Priam's sons
who had escaped from Pyrrhus' slaughter, down
long porticoes, past enemies and arrows,
races, wounded, across the empty courts.   710
But after him, and hot to thrust, is Pyrrhus;
now, even now he clutches, closing in;
he presses with his shaft until at last
Polites falls before his parents' eyes,

within their presence; he pours out his life   715
in streams of blood. Though in the fist of death,
at this, Priam does not spare voice or wrath:
'If there is any goodness in the heavens
to oversee such acts, for this offense
and outrage may you find your fitting thanks   720
and proper payment from the gods, for you
have made me see the murder of my son,
defiled a father's face with death. Achilles—
you lie to call him father—never dealt
with Priam so—and I, his enemy;   725
for he had shame before the claims and trust
that are a suppliant's. He handed back
for burial the bloodless corpse of Hector
and sent me off in safety to my kingdom.'
The old man spoke; his feeble spear flew off—   730
harmless; the hoarse bronze beat it back at once;
it dangled, useless now, from the shield's boss.
And Pyrrhus: 'Carry off these tidings; go
and bring this message to my father, son
of Peleus; and remember, let him know   735
my sorry doings, how degenerate
is Neoptolemus. Now die.' This said,
he dragged him to the very altar stone,
with Priam shuddering and slipping in
the blood that streamed from his own son. And Pyrrhus 740
with his left hand clutched tight the hair of Priam;
his right hand drew his glistening blade, and then
he buried it hilt-high in the king's side.
This was the end of Priam's destinies,
the close that fell to him by fate: to see   745
his Troy in flames and Pergamus laid low—
who once was proud king over many nations
and lands of Asia. Now he lies along
the shore, a giant trunk, his head torn from
his shoulders, as a corpse without a name.   750

"This was the first time savage horror took me.
I was astounded; as I saw the king
gasping his life away beneath a ruthless
wound, there before me rose the effigy
of my dear father, just as old as Priam;   755
before me rose Creüsa, left alone,

my plundered home, the fate of small Iülus.
I look behind and scan the troops around me;
all of my men, worn out, have quit the battle,
have cast their bodies down along the ground   760
or fallen helplessly into the flames.

"And now that I am left alone, I see
the daughter of Tyndareos clinging
to Vesta's thresholds, crouching silently
within a secret corner of the shrine;   765
bright conflagrations give me light as I
wander and let my eyes read everything.
For she, in terror of the Trojans—set
against her for the fall of Pergamus—
and of the Danaans' vengeance and the anger   770
of her abandoned husband; she, the common
Fury of Troy and of her homeland, she
had hid herself; she crouched, a hated thing,
beside the altars. In my mind a fire
is burning; anger spurs me to avenge   775
my falling land, to exact the debt of crime.
'Is she to have it so: to leave unharmed,
see Sparta and her home Mycenae, go—
a victor queen in triumph—to look on
her house and husband, parents, children, trailing   780
a train of Trojan girls and Phrygian slaves?
Shall Troy have been destroyed by fire, Priam
been beaten by the blade, the Dardan shore
so often soaked with blood, to this end? No.
For though there is no memorable name   785
in punishing a woman and no gain
of honor in such victory, yet I
shall have my praise for blotting out a thing
of evil, for my punishing of one
who merits penalties; and it will be   790
a joy to fill my soul with vengeful fire,
to satisfy the ashes of my people.'

"And carried off by my mad mind, I was
still blurting out these words when, with such brightness
as I had never seen, my gracious mother   795
stood there before me; and across the night
she gleamed with pure light, unmistaken goddess,

as lovely and as tall as she appears
whenever she is seen by heaven's beings.
And while she caught and held my right hand fast,   800
she spoke these words to me with her rose lips:
'My son, what bitterness has kindled this
fanatic anger? Why this madness? What
of all your care for me—where has it gone?
Should you not first seek out your father, worn   805
with years, Anchises, where you left him; see
if your own wife, Creüsa, and the boy
Ascanius are still alive? The Argive
lines ring them all about; and if my care
had not prevented such an end, by now   810
flames would have swept them off, the hostile sword
have drunk their blood. And those to blame are not
the hated face of the Laconian woman,
the daughter of Tyndareos, or Paris:
it is the gods' relentlessness, the gods',   815
that overturns these riches, tumbles Troy
from its high pinnacle. Look now—for I
shall tear away each cloud that cloaks your eyes
and clogs your human seeing, darkening
all things with its damp fog: you must not fear   820
the orders of your mother; do not doubt,
but carry out what she commands. For here,
where you see huge blocks ripped apart and stones
torn free from stones and smoke that joins with dust
in surges, Neptune shakes the walls, his giant   825
trident is tearing Troy from its foundations;
and here the first to hold the Scaean gates
is fiercest Juno; girt with iron, she
calls furiously to the fleet for more
Greek troops. Now turn and look: Tritonian Pallas   830
is planted there; upon the tallest towers
she glares with her storm cloud and her grim Gorgon.
And he who furnishes the Greeks with force
that favors and with spirit is the Father
himself, for he himself goads on the gods   835
against the Dardan weapons. Son, be quick
to flee, have done with fighting. I shall never
desert your side until I set you safe
upon your father's threshold.' So she spoke,
then hid herself within the night's thick shadows.   840

Ferocious forms appear—the fearful powers
of gods that are the enemies of Troy.

"At this, indeed, I saw all Ilium
sink down into the fires; Neptune's Troy
is overturned: even as when the woodsmen   845
along a mountaintop are rivals in
their striving to bring down an ancient ash,
hacked at with many blows of iron and ax;
it always threatens falling, nodding with
its trembling leaves and tossing crest until,   850
slowly, slowly, the wounds have won; it gives
one last great groan, then wrenches from the ridges
and crashes into ruin. I go down
and, guided by a god, move on among
the foes and fires; weapons turn aside,   855
the flames retire where I make my way.

"But now, when I had reached my father's threshold,
Anchises' ancient house, our home—and I
longed so to carry him to the high mountains
and sought him first—he will not let his life   860
be drawn out after Troy has fallen, he
will not endure exile: 'You whose lifeblood
is fresh, whose force is still intact and tough,
you hurry your escape; if heaven's lords
had wanted longer life for me, they would   865
have saved my home. It is enough—and more—
that I have lived beyond one fall and sack
of Troy. Call out your farewell to my body
as it is now, thus laid out, thus; and then
be gone. I shall find death by my own hand;   870
the enemy will pity me and seek
my spoils. The loss of burial is easy.
For hated by the gods and useless, I
have lingered out my years too long already,
since that time when the father of the High Ones   875
and king of men let fly his thunderbolt
against me with the winds, touched me with lightning.'

"These were the words he used. He did not move.
We stood in tears—my wife, Creüsa, and
Ascanius and all the household—begging   880

my father not to bring down everything
along with him and make our fate more heavy.
He will not have it. What he wants is set;
he will not leave his place. Again I take
to arms and, miserable, long for death.   885
What other stratagem or chance is left?
And then I ask: 'My father, had you thought
I could go off and leave you here? Could such
unholiness fall from a father's lips?
For if it please the High Ones that no thing   890
be left of this great city, if your purpose
must still persist, if you want so to add
yourself and yours to Ilium's destruction—
why then, the door to death is open: Pyrrhus—
who massacres the son before his father's   895
eyes, and then kills the father at the altars—
still hot from Priam's blood, will soon be here.
And was it, then, for this, my gracious mother,
that you have saved me from the blade, the fire—
that I might see the enemy within   900
the heart of home, my son Ascanius,
my father, and Creüsa at their side,
all butchered in each other's blood? My men,
bring arms; the last light calls upon the beaten.
Let be, and let me at the Greeks again,   905
to make my way back to new battles. Never
shall we all die this day without revenge.'

"At that I girded on my sword again
and fixed it firm, passing my left hand through
my shield strap as I hurried from the house.   910
But suddenly Creüsa held me fast
beside the threshold; clinging to my feet,
she lifted young Iülus to his father:
'If you go off to die, then take us, too,
to face all things with you; but if your past   915
still lets you put your hope in arms, which now
you have put on, then first protect this house.
To whom is young Iülus left, to whom
your father and myself, once called your wife?'

"So did Creüsa cry; her wailing filled   920
my father's house. But even then there comes

a sudden omen—wonderful to tell:
between the hands, before the faces of
his grieving parents, over Iülus' head
there leaps a lithe flametip that seems to shed   925
a radiance; the tongue of fire flickers,
harmless, and plays about his soft hair, grazes
his temples. Shuddering in our alarm,
we rush to shake the flames out of his hair
and quench the holy fire with water. But   930
Anchises raised his glad eyes to the stars
and lifted heavenward his voice and hands:
'O Jupiter, all-able one, if you
are moved by any prayers, look on us.
I only ask you this: if by our goodness   935
we merit it, then, Father, grant to us
your help and let your sign confirm these omens.'

"No sooner had the old man spoken so
than sudden thunder crashed upon the left,
and through the shadows ran a shooting star,   940
its trail a torch of flooding light. It glides
above the highest housetops as we watch,
until the brightness that has marked its course
is buried in the woods of Ida: far
and wide the long wake of that furrow shines,   945
and sulphur smokes upon the land. At last,
won over by this sign, my father rises,
to greet the gods, to adore the sacred star:
'Now my delay is done; I follow; where
you lead, I am. Gods of my homeland, save   950
my household, save my grandson. Yours, this omen;
and Troy is in your keeping. Yes, I yield.
My son, I go with you as your companion.'

"These were his words. But now the fire roars
across the walls; the tide of flame flows nearer.   955
'Come then, dear father, mount upon my neck;
I'll bear you on my shoulders. That is not
too much for me. Whatever waits for us,
we both shall share one danger, one salvation.
Let young Iülus come with me, and let   960
my wife Creüsa follow at a distance.
And servants, listen well to what I say:

along the way, just past the city walls,
in an abandoned spot there is a mound,
an ancient shrine of Ceres; and nearby   965
an ancient cypress stands, one that our fathers'
devotion kept alive for many years.
From different directions, we shall meet
at this one point. My father, you will carry
the holy vessels and our homeland's gods.   970
Filthy with war, just come from slaughter, I
must never touch these sacred things until
I bathe myself within a running stream.'

"This said, I spread a tawny lion skin
across my bent neck, over my broad shoulders,   975
and then take up Anchises; small Iülus
now clutches my right hand; his steps uneven,
he is following his father; and my wife
moves on behind. We journey through dark places;
and I, who just before could not be stirred   980
by any weapons cast at me or by
the crowds of Greeks in charging columns, now
am terrified by all the breezes, startled
by every sound, in fear for son and father.

"And now, as I approached the gates and thought   985
I had found the way of my escape, the sudden
and frequent tramp of feet was at my ears;
and peering through the shades, Anchises cries:
'My son, take flight; my son, they are upon us.
I see their gleaming shields, the flashing bronze.'   990
At this alarm I panicked: some unfriendly
god's power ripped away my tangled mind.
For while I take a trackless path, deserting
the customary roads, fate tears from me
my wife Creüsa in my misery.   995
I cannot say if she had halted or
had wandered off the road or slumped down, weary.
My eyes have never had her back again.
I did not look behind for her, astray,
or think of her before we reached the mound   1000
and ancient, sacred shrine of Ceres; here
at last, when all were gathered, she alone
was missing—gone from husband, son, companions.
             ✿   ✿   ✿

"What men, what gods did I in madness not
accuse? Did I see anything more cruel　　　　　1005
within the fallen city? I commit
Ascanius, Anchises, and the gods
of Troy to my companions, hiding them
inside a winding valley. I myself
again seek out the city, girding on　　　　　1010
my gleaming arms. I want to meet all risks
again, return through all of Troy, again
give back my life to danger. First I seek
the city walls, the gateway's shadowed thresholds
through which I had come before. And I retrace　　1015
my footsteps; through the night I make them out.
My spirit is held by horror everywhere;
even the very silence terrifies.
Then I move homeward—if by chance, by chance,
she may have made her way there. But the Danaans　1020
had flooded in and held the house. At once
the hungry conflagration rolls before
the wind, high as the highest rooftop; flames
are towering overhead, the boiling tide
is raging to the heavens. I go on;　　　　　1025
again I see the house of Priam and
the fortress. Down the empty porticoes,
in Juno's sanctuary, I can see
both Phoenix and the fierce Ulysses, chosen
as guardians, at watch over the booty.　　　　1030
And here, from every quarter, heaped together,
are Trojan treasures torn from burning altars—
the tables of the gods, and plundered garments,
and bowls of solid gold; and Trojan boys
and trembling women stand in a long line.　　　1035

"And more, I even dared to cast my cries
across the shadows; in my sorrow, I—
again, again, in vain—called for Creüsa;
my shouting filled the streets. But as I rushed
and raged among the houses endlessly,　　　　1040
before my eyes there stood the effigy
and grieving shade of my Creüsa, image
far larger than the real. I was dismayed;
my hair stood stiff, my voice held fast within
my jaws. She spoke; her words undid my cares:　　1045

" 'O my sweet husband, is there any use
in giving way to such fanatic sorrow?
For this could never come to pass without
the gods' decree; and you are not to carry
Creüsa as your comrade, since the king   1050
of high Olympus does not grant you that.
Along your way lie long exile, vast plains
of sea that you must plow; but you will reach
Hesperia, where Lydian Tiber flows,
a tranquil stream, through farmer's fruitful fields.   1055
There days of gladness lie in wait for you:
a kingdom and a royal bride. Enough
of tears for loved Creüsa. I am not
to see the haughty homes of Myrmidons
or of Dolopians, or be a slave   1060
to Grecian matrons—I, a Dardan woman
and wife of Venus' son. It is the gods'
great Mother who keeps me upon these shores.
And now farewell, and love the son we share.'

"When she was done with words—I weeping and   1065
wanting to say so many things—she left
and vanished in transparent air. Three times
I tried to throw my arms around her neck;
three times the Shade I grasped in vain escaped
my hands—like fleet winds, most like a winged dream.   1070

"And so at last, when night has passed, I go
again to my companions. Here I find,
to my surprise, new comrades come together,
vast numbers, men and women, joined for exile,
a crowd of sorrow. Come from every side,   1075
with courage and with riches, they are ready
for any lands across the seas where I
may lead them. Now the star of morning rose
above high Ida's ridges, guiding the day.
The Danaans held the gates' blockaded thresholds.   1080
There was no hope of help. Then I gave way
and, lifting up my father, made for the mountains."

Polyphemus

BOOK III

"'THE POWER OF Asia and Priam's guiltless race
are overturned, proud Ilium is fallen,
and all of Neptune's Troy smokes from the ground;
this the Highest Ones were pleased to do.
Then we are driven by divine commands   5
and signs to sail in search of fields of exile
in distant and deserted lands. We build
a fleet beneath Antandros, in the foothills
of Phrygian Ida, knowing not where fate
will carry us or where we are to settle;   10
and there we gather up our men. No sooner
was summer come upon us than my father
Anchises bid us spread our sails to fate.
Weeping, I must give up the shores, the harbors
that were my home, the plain that once was Troy.   15
An exile, I go out across the waters
together with my comrades and my son,
my gods of hearth and home and the Great Gods.

"The land of Mars is not far off: vast plains
the Thracians till, once ruled by fierce Lycurgus,   20
a land that had long been a friend to us,
with household gods allied to Troy until

our fortunes fell away. I sail to Thrace.
Along that curving shore I trace our first
walls—but beneath unkindly fates. That city   25
receives its name from mine: Aeneadae.

"So that the gods may guard our undertaking,
I offer sacrifices to my mother,
Dione's daughter, and to the other powers,
slaughtering along that beach a gleaming   30
white bull to the high king of heaven-dwellers.

"Nearby, above a mound, a copse of dogwood
and myrtle bushes bristle, thick with shoots.
I try to tear a green branch from the soil
to serve as leafy cover for our altars—   35
but see an awful omen, terrible
to tell. For from that first tree's severed roots
drops of black blood drip down. They stain the ground
with gore. My body shudders, cold. My blood
is frozen now with terror. I try again   40
and tear the tenacious stem of a second shoot
that I may reach the deep, the secret root.
And from that second bark, black blood flows down.

"Dismayed, I pray both to the rural nymphs
and Father Mars, who guards the fields of Thrace,   45
to make the vision kind and not a menace.
But when, knees hard against the stubborn sand,
I strained, with greater force, to wrestle free
a third stem—shall I speak or hold my tongue?—
a moan rose from the bottom of the mound,   50
a lamentable voice returned to me:
'Why are you mangling me, Aeneas? Spare
my body. I am buried here. Do spare
the profanation of your pious hands.
I am no stranger to you; I am Trojan.   55
The blood you see does not flow from a stem.
Flee from these cruel lands, this greedy shore,
for I am Polydorus; here an iron
harvest of lances covered my pierced body;
for this, sharp javelins have grown above me.'   60
And then, indeed, my mind weighed down by doubt
and dread, I was astounded, and my hair

stood stiff, my voice held fast within my jaws.

"When luckless Priam first despaired of Dardan
arms, when he saw the city ringed by siege,   65
he sent young Polydorus out in secret,
along with much gold, to the king of Thrace,
who was to care for him. But when the might
of Troy is shattered and her fortune gone,
that king makes common cause with Agamemnon.   70
He breaks with every sacred trust; he murders
this Polydorus, takes his gold by force.
To what, accursed lust for gold, do you
not drive the hearts of men? When fear has left
my bones, I bring the omens of the gods   75
before my people's chieftains—with my father
Anchises first; I want to hear their judgment.
And all are of one mind: to leave that land
of crime, a place where friendship was profaned,
to let the south winds take our sails. And thus   80
we give fresh funerals to Polydorus
and heap earth high upon his mound and build
our altars to the Shades, with melancholy
dark garlands and black cypress; and around us
the Trojan women stand; their streaming hair   85
is loosened as our custom bids. We offer
bowls foaming with warm milk and cups of victims'
blood; then we lay the spirit in his grave
and, for the last time, call his name aloud.

"Then, just as soon as we can trust the sea,   90
as soon as the air allows us tranquil waters
and while the south wind, softly whispering,
invites to journeying, my comrades crowd
the beach to launch our fleet. We leave the harbor.
Our eyes have lost the cities and the land.   95

"Midsea a sacred island lies, loved by
the Nereids' mother and Aegean Neptune.
The grateful Archer God had found it drifting
around the coasts and shores; he bound it fast
to towering Myconos and Gyaros—   100
stable, habitable, scorning the winds.
And there I sail; this island grants calm entry,

safe harbor to our weary company.
On landing we revere Apollo's city.
King Anius, both king of men and priest   105
of Phoebus, garlands on his brow and holy
laurel, hurries to meet us, recognizing
Anchises, his old friend. We clasp right hands
in greeting, and we pass beneath his roof.

"At once I offered homage to the temple   110
of Phoebus, built of ancient stone: 'Give us,
o god of Thymbra, our own home; give us—
the weary—walls and sons, a lasting city;
preserve the second citadel of Troy,
the remnant left by Greeks and pitiless   115
Achilles. Whom are we to follow? Where
are we to go, to found our home? Father,
give us an omen, entering our hearts!'

"No sooner had I spoken so when all—
the gateways and the laurels of the gods—   120
seemed suddenly to tremble, and the whole
mountain began to sway, the tripod moaned,
the sacred shrine lay open. We bow low
upon the ground. A voice is carried to us:
'O iron sons of Dardanus, the land   125
that gave you birth, the land of your ancestors,
will welcome you again, returned to her
generous breast. Seek out your ancient mother.
For there Aeneas' house will rule all coasts,
as will his sons' sons and those born of them.'   130

"So said Apollo. Our great joy was mixed
with turbulence. All ask, 'Where are those walls
to which Apollo calls the wanderers,
asking for our return?' And then my father
thinks back upon his memories of old.   135
'O chieftains, listen, understand your hopes,'
he says. 'Out in the middle of the sea
lies Crete, the island of great Jupiter.
There is Mount Ida, cradle of our people.
The Cretans have a hundred splendid cities,   140
the richest realms. If I remember rightly

what I have heard, our greatest father, Teucer,
sailed out from Crete to the Rhoetean coasts
and chose a place fit for his kingdom. Ilium,
the towers of Pergamus were not yet built.   145
Men lived deep in the valleys. And from Crete
the Mother Goddess came to Cybele,
as did the Corybantes' brazen cymbals
within the grove of Ida; and from Crete
she brought the reverential silence of   150
her mysteries; the team of harnessed lions
that draw her chariot—a Cretan custom.
Then let us follow where the gods have led.
Let us appease the winds and seek the shores
of Cnossus. They are not too far from here;   155
if only Jupiter be gracious to us,
our fleet will land at Crete on the third day.'
This said, he slaughtered seemly sacrifices:
a bull to Neptune; one to you, Apollo;
a black sheep to the Winter, god of storms;   160
and to the favoring west winds, a white.

"We hear a rumor that Idomeneus,
the prince of Crete, is exiled from his father's
lands, that the coasts of Crete have been abandoned,
there are no enemies, deserted houses   165
await us there. We leave the port of Delos
and wing across the sea, skimming past Naxos,
where on the hills Bacchantes wanton, past
the green Donysa and Olearos
and snow-white Paros and the Cyclades   170
that stud the waters, through excited seas
that foam at frequent islands. And the oarsmen
cry out as they contend. My comrades urge:
'Drive on to Crete and to our ancestors!'

"The wind wakes at our stern. At length we glide   175
on to the ancient coasts of the Curetes.
There eagerly I raise the longed-for city's
walls, and I call it Pergamum. I spur
my people, happy in that name, to love
their home, to build a citadel on high.   180
   ❋   ❋   ❋

"And now our boats had just been drawn up on
dry beaches, with our young men busy at
new weddings and new plowings—I was giving
us laws, assigning dwellings—when a sudden
and wasting pestilence fell on our bodies   185
from some polluted quarter of the sky:
death's time, and terrible for trees and crops.
Men left sweet life or dragged their tainted bones.
The Dog Star burned the fields to barrenness.
The grass was parched. Sick grain denied us food.   190

"My father calls on us to cross again
the sea to Delos and the oracle
of Phoebus at Ortygia, to implore
his kindness, ask what end he will allot
our tired destinies, where to seek help   195
in our distress, and where to set our course.

"Night. Sleep held every living thing on earth.
The sacred statues of the deities,
the Phrygian household gods whom I had carried
from Troy out of the fires of the city,   200
as I lay sleeping seemed to stand before me.
And they were plain to see in the broad light
where full moon flowed through windows in the walls.
These were their words, and these erased my cares:
'Unasked, Apollo sends us to your threshold;   205
for here he prophesies just as he would
had you again traced back the seas to Delos.
We followed you, your men, from burning Troy
and crossed the swollen waters in your care
together with your ships; and we shall raise   210
your children to the stars and build an empire
out of their city. For the great make ready
great walls, do not desert the tedious
trials of your journeying. Your home is elsewhere.
For Delian Apollo did not call   215
the coasts of Crete your site for settlement.
There is a place the Greeks have named Hesperia—
an ancient land with strong arms and fat soil.
The men who lived there were Oenotrians;
but now it is said that their descendants call   220
the country "Italy" after their leader.

That is the home for us. Iasius—
our father, founder of the Trojan race—
and Dardanus were both born there. Rise up
and bring to old Anchises these sure words: 225
to seek out Corythus, Ausonia;
for Jupiter denies you Dicte's fields.'

"These visions and the voice of gods were too
astonishing: I did not dream, I knew
their faces and the fillets in their hair,   230
those trusted images that stood before me.
An icy sweat was wrapped around my body.
I tear myself from bed and lift my voice
and hands to heaven; on the hearth I pour
unwatered wine. This ceremony done,   235
I gladly tell Anchises all they said.
At this, he saw our double lineage,
twin parentage, how he had been mistaken
through new confusion over ancient places.
'My son, Cassandra was the only one   240
who saw this destiny for us—Cassandra,
so battered by Troy's fates. Now I remember:
she prophesied what lay in wait, and often
she named Hesperia and Italy.
But who could then believe the Teucrians   245
would reach the harbors of Hesperia?
Who then could heed Cassandra's prophecy?
But let us trust in Phoebus; warned by him,
let us pursue a better destiny.'
His speech is done; in gladness we obey.   250
We leave the walls of Pergamum; only
a few remain, the rest of us set sail
across the wide seas in our hollow keels.

"But after we were well upon the waters,
with land no longer to be seen—the sky   255
was everywhere, and everywhere the sea—
a blue-black cloud ran overhead; it brought
the night and storm and breakers rough in darkness.
The winds roll up the sea, great waters heave.
And we are scattered, tossed upon the vast   260
abyss; clouds cloak the day; damp night annuls
the heavens; frequent lightning fires flash

through tattered clouds; cast from our course, we wander
across the blind waves. Even Palinurus
can not tell day from night upon the heavens,   265
can not recall our way among the waters.

"We wander for three days in sightless darkness
and for as many nights without a star.
At last, upon the fourth, the land rose up
with twining smoke and mountains seen far off.   270
The sails are dropped. Our crewmen take their oars;
they do not wait. The straining rowers lash
the spray, they sweep across the blue-gray waters.

"When I am safe at last from waves, the first
coast to receive me is the Strophades':   275
the Strophades that bear a Grecian name,
islands within the great Ionian sea.
They are the home of horrible Celaeno
and all her sister Harpies since the time
that Phineus shut his house against them and,   280
in fear, they fled their former feasts. No monster
is more malevolent than these, no scourge
of gods or pestilence more savage ever
rose from the Stygian waves. These birds may wear
the face of virgins, but their bellies drip   285
with a disgusting discharge, and their hands
are talons, and their features pale and famished.

"On entering that harbor, we can see
glad herds of cattle scattered through the fields
and flocks of goats, unguarded, on the grass.   290
We fall upon them with our swords; we call
the gods and Jove himself to share our spoils.
Along the curving coast we build our couches.
We feast on those rich meats. But suddenly,
shaking out their wings with a great clanging,   295
the Harpies, horrible, swoop from the hilltops;
and plundering our banquet with the filthy
touch of their talons, they foul everything.
Their terrifying scream leaps from that stench.

"But in the shelter of a hollowed rock,   300
shut in by trees and trembling shadows, we

again set out our tables and replace
the fire on the altars. But again,
though from another quarter of the heavens
and from dark dens, the clanging crowd descends;   305
they fall upon their prey with crooked talons,
defiling all our feast. I call my comrades
to arms, to war against the cruel tribe.
They do as they are commanded; all conceal
their swords beneath the grass; they hide their shields.   310
And when along the winding shore the shrill
Harpies swoop down on us, Misenus signals;
his hollow trumpet sounds from his high lookout.

"My comrades now attack in strangest struggle,
hacking at these lewd birds come from the sea.   315
No blow can wound their wings or scar their backs.
Beneath the stars they glide in headlong flight.
They leave behind half-eaten prey and filth.

"One only—prophetess of misery,
Celaeno—perches on a towering rock.   320
Her cry breaks out: 'Sons of Laomedon,
we let you slaughter oxen, kill our bullocks;
but in return you wage a war to drive
the guiltless Harpies from their father's kingdom.
Therefore, receive these words of mine: fix them   325
within your mind. What the all-able Father
foretold to Phoebus, Phoebus unto me,
now I, the Furies' chief, reveal to you.
The place you seek is Italy, and you
will go to Italy with winds that you   330
invoke; you will not be denied its harbors.
But you will not wall in your promised city
until an awful hunger and your wrong
in slaughtering my sisters has compelled
your jaws to gnaw as food your very tables.'   335
She spoke and then flew back into the forest.

"My comrades' blood ran cold with sudden fear.
Their spirits fell. They'd have me plead for peace
with vows and prayers, not weapons—whether these
be goddesses or awful, obscene birds.   340
Then from the shore, with hands outstretched, Anchises

calls on the great gods, offers sacrifices:
'Gods, keep these threats from us, let such disaster
be distant, and be gracious to the pious.'
He has us tear our cable free from shore,   345
uncoil our ropes to loosen up the sails.
Then south winds stretch our sheets; we flee across
the foam, where wind and pilot called our course.
And now among the waves we see the wooded
Zacynthus and Dulichium and Same   350
and steep-cliffed Neritos. We shun the shoals
of Ithaca, Laertes' land, and curse
the earth that once had nursed the fierce Ulysses.
Soon we can see Apollo's shrine above
Leucata's stormy peaks that panic sailors.   355
Now weary, we approach the little city.
Our anchor is down, the sterns stand on the shore.

"And having gained unhoped-for land, we kindle
the altars with our offerings. We give
our gifts to Jupiter and crowd the beaches   360
of Actium with Trojan games. My comrades
strip naked; sleek with oil, they try their strength
in Ilian wrestling matches, glad to have
slipped past so many Argive towns, held fast
to flight among a crowd of enemies.   365

"Meanwhile the sun wheels round the full year's circle;
the icy winter's north winds bring rough waves.
I fasten to the temple door a shield
of hollow brass that once belonged to mighty
Abas. Beneath it I inscribe this verse: 370
Aeneas took these arms from Grecian victors.
I then command my men to leave the harbor,
to take their places at the rowing benches.
My comrades lash the waves; in rivalry
they sweep the plain of sea. We soon lose sight   375
of the airy heights of the Phaeacians;
we skirt the coastline of Epirus, then
we sail into the harbor of Chaonia,
approaching the steep city of Buthrotum.

"A rumor of incredible events   380
awaits us here: that Helenus, the son

of Priam, is a king of Grecian cities,
that he has won the wife and scepter of
Pyrrhus, Achilles' son; that once again
Andromache is given to a husband   385
of her own country. And I was amazed.
My heart burned with extraordinary longing
to speak to him, to learn of such great happenings.
Just then—when I had left the harbor and
my boat, drawn up along the beaches—there,   390
within a grove that stood before the city,
alongside waves that mimed the Simois,
Andromache was offering to the ashes
a solemn banquet and sad gifts, imploring
the Shade of Hector's empty tomb that she   395
had raised out of green turf with double altars
and consecrated as a cause for tears.

"And when, distracted, she caught sight of me
and saw our Trojan armor all around her,
in terror of these mighty omens, she   400
grew stiff; heat left her bones; she fell, fainting.
But after long delay, at last she asks:
'Are you, born of a goddess, a true body,
a real messenger who visits me?
Are you alive? Or if the gracious light   405
of life has left you, where is Hector?' So
she spoke. Her tears were many and her cries
filled all the grove. She is so frenzied, I—
disquieted—must stammer scattered words:
'Indeed I live and drag my life through all   410
extremities; do not doubt—I am real.
But you, what fate has overtaken you,
divided from so great a husband, or
what kindly fortune comes again to Hector's
Andromache? Are you still wed to Pyrrhus?' 415
Her eyes downcast, she spoke with murmured words:

" 'O happy past all others, virgin daughter
of Priam, made to die beside our foeman's
tomb, underneath the towering walls of Troy;
o you, for whom no lots were cast, who never   420
as captive touched the couch of a conquering master!
But we, our homeland burned, were carried over

strange seas, and we endured the arrogance
of Pyrrhus and his youthful insolence,
to bear him children in our slavery;　　　　　　425
until he sought Hermione, the daughter
of Leda, and a Spartan wedding, handing
me to Helenus, a slave to a slave.
But then Orestes, goaded by his great
passion for his lost bride and fired by　　　　　430
the Furies of his crimes, surprises Pyrrhus
and cuts him down beside his father's altars.
At Pyrrhus' death a portion of his kingdom
passed on to Helenus, who named the plains
Chaonian—all the land Chaonia,　　　　　　435
for Trojan Chaon—placing on the heights
a Pergamus and this walled Ilium.
But what winds and what fates have given you
a course to steer? What god has driven you,
unknowing, to our shores? Where is your boy　　440
Ascanius—while Troy still stood, Creüsa
would carry him to you—does he still live
and feed upon the air? Is any care
for his lost mother still within the boy?
Do both his father and his uncle, Hector,　　445
urge him to ancient courage, manliness?'

"Andromache was weeping, calling up
long, needless tears, when the hero Helenus,
the son of Priam, with a crowd behind him,
approaches from the city walls. And he　　　450
knows us as his own kinsmen. Glad, he leads
the way up to the thresholds and, between
each word, sheds many tears. As I advance,
I see a little Troy, a Pergamus
that mimes the great one, and a dried-up stream　455
that takes its name from Xanthus. I embrace
the portals of the Scaean gates. My Trojans
also enjoy the kindly city where
the king has welcomed them to spacious porches.
They pour the cups of Bacchus in the hall.　　460
The feast is served on gold. They lift the goblets.

"Day follows day, the breezes call our canvas,
and now the swelling south wind fills our sails.

And I approach the prophet with these words:
'O son of Troy, interpreter of gods,   465
you who can understand the will of Phoebus,
the tripods and the laurel of Apollo,
the stars, the tongues of birds, the swift-winged omens,
come, tell me—for the heavens have foretold
with words of blessing all my voyage, all   470
the gods have counseled me to Italy,
to seek out and explore that far-off land:
only Celaeno, chieftain of the Harpies,
has chanted strange portents, monstrous to tell,
predicting awful vengeance, foul starvation—   475
what dangers shall I first avoid? Tell me
the course I need to overcome such trials.'

"First steers are sacrificed, then Helenus
loosens the garlands from his hallowed head;
he prays the gods for grace; with his own hand   480
he leads me to your portals, Phoebus, awed
before your mighty presence, as he chants
these priestly words from his inspired lips:

" 'Aeneas, goddess-born—since you must surely
have crossed the seas beneath high auspices—   485
so does the king of gods allot the fates,
revolving every happening, this is
the circling order; few things out of many
I shall unfold in words, that you may find
the waters friendly and the crossing tranquil   490
and reach the harbor of Ausonia.
The Fates will not let Helenus know more;
Saturnian Juno will not let me speak.
But first, the Italy you now think close—
preparing, in your ignorance, to rush   495
into its nearby harbors—is far off:
a long and pathless way through spacious lands
divides you from her. For your oar must bend
beneath the waters of Trinacria,
your ships must cross Ausonia's salt sea,   500
and you must pass the lakes below the earth,
and then the island of Aeaean Circe,
before you find safe ground to build your city.
          ❂   ❂   ❂

" 'I give you signs: hold them fast in your mind.
For when, in your perplexity, you find   505
beside the waters of a secret stream,
along the banks beneath the branching ilex,
a huge white sow stretched out upon the ground
together with a new-delivered litter
of thirty suckling white pigs at her teats,   510
that place will be the site set for your city;
that place will bring sure rest from all your toils.
And do not fear your gnawing at the tables
that was forewarned; for fate will find a way;
Apollo will be present when you call.   515

" 'But shun those lands and that Italian coast
nearest to us and washed by our own sea:
for all those walls are manned by hostile Greeks;
there the Narycian Locrians built their cities
and there Idomeneus of Lyctos with   520
his warriors blocks the Sallentini's plains;
and there the small Petelia of Philoctetes,
the Meliboean chief, stands in its walls.
Moreover, when your ships have crossed and anchor
along the other coast, when you are pledging   525
your vows upon the altars by the shore,
conceal your head beneath a purple mantle,
that while you are at worship there, no hostile
face may appear to you among the sacred
and sacrificial fires to spoil the omens.   530
And let your comrades, too, keep fast this practice
of sacrifice; yourself maintain the custom;
and may your pious sons continue it.

" 'But when you have departed, when the wind
has carried you to the Sicilian coast,   535
just where the strait gates of Pelorus open,
then—though the way be long—you must still shun
the shoreline and the waters to the right;
seek out the left-hand seas, the left-hand coast.
When these two lands were an unbroken one   540
in ancient times, they say, a vast convulsion
tore them apart by force (through time's long lapse,
such overwhelming changes come to pass).
Between them violently burst the sea;

waves split apart the shores of Italy   545
and Sicily. Along the severed coasts
a narrow tideway bathes the fields and cities.

" 'Now Scylla holds the right; insatiable
Charybdis keeps the left. Three times she sucks
the vast waves into her abyss, the deepest   550
whirlpool within her vortex, then she hurls
the waters high, lashing the stars with spray.
But Scylla is confined to blind retreats,
a cavern; and her mouths thrust out to drag
ships toward the shoals. Her upper parts are human;   555
down to the pubes, she seems a lovely-breasted
virgin; but underneath she is a monster
come from the sea, a terrifying body:
a dolphin's tail that joins a wolfish groin.
Therefore I tell you: better to be slow—   560
to round the promontory of Pachynus,
to take the longer way—than to behold
misshapen Scylla in her savage cavern,
the rocks that echo with her sea-green dogs.

" 'Above all, if the prophet merit trust,   565
if any prudence be in Helenus
and if Apollo fill his soul with truth,
then this one thing, Aeneas, goddess-born,
this more than any thing, I conjure you,
repeating it again, again, as warning: 570
first, do adore the power of mighty Juno
with prayers and pledge your vows to mighty Juno
with willingness, to win that mighty mistress
with pleasing gifts—and then, victorious,
to leave Trinacria for Italy.   575

" 'When on your way you reach the town of Cumae,
the sacred lakes, the loud wood of Avernus,
there you will see the frenzied prophetess.
Deep in her cave of rock she charts the fates,
consigning to the leaves her words and symbols.   580
Whatever verses she has written down
upon the leaves, she puts in place and order
and then abandons them inside her cavern.
When all is still, that order is not troubled;

but when soft winds are stirring and the door,   585
turning upon its hinge, disturbs the tender
leaves, then she never cares to catch the verses
that flutter through the hollow grotto, never
recalls their place or joins them all together.
Her visitors, when they have had no counsel,   590
depart, and then detest the Sibyl's cavern.
Let no expense of time be counted here,
though comrades chide and though the journey urge
your sails to take the waves or favoring
sea breezes swell their folds for voyaging.   595
But visit her, the prophetess, with prayers,
that she reveal the oracles herself
and willingly unlock her voice and lips.
She will unfold for you who are the peoples
of Italy, the wars that are to come,   600
and in what way you are to flee or face
each crisis. Worshiped properly, she grants
prosperous voyages. These things are all
the gods allow my tongue to chant and tell.
Now go your way, and with your acts exalt   605
the mightiness of Troy as high as heaven.'

"The seer had finished with his friendly words.
He asks that gifts of chiseled ivory
and massive gold be carried to our galleys;
he stows much silver in the holds, Dodona   610
caldrons, a corselet joined with links of three-
ply gold—the gear of Neoptolemus—
and presents for my father. Then he adds
new oarsmen for our crew and guides and horses;
he furnishes my fighting men with weapons.   615

"Meanwhile Anchises has our sails made ready
that no delay rob us of driving winds.
With deep respect Apollo's spokesman greets him:
'Anchises, honored as high mate of Venus,
Anchises, whom the gods care for, twice saved   620
from Troy in ruins: now Ausonia
is yours, bear down upon it with your sails.
And yet you must bypass the coast you see;
Apollo has disclosed a farther country.
Go, blessed in the affection of your son.   625

But why do I talk on? My tongue must not
keep back the surging south winds from your sails.'

"Andromache mourns deeply at our last
leavetaking, bringing robes adorned with threads
of gold, a Phrygian mantle for my son—   630
she does not yield in doing honor—weighting
Ascanius with woven gifts, then tells him:
'Receive these, too, my boy: memorials
of my own handiwork; and let them serve
as witness to Andromache's long love   635
as wife of Hector. Take with you these last
gifts of your people—you, the only image
that still is left of my Astyanax:
so did he bear his eyes, his hands, his face;
so would he now be entering his youth,   640
were he alive, his years the same as yours.'

"My parting words were said with rising tears:
'Your fate is here, then live it happily.
But we are called from one fate to another.
For you can rest: no need to plow the seas   645
or seek the fleeing fields of Italy.
Here you can see the image of new Xanthus
and of the Troy your hands have built beneath
more kindly auspices, I hope—a city
less open to the Greeks than was old Troy.   650
If ever I shall enter on the Tiber
and on the lands that lie along the Tiber
and see the ramparts given to my race,
then we, in time to come, shall build one Troy
in spirit from our sister cities in   655
Epirus and Hesperia and from
our kindred peoples—those who share one founder
in Dardanus and share one destiny.
May this become the care of all our sons.'

"We speed along the sea and past the nearby   660
cliffs of Ceraunia, the shortest passage
across the waves, the way to Italy.
The sun has set, the hills are dark with shadow.
We disembark. When we had assigned by lot
our turns to watch the oars, we stretch out on   665

the lap of longed-for land beside the water;
and all along the dry beach we renew
our bodies; sleep is dew for weary limbs.

"Night, driven by the Hours, has not yet reached
the middle of her path when Palinurus   670
springs quickly from his couch, takes note of all
the winds, and with his keen ear tries to catch
the breath of a breeze. He watches all the stars
that glide through silent skies: he marks Arcturus,
the twin Bears and the rainy Hyades,   675
Orion armed with gold; and seeing all
together in the tranquil heavens, loudly
he signals from the stern. We break up camp
and try our course with spreading canvas wings.

"And now Aurora reddens as the stars   680
take flight. We sight the dim and distant hills,
the low coastline of Italy. Achates
is first to cry out, 'Italy'; with joy
the rest shout, 'Italy.' Anchises crowns
a great bowl with a garland, fills it up   685
with wine, and from the steep stern summons all
the deities: 'O gods who govern sea
and land and tempests, grant us easy passage
and breathe upon us with your kindliness.'

"The wished-for winds have quickened now; nearby   690
a harbor opens up. We can make out
a temple standing on Minerva's Height.
My comrades furl the sails; they turn the prow
toward shore. The eastern waves have hollowed out
that port into a bow; the thrusting reefs   695
churn up salt spray; the harbor is concealed.
Like drooping arms, a double wall runs down
from towering crags; the shrine is set far back
from shore, and here, as our first omen, I
could see four snow-white horses grazing far   700
and wide along the grassy plain. Anchises
cries out: 'O stranger land, the tale you tell
is war; these horses wear the harnesses
of war; these herds mean war. Yet these same stallions
have yielded to the chariot beneath   705

the yoke and reins of peace. Then there is also
some hope for peace.' We pray unto the holy
power of Pallas, clangorous with arms,
the first to hear our joyous shout. We cover
our heads with Trojan veils before the altars;   710
and just as Helenus ordained, we offer
burnt sacrifices to the Argive Juno.

"No lingering; our vows are done. We turn
to sea our sail-draped spars with tapering horns.
We leave behind the homes of the Grecian-born,   715
the fields that we distrust. We sight the town
of Hercules—Tarentum's gulf (if what
they tell as tale be true); then, facing us,
Lacinian Juno's temple rises; next
the fortresses of Caulon; after that   720
the city known for shipwrecks—Scylaceum.

"Then far across the waters we can see
Sicilian Etna; far across we hear
the mighty moan of breakers, pounded stones
and broken echoes on the beach, and shoals   725
that leap and sands that mingle with the surge.
Anchises cries, 'This surely is Charybdis;
these are the crags, and these the fearful rocks
that Helenus predicted. Save yourselves;
my comrades, stroke as one upon the oars!'   730

"They do as they are told. First Palinurus
turned round the groaning prow to larboard waters;
the crew then sought the left with wind and oar.
We rise to heaven on the bending wave
and, as the surge slips back, we sink again   735
down to the deepest Shades. Three times the crags
cried out among the eaves of rock, three times
we saw the heaving spray, the dripping stars.
But then the sun has set, the wind has left
our weary crew; not knowing where we go,   740
we drift upon the beaches of the Cyclops.

"That harbor is wide and free from winds; but Etna
is thundering nearby with dread upheavals.
At times it belches into upper air

dark clouds with tar-black whirlwinds, blazing lava,   745
while lifting balls of flame that lick the stars.
At times it vomits boulders as the crater's
bowels are torn; it moans and tosses molten
stones up to heaven; from its deep bedrock
the mountain boils and foams. The tale is told   750
that, charred by lightning bolts, the body of
Enceladus lies pressed beneath this mass;
that mighty Etna, piled above him, breathes
and blazes from its bursting furnaces;
and that as often as Enceladus   755
shifts on his weary side, all Sicily
shudders and groans, and smoke blots out the sky.
That night we hide within the forest, fiendish
horrors upon us, but we cannot see
the cause of all that clamoring; the stars   760
had lost their fires, the heavens had no brightness
but only mists on darkened skies; the dead
of night had clutched the moon within a cloud.

"Tomorrow now was rising with first light,
Aurora had banned damp shadows from the sky,   765
when suddenly a tattered stranger, gaunt
with final hunger, staggers from the woods
and stretches pleading hands toward shore. We turn
to look at him: his filth is ghastly—his beard
is tangled and his clothing hooked by thorns;   770
and yet he is a Greek—one who was sent
to Troy with Argive arms. And when far off
he saw our Dardan dress, our Trojan weapons,
his terror held him for a time, he stayed
his steps, then dashed headlong upon the shore   775
with tears and prayers: 'By stars and gods above,
and by the light of heaven that we breathe,
I conjure you to take me with you, Trojans,
to carry me wherever you may go.
I ask no more than this. I know that I   780
am from the ships of Danaans and confess
I warred against the gods of Troy; for this,
if it be such great wrong, dismember me
upon the waters, plunge me in vast seas.
For if I must die now, then I shall be   785

content to perish at the hands of humans.'

"Such was his outcry. Groveling, he clasped
my knees and held me fast. We urge him on,
to tell us who he is, who are his people,
what fortune harries him. Father Anchises   790
does not wait long to offer him his hand
and steadies the young man with that strong pledge.
At last he lays aside his fear and says:

" 'I am of Ithaca and sailed for Troy,
a comrade of unfortunate Ulysses;   795
my name is Achaemenides, the son
of Adamastus, a poor father—would
my lot had never changed! My comrades left me,
forgotten in the great cave of the Cyclops,
while they escaped in haste those savage thresholds.   800

" 'It is a house of gore and gruesome feasts,
both black and vast within. The towering Cyclops
is tall enough to strike the high stars—gods,
keep such a plague away from earth!—and hardly
easy to look upon; no one can reach him   805
with speech. He feeds upon the guts and dark
blood of his victims. I myself have seen him
snatch up a pair of us in his huge paw,
then, stretched along the middle of the cavern,
bash both of them against a boulder; then   810
the entrance swam with splattered gore. I saw
him crunch their limbs that dripped with blood; I saw
their warm joints quivering within his jaws.

" 'But he has had to pay for this. Such slaughter
was too much for Ulysses; facing it,   815
the Ithacan did not forget himself.
As soon as Polyphemus, banquet-bloated,
buried in wine, reclined his drooping neck
and, monstrous, lay along the cavern, belching
his morsels mixed with dripping blood and wine,   820
we prayed to the great gods, we drew our lots;
then we surrounded him on every side
and with a pointed weapon pierced his eye—
hidden, it lay beneath his sullen brow,

alone, enormous, like an Argive shield   825
or like the lamp of Phoebus—and at last,
in joy, avenged the Shades of our companions.

" 'But, miserable men, cut loose your cable
from shore and flee now, flee! For just as huge
as Polyphemus—he who pens his herds   830
of woolly sheep within his hollow cavern
and squeezes out their teats—there are a hundred
other ferocious Cyclops. And they crowd
these curving coasts and climb across these mountains.
Three times the moon has filled her horns with light   835
since I began to drag out my poor life
within the woods, among the desert dens
and dwellings of wild beasts, and from a rock
to watch the huge Cyclops, to tremble at
their tramping feet, their voices' clamoring.   840
I feed on wretched food, on stony cornels
and berries from the branches, and I eat
roots torn from plants. I have scanned every view,
but yours is the first fleet I have seen landing
upon these shores. Whatever happens, I   845
am given up to you. It is enough
for me to have escaped that cursed tribe.
By any death whatever, take this life!'

"His words were hardly ended when we saw
upon a peak the shepherd Polyphemus;   850
he lugged his mammoth hulk among the flocks,
searching along familiar shores—an awful
misshapen monster, huge, his eyelight lost.
His steps are steadied by the lopped-off pine
he grips. His woolly sheep are at his side—   855
his only joy and comfort for his loss.
As soon as he had reached the open sea
and touched deep waves, he bathed the blood trickling
down from the socket of his dug-out light.
Groaning, gnashing his teeth, he strides the waters.   860
The wave has not yet wet his giant thighs.

"Alarmed, we rush our flight. The suppliant,
who merited as much, is taken on
shipboard. We cut the cable silently

and, bending, sweep the waves with straining oars.   865
The monster sensed as much. He wheeled around.
He is following our voices, but without
a chance to clutch us with his right hand or
to match Ionian waves in chasing us.
His roaring is tremendous, and the sea   870
and all the waters quake together; far
inland a terror takes all Italy,
and Etna bellows in her curving caves.

"But down from woods and mountains in alarm
the tribe of Cyclops hurry toward the harbor.   875
They crowd the beaches. Brotherhood of Etna,
they stand, helpless, with sullen eyes, their heads
raised high to heaven—horrible conclave,
as when, upon a summit, giant oaks
or cypresses, cone-bearing, mass together: 880
Diana's grove or Jupiter's tall forest.
Keen terror urges us headlong to shake
our rigging where we can, to stretch our sails
to favorable winds. But Helenus
had warned us we were not to hold our course   885
through Scylla and Charybdis, where each way
is neighbor to our death. We must sail back.
And from the narrow fastness of Pelorus
the north wind comes to meet us. I sail past
the mouth of the Pantagias, living rock,   890
the bays of Megara, and then flat Thapsus.
These were the coasts that Achaemenides,
the comrade of unfortunate Ulysses,
showed us as he retraced his former wanderings.

"Along a bay of Sicily there lies   895
the sea-drenched island of Plemyrium.
Of old, Ortygia was its name. The story
tells us that here Alpheus, Elis' river,
forced secret passage underneath the sea,
and mingles now with your mouth, Arethusa,   900
in these Sicilian waves. Obedient,
we venerate the high gods of that place,
then pass Helorus with its fat marshlands.
We skirt the high reefs and the thrusting rocks
along the promontory of Pachynus;   905

then Camarina, whom the Fates forbade
to be dislodged, is seen far off; the plains
of Gela and the town that also takes
its name of Gela from its rushing river.
Steep Acragas, which once bred noble horses,   910
next shows its mighty ramparts in the distance.
I leave behind Selinus, palmy city,
with kindly winds, then skim past Lilybaeum
and shallows that are rough with hidden rocks.

"Then Drepanum's unhappy coast and harbor   915
receive me. It is here that—after all
the tempests of the sea—I lose my father,
Anchises, stay in every care and crisis.
For here, o best of fathers, you first left
me to my weariness, alone—Anchises,   920
you who were saved in vain from dreadful dangers.
Not even Helenus, the prophet, nor
the horrible Celaeno, when they warned
of many terrors, told this grief to come.
And this was my last trial; this was the term   925
of my long journeying. I left that harbor.
And then the god drove me upon your shore."

And thus, with all of them intent on him,
father Aeneas told of destinies
decreed by gods and taught his wanderings.   930
At last he ended here, was silent, rested.

IV·914

BOOK IV

Too late. The queen is caught between love's pain
and press. She feeds the wound within her veins;
she is eaten by a secret flame. Aeneas'
high name, all he has done, again, again
come like a flood. His face, his words hold fast   5
her breast. Care strips her limbs of calm and rest.

A new dawn lights the earth with Phoebus' lamp
and banishes damp shadows from the sky
when restless Dido turns to her heart's sharer:
"Anna, my sister, what dreams make me shudder?   10
Who is this stranger guest come to our house?
How confident he looks, how strong his chest
and arms! I think—and I have cause—that he
is born of gods. For in the face of fear
the mean must fall. What fates have driven him!   15
What trying wars he lived to tell! Were it not
my sure, immovable decision not
to marry anyone since my first love
turned traitor, when he cheated me by death,
were I not weary of the couch and torch,   20
I might perhaps give way to this one fault.
For I must tell you, Anna, since the time

Sychaeus, my poor husband, died and my
own brother splashed our household gods with blood,
Aeneas is the only man to move   25
my feelings, to overturn my shifting heart.
I know too well the signs of the old flame.
But I should call upon the earth to gape
and close above me, or on the almighty
Father to take his thunderbolt, to hurl   30
me down into the shades, the pallid shadows
and deepest night of Erebus, before
I'd violate you, Shame, or break your laws!
For he who first had joined me to himself
has carried off my love, and may he keep it   35
and be its guardian within the grave."
She spoke. Her breast became a well of tears.

And Anna answers: "Sister, you more dear
to me than light itself, are you to lose
all of your youth in dreary loneliness,   40
and never know sweet children or the soft
rewards of Venus? Do you think that ashes
or buried Shades will care about such matters?
Until Aeneas came, there was no suitor
who moved your sad heart—not in Libya nor,   45
before, in Tyre: you always scorned Iarbas
and all the other chiefs that Africa,
a region rich in triumphs, had to offer.
How can you struggle now against a love
that is so acceptable? Have you forgotten   50
the land you settled, those who hem you in?
On one side lie the towns of the Gaetulians,
a race invincible, and the unbridled
Numidians and then the barbarous Syrtis.
And on the other lies a barren country,   55
stripped by the drought and by Barcaean raiders,
raging both far and near. And I need not
remind you of the wars that boil in Tyre
and of your brother's menaces and plots.
For I am sure it was the work of gods   60
and Juno that has held the Trojan galleys
fast to their course and brought them here to Carthage.
If you marry Aeneas, what a city

and what a kingdom, sister, you will see!   65
With Trojan arms beside us, so much greatness
must lie in wait for Punic glory! Only
pray to the gods for their good will, and having
presented them with proper sacrifices,
be lavish with your Trojan guests and weave
excuses for delay while frenzied winter   70
storms out across the sea and shatters ships,
while wet Orion blows his tempest squalls
beneath a sky that is intractable."

These words of Anna fed the fire in Dido.
Hope burned away her doubt, destroyed her shame.   75
First they move on from shrine to shrine, imploring
the favor of the gods at every altar.
They slaughter chosen sheep, as is the custom,
and offer them to Ceres the lawgiver,
to Phoebus, Father Bacchus, and—above all—   80
to Juno, guardian of marriage. Lovely
Dido holds the cup in her right hand;
she pours the offering herself, midway
between a milk-white heifer's horns. She studies
slit breasts of beasts and reads their throbbing guts.   85
But oh the ignorance of augurs! How
can vows and altars help one wild with love?
Meanwhile the supple flame devours her marrow;
within her breast the silent wound lives on.
Unhappy Dido burns. Across the city   90
she wanders in her frenzy—even as
a heedless hind hit by an arrow when
a shepherd drives for game with darts among
the Cretan woods and, unawares, from far
leaves winging steel inside her flesh; she roams   95
the forests and the wooded slopes of Dicte,
the shaft of death still clinging to her side.
So Dido leads Aeneas around the ramparts,
displays the wealth of Sidon and the city
ready to hand; she starts to speak, then falters   100
and stops in midspeech. Now day glides away.
Again, insane, she seeks out that same banquet,
again she prays to hear the trials of Troy,
again she hangs upon the teller's lips.
        ✿   ✿   ✿

But now the guests are gone. The darkened moon,   105
in turn, conceals its light, the setting stars
invite to sleep; inside the vacant hall
she grieves alone and falls upon the couch
that he has left. Absent, she sees, she hears
the absent one or draws Ascanius,   110
his son and counterfeit, into her arms,
as if his shape might cheat her untellable love.

Her towers rise no more; the young of Carthage
no longer exercise at arms or build
their harbors or sure battlements for war;   115
the works are idle, broken off; the massive,
menacing rampart walls, even the crane,
defier of the sky, now lie neglected.

As soon as Jove's dear wife sees that her Dido
is in the grip of such a scourge and that   120
no honor can withstand this madness, then
the daughter of Saturn faces Venus: "How
remarkable indeed: what splendid spoils
you carry off, you and your boy; how grand
and memorable is the glory if   125
one woman is beaten by the guile of two
gods. I have not been blind. I know you fear
our fortresses, you have been suspicious of
the houses of high Carthage. But what end
will come of all this hate? Let us be done   130
with wrangling. Let us make, instead of war,
an everlasting peace and plighted wedding.
You have what you were bent upon: she burns
with love; the frenzy now is in her bones.
Then let us rule this people—you and I—   135
with equal auspices; let Dido serve
a Phrygian husband, let her give her Tyrians
and her pledged dowry into your right hand."

But Venus read behind the words of Juno
the motive she had hid: to shunt the kingdom   140
of Italy to Libyan shores. And so
she answered Juno: "Who is mad enough
to shun the terms you offer? Who would prefer
to strive with you in war? If only fortune

favor the course you urge. For I am ruled   145
by fates and am unsure if Jupiter
would have the Trojans and the men of Tyre
become one city, if he likes the mingling
of peoples and the writing of such treaties.
But you are his wife and it is right for you   150
to try his mind, to entreat him. Go. I'll follow."

Queen Juno answered her: "That task is mine.
But listen now while in few words I try
to tell you how I mean to bring about
this urgent matter. When tomorrow's Titan   155
first shows his rays of light, reveals the world,
Aeneas and unhappy Dido plan
to hunt together in the forest. Then
while horsemen hurry to surround the glades
with nets, I shall pour down a black raincloud,   160
in which I have mixed hail, to awaken all
the heavens with my thundering. Their comrades
will scatter under cover of thick night.
Both Dido and the Trojan chief will reach
their shelter in the same cave. I shall be there.   165
And if I can rely on your goodwill,
I shall unite the two in certain marriage
and seal her as Aeneas' very own;
and this shall be their wedding." Cytherea
said nothing to oppose the plan; she granted   170
what Juno wanted, smiling at its cunning.

Meanwhile Aurora rose; she left the Ocean.
And when her brightness fills the air, select
young men move from the gates with wide-meshed nets
and narrow snares and broad-blade hunting spears,   175
and then Massylian horsemen hurry out
with strong, keen-scented hounds. But while the chieftains
of Carthage wait at Dido's threshold, she
still lingers in her room. Her splendid stallion,
in gold and purple, prances, proudly champing   180
his foaming bit. At last the queen appears
among the mighty crowd; upon her shoulders
she wears a robe of Sidon with embroidered
borders. Her quiver is of gold, her hair
has knots and ties of gold, a golden clasp   185

holds fast her purple cloak. Her Trojan comrades
and glad Ascanius advance behind her.
Aeneas, who is handsome past all others,
himself approaches now to join her, linking
his hunting band to hers. Just as Apollo,   190
when in the winter he abandons Lycia
and Xanthus' streams to visit his maternal
Delos, where he renews the dances—Cretans,
Dryopians, and painted Agathyrsi,
mingling around the altars, shout—advances   195
upon the mountain ridges of high Cynthus
and binds his flowing hair with gentle leaves
and braids its strands with intertwining gold;
his arrows clatter on his shoulder: no
less graceful is Aeneas as he goes;   200
an equal beauty fills his splendid face.
And when they reach the hills and pathless thickets,
the wild she-goats, dislodged from stony summits,
run down the ridges; from another slope
stags fling themselves across the open fields;   205
they mass their dusty bands in flight, forsaking
the hillsides. But the boy Ascanius
rides happy in the valleys on his fiery
stallion as he passes on his course
now stags, now goats; among the lazy herds   210
his prayer is for a foaming boar or that
a golden lion come down from the mountain.

Meanwhile confusion takes the sky, tremendous
turmoil, and on its heels, rain mixed with hail.
The scattered train of Tyre, the youth of Troy,   215
and Venus' Dardan grandson in alarm
seek different shelters through the fields; the torrents
roar down the mountains. Dido and the Trojan
chieftain have reached the same cave. Primal Earth
and Juno, queen of marriages, together   220
now give the signal: lightning fires flash,
the upper air is witness to their mating,
and from the highest hilltops shout the nymphs.
That day was her first day of death and ruin.
For neither how things seem nor how they are deemed   225
moves Dido now, and she no longer thinks
of furtive love. For Dido calls it marriage,

and with this name she covers up her fault.

Then, swiftest of all evils, Rumor runs
straightway through Libya's mighty cities—Rumor,   230
whose life is speed, whose going gives her force.
Timid and small at first, she soon lifts up
her body in the air. She stalks the ground;
her head is hidden in the clouds. Provoked
to anger at the gods, her mother Earth   235
gave birth to her, last come—they say—as sister
to Coeus and Enceladus; fast-footed
and lithe of wing, she is a terrifying
enormous monster with as many feathers
as she has sleepless eyes beneath each feather   240
(amazingly), as many sounding tongues
and mouths, and raises up as many ears.
Between the earth and skies she flies by night,
screeching across the darkness, and she never
closes her eyes in gentle sleep. By day   245
she sits as sentinel on some steep roof
or on high towers, frightening vast cities;
for she holds fast to falsehood and distortion
as often as to messages of truth.
Now she was glad. She filled the ears of all   250
with many tales. She sang of what was done
and what was fiction, chanting that Aeneas,
one born of Trojan blood, had come, that lovely
Dido has deigned to join herself to him,
that now, in lust, forgetful of their kingdom,   255
they take long pleasure, fondling through the winter,
the slaves of squalid craving. Such reports
the filthy goddess scatters everywhere
upon the lips of men. At once she turns
her course to King Iarbas; and his spirit   260
is hot, his anger rages at her words.

Iarbas was the son of Hammon by
a ravished nymph of Garamantia.
In his broad realm he had built a hundred temples,
a hundred handsome shrines for Jupiter.   265
There he had consecrated sleepless fire,
the everlasting watchman of the gods;
the soil was rich with blood of slaughtered herds,

and varied garlands flowered on the thresholds.
Insane, incited by that bitter rumor,   270
he prayed long—so they say—to Jupiter;
he stood before the altars in the presence
of gods, a suppliant with upraised hands:
"All-able Jove, to whom the Moorish nation,
feasting upon their figured couches, pour   275
Lenaean sacrifices, do you see
these things? Or, Father, are we only trembling
for nothing when you cast your twisting thunder?
Those fires in the clouds that terrify
our souls—are they but blind and aimless lightning   280
that only stirs our empty mutterings?
A woman, wandering within our borders,
paid for the right to build a tiny city.
We gave her shore to till and terms of tenure.
She has refused to marry me, she has taken   285
Aeneas as a lord into her lands.
And now this second Paris, with his crew
of half-men, with his chin and greasy hair
bound up beneath a bonnet of Maeonia,
enjoys his prey; while we bring offerings   290
to what we have believed to be your temples,
still cherishing your empty reputation."

And as he prayed and clutched the altar stone,
all-able Jupiter heard him and turned
his eyes upon the royal walls, upon   295
the lovers who had forgotten their good name.
He speaks to Mercury, commanding him:
"Be on your way, my son, call up the Zephyrs,
glide on your wings, speak to the Dardan chieftain
who lingers now at Tyrian Carthage, paying   300
not one jot of attention to the cities
the Fates have given him. Mercury, carry
across the speeding winds the words I urge:
his lovely mother did not promise such
a son to us; she did not save him twice   305
from Grecian arms for this—but to be master
of Italy, a land that teems with empire
and seethes with war; to father a race from Teucer's
high blood, to place all earth beneath his laws.
But if the brightness of such deeds is not   310

enough to kindle him, if he cannot
attempt the task for his own fame, does he—
a father—grudge Ascanius the walls
of Rome? What is he pondering, what hope
can hold him here among his enemies,   315
not caring for his own Ausonian sons
or for Lavinian fields. He must set sail.
And this is all; my message lies in this."

His words were ended. Mercury made ready
to follow his great father's orders. First   320
he laces on his golden sandals: winged
to bear him, swift as whirlwinds, high across
the land and water. Then he takes his wand;
with this he calls pale spirits up from Orcus
and down to dreary Tartarus sends others;   325
he uses this to give sleep and recall it,
and to unseal the eyes of those who have died.
His trust in this, he spurs the winds and skims
the troubled clouds. And now in flight, he sights
the summit and high sides of hardy Atlas   330
who props up heaven with his crest—Atlas,
whose head is crowned with pines and battered by
the wind and rain and always girdled by
black clouds; his shoulders' cloak is falling snow;
above the old man's chin the rivers rush;   335
his bristling beard is stiff with ice. Here first
Cyllene's god poised on his even wings
and halted; then he hurled himself headlong
and seaward with his body, like a bird
that, over shores and reefs where fishes throng,   340
swoops low along the surface of the waters.
Not unlike this, Cyllene's god between
the earth and heaven as he flies, cleaving
the sandy shore of Libya from the winds
that sweep from Atlas, father of his mother.   345

As soon as his winged feet have touched the outskirts,
he sees Aeneas founding fortresses
and fashioning new houses. And his sword
was starred with tawny jasper, and the cloak
that draped his shoulders blazed with Tyrian purple—   350
a gift that wealthy Dido wove for him;

she had run golden thread along the web.
And Mercury attacks at once. "Are you
now laying the foundation of high Carthage,
as servant to a woman, building her   355
a splendid city here? Are you forgetful
of what is your own kingdom, your own fate?
The very god of gods, whose power sways
both earth and heaven, sends me down to you
from bright Olympus. He himself has asked me   360
to carry these commands through the swift air:
what are you pondering or hoping for
while squandering your ease in Libyan lands?
For if the brightness of such deeds is not
enough to kindle you—if you cannot   365
attempt the task for your own fame—remember
Ascanius growing up, the hopes you hold
for Iülus, your own heir, to whom are owed
the realm of Italy and land of Rome."
So did Cyllene's god speak out. He left   370
the sight of mortals even as he spoke
and vanished into the transparent air.

This vision stunned Aeneas, struck him dumb;
his terror held his hair erect; his voice
held fast within his jaws. He burns to flee   375
from Carthage; he would quit these pleasant lands,
astonished by such warnings, the command
of gods. What can he do? With what words dare
he face the frenzied queen? What openings
can he employ? His wits are split, they shift   380
here, there; they race to different places, turning
to everything. But as he hesitated,
this seemed the better plan: he calls Sergestus
and Mnestheus and the strong Serestus, and
he asks them to equip the fleet in silence,   385
to muster their companions on the shore,
to ready all their arms, but to conceal
the reasons for this change; while he himself—
with gracious Dido still aware of nothing
and never dreaming such a love could ever   390
be broken—would try out approaches, seek
the tenderest, most tactful time for speech,
whatever dexterous way might suit his case.

And all are glad. They race to carry out
the orders of Aeneas, his commands.   395

But Dido—for who can deceive a lover?—
had caught his craftiness; she quickly sensed
what was to come; however safe they seemed,
she feared all things. That same unholy Rumor
brought her these hectic tidings: that the boats   400
were being armed, made fit for voyaging.
Her mind is helpless; raging frantically,
inflamed, she raves throughout the city—just
as a Bacchante when, each second year,
she is startled by the shaking of the sacred   405
emblems, the orgies urge her on, the cry
"o Bacchus" calls to her by night; Cithaeron
incites her with its clamor. And at last
Dido attacks Aeneas with these words:

"Deceiver, did you even hope to hide   410
so harsh a crime, to leave this land of mine
without a word? Can nothing hold you back—
neither your love, the hand you pledged, nor even
the cruel death that lies in wait for Dido?
Beneath the winter sky are you preparing   415
a fleet to rush away across the deep
among the north winds, you who have no feeling?
What! Even if you were not seeking out
strange fields and unknown dwellings, even if
your ancient Troy were still erect, would you   420
return to Troy across such stormy seas?
Do you flee me? By tears, by your right hand—
this sorry self is left with nothing else—
by wedding, by the marriage we began,
if I did anything deserving of you   425
or anything of mine was sweet to you,
take pity on a fallen house, put off
your plan, I pray—if there is still place for prayers.
Because of you the tribes of Libya, all
the Nomad princes hate me, even my   430
own Tyrians are hostile; and for you
my honor is gone and that good name that once
was mine, my only claim to reach the stars.
My guest, to whom do you consign this dying

woman? I must say 'guest': this name is all   435
I have of one whom once I called my husband.
Then why do I live on? Until Pygmalion,
my brother, batters down my walls, until
Iarbas the Gaetulian takes me prisoner?
Had I at least before you left conceived   440
a son in me; if there were but a tiny
Aeneas playing by me in the hall,
whose face, in spite of everything, might yet
remind me of you, then indeed I should
not seem so totally abandoned, beaten."   445

Her words were ended. But Aeneas, warned
by Jove, held still his eyes; he struggled, pressed
care back within his breast. With halting words
he answers her at last: "I never shall
deny what you deserve, the kindnesses   450
that you could tell; I never shall regret
remembering Elissa for as long
as I remember my own self, as long
as breath is king over these limbs. I'll speak
brief words that fit the case. I never hoped   455
to hide—do not imagine that—my flight;
I am not furtive. I have never held
the wedding torches as a husband; I
have never entered into such agreements.
If fate had granted me to guide my life   460
by my own auspices and to unravel
my troubles with unhampered will, then I
should cherish first the town of Troy, the sweet
remains of my own people and the tall
rooftops of Priam would remain, my hand   465
would plant again a second Pergamus
for my defeated men. But now Grynean
Apollo's oracles would have me seize
great Italy, the Lycian prophecies
tell me of Italy: there is my love,   470
there is my homeland. If the fortresses
of Carthage and the vision of a city
in Libya can hold you, who are Phoenician,
why, then, begrudge the Trojans' settling on
Ausonian soil? There is no harm: it is   475
right that we, too, seek out a foreign kingdom.

For often as the night conceals the earth
with dew and shadows, often as the stars
ascend, afire, my father's anxious image
approaches me in dreams. Anchises warns   480
and terrifies; I see the wrong I have done
to one so dear, my boy Ascanius,
whom I am cheating of Hesperia,
the fields assigned by fate. And now the gods'
own messenger, sent down by Jove himself—   485
I call as witness both our lives—has brought
his orders through the swift air. My own eyes
have seen the god as he was entering
our walls—in broad daylight. My ears have drunk
his words. No longer set yourself and me   490
afire. Stop your quarrel. It is not
my own free will that leads to Italy."

But all the while Aeneas spoke, she stared
askance at him, her glance ran this way, that.
She scans his body with her silent eyes.   495
Then Dido thus, inflamed, denounces him:

"No goddess was your mother, false Aeneas,
and Dardanus no author of your race;
the bristling Caucasus was father to you
on his harsh crags; Hyrcanian tigresses   500
gave you their teats. And why must I dissemble?
Why hold myself in check? For greater wrongs?
For did Aeneas groan when I was weeping?
Did he once turn his eyes or, overcome,
shed tears or pity me, who was his loved one?   505
What shall I cry out first? And what shall follow?
No longer now does mighty Juno or
our Father, son of Saturn, watch this earth
with righteous eyes. Nowhere is certain trust.
He was an outcast on the shore, in want.   510
I took him in and madly let him share
my kingdom; his lost fleet and his companions
I saved from death. Oh I am whirled along
in fire by the Furies! First the augur
Apollo, then the Lycian oracles,   515
and now, sent down by Jove himself, the gods'

own herald, carrying his horrid orders.
This seems indeed to be a work for High Ones,
a care that can disturb their calm. I do not
refute your words. I do not keep you back.   520
Go then, before the winds, to Italy.
Seek out your kingdom overseas; indeed,
if there be pious powers still, I hope
that you will drink your torments to the lees
among sea rocks and, drowning, often cry   525
the name of Dido. Then, though absent, I
shall hunt you down with blackened firebrands;
and when chill death divides my soul and body,
a Shade, I shall be present everywhere.
Depraved, you then will pay your penalties.   530
And I shall hear of it, and that report
will come to me below, among the Shadows."

Her speech is broken off; heartsick, she shuns
the light of day, deserts his eyes; she turns
away, leaves him in fear and hesitation,   535
Aeneas longing still to say so much.
As Dido faints, her servants lift her up;
they carry her into her marble chamber;
they lay her body down upon the couch.

But though he longs to soften, soothe her sorrow   540
and turn aside her troubles with sweet words,
though groaning long and shaken in his mind
because of his great love, nevertheless
pious Aeneas carries out the gods'
instructions. Now he turns back to his fleet.   545

At this the Teucrians indeed fall to.
They launch their tall ships all along the beach;
they set their keels, well-smeared with pitch, afloat.
The crewmen, keen for flight, haul from the forest
boughs not yet stripped of leaves to serve as oars   550
and timbers still untrimmed. And one could see them
as, streaming, they rushed down from all the city:
even as ants, remembering the winter,
when they attack a giant stack of spelt
to store it in their homes; the black file swarms   555
across the fields; they haul their plunder through

the grass on narrow tracks; some strain against
the great grains with their shoulders, heaving hard;
some keep the columns orderly and chide
the loiterers; the whole trail boils with work.   560

What were your feelings, Dido, then? What were
the sighs you uttered at that sight, when far
and wide, from your high citadel, you saw
the beaches boil and turmoil take the waters,
with such a vast uproar before your eyes?   565
Voracious Love, to what do you not drive
the hearts of men? Again, she must outcry,
again, a suppliant, must plead with him,
must bend her pride to love—and so not die
in vain, and with some way still left untried.   570

"Anna, you see them swarm across the beaches;
from every reach around they rush to sea:
the canvas calls the breezes, and already
the boisterous crewmen crown the sterns with garlands.
But I was able to foresee this sorrow;   575
therefore I can endure it, sister; yet
in wretchedness I must ask you for this
one service, Anna. Treacherous Aeneas
has honored you alone, confiding even
his secret feelings unto you; and you   580
alone know all his soft approaches, moods.
My sister, go—to plead with him, to carry
this message to my arrogant enemy.
I never trafficked with the Greeks at Aulis
to root the Trojans out, I never sent   585
a fleet to Pergamus, never disturbed
his father's ashes or Anchises' Shade,
that now Aeneas should ward off my words
from his hard ears. Where is he hurrying?
If he would only grant his wretched lover   590
this final gift: to wait for easy sailing
and favoring winds. I now no longer ask
for those old ties of marriage he betrayed,
nor that he lose his kingdom, be deprived
of lovely Latium; I only ask   595
for empty time, a rest and truce for all
this frenzy, until fortune teaches me,

defeated, how to sorrow. I ask this—
pity your sister—as a final kindness.
When he has granted it, I shall repay   600
my debt, and with full interest, by my death."

So Dido pleads, and her poor sister carries
these lamentations, and she brings them back.
For lamentation cannot move Aeneas;
his graciousness toward any plea is gone.   605
Fate is opposed, the god makes deaf the hero's
kind ears. As when, among the Alps, north winds
will strain against each other to root out
with blasts—now on this side, now that—a stout
oak tree whose wood is full of years; the roar   610
is shattering, the trunk is shaken, and
high branches scatter on the ground; but it
still grips the rocks; as steeply as it thrusts
its crown into the upper air, so deep
the roots it reaches down to Tartarus: 615
no less than this, the hero; he is battered
on this side and on that by assiduous words;
he feels care in his mighty chest, and yet
his mind cannot be moved; the tears fall, useless.

Then maddened by the fates, unhappy Dido   620
calls out at last for death; it tires her
to see the curve of heaven. That she may
not weaken in her plan to leave the light,
she sees, while placing offerings on the altars
with burning incense—terrible to tell—   625
the consecrated liquid turning black,
the outpoured wine becoming obscene blood.
But no one learns of this, not even Anna.
And more: inside her palace she had built
a marble temple to her former husband   630
that she held dear and honored wonderfully.
She wreathed that shrine with snow-white fleeces and
holy-day leaves. And when the world was seized
by night, she seemed to hear the voice and words
of her dead husband, calling out to Dido.   635
Alone above the housetops, death its song,
an owl often complains and draws its long
slow call into a wailing lamentation.

More, many prophecies of ancient seers
now terrify her with their awful warnings. 640
And in her dreams it is the fierce Aeneas
himself who drives her to insanity;
she always finds herself alone, abandoned,
and wandering without companions on
an endless journey, seeking out her people, 645
her Tyrians in a deserted land:
even as Pentheus, when he is seized by frenzy,
sees files of Furies, and a double sun
and double Thebes appear to him; or when
Orestes, son of Agamemnon, driven 650
across the stage, flees from his mother armed
with torches and black serpents; on the threshold
the awful goddesses of vengeance squat.

When she had gripped this madness in her mind
and, beaten by her grief, resolved to die, 655
she plotted with herself the means, the moment.
Her face conceals her meaning; on her brow
she sets serenity, then speaks to Anna:
"My sister, wish me well, for I have found
a way that will restore Aeneas to me 660
or free me of my love for him. Near by
the bounds of Ocean and the setting sun
lies Ethiopia, the farthest land;
there Atlas, the incomparable, turns
the heavens, studded with their glowing stars, 665
upon his shoulders. And I have been shown
a priestess from that land—one of the tribe
of the Massylians—who guards the shrine
of the Hesperides; for it was she
who fed the dragon and preserved the holy 670
branches upon the tree, sprinkling moist honey
and poppy, bringing sleep. She promises
to free, with chant and spell, the minds of those
she favors but sends anguish into others.
And she can stay the waters in the rivers 675
and turn the stars upon their ways; she moves
the nightly Shades; makes earth quake underfoot
and—you will see—sends ash trees down the mountains.
Dear sister, I can call the gods to witness,
and you and your dear life, that I resort 680

to magic arts against my will. In secret
build up a pyre within the inner courtyard
beneath the open air, and lay upon it
the weapons of the hero. He, the traitor,
has left them hanging in my wedding chamber.   685
Take all of his apparel and the bridal
bed where I was undone. You must destroy
all relics of the cursed man, for so
would I, and so the priestess has commanded."
This said, she is silent and her face is pale.   690
But Anna cannot dream her sister hides
a funeral behind these novel rites;
her mind is far from thinking of such frenzy;
and she fears nothing worse than happened when
Sychaeus died. And so, she does as told.   695

But when beneath the open sky, inside
the central court, the pyre rises high
and huge, with logs of pine and planks of ilex,
the queen, not ignorant of what is coming,
then wreathes the place with garlands, crowning it   700
with greenery of death; and on the couch
above she sets the clothes Aeneas wore,
the sword he left, and then his effigy.
Before the circling altars the enchantress,
her hair disheveled, stands as she invokes   705
aloud three hundred gods, especially
Chaos and Erebus and Hecate,
the triple-shaped Diana, three-faced virgin.
And she had also sprinkled waters that
would counterfeit the fountain of Avernus;   710
she gathered herbs cut down by brazen sickles
beneath the moonlight, juicy with the venom
of black milk; she had also found a love charm
torn from the forehead of a newborn foal
before his mother snatched it. Dido herself—   715
with salt cake in her holy hands, her girdle
unfastened, and one foot free of its sandal,
close by the altars and about to die—
now calls upon the gods and stars, who know
the fates, as witness; then she prays to any   720
power there may be, who is both just and watchful,
who cares for those who love without requital.
  ❀   ❀ ❀

Night. And across the earth the tired bodies
were tasting tranquil sleep; the woods and savage
waters were resting and the stars had reached   725
the midpoint of their gliding fall—when all
the fields are still, and animals and colored
birds, near and far, that find their home beside
the limpid lakes or haunt the countryside
in bristling thickets, sleep in silent night.   730
But not the sorrowing Phoenician; she
can not submit to sleep, can not admit
dark night into her eyes or breast; her cares
increase; again love rises, surges in her;
she wavers on the giant tide of anger.   735
She will not let things rest but carries on;
she still revolves these thoughts within her heart:
"What can I do? Shall I, whom he has mocked,
go back again to my old suitors, begging,
seeking a wedding with Numidians whom   740
I have already often scorned as bridegrooms?
Or should I sail away on Trojan ships,
to suffer there even their harshest orders?
Shall I do so because the Trojans once
received my help, and gratefulness for such   745
old service is remembered by the mindful?
But even if I wish it, would they welcome
someone so hated to their haughty ships?
For, lost one, do you not yet know, not feel
the treason of the breed of Laomedon?   750
What then? Shall I accompany, alone,
the exultant sailors in their flight? Or call
on all my Tyrians, on all my troops
to rush upon them? How can I urge on
those I once dragged from Sidon, how can I   755
now force them back again upon the sea
and have them spread their canvas to the winds?
No; die as you deserve, and set aside
your sorrow by the sword. My sister, you,
won over by my tears—you were the first   760
to weigh me down with evils in my frenzy,
to drive me toward my enemy. And why
was it not given me to lead a guiltless
life, never knowing marriage, like a wild
beast, never to have touched such toils? I have not   765

held fast the faith I swore before the ashes
of my Sychaeus." This was her lament.

Aeneas on the high stern now was set
to leave; he tasted sleep; all things were ready.
And in his sleep a vision of the god   770
returned to him with that same countenance—
resembling Mercury in everything:
his voice and coloring and yellow hair
and all his handsome body, a young man's—
and seemed to bring a warning once again: 775
"You, goddess-born, how can you lie asleep
at such a crisis? Madman, can't you see
the threats around you, can't you hear the breath
of kind west winds? She conjures injuries
and awful crimes, she means to die, she stirs   780
the shifting surge of restless anger. Why
not flee this land headlong, while there is time?
You soon will see the waters churned by wreckage,
ferocious torches blaze, and beaches flame,
if morning finds you lingering on this coast.   785
Be on your way. Enough delays. An ever
uncertain and inconstant thing is woman."
This said, he was at one with the black night.

The sudden apparition terrifies
Aeneas. And he tears his body free   790
from sleep. He stirs his crewmen: "Quick! Awake!
Now man the benches, comrades, now unfurl
our sails with speed! Down from the upper air
a god was sent to urge us on again,
to rush our flight, to slice our twisted cables.   795
O holy one among the gods, we follow
your way, whoever you may be; again
rejoicing, we shall do as you command.
Be present, help us with your kindness, bring
your gracious constellations to the heavens."   800
He spoke; and from his scabbard snatches up
his glowing sword; with drawn blade, strikes the hawsers.
And all are just as eager, hurrying
to leave the shore; the ships conceal the sea.
They strain to churn the foam and sweep blue waters.   805

❀   ❀   ❀

Now early Dawn had left Tithonus' saffron
bed, scattering new light upon the earth.
As soon as from her lookout on the tower
the queen could see the morning whitening,
the fleet move on with level sails, the shores   810
and harbors now abandoned, without oarsmen,
she beat against her lovely breast three times,
then four, and tore her golden hair, and cried:
"O Jupiter, you let him go, a stranger
who mocked our kingdom! Will my men not ready   815
their weapons, hunt him down, pour from my city
and rip the galleys from their moorings? Quick!
Bring torches, spread your sails, and ply your oars!
What am I saying? Where am I? What madness
has turned awry what I had meant to do?   820
Poor Dido, does his foulness touch you now?
It should have then, when you gave him your scepter.
This is the right hand, this the pledge of one
who carries with him, so they say, the household
gods of his land, who bore upon his shoulders   825
his father weak with years. And could I not
have dragged his body off, and scattered him
piecemeal upon the waters, limb by limb?
Or butchered all his comrades, even served
Ascanius himself as banquet dish   830
upon his father's table? True enough—
the battle might have ended differently.
That does not matter. For, about to die,
need I fear anyone? I should have carried
my torches to his camp and filled his decks   835
with fire, destroyed the son, the father, that
whole race, and then have thrown myself upon them.
You, Sun, who with your flames see all that is done
on earth; and Juno, you, interpreter
and witness of my sorrows; Hecate,   840
invoked with shrieks, by night, at every city's
crossways; and you, the Furies; and the gods
that guard dying Elissa—hear these words
and turn your power toward my pain; as I
deserve, take up my prayers. If it must be   845
that he, a traitor, is to touch his harbor,
float to his coasts, and so the fates of Jove

demand and if this end is fixed; yet let
him suffer war and struggles with audacious
nations, and then—when banished from his borders   850
and torn from the embrace of Iülus—let him
beg aid and watch his people's shameful slaughter.
Not even when he has bent low before
an unjust peace may he enjoy his kingdom,
the light that he has wished for. Let him fall   855
before his time, unburied in the sand.
These things I plead; these final words I pour
out of my blood. Then, Tyrians, hunt down
with hatred all his sons and race to come;
send this as offering unto my ashes.   860
Do not let love or treaty tie our peoples.
May an avenger rise up from my bones,
one who will track with firebrand and sword
the Dardan settlers, now and in the future,
at any time that ways present themselves.   865
I call your shores to war against their shores,
your waves against their waves, arms with their arms.
Let them and their sons' sons learn what is war."

This said, she ran her mind to every side,
for she was seeking ways with which to slice—   870
as quickly as she can—the hated light;
and then, with these brief words, she turned to Barce,
Sychaeus' nurse—for Dido's own was now
black ashes in Phoenicia, her old homeland:
"Dear nurse, call here to me my sister Anna;   875
and tell her to be quick to bathe her body
with river water; see that she brings cattle
and all that is appointed for atonement.
So must my sister come; while you yourself
bind up your temples with a pious fillet.   880
I mean to offer unto Stygian Jove
the sacrifices that, as is ordained,
I have made ready and begun, to put
an end to my disquiet and commit
to flames the pyre of the Trojan chieftain."   885
So Dido spoke. And Barce hurried off;
she moved with an old woman's eagerness.

But Dido, desperate, beside herself
with awful undertakings, eyes bloodshot

and rolling, and her quivering cheeks flecked   890
with stains and pale with coming death, now bursts
across the inner courtyards of her palace.
She mounts in madness that high pyre, unsheathes
the Dardan sword, a gift not sought for such
an end. And when she saw the Trojan's clothes   895
and her familiar bed, she checked her thought
and tears a little, lay upon the couch
and spoke her final words: "O relics, dear
while fate and god allowed, receive my spirit
and free me from these cares; for I have lived   900
and journeyed through the course assigned by fortune.
And now my Shade will pass, illustrious,
beneath the earth; I have built a handsome city,
have seen my walls rise up, avenged a husband,
won satisfaction from a hostile brother: 905
o fortunate, too fortunate—if only
the ships of Troy had never touched our coasts."
She spoke and pressed her face into the couch.
"I shall die unavenged, but I shall die,"
she says. "Thus, thus, I gladly go below   910
to shadows. May the savage Dardan drink
with his own eyes this fire from the deep
and take with him the omen of my death."

Then Dido's words were done, and her companions
can see her fallen on the sword; the blade   915
is foaming with her blood, her hands are bloodstained.
Now clamor rises to the high rooftop.
Now rumor riots through the startled city.
The lamentations, keening, shrieks of women
sound through the houses; heavens echo mighty   920
wailings, even as if an enemy
were entering the gates, with all of Carthage
or ancient Tyre in ruins, and angry fires
rolling across the homes of men and gods.

And Anna heard. Appalled and breathless, she   925
runs, anxious, through the crowd, her nails wounding
her face; her fists, her breasts; she calls the dying
Dido by name: "And was it, then, for this,
my sister? Did you plan this fraud for me?
Was this the meaning waiting for me when   930
the pyre, the flames, the altar were prepared?

What shall I now, deserted, first lament?
You scorned your sister's company in death;
you should have called me to the fate you met;
the same sword pain, the same hour should have taken 935
the two of us away. Did my own hands
help build the pyre, and did my own voice call
upon our fathers' gods, only to find
me, heartless, far away when you lay dying?
You have destroyed yourself and me, my sister,   940
the people and the elders of your Sidon,
and all your city. Let me bathe your wounds
in water, and if any final breath
still lingers here, may my lips catch it up."
This said, she climbed the high steps, then she clasped 945
her half-dead sister to her breast, and moaning,
embraced her, dried the black blood with her dress.
Trying to lift her heavy eyes, the queen
falls back again. She breathes; the deep wound in
her chest is loud and hoarse. Three times she tried   950
to raise herself and strained, propped on her elbow;
and three times she fell back upon the couch.
Three times with wandering eyes she tried to find
high heaven's light and, when she found it, sighed.

But then all-able Juno pitied her   955
long sorrow and hard death and from Olympus
sent Iris down to free the struggling spirit
from her entwining limbs. For as she died
a death that was not merited or fated,
but miserable and before her time   960
and spurred by sudden frenzy, Proserpina
had not yet cut a gold lock from her crown,
not yet assigned her life to Stygian Orcus.
On saffron wings dew-glittering Iris glides
along the sky, drawing a thousand shifting   965
colors across the facing sun. She halted
above the head of Dido: "So commanded,
I take this lock as offering to Dis;
I free you from your body." So she speaks
and cuts the lock with her right hand; at once   970
the warmth was gone, the life passed to the winds.

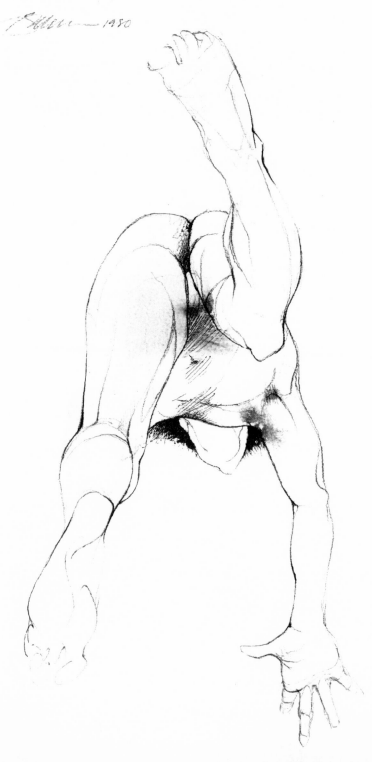

Palinurus

J. Allen — 1980

BOOK V

MEANWHILE AENEAS, well upon his way,
was sailing steadfast with his galleys, cutting
the waves blown black beneath the north wind, gazing
back—watching where the walls of Carthage glowed
with sad Elissa's flames. They cannot know   5
what caused so vast a blaze, and yet the Trojans
know well the pain when passion is profaned
and how a woman driven wild can act;
their hearts are drawn through dark presentiments.

But when the fleet had reached the open waters,   10
with land no longer to be seen—the sky
was everywhere and everywhere the sea—
a blue-black cloud ran overhead; it brought
the night and storm and breakers rough in darkness.
And from the high stern, even Palinurus,   15
the pilot, cries: "And why these tempest clouds
surrounding heaven? Father Neptune, what
are you preparing?" After this he orders
the crews to gather in the rigging, bend
upon their sturdy oars; he trims the sails   20
to slant across the wind; his words are these:
"Aeneas, great of heart, not even if

high Jupiter himself should guarantee
his promise, could I hope to reach the coast
of Italy beneath a sky like this.   25
The wind has shifted; now it blows across
our path and rises from the black west, now
the air has thickened into mist. We cannot
hold out against it, cannot keep on course.
Since Fortune has the better of us now,   30
let us obey and turn aside where she
has called. I think the faithful shores of Eryx,
your brother, and Sicilian ports are not
far off, if only I remember right
and can retrace the stars I watched before."   35

Pious Aeneas answered: "Even I
have seen, long since, that this is what the winds
demand, that it is useless now to struggle;
then, Palinurus, let our course be like
our sails. Can any country please me more   40
or offer me more welcome harbor than
the land that holds my Dardan friend Acestes,
that in its bosom keeps my father's bones?"
This said, they head for harbor; kind winds swell
their sails; the fleet runs swift across the surge;   45
at last, and glad, they reach familiar sands.

But far off, from a high hill crest, Acestes,
amazed to see the friendly ships arrive,
has hurried down to meet them. He is bristling
with javelins and an African bearskin—   50
Acestes, who was fathered by Crinisus,
the river-god, out of a Trojan mother.
And not forgetting his old parentage,
Acestes welcomes their return with joy;
he greets them with his rustic treasures and   55
he cheers their weariness with generous stores.

And when the next bright day has put to flight
the stars at early dawn, Aeneas calls
his comrades in from all along the beach;
then from a mound he tells the gathered Trojans: 60
"Great sons of Dardanus, a race born of
the high blood of the gods: the circling year

completes its months since we entombed in earth
the bones and remnants of my godlike father.
Unless I err, that anniversary   65
is here, the day that I shall always keep
in grief and honor (so you gods have willed).
Were I to find myself this day an exile
among the quicksands of Gaetulia
or, taken by surprise, upon the sea   70
of Greece or in the city of Mycenae—
then, even then, I should fulfill, as due,
my yearly vows, the solemn funeral
observances, and heap the shrines with gifts.
But more than this, we find ourselves this day   75
beside my father's very bones and ashes—
and I believe it is the will and power
of gods that brought us to these friendly harbors.
Come, then, and let us celebrate in gladness
these sacrifices; let us pray for winds,   80
and may he grant that, when I build a city,
I may observe these rites year after year
in temples dedicated unto him.
Acestes, born of Troy, gives to each ship
two head of cattle; summon to the feast   85
your homeland's household gods and those your host
Acestes worships here. Moreover, should
the ninth dawn bring a gracious day to mortals
and with her rays reveal the world, I shall
ordain these competitions for the Trojans: 90
first we shall hold a race for our swift ships;
then for our fastest runner; and for him
who is the best at hurling, strong and bold,
the javelin or light arrows; and for those
who dare to box with rawhide gauntlets—all   95
stand ready to seek out the victor's prize
and palm. But now let everyone keep solemn
silence; let us all wreathe our brows with leaves."

This said, Aeneas binds his brows with myrtle,
the plant dear to his mother; and so, too,   100
does Helymus, and so Acestes, ripe
in years, and so the boy Ascanius,
whom all the young men follow. Then Aeneas
moved on from that assembly to the tomb

with many thousands, a great retinue.   105
And here he pours a ritual libation
out on the ground: two bowls of pure wine and
two bowls of new milk, two of victims' blood;
he scatters brilliant flowers as he cries:
"Hail, sacred father, once again; I hail   110
you, ashes, Shade, and spirit of my father,
you, saved in vain from Troy! For I was not
allowed to seek the fated boundaries
and fields of Italy with you and not—
whatever it may be—Ausonian Tiber."   115

So he had spoken when a slippery serpent
dragged from the bottom of the shrine its seven
enormous coils that wound in seven spirals,
while twining gently around the burial mound,
gliding between the altars; and its back   120
was marked with blue-gray spots, its scales were flecked
with gold that kindled into brightness—just
as in the clouds, across the facing sun,
a rainbow casts a thousand shifting colors.
Aeneas was astonished at the sight.   125
The serpent, weaving slowly through the bowls
and polished goblets, tasted of the feast,
then, harmless, made its way back to the tomb
and left the altars it had fed upon.
And so, even more eager now, Aeneas   130
resumes his father's rites, uncertain if
that serpent is the genius of the place
or the attendant spirit of Anchises.
As custom asks, he kills a pair of sheep,
two swine, as many black-backed steers; he pours   135
wine out of bowls and calls on great Anchises'
soul, on his Shade set free from Acheron.
And as he does, so each of his companions
brings gladly what he can as offering;
some heap the altars high and slaughter oxen,   140
while others, in their turn, set out bronze caldrons
and, stretched along the grass, place burning coals
beneath the spits and roast the victims' entrails.

The wished-for day had come, and Phaethon's horses
now drew the ninth dawn through the tranquil light.   145

The news and bright Acestes' name had roused
the neighbors; gladly gathering, they crowded
along the beaches, some of them to see
Aeneas' men and some prepared for contests.
But first the prizes are displayed along   150
the middle of the ring: the sacred tripods,
green garlands, palms, rewards for victory,
and armor, garments dyed in purple, talents
of gold and silver. From the central mound
the trumpet blares; the games have now begun.   155

The first event is entered by four galleys,
matched evenly, each heavy-oared and chosen
from all the fleet. With his tenacious crew,
Mnestheus directs the swift "Shark"—Mnestheus, soon
to be Italian, the chief from whom   160
the line of Memmians will take their name.
And Gyas drives the huge "Chimaera," huge
in bulk, a city's size, with triple tiers
of oars, rowed by three files of Dardan youths.
Sergestus, founder of the Sergian house,   165
rides on the giant "Centaur." Last, Cloanthus
rides sea-green "Scylla": it is he from whom
you take your name, Roman Cluentius.

Well out at sea, facing the foaming shores,
there stands a rock at times submerged and battered   170
by swollen breakers when the winter's stormy
northwesters hide the stars; but in the calm
it rises, silent, over tranquil waters,
a tableland, a welcome resting place
for sea gulls as they take the sun. And here   175
father Aeneas hangs a leafy branch
of ilex as a signal for his crews,
the goal at which they are to turn around,
to wheel back on their long way. Then they choose
places by lot; above the sterns, far off,   180
the captains gleam in purple, gold; the oarsmen
are crowned with poplar leaves, their naked shoulders
are glistening, wet with oil. They man the benches;
their arms are tense upon the oars; they wait,
expectant, for the start as throbbing fear   185
and eager love of praise drain their high hearts.

        ✿   ✿   ✿

At last, with the bright trumpet blast, at once
they all shoot from their starting places; shouts
of sailors beat against the skies, the waters
are turned to foam beneath the stroking arms.   190
They cleave the furrows with their equal thrusts;
the whole sea gapes, torn by the oars, the ships'
three-pointed beaks. Not even chariots,
when with their racing teams they seize the field
and rush out of their starting stalls, are so   195
swift, so headlong; not even charioteers
can shake their waving reins above their breakneck
horses and bend to beat and lash with so
much power. Then the cheers and the applause,
the cries and eager calls of followers,   200
fill all the woods; the hemmed-in beach rolls on
the echo, and struck hills give back that roar.

Among that clamor and confusion Gyas
flies on before the others, gliding first
across the waves. Cloanthus follows close;   205
his crew is better, but his bulky ship
has slowed him with its weight. At equal distance
behind these two, the "Shark" and "Centaur" strive
to take first place; the "Shark" is now ahead,
and now the giant "Centaur" makes its way,   210
now both ride on together, prows abreast,
cleaving the salt waves with their lengthy keels.
And all were drawing near the midpoint rock
when Gyas, who has led through half the course,
shouts, as a victor, to his galley's pilot,   215
Menoetes: "Why so hard to starboard? Turn;
hold close the boulder; let the oar blades scrape
along the shoals upon our left; let others
keep to the deeper waters!" He said this;
but fearing hidden reefs, Menoetes twists   220
his prow seaward. "Why so off course? Make for
the rocks, Menoetes!" Once again he shouts
to call his pilot back; then looking round,
he sees Cloanthus driving right behind him
and on the nearer course. Between the galley   225
of Gyas and the roaring reefs, Cloanthus
now shaves the left-hand channel, quickly takes
the lead and, past the mark, already gains

safe waters. Then indeed great anger burned
deep in young Gyas' bones, his cheeks were not   230
without their tears; and now, forgetting his
own dignity and, too, his comrades' safety,
he hurls the slow Menoetes headlong from
the high stern down into the sea; and strides,
himself both helmsman and commander, toward   235
the tiller; he spurs on his oarsmen, turns
the rudder toward the shore. But when at last
Menoetes, heavy, rose up from the sea,
struggling and old and dripping with drenched clothes,
he clambered up the reef, and at the top   240
he squatted on dry stones. The Teucrians
laughed as he fell, then as he swam; they laugh
as he spits out salt water from his chest.

As Gyas slowed, the pair behind—Sergestus
and Mnestheus—took new heart; they hoped to catch
    him.   245
Sergestus is the first to gain the channel
beside the rock—but not enough to take
a boat-length lead, only a part; the "Shark,"
his rival, overlaps him with her prow.
But Mnestheus, pacing midships, spurs his sailors: 250
"Now, now rise to your oars, comrades of Hector,
the ranks I chose in Troy's last agony;
now, now put forth the powers, now the heart
you showed in the Gaetulian quicksands,
in the Ionian sea, in Malea's   255
pursuing waves! I, Mnestheus, do not seek
the first prize anymore or try to conquer
(Neptune, let those whom you so choose be victors),
and yet it would be shameful to be last;
my countrymen, at least shun that disgrace!"   260
They thrust upon their oars, they give their all;
the brazen galley quakes with hefty strokes;
the seabed is drawn out from under them;
their hurried panting shakes their limbs and parched
throats; sweat is streaming everywhere. But chance   265
itself brings them the longed-for victory.
For while Sergestus, wild in spirit, drove
his prow beside the shoals, upon the inside—
a gap too strait and dangerous—luckless,

he struck against the jutting reefs. The rocks   270
were jarred; the oars, jammed up against the sharp
and jagged edges, snapped; the crashing hull
hung fast. The crewmen shout aloud, leap up
as one at this delay; with iron-plated
boat hooks and pointed poles, they gather in   275
their shattered oars out of the sea. And Mnestheus,
still keener now, and glad with his success,
with rapid strokes and calling on the winds,
makes for the sloping, shoreward waters, glides
straight down the open sea. Just as a dove,   280
who has her home and nestlings in a secret
cliffside, when she is startled from her cavern,
flies toward the fields; for, frightened in her den,
she loudly flaps her wings, but soon she glides
upon the quiet air, and skims her liquid   285
path, does not move her rapid pinions: even
so Mnestheus, so the "Shark," self-driven, cuts
the final stretch of waters in her flight,
her first impulse enough to drive her on.
Now Mnestheus leaves behind the floundering   290
Sergestus on the steep reef in the shallows
as he calls out in vain for help and learns
to race with broken oars. Then Mnestheus passes
Gyas who rides the giant-hulked "Chimaera";
and having lost her helmsman, she gives way.   295

And now the goal is near—only Cloanthus
is left; and Mnestheus makes for him and, straining
with all his power, presses forward. Then
indeed the shouting doubles as the chase
is urged along by many cheers; the heavens   300
reecho with the roar. Cloanthus' crewmen
now think it a disgrace to fail to keep
the fame and honor they themselves have won,
and they would give their very lives for glory;
but Mnestheus' men are strengthened by success,   305
they have the power because they feel they have it.
And now perhaps, both prows abreast, the men
of Mnestheus would have won the prize had not
Cloanthus, stretching seaward both his hands,
poured prayers and called upon the gods with vows: 310
"You gods who rule the kingdom of the seas,

whose waters I now race upon: to keep
the promise that I pledge, I shall with gladness
offer a snow-white bull before your altars
along this beach, and I shall fling its entrails   315
into your salt waves and pour out pure wine."
He spoke; and all the company of Nereids
beneath the sea heard him; father Portunus
drove on Cloanthus' ship with his great hand.
She flies to land faster than south wind or   320
swift arrow; then she rests in that deep harbor.

At this, Anchises' son, following custom,
assembles everyone, then has the herald's
loud voice proclaim Cloanthus as the victor;
he crowns his temples with green laurel, and   325
he has him choose three bullocks for each crew,
and wine and an enormous silver talent;
and for the captains he has special honors.
A gold-embroidered cape goes to the victor;
around its borders ran a double fringe   330
of Meliboean purple, sinuous
and rich; and woven in it Ganymede,
the royal boy, with javelin gives keen
chase—he is panting—tiring running stags;
and Jove's swift armor-bearer sweeps him up   335
from Ida in his talons; and the boy's
old guardians in vain implore the stars;
the savage barking of the dogs disturbs
the skies. To him who has earned second place,
Aeneas gives, to keep as shield in battle   340
and as an ornament, a corselet made
of triple-plated gold in polished chains;
this he himself had torn, as victor, from
Demoleos beside swift Simois
beneath high Ilium. And even with   345
their straining shoulders Sagaris and Phegeus,
the servants, find that massive chainwork almost
too much for them to carry off; and yet,
while wearing this, Demoleos used once
to chase the straggling Trojans. As third prize   350
he then presents a pair of brazen caldrons
and bowls of silver, rough with high relief.
    ❉   ❉   ❉

The victors had received their gifts and, proud
of their rewards, were moving on, their prows
entwined with purple ribbons when—dislodged   355
with difficulty from the ruthless rock,
oars lost, with one disabled tier—Sergestus
brought in his mocked-at ship, inglorious.
And just as, often, when a snake—surprised
upon the highroad and run over by   360
a brazen wheel that slants across him, or
else beaten by a traveler's heavy blow
and left half-dead and mangled by a stone—
will try in vain to run away and writhes
his body in long coils; a part of him   365
is fierce, his eyes are glowing, and he lifts
his hissing throat on high; a part, maimed by
the wound, prevents his moves—he twists and twines
and folds himself on his own limbs: so did
the ship move slowly on with her slow oars.   370
And yet she spreads her sails; her canvas full,
she rides into the harbor. Then Aeneas,
glad that the galley is saved, his comrades back,
presents Sergestus with the promised prize:
a female slave, the Cretan Pholoë,   375
one not unskillful in Minerva's arts,
a woman bearing twin sons at her breast.

This contest done, pious Aeneas moves
into a grassy plain, surrounded by
wooded and winding hills on every side;   380
the center of that valley took the shape
of an arena; there, with many thousands,
the hero went; he sat on a raised seat.
And here he tempts the minds of those who now
may want to face a swift footrace; he sets   385
rewards and prizes. From all sides they gather:
the Teucrians, Sicilians, together.
The first are Nisus and Euryalus—
Euryalus renowned for handsomeness
and for his fresh youth, Nisus for his honest   390
love of the boy. Behind them came the princely
Diores, from the noble line of Priam;
then Salius and Patron came together—
the one Acarnian, the other born

out of Arcadian blood, a Tegean;   395
and then two young Sicilians, Helymus
and Panopes, familiar with the forests
and both companions of the old Acestes;
and others came, whose fame is now in darkness.
These were the words Aeneas spoke to them: 400
"Now let your hearts hear this, pay glad attention.
Not one of you shall leave without a gift.
At race's end, each one of you shall have
two Gnosian shafts that gleam with polished steel,
together with an ax embossed with silver.   405
Each one of you who runs shall have these prizes.
Three will be given even more rewards
and pale-green olive garlands on their heads.
The first, as victor, is to have a horse
with splendid trappings; and the second takes   410
an Amazonian quiver, full of Thracian
arrows and girdled by a broad gold belt—
the clasp that holds it fast, a polished gem;
the third will be content with this Greek helmet."

This said, they take their places; suddenly   415
the signal sounds; they are on their way; they leave
the starting point; they stream out like a storm cloud,
their eyes upon the goal. The first to go
is Nisus, darting past all others, swifter
than winds or than winged lightning; after him,   420
but still far back, is Salius; and third,
though well behind, Euryalus; the next
is Helymus; and hard upon him—look!—
Diores darts and now treads heel to heel
and presses at his shoulder; if there were   425
more ground remaining, he would even pass
or else at least be tied with Helymus.
Now, almost at the end and tired out,
they all are near the goal when luckless Nisus
slides on some slippery blood that had been spilled 430
by chance where steers were slaughtered, soaking both
the ground and its grass cover. Even as
the youth rejoiced in victory, the earth
slid out from under him, and he could not
hold fast his stumbling footsteps. Nisus fell   435

headlong upon the filthy slime itself
and in the sacrificial blood. And yet
he did not once forget Euryalus,
not even then forget his love; for rising
above the slippery soil, he threw himself　　　　440
across the path of Salius, who tumbled
backward on the thick sand. Euryalus
now runs ahead and gains first place, a winner
because of his friend's kindness; he flies on,
cheered by applause and shouts. And Helymus　　445
is next, and then Diores takes third prize.

At this, the loud outcries of Salius
reach everyone within that vast arena:
the elders in the front rows and the crowd.
He asks that what was snatched from him by fraud　450
be given back. But popularity
protects Euryalus, together with
his graceful tears and worth that please the more
since they appear in such a handsome body.
The protests of Diores also help;　　　　455
he then was nearing to receive his palm
and would have come in vain to claim third prize
if Salius were given back first honors.
Then, "Your rewards will not be touched," said father
Aeneas. "Men, no one will change the order　　460
of prizes: let it be for me to pity
the way things turned against my blameless friend."
This said, he gives as gift to Salius
the giant hide of a Gaetulian lion,
heavy with shaggy hair and gilded claws.　　　465
But Nisus cries: "If this is for the losers
and you take so much pity on the fallen,
what worthy gift can now be given Nisus,
who would have won the first prize by his merit
had not malicious Fortune hampered me,　　　470
even as she did Salius!" With this,
he showed his face and limbs fouled with wet filth.
The best of fathers smiled on him and ordered
a shield brought from the ships, the handiwork
of Didymaon that had been wrenched free　　　475
from Neptune's sacred doorpost by the Danaans.
He gives the noble youth so bright a prize.
　　　　❋　　　　❋　　　　❋

Then, with the races done, the gifts all given:
"And now, if any one of you has courage,
a keen heart in his breast, let him step forward   480
and lift his hands bound up with leather gauntlets."
The contest is announced; Aeneas sets
two prizes for the boxing match: the victor
will gain a bullock dressed in gold and garlands;
a sword and stately helmet will console   485
the loser. There is no delay. Straightway,
among the mighty murmurs of the crowd,
the Trojan Dares stands; he shows himself
in all his overwhelming power—Dares,
the only one who used to box with Paris;   490
he who, nearby the mound where matchless Hector
now lies, had beaten down the champion Butes
(a son of Amycus' Bebrycian house
who stalked along with his tremendous bulk)
and stretched him dying on the yellow sands.   495
For such is Dares, he who is the first
to raise his head high for the contest, show
his massive shoulders, toss his arms about
in turn, and stretch, and beat the air with blows.
They look for a contender but no one   500
in that great crowd will dare to box or bind
his hands with gauntlets. So, in eagerness,
and thinking no one else would claim the prize,
Dares stood up before Aeneas; then
without delay he grips the bullock's horns   505
in his left hand and speaks out: "Goddess-born,
if no one dares to trust himself to face me,
how long am I to stand? How long to linger?
Then order me to lead away my gift."
As one, all Dardans shouted their approval   510
and asked that he receive the promised prize.

At this, Acestes sternly takes to task
Entellus where, on the green couch of grass,
he sat nearby: "Entellus, once the bravest
of heroes—but how useless now—will you   515
so quietly allow such splendid prizes
to be removed without a contest? Where
are we to look for Eryx, he who was
your god and teacher, celebrated by us

in vain? And where is your Sicilian fame,   520
those trophies hanging in your halls?" To this
Entellus: "It is not that love of praise
or fame has left me, driven off by fear,
but that my blood is chilled and dulled by slow
old age, my body's force is numb, is cold.   525
If I could only have what once was mine,
the youth of which that shameless fellow there
so confidently brags, I should have boxed,
and not because a prize or handsome bullock
had tempted me; I do not need rewards!"   530
Then, having spoken so, Entellus tossed
his two tremendous gloves into the ring—
those gloves with which fierce Eryx used to box
when he had bound his arms with their tough hide.
The crowd was stunned, so giant were the oxen   535
whose seven mighty skins were stiff with lead
and iron sewn inside. Above all, Dares
himself is startled, and he shrinks far back.

The generous Aeneas feels their weight
and turns this way and that the twisting, vast   540
thongs. Then the old Entellus said to him:
"And what if you had seen the gauntlets and
the arms of Hercules himself, the sad
encounter on these very sands? Your kinsman
Eryx once used to wear these gloves, you can   545
still see them stained with blood and spattered brains.
With these he stood against the great Alcides,
with these I used to box, so long as better
blood still could give me strength and envious
old age had not yet scattered its white hairs   550
across my temples. But if Trojan Dares
declines to face my weapons, then—should pious
Aeneas so decide, and my adviser
Acestes lend approval—let us meet
as equals. Dares, I give up the hides   555
of Eryx for your sake (forget your fear),
and for your part, put off your Trojan gauntlets."
And when Entellus made this offer, he
threw down the double cloak that draped his shoulders,
laid bare his giant joints and limbs, the giant   560
bones and the sinews of his arms; he stood,
enormous, at the center of the field.

    ❋   ❋   ❋

Presiding at the bout, Anchises' son
brought equal gauntlets out and bound the hands
of both with well-matched weapons. And straightway   565
each stood erect and poised and undismayed;
each lifted high his arms and held them there.
They draw their towering heads back, out of range
of blows, spar hand-to-hand, and so provoke
attack. The Trojan is better in his footwork,   570
relying on his youth; the other is strong
in bulk and body, but his knees are slack
and totter, trembling; his tremendous limbs
are racked by his sick gasping. Without sure
result they let loose many blows; they pound   575
each other's hollow flanks, again, again,
and heavy thuds reecho from their chests;
the quick hands play about their temples, ears;
their jawbones rattle under solid strokes.
Entellus, motionless and heavy, keeps   580
the same stance, using only his body and
his watchful eyes to dodge the blows of Dares.
The other—just as one who drives against
a towering city with siegeworks, or camps
with arms beneath a mountain fortress—scans   585
now this approach, now that, explores the ground
with skill, and tries, in vain, shifting attacks.
Entellus, rising, stretched his right hand high;
but Dares, quick to see the coming blow,
had slipped aside and dodged with his quick body.   590
Entellus spent his strength upon the wind;
his own weight, his own force, had carried him
heavy, and heavily, with his huge hulk
down to the ground; just as at times a hollow
pine, torn up from its roots on Erymanthus   595
or on the slopes of giant Ida, falls.
The Trojan and Sicilian boys leap up;
their shouting takes the sky; and first Acestes
runs to the ring; with pity he lifts up
his friend, as old as he is. But the hero,   600
not checked and not to be delayed, returns
more keenly to the bout, his anger spurs
his force. His shame, his knowledge of his worth
excite his power; furiously he
drives Dares headlong over all the field,   605
and now his right hand doubles blows and now

his left; he knows no stay or rest; just as
storm clouds that rattle thick hail on the roofs,
so do the hero's two hands pummel, pound
at Dares, blow on blow, from every side.   610

But then father Aeneas would not let
such fury go unchecked; he would not have
Entellus rage in bitterness. He stopped
the boxing, snatched away exhausted Dares,
and when he spoke to him, used soothing words: 615
"Poor man, what madness has possessed your mind?
Your forces are not matched—can't you see that?—
the gods have shifted to the other side.
Give way to heaven." So he spoke; his orders
ended the bout. But Dares' faithful comrades   620
now lead him to the ships; he drags along
his weak knees, and his head sways back and forth;
he spits thick gore out of his mouth, and teeth
that mingle with his blood. And his companions
are called to take the helmet and the sword;   625
they leave the palm and bullock for Entellus.
At this, the victor, high in heart and proud
to win the bull, cries out: "You, goddess-born,
and you, the Trojans, learn what strength was once
in my young body, and from what a death   630
you have just rescued and recalled your Dares."
He spoke and then he faced that contest's prize,
the bullock standing nearby; drawing back
his right hand, straight between the towering horns
he planted his tough gauntlets; and he smashed   635
the bones, dashed in the brains. The ox is flat;
it trembles, lifeless, on the ground. Entellus,
above the ox, pours these words from his breast:
"O Eryx, unto you I offer up
this better life instead of Dares' death;   640
here—victor—I lay down my gloves, my art."

At once Aeneas calls for all who want
to join a match with their swift shafts; he raises
with his great hand a mast brought from Serestus'
galley; and as a target for their arrows,   645
he hangs a fluttering dove, tied by a cord,
on top. The archers gather; in a helmet

of bronze the lots are cast. The first turn falls,
backed by loud cheering, to Hippocoön,
the son of Hyrtacus; the second falls   650
to Mnestheus, recent victor in the boat race,
a garland of green olive around his head;
the third, Eurytion—who is your brother,
most famous Pandarus, you who, when ordered
to break the treaty, were the first to cast   655
your shaft at the Achaeans. And the last
lot, deep within the helmet, is Acestes';
for even he dares try a young man's task.

Then solid, sturdy, each one for himself,
they bend and curve their bows and draw their arrows 660
out of their quivers. The first steel to cleave
the winged air, through the sky, from its shrill string:
the shaft shot by the son of Hyrtacus;
it sinks into the wood of the ship's mast.
The mast shook, and the bird, in terror, fluttered   665
her wings, and everyone applauded loudly.
And next keen Mnestheus took his stand; bow bent
and aiming high, he leveled both his arrow
and sight. But fortune was not his, he could
not reach the bird herself; instead, his shaft   670
broke off the knots and cords of hemp that held
her foot bound fast where she hung from the mast.
She flew up to the south wind and black clouds.
Then quickly—for his bow was long since ready,
his shaft drawn taut—Eurytion called on   675
his brother, Pandarus, in prayer; then marked
the dove as, glad, she flapped her wings beneath
the open sky; and under a dark cloud
he pierces her. She dropped down, dead; she left
her life among the stars of the high air   680
and, as she fell, brought back the piercing shaft.
Only Acestes, knowing that the prize
is lost, remained to shoot; nevertheless
that father whirled his dart into the air
to show his sounding bow, to show his art.   685
And here a sudden prodigy appears
that is to be a mighty augury;
for afterward its massive meaning showed;
in later days tremendous prophets hailed it.

As it flew through the liquid clouds, the reed   690
caught fire and marked its track by flames until,
consumed, it vanished in thin air; just as,
set loose from heaven, often shooting stars
will race and in their wake leave trailing tresses.
The Trojans and Sicilians stood, amazed,   695
in prayer to the High Ones; nor did great
Aeneas shun the omen; he embraced
the glad Acestes, loading him with handsome
offerings, saying, "Take them, Father, for
the great king of Olympus, with these signs   700
has willed that you have extraordinary
honors. You are to have this gift that once
was old Anchises' own—a bowl engraved
with figures, which the Thracian Cisseus gave
my father as a splendid gift, to bear   705
as a memorial and pledge of love."
This said, he binds Acestes' brows with green
garlands of laurel, naming him the victor,
first over all. The good Eurytion
did not begrudge this preference and prize—   710
and this although he was himself the only
bowman to bring the bird down from the sky.
And after these, the next to take his gift
is Mnestheus, he who broke the cord; the last,
Hippocoön, whose swift shaft pierced the mast.   715

But while that contest still was underway,
father Aeneas calls for Epytides,
the guardian and companion of young Iülus,
and whispers this into his trusted ear:
"Go now and tell Ascanius that if   720
his band of boys is ready with him, if
his horses are arrayed for the maneuvers,
then he can lead his squadrons out to honor
Anchises and can show himself in arms."
Then he himself calls for the crowding throng   725
to quit the long arena, clear the field.
The boys advance high on their bridled horses;
in even ranks, before their parents' eyes,
they glitter; as they pass, the men of Troy
and Sicily admiringly murmur.   730
And all, as custom calls for, have their hair
bound with a wreath of clipped leaves; and each bears

two cornel lances tipped with iron heads;
and some have polished quivers on their shoulders;
and high upon his chest, down from the neck,   735
each wears a pliant chain of twisted gold.
The squads are three in number, and three captains
parade, with twice-six boys behind each captain;
they gleam in ranks of six, each with a leader.
One band of boys is led by a triumphant   740
small Priam, who renews the name of his
grandfather—your bright son, Polites, destined
to swell the race of the Italians;
he rides upon a dappled Thracian stallion,
spotted with white, which as it paces, shows   745
white pasterns and a forehead high and white.
Next Atys rides, from whom the Atian
Latins have drawn their lineage—the little
Atys, a boy loved by the boy Iülus.
The last, and handsomest of all, Iülus,   750
is mounted on a horse from Sidon, one
fair Dido gave him as memorial
and pledge of love. The other boys ride on
Sicilian horses from Acestes' stable.

The cheering Dardans greet the anxious squadrons   755
and, watching those young faces, recognizing
the features of their ancestors, are glad.
And when the boys had crossed the whole enclosure,
had ridden happily before their elders,
then Epytides gave the signal shout   760
from far and cracked his whip. They rode apart,
to right and left, in equal ranks; the three
squadrons had split their columns into two
separate bands; and then, called back again,
they wheeled around and charged like enemies   765
with leveled lances. Now they start new marches
and countermarches in the space between them;
and interweaving circle into circle
in alternation, armed, they mime a battle.
And now they bare their backs in flight, and now,   770
peace made between them, gallop side by side.
As once, in ancient days, so it is said,
the labyrinth in high Crete had a path
built out of blind walls, an ambiguous
maze of a thousand ways, a winding course   775

that mocked all signs of finding a way out,
a puzzle that was irresolvable
and irretraceable: in such a course,
so intricate, the sons of Troy maneuver;
they interweave in sport of flight and battle   780
like dolphins which, when swimming liquid seas,
will cleave the Libyan and Carpathian deeps
and play among the waves. Ascanius
renewed, in later days, this way of riding,
these contests, when he girded Alba Longa   785
with walls and taught the early Latins how
to celebrate these games as he had done
beside the Trojan boys when he was young.
The Albans taught their sons, and after them
great Rome received these games and carried on   790
this same ancestral celebration; now
the boys are called "Troy" and their band, the "Trojans."
Such were the competitions they observed
in honor of Aeneas' holy father.

Here fortune shifted, first turned treacherous.   795
For while the solemn anniversary
is paid with varied games before the tomb,
Saturnian Juno orders Iris down
from heaven to the Trojan fleet, breathing
brisk winds to favor Iris on her way,   800
still pondering new stratagems, her old
resentment still unsatisfied. The virgin
now speeds along her thousand-colored rainbow,
along her sloping path, noticed by none.
She sees the giant crowd and scans the shores;   805
she sees the bay deserted and the fleet
abandoned. But far off, on a lonely beach,
the Trojan women wept for lost Anchises,
all gazing over the deep waters, wailing:
"O that so many shoals, so wide a sea,   810
are still left for the weary!" This one cry
came from them all. They pray to have a city;
they are tired of their trials at sea. And Iris,
since she is not unskilled at stirring evil,
then throws herself among them, sets aside   815
the dress and the appearance of a goddess,
becoming Beroë, the aged wife

of Tmarian Doryclus, she who once had
her fame and family and sons; and thus
she shows herself among the Dardan women.   820
"O miserable ones, we whom the Achaean
soldiers did not drag off to death in battle
beneath our country's walls!" she cries. "Unhappy
race, what an end has fortune saved for you!
The seventh summer since the fall of Troy   825
is fading; we have measured in our journey
all waters, lands, with many rocks and stars
so inhospitable; from wave to wave,
on vast seas, we chase fleeing Italy.
Here are the fields of kindly Eryx and   830
our friend Acestes; then what can prevent
our building walls, giving our men a city?
My homeland and my household gods—o you
we saved in vain from enemies—shall no
walls ever take the name of Troy again?   835
And shall I never see the Simois
and Xanthus, Hector's rivers? No! Come now
and burn these damned ships with me! In my sleep
the image of the prophetess Cassandra
appeared and offered blazing brands. 'Look here   840
for Troy; here is your home!' she cried. The time
to act is now; such signs do not allow
delay. Here are four altars raised to Neptune;
the god himself gives us the will, the torches."
And shouting this, she is the first to snatch   845
the deadly fire with force; and swinging back
her lifted arm, she strives, then brandishes
and flings the flame. She has stunned the minds, dismayed
the Trojan women's hearts. Among the crowd
the eldest of them—Pyrgo, royal nurse   850
of many sons of Priam—now cries out:
"O mothers, this is not the Trojan wife
of Doryclus; this is not Beroë.
Her signs of godly beauty are enough—
what flashing eyes, what fire, what features, what   855
a tone of voice, what measure in her walk.
For I myself just now left Beroë
behind; and she was sick, complaining, grumbling
that she alone would miss our mourning here,
neglect the honors that are owed Anchises."   860

                ❖   ❖   ❖

So Pyrgo spoke. And yet at first the matrons,
though looking at the ships maliciously,
were doubtful, hesitant between two wretched
loves: one that held them to their present land;
the other, to the land where fate had called them.   865
But then the goddess, poised upon her wings,
rose high across the sky; and in her flight
she cut a giant bow beneath the clouds.
And now indeed, stunned by this prodigy
and driven mad, the matrons shout; and some   870
snatch fire from the inner hearths, and others
strip down the altars, flinging leaves and branches
and firebrands. Across the oars and benches
and painted pine hulls, Vulcan, ruthless, rages.

Eumelus now brings back to Anchises' tomb   875
and to the crowded theater the news
of burning Trojan ships; it is enough
to turn and see black ashes in a cloud.
And first Ascanius, just as he was—
glad, leading on his ranging horsemen—spurred   880
his eager stallion toward the panicked camp;
his breathless guardians cannot hold him back.
"What strange madness is this? Where now? Where to?"
he cries. "O wretched women, it is not
the enemy, the Argive's hostile camp,   885
it is your hopes you burn. Look, I am your
Ascanius!" And at his feet he casts
the empty helmet that had been his headdress
when he had played at miming war. Aeneas
has also hurried here, with Trojan squadrons.   890
But, terrified, the Dardan women scatter
this way and that along the shore; in stealth
they search for any woods and hollow rocks;
they hate what they have done, they shun the light;
now changed, they recognize their countrymen,   895
and Juno has been shaken from their hearts.

Yet not for that did flame and conflagration
relax their tameless force; alive, the tow
still burns beneath the soggy timbers, belches
its lazy smoke; slow heat consumes the keels;   900
the plague sinks into all that frame; the strength
of heroes, streams of water cannot help.

When he saw this, pious Aeneas tore
the mantle from his shoulders; stretching out
his hands, he called upon the gods for help: 905
"All-able Jupiter, if you do not
detest the Trojans down to their last man,
if your old kindness still has care for human
trials, Father, let this fleet escape the flames
and snatch away the Teucrians' thin fortunes   910
from ruin; or, if I deserve it, let
your hating thunderbolt send down to death
the little that is left; let your right hand
annihilate us here." He had just said this
when pouring rains, a lawless, furious   915
dark tempest, rage across the hills and plains
that tremble with the thunder; all the heavens
let fall a murky storm of water, black
with heavy south winds. From above the ships
are filled, charred timbers soaked, until the heat   920
and smoke are spent and all the hulls—except
four lost—are rescued from that pestilence.

But, battered by this bitter crisis, father
Aeneas now was mulling mighty cares
this way and that within his breast: whether   925
to settle in the fields of Sicily,
forgetful of the fates, or else to try
for the Italian coast. Then aged Nautes—
to whom especially Tritonian Pallas
had taught (and brought him fame for his great art)   930
how to explain the meaning of the gods'
great wrath or what the scheme of fate has asked—
consoles Aeneas, saying this to him:
"O goddess-born, there where the fates would have us
go forward or withdraw, there let us follow;   935
whatever comes, all fortune must be won
by our endurance. Like yourself, the Dardan
Acestes is a son of gods: take him
as comrade in your counsels, as a willing
friend; unto him entrust those who have lost   940
their ships and are superfluous; and choose
those who are tired of your vast attempt
and of your fortunes, and the old men spent
with years, and women weary of the sea,
and all who are weak and fear new dangers; let   945

the weary have their walls within these lands;
if you consent, their town's name is 'Acesta.' "

The words of his old friend disturb Aeneas;
his mind is torn apart by all his cares.
But when black Night rode high upon her chariot   950
and took possession of the heavens, then
down from the sky the image of his father
Anchises seemed to glide. His sudden words:
"Son, once more dear to me than life when life
was mine; son, battered by the fates of Troy!   955
Jove, who drove off the fire from your fleet
and from high heaven pitied you at last,
has sent me here. Obey the excellent
advice old Nautes gives; and take your chosen
young men, your bravest hearts, to Italy.   960
In Latium you must subdue a people
of steel, a race that has its rugged ways.
Yet first draw near the lower halls of Dis
and through the lands of deep Avernus seek,
my son, a meeting with me. I am not   965
among sad Shades, in impious Tartarus;
my home is in Elysium, among
the gracious gatherings of the pious ones.
You shall be shown the way there by the chaste
Sibyl—but after offering blood from many   970
black cattle. You will learn of all your race
and of the walls that have been given you.
And now farewell. Damp Night wheels on her way;
fierce Dawn, with panting stallions, breathes on me."
He spoke, then fled like smoke into thin air.   975
"Where are you rushing now, where hurrying?"
Aeneas cries. "Whom do you flee? Or who
keeps you from my embraces?" Saying this,
he stirs the embers and the sleeping fires,
and worships as a suppliant the Trojan   980
god of the hearth and the ancient Vesta's shrine
with sacred meal and with a full censer.

At once he calls his comrades—first Acestes—
and tells of Jove's command and his dear father's
advice and, too, what he himself has now   985

resolved. The meeting is not long; Acestes
does not object to what Aeneas asks.
They choose the women for the city, settling
a willing people, hearts that do not want
great fame. And they themselves renew the rowing   990
benches, and they repair the ships' charred timbers
and fit out oars and rigging—they are few
in number, but their hearts are keen for war.

And meanwhile with a plow Aeneas marks
the city's limits and allots the houses: 995
he calls one district "Troy," one "Ilium."
Acestes, born of Troy, delights in his
new kingdom; he proclaims a court of justice;
to the assembled elders he gives laws.
And then, close to the stars, above Mount Eryx,   1000
to Venus of Idalium they raise
a temple; and assign to Anchises' tomb
a priest within a sacred, spacious grove.

And now that everyone has feasted for
nine days, their offerings paid before the altars,   1005
calm breezes smooth the waters; blowing fresh,
the south wind calls again to voyaging.
A mighty wailing rises on the winding
beaches; and while embracing, they delay
a night, a day. The very men and matrons   1010
who once had found the face and name of the sea
so harsh and unendurable now want
to journey on, to test the trials of exile.
With kindly words, Aeneas comforts them;
and weeping, he commends them to his kinsman   1015
Acestes. Then he offers up three calves
to Eryx; for the Tempests, he commands
a lamb as sacrifice; that done, he has
the cable duly loosened. He himself,
a garland of stripped olive on his brow,   1020
now stands apart upon the prow; he holds
a bowl and throws the entrails to the salt
waves, and he pours pure wine. As they sail out,
the wind awakes astern. His comrades lash
the seas in rivalry, they sweep the waters.   1025

But meanwhile Venus is distressed, and this
lament pours from her breast; she says to Neptune:
"Juno's fanatic wrath, that heart of hers
that is insatiable, have made me stoop
to every sort of prayer; but she can never   1030
be softened, Neptune, neither by time's lapse
nor by the honors paid her; she can never
accept the Fates' or Jupiter's decrees.
It is not enough that her abominable
hatred devoured the city of the Phrygians,   1035
tearing their very heart, then dragged their remnant
through every punishment—she now pursues
the rest: the ashes, bones of ruined Troy.
Let her be very sure she has good reasons
for such madness. And you yourself can be   1040
my witness: what a sudden thrashing she
just now let loose upon the Libyan waters;
she mingled all the seas with heaven, trusting
in vain the huricanes of Aeolus;
and this she dared to do within your kingdom.   1045
And criminally, too, she drove the Trojan
women and foully burned their ships; and since
the fleet is lost, she has forced them to abandon
their comrades in an unknown land. I pray:
permit this remnant to entrust their sails   1050
safely across the waters. Let them reach
Laurentine Tiber if what I beseech
is just, if fate has given them those walls."

Then Saturn's son, who tames the deep sea, answered:
"O Cytherean, you have every right   1055
to put your trust in this my kingdom; you
yourself were born here. I have earned this trust,
for I have often checked the frenzy and
great anger of the sea and sky. No less
on land—I call to witness Simois   1060
and Xanthus—I have cared for your Aeneas.
For when in his pursuit Achilles dashed
the breathless Trojan ranks against the walls
and gave to death so many thousands, when
choked rivers groaned and Xanthus could not find   1065
a path or roll into the sea, then I
caught up Aeneas in a hollow cloud
as he encountered Peleus' son, with neither

the gods nor force upon his side; and this
although I wanted so to overturn   1070
the walls of perjured Troy, which I had built
with my own hands. My mind is still as kind;
then set your fear aside. Just as you ask,
he will safely reach the harbor of Avernus.
And you will only have to mourn one Trojan,   1075
one lost within the eddies of the sea;
one life shall be enough instead of many."

When he has soothed and cheered the goddess' heart,
the Father harnesses his fiery horses
with gold and fastens foaming bits and lets   1080
the reins run slack. Upon his azure chariot
he lightly glides across the waters' surface.
Beneath his thundering axletree the swollen
waves of the sea are smoothed, the cloud banks flee
the vast sky. Then his retinue appears   1085
in shapes so various: enormous whales,
the ancient company of Glaucus, and
Palaemon, son of Ino; and the rapid
Tritons have come, and all the band of Phorcus.
And on the left are Melite and Thetis,   1090
the virgin Panopea and Nesaea,
Thalia, Spio, and Cymodoce.

At this a healing joy restores the restless
spirit of father Aeneas; and he orders
that all the masts be raised with speed, the yards   1095
be spread with canvas. All the crewmen fasten
the sheets; at once, together, they let loose
the sails, to port, to starboard; and as one,
they shift and turn the high yardarms; kind winds
drive on the fleet. The first in that close squadron   1100
is Palinurus, leading; everyone
takes this command: to steer their course by him.

And now damp Night had almost reached her midpoint
along the skies; beneath their oars the sailors
were stretching out on their hard rowing benches,   1105
their bodies sinking into easy rest,
when, gliding lightly from the stars of heaven,
Sleep split the darkened air, cast back the shadows,

searching for you, o Palinurus, bringing
his dismal dreams to you, an innocent.   1110
The god sat down upon the high stern, taking
the shape of Phorbas, pouring out these words:
"Palinurus, son of Iasus,
the seas themselves bear on the fleet; the breezes
blow steadily; this is a time for rest.   1115
Lay down your head and steal your tired eyes
from trials; and for a brief while I myself
will take your place, your duties." Palinurus,
who scarcely lifts his eyes, makes this reply:
"And are you asking me to act as if   1120
I did not know the face of this calm sea
and its still waves? Do you ask me to trust
this monster? Why should I confide Aeneas
to the deceiving winds—I who have been
cheated so often by the treachery   1125
of tranquil skies?" He held the tiller fast;
not once did he let loose his grasp; his eyes
were fixed upon the stars. But—look—the god
now shakes a bough that drips with Lethe's dew,
drenched with the stupefying power of Styx,   1130
on Palinurus' temples; as he struggles,
his swimming eyes relax. That sudden rest
had just begun to let his limbs fall slack
when, bending down, the god cast him headlong
into the limpid waters; as he fell,   1135
he tore away part of the stern and helm,
and often cried, in vain, to his companions.
The god himself soared off upon his wings
into thin air. Nevertheless the fleet
runs safely on its way across the sea—   1140
even as father Neptune promised—carried
without alarm. Now, swept along, it neared
the Sirens' reefs, long since so dangerous,
white with the bones of many. When, far off,
the rocks were roaring, hoarse with ceaseless surf,   1145
father Aeneas felt his ship drift, aimless,
its pilot lost; he took the helm himself
and steered his galley through the midnight waters,
while sighing often, stunned by the disaster
fallen upon his friend: "O Palinurus,   1150
too trustful of the tranquil sky and sea,
you will lie naked on an unknown shore."

The Golden Bough

BOOK VI

THESE WERE THE words he wept and said. He lets
the reins that curb the fleet fall slack; at last
he glides to the Euboean coast of Cumae.
The Trojans turn their prows around to sea;
tenacious teeth, their anchors grip the ships;   5
the curving keels line up, they fringe the beach.
A band of keen young men leap toward the land
that is Hesperia. Some seek the seeds
of fire hidden in the veins of flint,
some scour the forest and the tangled dens   10
of beasts and point to newfound streams. But pious
Aeneas seeks the peaks where high Apollo
is king and, in a deep, enormous grotto,
the awful Sibyl has her secret home,
for there the seer of Delos so inspires   15
her mind and soul that she may know the future.
And now they come upon Diana's grove,
and now they reach the shrine, the roof of gold.

When Daedalus—for so the tale is told—
fled Minos' kingdom on swift wings and dared   20
to trust his body to the sky, he floated
along strange ways, up toward the frozen North,

until he gently came to rest upon
the mountaintop of Chalcis. Here he was
returned to earth, and here he dedicated   25
his oar-like wings to you, Apollo; here
he built a splendid temple in your honor.
Upon the gates he carved Androgeos' death,
and then the men of Athens, made to pay
each year with seven bodies of their sons;   30
before them stands the urn, the lots are drawn.
And facing this, he set another scene:
the land of Crete, rising out of the sea;
the inhuman longing of Pasiphaë,
the lust that made her mate the bull by craft;   35
her mongrel son, the two-formed Minotaur,
a monument to her polluted passion.
And here the inextricable labyrinth,
the house of toil, was carved; but Daedalus
took pity on the princess Ariadne's   40
deep love, and he himself helped disentangle
the wiles and mazes of the palace; with
a thread he guided Theseus' blinded footsteps.
And Icarus, you also would have played
great part in such work, had your grief allowed;   45
twice he had tried to carve your trials in gold,
and twice a father's hand had failed. The Trojans
would surely have looked closely at each scene
had not Achates, sent on in advance,
returned together with Deiphobe,   50
the priestess of Apollo and Diana,
and daughter of Glaucus. She tells king Aeneas:
"This is no time to gape at spectacles.
Far better now to slaughter seven steers
drawn from a herd the yoke has never touched,   55
to choose as many sheep as custom asks."
And having spoken so—Aeneas' men
are quick to sacrifice at her command—
she calls the Trojans into that high temple.

The giant flank of that Euboean crag   60
has been dug out into a cave; a hundred
broad ways lead to that place, a hundred gates;
as many voices rush from these—the Sibyl's
replies. Just as the Trojans reached the threshold,

the virgin cried: "Now call upon the Fates   65
for oracles. The god is here! The god!"
As she says this before the doors, her face
and color alter suddenly; her hair
is disarrayed; her breast heaves, and her wild
heart swells with frenzy; she is taller now;   70
her voice is more than human, for the power
of god is closing in, he breathes upon her.
"And are you slow to offer vows and prayers,
Trojan Aeneas? Are you slow?" she shouts.
"The terrifying house will never open   75
its giant jaws before your vows are spoken."

The Sibyl spoke and then was still. The Trojans'
tough bones were shaken by chill shuddering.
Their king pours prayers from his deepest breast:
"Phoebus, you always pitied Troy's hard trials,   80
you guided Dardan spears and Paris' hand
against the body of Achilles; you
yourself led me along so many seas
that bathe broad lands of far Massylian
tribesmen, past fields fringed by the Syrtes' sands;   85
but after this, and at long last, we grasp
the shores of fleeing Italy; may Troy's
fortune have followed us so far—no farther!
Now all you gods and goddesses who took
offense at Troy and at the Dardans' glory   90
can justly spare the sons of Pergamus.
And you, most holy priestess, you who know
what is to come (I do not ask for any
lands that have not been promised by my fates),
o let the Trojans rest in Latium   95
together with their wandering deities
and Troy's tormented gods. Then I shall raise
a temple to Apollo and Diana
built out of solid marble and decree
feast days in Phoebus' name. Great shrines await   100
you, priestess, too, within our Latin kingdom;
for there I shall set up your oracles
and secret omens spoken to my people
and consecrate to you, generous one,
our chosen men. Only do not entrust   105
your verses to the leaves, lest they fly off

in disarray, the play of rapid winds:
chant them yourself, I pray." His words were ended.

But she has not yet given way to Phoebus:
she rages, savage, in her cavern, tries   110
to drive the great god from her breast. So much
the more, he tires out her raving mouth;
he tames her wild heart, shapes by crushing force.
And now the hundred great gates of the house
swing open of their own accord. They bear   115
the answers of the priestess through the air:
"O you who are done, at last, with those great dangers
that lie upon the sea—worse wait on land—
the sons of Dardanus will reach Lavinium's
kingdom (for you can now be sure of this)   120
and yet shall wish that they had never come.
I see wars, horrid wars, the Tiber foaming
with much blood. You shall have your Simois,
your Xanthus, and your Doric camp; already
there is in Latium a new Achilles—   125
he, too, son of a goddess. Nor will Juno
fail anywhere to hound the Teucrians,
while you, a beggar in your need, implore
the towns, the tribes through all of Italy!
The cause of so much Trojan misery: 130
again, a foreign bride, a foreign wedding.
Do not relent before distress, but be
far bolder than your fortune would permit.
The first path to your safety, though it seem
unlikely, shall yet be a Grecian city."   135

These are the words that from her shrine the Sibyl
of Cumae chants; and these hard oracles
come roaring from her cavern, mingling true
sayings with darkness. So Apollo urges
the reins as she raves on; he plies the spurs   140
beneath her breast. But when her frenzy is done,
her raging lips are hushed, hero Aeneas
begins: "None of the trials you tell of, virgin,
is strange or unexpected: all of these
I have foreseen and journeyed in my thought.   145
One thing I ask: since here is said to be
the gateway of the lower king and here

the marsh of overflowing Acheron,
may it be granted me to go before
the face and presence of my dearest father? 150
Teach me the way, open the holy doors.
For through the fire, a thousand spears behind us,
I carried him upon these shoulders; from
the press of enemies I drew him on;
he was the comrade of my journeying; 155
with me he suffered all the seas and all
the threats of sky and wave—and these beyond
the power or the portion of old age—
however weak he was. Indeed, he prayed
and charged me to seek out and find your threshold. 160
Kind prophetess, I plead, take pity on
one who is both a father and a son;
your power touches all, and not for nothing
has Hecate assigned Avernus' woods
to your safekeeping. For if Orpheus could 165
recall the spirit of his wife, relying
upon his Thracian lyre's enchanting strings,
if Pollux could redeem his brother by
the death he alternates with him, and goes
and comes time after time on this same road. . . 170
I need not speak of mighty Theseus or
of Hercules. I, too, stem from high Jove."

And so Aeneas prayed, clasping the altar;
the prophetess began: "Born of the blood
of gods and son of Troy's Anchises, easy— 175
the way that leads into Avernus: day
and night the door of darkest Dis is open.
But to recall your steps, to rise again
into the upper air: that is the labor;
that is the task. A few, whom Jupiter 180
has loved in kindness or whom blazing worth
has raised to heaven as gods' sons, returned.
Through all the central region runs a forest
encircled by the black curves of Cocytus.
But if your mind is moved by such a love, 185
so great a longing, twice to swim the lake
of Styx and twice to see black Tartarus,
and you are pleased to try this mad attempt,
then, Trojan, hear what you must first accomplish.

A bough is hidden in a shady tree;   190
its leaves ànd pliant stem are golden, set
aside as sacred to Proserpina.
The grove serves as its screen, and shades enclose
the bough in darkened valleys. Only he
may pass beneath earth's secret spaces who   195
first plucks the golden-leaved fruit of that tree.
Lovely Proserpina ordained that this
be offered her as gift. And when the first
bough is torn off, a second grows again—
with leaves of gold, again of that same metal.   200
So let your eyes search overhead; and when
the bough is found, then pluck it down by hand
as due: for if the Fates have summoned you,
the bough will break off freely, easily;
but otherwise, no power can overcome it,   205
hard iron cannot help to tear it off.
And more, the lifeless body of your friend
now lies—but you have still to learn of this—
defiling all your fleet with death, while you
still ask your destiny and linger at   210
our threshold. First, you are to carry him
to his own place of rest and burial
and bring black cattle as peace offering.
And so, at last, your eyes shall see the groves
of Styx, the lands the living never pass."   215
She spoke and then was silent. Her lips closed.

Aeneas, sad and staring, takes his way.
He leaves the cavern, thinking on the strange
events, and at his side the same concerns
disturb the true Achates as he goes.   220
Their talk is long and varied as they walk.
Of what dead comrade did the priestess speak?
What body did she mean for them to bury?
But when they reach the shore again, they see
Misenus on the dry beach, beaten by   225
a death he did not merit: Misenus, son
of Aeolus, a man no one surpassed
in waking warriors with his trumpet blast,
in kindling with his clang the god of war.
For he had been a comrade of great Hector   230
and famous for his clarion and spear;
with Hector he had hurried into battle.

But when Achilles, victor, stripped his leader
of life, Misenus joined himself to Dardan
Aeneas, following no lesser banner.   235
And then he fell to madness: happening
to make the waves ring with his hollow shell,
blaring, he challenges the gods to contest;
and jealous Triton—if the tale can be
believed—snatched up Misenus, dashing him   240
in foaming shoals and breakers. Now, around him,
all mourned aloud, especially the pious
Aeneas. Then they rush to carry out,
in tears, the Sibyl's orders, strive to heap
an altar for his tomb, to build it high   245
to heaven, searching through the ancient forest,
deep dens of animals. The pitch pines fall;
the ilex rings beneath ax strokes; their wedges
now cleave the trunks of ash and splintering oaks.
They roll the giant rowans down the mountain.   250

Aeneas, first in that work, also girds
himself with tools like theirs; he cheers his comrades.
But gazing on the giant forest, he
is sad within his heart and prays: "If only
that golden bough might show itself to us   255
upon some tree in this great wood; for in
all things that had to do with you, Misenus,
the priestess has foreseen only too truly."
No sooner was this said than from the sky
twin doves descended, there, before his eyes,   260
settling along the green grass. And the chief
of heroes recognized his mother's birds
and prayed with gladness: "Be my guides if there
is any passage, strike across the air
to that grove where the rich bough overshadows   265
the fertile ground. And you, my goddess mother,
be true to me in my uncertainty."
As he said this, he stayed his steps. He watched
for omens, for the way the birds would turn.
Then, as they fed, they flew along as far   270
as sight could follow. But when they have reached
the jaws of foul Avernus, there they rise
and swiftly glide along the liquid air;
they settle, twins, on their desired treetop.
The gleam of gold was different, flickering   275

across the boughs. As in the winter's cold,
among the woods the mistletoe—no seed
of where it grows—is green with new leaves, girding
the tapering stems with yellow fruit: just so
the gold leaves seemed against the dark-green ilex;   280
so, in the gentle wind, the thin gold leaf
was crackling. And at once Aeneas plucks it
and, eager, breaks the hesitating bough
and carries it into the Sibyl's house.

Meanwhile along the shore the Teucrians   285
were weeping for Misenus, offering
their final tributes to his thankless ashes.
First they build high a giant pyre, rich
with pine and planks of oak. They interweave
the sides with somber leaves, in front they set   290
funeral cypresses, with gleaming weapons
as ornament above. And some make ready
hot water, caldrons bubbling on the flames;
they bathe and then anoint their friend's cold body.
Their lamentation is done, they place his limbs,   295
wept on, across the bier; and over them,
they throw his purple robes, familiar clothes.
Then some, as their sad office, raised the massive
barrow and, in their fathers' manner, faces
averted, set the firebrand below.   300
The offerings of frankincense and meats
and bowls of flowing oil are heaped together
and burned. The ashes sank, the flame was still;
they washed the remnants and the thirsty embers
with wine; and Corynaeus hid the gathered   305
bones in an urn of bronze. Three times he circled
around his comrades with clear water, and
with light spray from a fruitful olive bough,
he sprinkled them and purified the Trojans
and spoke the final words. Pious Aeneas   310
sets up a mighty tomb above Misenus
bearing his arms, a trumpet and an oar;
it stands beneath a lofty promontory,
now known as Cape Misenus after him:
it keeps a name that lasts through all the ages.   315

This done, he now moves swiftly to fulfill
all the commands and warnings of the Sibyl.
There was a wide-mouthed cavern, deep and vast
and rugged, sheltered by a shadowed lake
and darkened groves; such vapor poured from those   320
black jaws to heaven's vault, no bird could fly
above unharmed (for which the Greeks have called
the place "Aornos," or "The Birdless"). Here
the priestess places, first, four black-backed steers;
and she pours wine upon their brows and plucks   325
the topmost hairs between their horns and these
casts on the sacred fires as offering,
calling aloud on Hecate, the queen
of heaven and of hell. Then others slit
the victims' throats and catch warm blood in bowls.   330
Aeneas sacrifices with his sword
a black-fleeced lamb for Night, the Furies' mother,
and Terra, her great sister; and for you,
Proserpina, he kills a barren heifer.
And then for Pluto, king of Styx, he raises   335
nocturnal altars, laying on their fires
whole carcasses of bulls; he pours fat oil
across the burning entrails. But no sooner
are dawn and brightness of the early sun
upon them than the ground roars underfoot,   340
the wooded ridges shudder, through the shadows
dogs seem to howl as Hecate draws near.
"Away, away, you uninitiated,"
the priestess shrieks, "now leave the grove: only
Aeneas move ahead, unsheathe your sword;   345
you need your courage now; you need your heart."
This said, she plunges, wild, into the open
cavern; but with unfaltering steps Aeneas
keeps pace beside his guide as she advances.

You gods who hold dominion over spirits;   350
you voiceless Shades; you, Phlegethon and Chaos,
immense and soundless regions of the night:
allow me to retell what I was told;
allow me by your power to disclose
things buried in the dark and deep of earth!   355

They moved along in darkness, through the shadows,
beneath the lonely night, and through the hollow
dwelling place of Dis, his phantom kingdom:
even as those who journey in a forest
beneath the scanty light of a changing moon,   360
when Jupiter has wrapped the sky in shadows
and black night steals the color from all things.
Before the entrance, at the jaws of Orcus,
both Grief and goading Cares have set their couches;
there pale Diseases dwell, and sad Old Age,   365
and Fear and Hunger, that worst counsellor,
and ugly Poverty—shapes terrible
to see—and Death and Trials; Death's brother, Sleep,
and all the evil Pleasures of the mind;
and War, whose fruits are death; and facing these,   370
the Furies' iron chambers; and mad Strife,
her serpent hair bound up with bloody garlands.

Among them stands a giant shaded elm,
a tree with spreading boughs and aged arms;
they say that is the home of empty Dreams   375
that cling, below, to every leaf. And more,
so many monstrous shapes of savage beasts
are stabled there: Centaurs and double-bodied
Scyllas; the hundred-handed Briareus;
the brute of Lerna, hissing horribly;   380
Chimaera armed with flames; Gorgons and Harpies;
and Geryon, the shade that wears three bodies.
And here Aeneas, shaken suddenly
by terror, grips his sword; he offers naked
steel and opposes those who come. Had not   385
his wise companion warned him they were only
thin lives that glide without a body in
the hollow semblance of a form, he would
in vain have torn the shadows with his blade.

Here starts the pathway to the waters of   390
Tartarean Acheron. A whirlpool thick
with sludge, its giant eddy seething, vomits
all of its swirling sand into Cocytus.
Grim Charon is the squalid ferryman,
is guardian of these streams, these rivers; his   395
white hairs lie thick, disheveled on his chin;

his eyes are fires that stare, a filthy mantle
hangs down his shoulder by a knot. Alone,
he poles the boat and tends the sails and carries
the dead in his dark ship, old as he is;   400
but old age in a god is tough and green.

And here a multitude was rushing, swarming
shoreward, with men and mothers, bodies of
high-hearted heroes stripped of life, and boys
and unwed girls, and young men set upon   405
the pyre of death before their fathers' eyes:
thick as the leaves that with the early frost
of autumn drop and fall within the forest,
or as the birds that flock along the beaches,
in flight from frenzied seas when the chill season   410
drives them across the waves to lands of sun.
They stand; each pleads to be the first to cross
the stream; their hands reach out in longing for
the farther shore. But Charon, sullen boatman,
now takes these souls, now those; the rest he leaves;   415
thrusting them back, he keeps them from the beach.

That disarray dismays and moves Aeneas:
"O virgin, what does all this swarming mean?
What do these spirits plead? And by what rule
must some keep off the bank while others sweep   420
the blue-black waters with their oars?" The words
the aged priestess speaks are brief: "Anchises'
son, certain offspring of the gods, you see
the deep pools of Cocytus and the marsh
of Styx, by whose divinity even   425
the High Ones are afraid to swear falsely.
All these you see are helpless and unburied.
That ferryman is Charon. And the waves
will only carry souls that have a tomb.
Before his bones have found their rest, no one   430
may cross the horrid shores and the hoarse waters.
They wander for a hundred years and hover
about these banks until they gain their entry,
to visit once again the pools they long for."

Anchises' son has stopped; he stays his steps   435
and ponders, pitying these unkind fates.

There he can see the sorrowing Leucaspis,
Orontes, captain of the Lycian fleet:
both dead without death's honors, for the south wind
had overwhelmed them, sinking ships and sailors,   440
when they were crossing stormy seas from Troy.

And there the pilot, Palinurus, passed:
lately, upon the Libyan voyage, as
he scanned the stars, he had fallen from the stern,
cast down into the center of the sea.   445
And when at last in that deep shade Aeneas
had recognized his grieving form, he was
the first to speak: "O Palinurus, what
god tore you from us, plunged you in midsea?
O tell me. For Apollo, who had never   450
been false before, in this one oracle
deceived me; he had surely prophesied
that you would be unharmed upon the waters
and reach the coastline of Ausonia.
Is this the way he keeps his word?" He answered: 455
"Anchises' son, my captain, you must know:
Apollo's tripod did not cheat, no god
hurled me into the waves. For as it happened,
the rudder that, as my appointed charge,
I clutched, to steer our course, was twisted off   460
by force; I dragged it down headlong with me.
I swear by those harsh seas that I was taken
by no fear for myself; I was afraid
your ship, without its gear, without a helmsman,
might swamp in such a surge. Three nights of winter,   465
along vast fields of sea, across the waters,
the south wind lashed me violently; only
on my fourth dawn, high on a wave crest, I
saw Italy, dimly. I swam toward land
slowly and was just at the point of safety—   470
my sea-drenched clothing heavy, my hooked hands
were clinging to a jagged cliffside—when
barbarians attacked me with the sword,
ignorantly thinking me a prize.
And now I am the breakers', beach winds toss me. . . .   475
I beg you, therefore, by the gentle light
and winds of heaven, undefeated one,
and by your father, by your growing son,
Iülus, save me from these evils: either

cast earth upon my body—for you can—   480
and seek again the port of Velia; or
if there be any way, if you are given
such power by your goddess mother (for
I cannot think that you are now prepared
to cross such mighty rivers and the marsh   485
of Styx without the gods' protection), give
your own right hand to wretched Palinurus
and take me with you past the waters, that
at least in death I find a place of rest."

But then the priestess turned on the dead pilot.   490
"Where was it, Palinurus, that you learned
such dread desire? For how can you, unburied,
look at the waves of Styx, upon the Furies'
stern river, and approach its shore, unasked?
Leave any hope that prayer can turn aside   495
the gods' decrees. But keep in memory
these words as comfort in your cruel trial:
for all around, the neighboring cities will
be goaded by the plague, a sign from heaven
to make peace with your bones; and they will build   500
a tomb and send their solemn sacrifices;
the place will always be named Palinurus."
These words have set his cares to rest, his sorrow
is exiled for a while from his sad heart.
The land that bears his name has made him glad.   505

The journey they began can now continue.
They near the riverbank. Even the boatman,
while floating on the Styx, had seen them coming
across the silent grove and toward the shore.
He does not wait for greeting but attacks,   510
insulting with these words: "Enough! Stop there!
Whoever you may be who make your way,
so armed, down to our waters, tell me now
why you have come. This is the land of shadows,
of Sleep and drowsy Night; no living bodies   515
can take their passage in the ship of Styx.
Indeed, I was not glad to have Alcides
or Theseus or Pirithoüs cross the lake,
although the three of them were sons of gods
and undefeated in their wars. Alcides   520
tried to drag off in chains the guardian

of Tartarus; he tore him, trembling, from
the king's own throne. The others tried to carry
the queen away from Pluto's wedding chamber."

Apollo's priestess answered briefly: "We   525
bring no such trickery; no need to be
disturbed; our weapons bear no violence;
for us, the mighty watchman can bark on
forever in his cavern, frightening
the bloodless shades; Proserpina can keep   530
the threshold of her uncle faithfully.
Trojan Aeneas, famed for piety
and arms, descends to meet his father, down
into the deepest shades of Erebus.
And if the image of such piety   535
is not enough to move you, then"—and here
she shows the branch concealed beneath her robe—
"you may yet recognize this bough." At this
the swollen heart of Charon stills its anger.
He says no more. He wonders at the sacred   540
gift of the destined wand, so long unseen,
and turns his blue-black keel toward shore. He clears
the other spirits from the gangways and
long benches and, meanwhile, admits the massive
Aeneas to the boat, the vessel's seams   545
groaning beneath the weight as they let in
marsh water through the chinks. At last he sets
the priestess and the soldier safe across
the stream in ugly slime and blue-gray sedge.

These regions echo with the triple-throated   550
bark of the giant Cerberus, who crouches,
enormous, in a cavern facing them.
The Sibyl, seeing that his neck is bristling
with snakes, throws him a honeyed cake of wheat
with drugs that bring on sleep. His triple mouths   555
yawn wide with rapid hunger as he clutches
the cake she cast. His giant back falls slack
along the ground; his bulk takes all the cave.
And when the beast is buried under sleep,
Aeneas gains the entrance swiftly, leaves   560
the riverbank from which no one returns.

   ✿   ✿   ✿

Here voices and loud lamentations echo:
the souls of infants weeping at the very
first threshold—torn away by the black day,
deprived of their sweet life, ripped from the breast,   565
plunged into bitter death. And next to them
are those condemned to die upon false charges.
These places have not been assigned, indeed,
without a lot, without a judge; for here
Minos is magistrate. He shakes the urn   570
and calls on the assembly of the silent,
to learn the lives of men and their misdeeds.
The land that lies beyond belongs to those
who, although innocent, took death by their
own hands; hating the light, they threw away   575
their lives. But now they long for the upper air,
and even to bear want and trials there.
But fate refuses them: the melancholy
marshland, its ugly waters, hem them in,
the prisoners of Styx and its nine circles.   580

Nearby, spread out on every side, there lie
the Fields of Mourning: this, their given name.
And here, concealed by secret paths, are those
whom bitter love consumed with brutal waste;
a myrtle grove encloses them; their pains   585
remain with them in death. Aeneas sees
Phaedra and Procris and sad Eriphyle,
who pointed to the wounds inflicted by
her savage son; he sees Pasiphaë
and then Evadne; and Laodamia   590
and Caeneus, once a youth and now a woman,
changed back again by fate to her first shape.

Among them, wandering in that great forest,
and with her wound still fresh: Phoenician Dido.
And when the Trojan hero recognized her   595
dim shape among the shadows (just as one
who either sees or thinks he sees among
the cloud banks, when the month is young, the moon
rising), he wept and said with tender love:
"Unhappy Dido, then the word I had   600
was true? That you were dead? That you pursued
your final moment with the sword? Did I

bring only death to you? Queen, I swear by
the stars, the gods above, and any trust
that may be in this underearth, I was   605
unwilling when I had to leave your shores.
But those same orders of the gods that now
urge on my journey through the shadows, through
abandoned, thorny lands and deepest night,
drove me by their decrees. And I could not   610
believe that with my going I should bring
so great a grief as this. But stay your steps.
Do not retreat from me. Whom do you flee?
This is the last time fate will let us speak."

These were the words Aeneas, weeping, used,   615
trying to soothe the burning, fierce-eyed Shade.
She turned away, eyes to the ground, her face
no more moved by his speech than if she stood
as stubborn flint or some Marpessan crag.
At last she tore herself away; she fled—   620
and still his enemy—into the forest
of shadows, where Sychaeus, once her husband,
answers her sorrows, gives her love for love.
Nevertheless, Aeneas, stunned by her
unkindly fate, still follows at a distance   625
with tears and pity for her as she goes.

He struggles on his given way again.
Now they have reached the borderlands of this
first region, the secluded home of those
renowned in war. Here he encounters Tydeus,   630
Parthenopaeus, famous soldier, and
the pale shade of Adrastus; here are men
mourned in the upper world, the Dardan captains
fallen in battle. And for all of these,
on seeing them in long array, he grieves: 635
for Glaucus, Medon, and Thersilochus,
the three sons of Antenor; Polyboetes,
who was a priest of Ceres; and Idaeus,
still clinging to his chariot, his weapons.
The spirits crowd Aeneas right and left,   640
and it is not enough to see him once;
they want to linger, to keep step with him,
to learn the reasons for his visit there.

But when the Grecian chieftains and the hosts
of Agamemnon see the hero and   645
his weapons glittering across the shadows,
they tremble with an overwhelming terror;
some turn their backs in flight, as when they once
sought out their ships; some raise a thin war cry;
the voice they now have mocks their straining throats.   650

And here Aeneas saw the son of Priam,
Deiphobus, all of his body mangled,
his face torn savagely, his face and both
his hands, his ears lopped off his ravaged temples,
his nostrils slashed by a disgraceful wound.   655
How hard it was to recognize the trembling
Shade as he tried to hide his horrid torments.
Aeneas does not wait to hear his greeting
but with familiar accents speaks to him:
"Deiphobus, great warrior, and born   660
of Teucer's brilliant blood, who made you pay
such brutal penalties? Who was allowed
to do such violence to you? For Rumor
had told me that on that last night, worn out
by your vast slaughter of the Greeks, you sank   665
upon a heap of tangled butchery.
Then I myself raised up an empty tomb
along Rhoeteum's shore; three times I called
loudly upon your Shade. Your name and weapons
now mark the place. I could not find you, friend,   670
or bury you, before I left, within
your native land." The son of Priam answered:

"My friend, you left no thing undone; you paid
Deiphobus and his dead Shade their due.
But I was cast into these evils by   675
my own fate and the deadly treachery
of the Laconian woman; it was she
who left me these memorials. You know
and must remember all too well how we
spent that last night among deceiving pleasures.   680
For when across high Pergamus the fatal
horse leaped and, in its pregnant belly, carried
armed infantry, she mimed a choral dance
and, shrieking in a Bacchic orgy, paced

the Phrygian women; it was she herself 685
who held a giant firebrand and, from
the citadel, called in the Danaans.
I lay, sleep-heavy, worn with cares, within
our luckless bridal chamber, taken by
a sweet, deep rest much like the peace of death. 690
And meanwhile my incomparable wife
has stripped the house of every weapon, even
removing from beneath my head my trusted
sword; and she throws the doorway open, calls
her Menelaeus to my palace, hoping 695
her lover surely will be grateful for
this mighty favor, and her infamy
for old misdeeds will be forgotten. Why
delay? They burst into my room. The son
of Aeolus joins them as a companion, 700
encourager of outrage. Gods, requite
the Greeks for this if with my pious lips
I ask for satisfaction. But, in turn,
come tell me what misfortunes bring you here
alive? Have you been driven here by sea 705
wanderings or by warnings of the gods?
What fate so wearies you that you would visit
these sad and sunless dwellings, restless lands?"

But as they talked together, through the sky
Aurora with her chariot of rose 710
had passed her midpoint; and they might have spent
all this allotted time with words had not
the Sibyl, his companion, warned him thus:
"The night is near, Aeneas, and we waste
our time with tears. For here the road divides 715
in two directions: on the right it runs
beneath the ramparts of great Dis, this is
our highway to Elysium; the wicked
are punished on the left—that path leads down
to godless Tartarus." Deiphobus: 720
"Do not be angry, mighty priestess, I
now leave to fill the count, return to darkness.
Go on, our glory, go; know better fates."
He said no more; his steps turned at these words.

    *   *   *

Aeneas suddenly looks back; beneath   725
a rock upon his left he sees a broad
fortress encircled by a triple wall
and girdled by a rapid flood of flames
that rage: Tartarean Phlegethon whirling
resounding rocks. A giant gateway stands   730
in front, with solid adamantine pillars—
no force of man, not even heaven's sons,
enough to level these in war; a tower
of iron rises in the air; there sits
Tisiphone, who wears a bloody mantle.   735
She guards the entrance, sleepless night and day.
Both groans and savage scourgings echo there,
and then the clang of iron and dragging chains.

Aeneas stopped in terror, and the din
held him. "What kind of crimes are these? Virgin, 740
o speak! What penalties are paid here? What
loud lamentations fill the air?" The priestess
began: "Great captain of the Teucrians,
no innocent can cross these cursed thresholds;
but when the goddess Hecate made me   745
the guardian of Avernus' groves, then she
revealed the penalties the gods decreed
and guided me through all the halls of hell.
The king of these harsh realms is Rhadamanthus
the Gnosian: he hears men's crimes and then   750
chastises and compels confession for
those guilts that anyone, rejoicing, hid—
but uselessly—within the world above,
delaying his atonement till too late,
beyond the time of death. Tisiphone   755
at once is the avenger, armed with whips;
she leaps upon the guilty, lashing them;
in her left hand she grips her gruesome vipers
and calls her savage company of sisters.
And now at last the sacred doors are opened,   760
their hinges grating horribly. You see
what kind of sentry stands before the entrance,
what shape is at the threshold? Fiercer still,
the monstrous Hydra lives inside; her fifty
black mouths are gaping. Tartarus itself   765

then plunges downward, stretching twice as far
as is the view to heaven, high Olympus.
And here the ancient family of Earth,
the sons of Titan who had been cast down
by thunderbolts, writhe in the deepest gulf.   770
Here, too, I saw the giant bodies of
the twin sons of Aloeus, those who tried
to rip high heaven with their hands, to harry
Jove from his realms above. I saw Salmoneus:
how brutal were the penalties he paid   775
for counterfeiting Jove's own fires and
the thunders of Olympus. For he drove
four horses, brandishing a torch; he rode
triumphant through the tribes of Greece and through
the city in the heart of Elis, asking   780
for his own self the honor due to gods:
a madman who would mime the tempests and
inimitable thunder with the clang
of bronze and with the tramp of horn-foot horses.
But through the thick cloud banks all-able Jove   785
let fly his shaft—it was no firebrand
or smoky glare of torches: an enormous
blast of the whirlwind drove Salmoneus headlong.
And I saw Tityos, the foster child
of Earth, mother of all, his body stretched   790
on nine whole acres; and a crooked-beaked
huge vulture feeds upon his deathless liver
and guts that only grow the fruits of grief.
The vulture has his home deep in the breast
of Tityos, and there he tears his banquets   795
and gives no rest even to new-grown flesh.
And must I tell you of Ixion and
Pirithoüs, the Lapithae? Of those
who always stand beneath a hanging black
flint rock that is about to slip, to fall,   800
forever threatening? And there are those
who sit before high banquet couches, gleaming
upon supports of gold; before their eyes
a feast is spread in royal luxury,
but near at hand reclines the fiercest Fury: 805
they cannot touch the tables lest she leap
with lifted torch and thundering outcries.
And here are those who in their lives had hated
their brothers or had struck their father or

deceived a client or (the thickest swarm)   810
had brooded all alone on new-won treasure
and set no share apart for kin and friends;
those slain for their adultery; those who followed
rebellious arms or broke their pledge to masters—
imprisoned, all await their punishment.   815
And do not ask of me what penalty,
what shape or fate has overwhelmed their souls.
For some are made to roll a giant boulder,
and some are stretched along the spokes of wheels.
Sad Theseus has to sit and sit forever;   820
and miserable Phlegyas warns them all—
his roaring voice bears witness through the darkness:
'Be warned, learn justice, do not scorn the gods!'
Here is one who sold his fatherland for gold
and set a tyrant over it; he made   825
and unmade laws for gain. This one assailed
the chamber of his daughter and compelled
forbidden mating. All dared horrid evil
and reached what they had dared. A hundred tongues,
a hundred mouths, an iron voice were not   830
enough for me to gather all the forms
of crime or tell the names of all the torments."

So did the aged priestess of Apollo
speak, and she adds, "But come now, on your way,
complete the task you chose. Let us be quick.   835
I see the walls the Cyclops forged, the gates
with arching fronts, where we were told to place
our gifts." She has spoken. Side by side they move
along the shaded path; and hurrying
across the space between, they near the doors.   840
Aeneas gains the entrance, and he sprinkles
his body with fresh water, then he sets
the bough across the threshold facing them.

Their tasks were now completed; they had done
all that the goddess had required of them.   845
They came upon the lands of gladness, glades
of gentleness, the Groves of Blessedness—
a gracious place. The air is generous;
the plains wear dazzling light; they have their very
own sun and their own stars. Some exercise   850
their limbs along the green gymnasiums

or grapple on the golden sand, compete
in sport, and some keep time with moving feet
to dance and chant. There, too, the Thracian priest,
the long-robed Orpheus, plays, accompanying   855
with seven tones; and now his fingers strike
the strings, and now his quill of ivory.

The ancient race of Teucer, too, is here,
most handsome sons, great-hearted heroes born
in better years: Assaracus and Ilus   860
and Dardanus, who founded Pergamus.
From far Aeneas wonders at their phantom
armor and chariots; their spears are planted,
fixed in the ground; their horses graze and range
freely across the plain. The very same   865
delight that once was theirs in life—in arms
and chariots and care to pasture their
sleek steeds—has followed to this underearth.

And here to right and left he can see others:
some feasting on the lawns; and some chanting   870
glad choral paeans in a fragrant laurel
grove. Starting here, Eridanus in flood
flows through a forest to the world above.
Here was the company of those who suffered
wounds, fighting for their homeland; and of those   875
who, while they lived their lives, served as pure priests:
and then the pious poets, those whose songs
were worthy of Apollo; those who had
made life more civilized with newfound arts;
and those whose merits won the memory   880
of men: all these were crowned with snow-white garlands.
And as they streamed around her there, the Sibyl
addressed them, and Musaeus before all—
he stood, his shoulders towering above
a thronging crowd whose eyes looked up to him: 885
"O happy souls and you the best of poets,
tell us what land, what place it is that holds
Anchises. It is for his sake we have come
across the mighty streams of Erebus."

The hero answered briefly: "None of us   890
has one fixed home: we live in shady groves

and settle on soft riverbanks and meadows
where fresh streams flow. But if the will within
your heart is bent on this, then climb the hill
and I shall show to you an easy path."   895
He spoke, and led the way, and from the ridge
he pointed out bright fields. Then they descend.

But in the deep of a green valley, father
Anchises, lost in thought, was studying
the souls of all his sons to come—though now   900
imprisoned, destined for the upper light.
And as it happened, he was telling over
the multitude of all his dear descendants,
his heroes' fates and fortunes, works and ways.
And when he saw Aeneas cross the meadow,   905
he stretched out both hands eagerly, the tears
ran down his cheeks, these words fell from his lips:

"And have you come at last, and has the pious
love that your father waited for defeated
the difficulty of the journey? Son,   910
can I look at your face, hear and return
familiar accents? So indeed I thought,
imagining this time to come, counting
the moments, and my longing did not cheat me.
What lands and what wide waters have you journeyed 915
to make this meeting possible? My son,
what dangers battered you? I feared the kingdom
of Libya might do so much harm to you."

Then he: "My father, it was your sad image,
so often come, that urged me to these thresholds.   920
My ships are moored on the Tyrrhenian.
O father, let me hold your right hand fast,
do not withdraw from my embrace." His face
was wet with weeping as he spoke. Three times
he tried to throw his arms around Anchises'   925
neck; and three times the Shade escaped from that
vain clasp—like light winds, or most like swift dreams.

Meanwhile, Aeneas in a secret valley
can see a sheltered grove and sounding forests
and thickets and the stream of Lethe flowing   930

past tranquil dwellings. Countless tribes and peoples
were hovering there: as in the meadows, when
the summer is serene, the bees will settle
upon the many-colored flowers and crowd
the dazzling lilies—all the plain is murmuring.   935
The sudden sight has startled him. Aeneas,
not knowing, asks for reasons, wondering
about the rivers flowing in the distance,
the heroes swarming toward the riverbanks.
Anchises answers him: "These are the spirits   940
to whom fate owes a second body, and
they drink the waters of the river Lethe,
the care-less drafts of long forgetfulness.
How much, indeed, I longed to tell you of them,
to show them to you face to face, to number   945
all of my seed and race, that you rejoice
the more with me at finding Italy."

"But, Father, can it be that any souls
would ever leave their dwelling here to go
beneath the sky of earth, and once again   950
take on their sluggish bodies? Are they madmen?
Why this wild longing for the light of earth?"
"Son, you will have the answer; I shall not
keep you in doubt," Anchises starts and then
reveals to him each single thing in order.   955

"First, know, a soul within sustains the heaven
and earth, the plains of water, and the gleaming
globe of the moon, the Titan sun, the stars;
and mind, that pours through every member, mingles
with that great body. Born of these: the race   960
of men and cattle, flying things, and all
the monsters that the sea has bred beneath
its glassy surface. Fiery energy
is in these seeds, their source is heavenly;
but they are dulled by harmful bodies, blunted   965
by their own earthly limbs, their mortal members.
Because of these, they fear and long, and sorrow
and joy, they do not see the light of heaven;
they are dungeoned in their darkness and blind prison.
And when the final day of life deserts them,   970
then, even then, not every ill, not all

the plagues of body quit them utterly;
and this must be, for taints so long congealed
cling fast and deep in extraordinary
ways. Therefore they are schooled by punishment   975
and pay with torments for their old misdeeds:
some there are purified by air, suspended
and stretched before the empty winds; for some
the stain of guilt is washed away beneath
a mighty whirlpool or consumed by fire.   980
First each of us must suffer his own Shade;
then we are sent through wide Elysium—
a few of us will gain the Fields of Gladness—
until the finished cycle of the ages,
with lapse of days, annuls the ancient stain   985
and leaves the power of ether pure in us,
the fire of spirit simple and unsoiled.
But all the rest, when they have passed time's circle
for a millennium, are summoned by
the god to Lethe in a great assembly   990
that, free of memory, they may return
beneath the curve of the upper world, that they
may once again begin to wish for bodies."

Anchises ended, drew the Sibyl and
his son into the crowd, the murmuring throng,   995
then gained a vantage from which he could scan
all of the long array that moved toward them,
to learn their faces as they came along:

"Listen to me: my tongue will now reveal
the fame that is to come from Dardan sons   1000
and what Italian children wait for you—
bright souls that are about to take your name;
in them I shall unfold your fates. The youth
you see there, leaning on his headless spear,
by lot is nearest to the light; and he   1005
will be the first to reach the upper air
and mingle with Italian blood; an Alban,
his name is Silvius, your last-born son.
For late in your old age Lavinia,
your wife, will bear him for you in the forest;   1010
and he will be a king and father kings;
through him our race will rule in Alba Longa.

Next Procas stands, pride of the Trojan race;
then Capys, Numitor, and he who will
restore your name as Silvius Aeneas,   1015
remarkable for piety and arms
if he can ever gain his Alban kingdom.
What young men you see here, what powers they
display, and how they bear the civic oak
that shades their brows! For you they will construct   1020
Nomentum, Gabii, Fidena's city,
and with the ramparts of Collatia,
Pometia and Castrum Inui,
and Bola, Cora, they will crown the hills.
These will be names that now are nameless lands.   1025

"More: Romulus, a son of Mars. He will
join Numitor, his grandfather, on earth
when Ilia, his mother, gives him birth
out of the bloodline of Assaracus.
You see the double plumes upon his crest: 1030
his parent Mars already marks him out
with his own emblem for the upper world.
My son, it is beneath his auspices
that famous Rome will make her boundaries
as broad as earth itself, will make her spirit   1035
the equal of Olympus, and enclose
her seven hills within a single wall,
rejoicing in her race of men: just as
the Berecynthian mother, tower-crowned,
when, through the Phrygian cities, she rides on   1040
her chariot, glad her sons are gods, embraces
a hundred sons of sons, and every one
a heaven-dweller with his home on high.

"Now turn your two eyes here, to look upon
your Romans, your own people. Here is Caesar   1045
and all the line of Iülus that will come
beneath the mighty curve of heaven. This,
this is the man you heard so often promised—
Augustus Caesar, son of a god, who will
renew a golden age in Latium,   1050
in fields where Saturn once was king, and stretch
his rule beyond the Garamantes and
the Indians—a land beyond the paths

of year and sun, beyond the constellations,
where on his shoulders heaven-holding Atlas   1055
revolves the axis set with blazing stars.
And even now, at his approach, the kingdom
of Caspia and land of Lake Maeotis
shudder before the oracles of gods;
the seven mouths of Nile, in terror, tremble.   1060
For even Hercules himself had never
crossed so much of the earth, not even when
he shot the brazen-footed stag and brought
peace to the groves of Erymanthus and
made Lerna's monster quake before his arrows;   1065
nor he who guides his chariot with reins
of vine leaves, victor Bacchus, as he drives
his tigers down from Nysa's steepest summits.
And do we, then, still hesitate to extend
our force in acts of courage? Can it be   1070
that fear forbids our settling in Ausonia?

"But who is he who stands apart, one crowned
with olive boughs and bearing offerings?
I recognize his hair and his white beard:
when called from humble Cures, a poor land,   1075
to mighty rulership, he will become
first king of Rome to found the city's laws.
And after Numa: Tullus, who will shatter
his country's idleness and wake to arms
the indolent and ranks unused to triumph.   1080
Beside him is the ever-boastful Ancus,
one even now too glad when people hail him.
And would you see the Tarquin kings? And, too,
the haughty spirit of avenging Brutus,
the fasces he regained? He will be first   1085
to win the power of a consul, to use
the cruel axes; though a father, for
the sake of splendid freedom he will yet
condemn his very sons who stirred new wars.
Unhappy man! However later ages   1090
may tell his acts, his love of country will
prevail, as will his passion for renown.

"Then see, far off, the Decii and Drusi;
Torquatus of the ruthless ax; Camillus

as he brings back the standards. But those spirits   1095
you see there—gleaming in their equal armor
and now, while night restrains them, still at peace—
if they but reach the light of life, how great
a war they will incite against each other,
what armies and what slaughter! There is Caesar,   1100
descending from the summits of the Alps,
the fortress of Monoecus, and Pompey,
his son-in-law, arrayed against him with
the legions of the East. My sons, do not
let such great wars be native to your minds,   1105
or turn your force against your homeland's vitals:
and Caesar, be the first to show forbearance;
may you, who come from heaven's seed, born of
my blood, cast down the weapon from your hand!

"And there is Mummius, who—famous for   1110
his slaying of Achaeans, conqueror
of Corinth—will yet drive his chariot
triumphantly to the high Capitol.
There stands Aemilius Paulus, the destroyer
of Agamemnon's own Mycenae and   1115
of Argos and the sons of Aeacus,
the seed of powerful-in-arms Achilles:
he will yet avenge the Trojan elders and
Minerva's outraged altars. Who could leave
to silence you, great Cato, or you, Cossus?   1120
Who can ignore the Gracchi or the Scipios,
twin thunderbolts of war, the lash of Libya;
Fabricius, so strong and with so little;
or you, Serranus, as you sow your furrow?
And Fabii, where does your prodding lead me—   1125
now weary—with your many deeds and numbers!
You are that Maximus, the only man
who, by delaying, gave us back our fortunes.
For other peoples will, I do not doubt,
still cast their bronze to breathe with softer features,   1130
or draw out of the marble living lines,
plead causes better, trace the ways of heaven
with wands and tell the rising constellations;
but yours will be the rulership of nations,
remember, Roman, these will be your arts: 1135
to teach the ways of peace to those you conquer,

to spare defeated peoples, tame the proud."

So, while Aeneas and the Sibyl marveled,
father Anchises spoke to them, then added:
"And see Marcellus there, as he advances   1140
in glory, with his splendid spoils, a victor
who towers over all! A horseman, he
will set the house of Rome in order when
it is confounded by great mutiny;
he will lay low the Carthaginians   1145
and rebel Gaul; then for a third time father
Quirinus will receive his captured arms."

At this, Aeneas had to speak; he saw
beside that Shade another—one still young,
of handsome form and gleaming arms, and yet   1150
his face had no gladness, his eyes looked down:
"Who, Father, moves beside this man? A son
or one of the great race of his sons' sons?
For how his comrades clamor as they crowd!
What presence—his! And yet, around his head   1155
black night is hovering with its sad shade!"

With rising tears Anchises answered him:
"My son, do not search out the giant sorrow
your people are to know. The Fates will only
show him to earth; but they will not allow   1160
a longer stay for him. The line of Rome,
o High Ones, would have seemed too powerful
for you, if his gifts, too, had been its own.
What cries of mourning will the Field of Mars
send out across that overwhelming city,   1165
what funerals, o Tiber, will you see
when you glide past the new-made tomb! No youth
born of the seed of Ilium will so
excite his Latin ancestors to hope;
the land of Romulus will never boast   1170
with so much pride of any of its sons.
I weep for righteousness, for ancient trust,
for his unconquerable hand: no one
could hope to war with him and go untouched,
whether he faced the enemy on foot   1175
or dug his foaming horse's flank with spurs.

O boy whom we lament, if only you
could break the bonds of fate and be Marcellus.
With full hands, give me lilies; let me scatter
these purple flowers, with these gifts, at least,   1180
be generous to my descendant's spirit,
complete this service, although it be useless."

And so they wander over all that region,
across the wide and misted plains, surveying
everything. And when father Anchises   1185
has shown his son each scene and fired his soul
with love of coming glory, then he tells
Aeneas of the wars he must still wage,
of the Laurentians, of Latinus' city,
and how he is to flee or face each trial.   1190

There are two gates of Sleep: the one is said
to be of horn, through it an easy exit
is given to true Shades; the other is made
of polished ivory, perfect, glittering,
but through that way the Spirits send false dreams   1195
into the world above. And here Anchises,
when he is done with words, accompanies
the Sibyl and his son together; and
he sends them through the gate of ivory.
Aeneas hurries to his ships, rejoins   1200
his comrades, then he coasts along the shore
straight to Caieta's harbor. From the prow
the anchor is cast. The sterns stand on the beach.

Camilla

BOOK VII

In DEATH, YOU too, Aeneas' nurse, Caieta,
have given to our coasts unending fame;
and now your honor still preserves your place
of burial; your name points out your bones
in broad Hesperia—if that be glory.   5

But having paid her final rites as due,
the mound above her tomb in order, pious
Aeneas, when the heavy seas have stilled,
sets out his sails to voyage, quits the harbor.
Night falls; the winds breathe fair; the brilliant moon   10
does not deny his way; the waters gleam
beneath the quivering light. The Trojans sail
close by the shore of Circe's island, where
the wealthy daughter of the Sun, with song
unending, fills her inaccessible groves;   15
she kindles fragrant cedarwood within
her handsome halls to light the night and runs
across her finespun web with a shrill shuttle.
The raging groans of lions fill her palace—
they roar at midnight, restless in their chains—   20
and growls of bristling boars and pent-up bears,
and howling from the shapes of giant wolves:

all whom the savage goddess Circe changed,
by overwhelming herbs, out of the likeness
of men into the face and form of beasts.   25
But lest the pious Trojans have to suffer
such horrors and be carried to this harbor
or land along these cruel coasts, Neptune
had swelled their sails with saving winds and helped
their flight. He carried them past the seething shoals.   30

And now the sea was red with sunrays, saffron
Aurora shone in her rose chariot;
the winds fell off, and from the high air every
harsh blast was ended suddenly, the oars
beat down against the waters' sluggish marble.   35
Then from his ship Aeneas spies a spacious
forest; and through the trees the Trojan sees
the Tiber, gracious river, hurrying
to sea, with yellow sands and rapid eddies.
And varied birds that knew the river's channel   40
and banks flew through the grove; and overhead
they soothed the air with song. Aeneas orders
his men to change their course; the prows are turned
to land; he enters, glad, the shadowed river.

Now, Erato, be with me, let me sing   45
of kings and times and of the state of things
in ancient Latium when the invaders
first beached their boats upon Ausonia's coasts,
and how it was that they began to battle.
O goddess, help your poet. I shall tell   50
of dreadful wars, of men who struggle, tell
of chieftains goaded to the grave by passion,
of Tuscan troops and all Hesperia
in arms. A greater theme is born for me;
I try a greater labor.

        King Latinus,   55
an old man now, ruled over fields and tranquil
towns in long-lasting peace. He was the son
of Faunus and Marica, a Laurentian
nymph—so we have been told. And Faunus' father
was Picus—he who calls you, Saturn, parent: 60
you are the earliest author of that line.

The edicts of the gods had left Latinus
no male descent; for as his son grew up,
he was cut off in early youth. One daughter
was all he had as heir for house and holdings;   65
and she was ripe now, ready for a husband;
her years were full for marriage. Many wooed her
from all Ausonia, wide Latium.
And Turnus, handsomest above all others,
had wooed her, too: he had mighty grandfathers   70
and great-grandfathers, and Latinus' royal
wife wished to see him as her son-in-law.
But in that wedding's way there stand the omens
of gods with many sinister alarms.
For in the inner courtyard of the palace   75
there stood a laurel tree with sacred leaves,
preserved with reverence for many years.
They say that it was found by King Latinus
himself, when he built his first fortresses,
and he had made it holy to Apollo;   80
from it, he gave the colonists their name:
Laurentians. At that laurel's crown—how strange
to tell—a thick and sudden swarm of bees,
borne, shrill, across the liquid air, had settled;
they twined their feet and hung from leafy branches.   85
At once the prophet cried: "In that direction
from which the swarm has come I see a stranger
approaching and an army nearing us;
I see them reach the palace, see them ruling
in our high citadel." More, while the virgin   90
Lavinia with pure and fragrant torches
kindled the altars, standing by her father,
she seemed—too terrible—to catch that fire
in her long tresses; all her ornaments
were burning in that crackling blaze, and burning,   95
her queenly hair, her crown set off with jewels;
then wrapped in smoke and yellow light, she scattered
her flames throughout the palace. This indeed
was taken as a sign of fear and wonder:
they sang she would be glorious in fame   100
and fate but bring great war to her own people.

Much troubled by these signs, Latinus visits
the oracle of Faunus, of his fate-

foretelling father; he consults the groves
of high Albunea. Deepest of forests,   105
it echoes with a holy fountain, breathing
a savage stench in darkness. Here the tribes
of Italy and all Oenotria
seek answers in uncertainty. And here
the priest would bring his gifts, then lie along   110
the outspread hides of slaughtered sheep, beneath
the silent night, asking for sleep, and see
so many phantoms hovering strangely
and hear various voices and enjoy
the conversation of the gods and speak   115
to Acheron in deep Avernus. Father
Latinus also came here, seeking answers.
He sacrificed a hundred woolly sheep,
as due, then rested on their hides and fleece.
A sudden voice was sent from that thick forest: 120
"O do not seek, my son, to join your daughter
in marriage to a Latin; do not trust
the readied wedding bed. For strangers come
as sons-in-law; their blood will raise our name
above the stars; and their sons' sons will see   125
all things obedient at their feet, wherever
the circling Sun looks on both sides of Ocean."
Latinus does not keep within himself
these answers told him by his father Faunus,
these warnings given under silent night.   130
But racing wide across Ausonia's cities,
swift Rumor had already carried them,
just at the time the Trojan crewmen fastened
their fleet along the grassy riverbank.

Aeneas, his chief captains, and the handsome   135
Iülus rest beneath a tall tree's branches
as they make ready for a feast with cakes
of wheat set out along the grass (for so
had Jove himself inspired them); and these
they use as platters, heaped with country fruits.   140
And here it happened, when their scanty food
was done, that—hungry still—they turned upon
the thin cakes with their teeth; they dared profane
and crack and gnaw the fated circles of
their crusts with hand and jaw; they did not spare   145

the quartered surfaces of their flat loaves.
"We have consumed our tables, after all,"
Iülus laughed, and said no more. His words,
began to bring an end to Trojan trials;
as they first fell from Iülus' lips, Aeneas   150
caught them and stopped his son's continuing;
he was astounded by the will of heaven.
He quickly cries: "Welcome, my promised land!
I hail the faithful household gods of Troy!
This is our home and country. For my father,   155
Anchises—now I can remember—left
such secrets of the fates to me, saying:
'My son, when you are carried overseas
to stranger shores, and when, your food consumed,
your hunger forces you to eat your tables,   160
remember in your weariness to hope
for homes, to set your hands to building dwellings
and raising walls around them.' And this was
the hunger that he had foretold; this was
the final trial to end our sorrows. Come,   165
and with the sun's first light let us explore
in different directions from this harbor—
and gladly—what these lands are, who lives here,
and where their city lies. Now let us pour
our cups to Jupiter, entreat my father   170
Anchises, set our wine back on the tables."

Then, having spoken so, Aeneas next
binds up his temples with a leafy branch,
entreats the genius of the place and Earth—
the first of gods—the nymphs, and rivers still   175
unknown; and then he prays to Night, the signs
that rise by night, and Jove of Ida and
the Phrygian mother, each in order; then
he calls on both his parents—one in heaven
and one in Erebus. When this was done,   180
the all-able Father thundered three times from
the clear sky overhead; from the high air
with his own hand he brandished—plainly showed—
a cloud that glowed with shafts of light and gold.
Then through the Trojan squadrons suddenly   185
this rumor runs: the day has come when they
must build their promised walls. In eagerness,

they feast again; made glad by that great omen,
they set the bowls and crown the wine with garlands.

And when the next day rose to scan the land   190
with its first light, they go by separate ways
to search the city out, its boundaries and
the coastline of that nation. These, they find,
are pools and fountains of Numicius;
and this, the river Tiber; here, the home   195
of sturdy Latins. Then Anchises' son
gives orders that a hundred emissaries,
men chosen from each rank, be sent—to go
before the king's majestic walls; all should
be shaded by Minerva's boughs and bring   200
gifts to the king and ask peace for the Trojans.
There is no lingering: they hurry off,
all carried by their rapid steps. Aeneas
himself now traces out a shallow trench
to mark the walls; he plans the site, surrounding   205
with mounds and battlements—just like a camp—
this their first settlement along the coast.
By now the Trojan band had found its way;
they saw the Latin towers and high roofs,
they neared the walls. Before the Latin city   210
boys and young men in their first flowering
practice their riding or break in fresh teams
for chariots along the dust, or bend
their keen long bows, or off their shoulders spin
tough-shafted javelins, or challenge one   215
another now to race or box; just then
a messenger, who has galloped on ahead,
reports to the old king that towering men
in unfamiliar dress have come to Latium.
Latinus orders that the strangers be   220
invited to the palace. At its center
he sat on his ancestral chair of state.

It was a stately dwelling, wide and high
and hundred-columned, towering above
the city; once the palace of Laurentian   225
Picus, an awesome place both for its forests
and for the sanctity of ancient worship.
Here Latin kings received their scepters, here

beneath its auspices first took their fasces;
this was the temple, this the senate house,   230
and these the seats for sacred feasts; and here
the elders, after slaughtering a ram,
would take their places at long rows of tables.
Here, too, the images of their forefathers
were carved in ancient cedar, placed in order   235
along the porch: first Italus and then
father Sabinus, planter of the vine,
shown holding his curved sickle underneath
his likeness; aged Saturn; two-faced Janus;
and all the other kings from the beginning;   240
and those who, fighting for their homeland, suffered
the wounds of war. Beside them many weapons
hang from the holy doorposts: captured chariots
and curving battle-axes, helmet crests
and massive bars of gates and shafts and shields   245
and beaks the Latins had wrenched free from ships.
With his Quirinal staff, his tunic short,
a shield in his left hand, Picus himself,
tamer of horses, sat: he whom his bride,
Circe, within the clutch of lust had struck   250
with her gold rod, transforming him by drugs
into a bird with wings of speckled colors.

This was the temple of the gods and here
Latinus, seated on his father's throne,
welcomed the Teucrians into his palace;   255
when they had entered, he spoke gentle words:
"You, sons of Dardanus—for we are not
that ignorant of both your stock and city;
we have heard about your journey on the sea—
do tell us what you seek. What cause or need   260
has brought your fleet to these Ausonian shores,
across so many blue-gray waters? Whether
you have been driven off your course by error
or tempest—sailors suffer many things
like these upon the sea—you now have entered   265
our riverbanks and moored within our harbor.
Then do not shun our welcome; do not forget
the Latins are a race of Saturn, needing
no laws and no restraint for righteousness;
they hold themselves in check by their own will   270

and by the customs of their ancient god.
And I remember, though the years obscure
the story, that the old men of Aurunca
would tell how Dardanus, raised in these lands,
had reached the towns of Phrygian Ida and   275
of Thracian Samos, now called Samothrace.
He came from here—from Corythus, his Tuscan
homeland—and starry heaven's golden palace
enthrones him now; his altars join the gods'."

He spoke. It was Ilioneus who answered: 280
"O King, great son of Faunus, no dark tempest
drove us across the waters to your lands;
no star, no coastline cast us off our way;
but by design and willing minds we all
have reached your city—exiled from a kingdom   285
that once excelled all that the Sun could see
in his long journeying from far Olympus.
Our race begins with Jove; the young of Troy
rejoice in Jove as ancestor; our king
himself is born of Jove's high race: the Trojan   290
Aeneas sends us to your gates. How great
a storm let loose by fierce Mycenae fell
upon the fields of Ida, by what fates
the worlds of Europe and of Asia clashed,
is known even to those the flung-back Ocean   295
keeps far away and those the pitiless
Sun separates from us, there where he stretches
across the middle of the world's four zones.
We sailed out from that flood across waste seas;
we only ask for some small settlement: 300
safe shore to house our native gods and air
and water free to all. We will not bring
disgrace upon your kingdom, and our praises
will not mean little for your reputation:
your graciousness will never be forgotten,   305
Ausonia will not repent the taking
of Troy into her bosom. By Aeneas'
fates and his right hand strong in trust and war
and arms I swear that many people, many
nations—and do not scorn us if we carry   310
these garlands, bring you willing words of peace—
have tried and wished to join themselves to us.

But we were driven forward by the fates
of gods and their commands to seek your lands.
Now Dardanus, born here, returns. Apollo   315
has urged us on by high decrees to find
the Tuscan Tiber and the sacred waters
that flow from the Numician fountain. More,
Aeneas gives to you these few poor emblems
of his old fortune, remnants snatched from Troy   320
in flames. Out of this golden bowl his father
Anchises poured libations at the altar;
and these were worn by Priam when he judged,
as custom was, his tribes in their assemblies;
his scepter and the sacred diadem,   325
and these his robes, the work of Trojan women."

And as Ilioneus says this, Latinus'
face is fixed fast upon the ground; only
his eyes, attentive, stir. Brocaded purple
and Priam's scepter do not move the king   330
as much as all his thoughts about his daughter's
wedding and bridal bed. Within his breast
he dwells upon old Faunus' oracle,
upon his son-in-law; the fates foretold
that he would come from stranger countries, called   335
to share Latinus' kingdom as an equal,
that out of this would come a race whose force
was famous, strong enough to take the world.
At last he speaks in gladness: "May the gods
now favor our attempt, their augury!   340
For, Trojan, you shall have what you have asked;
I do not scorn your gifts. While I am king,
you shall not lack the wealth of this rich land
or Troy's abundance. Only let Aeneas
approach in person, if he longs for us   345
and wants to join us as a friend, to bear
the name of ally. He need never fear
our friendly presence. One term of our peace
shall be for me to clasp your chief's right hand.
Now take, in turn, my answers to your king.   350
I have a daughter whom the oracles
of my paternal shrine and many omens
sent down from heaven will not let me wed
to any husband from our nations: sons

will come to us from foreign shores, their blood   355
will raise our name high as the stars—this is
the prophecy that waits for Latium.
And if my mind has augured anything
of truth, then I receive and, too, accept
this man himself as called upon by fate."   360

Father Latinus, having spoken so,
then chooses horses from his herds: three hundred
stood sleek in their high stalls. At once he calls
for those wing-footed ones to be led out—
in purple and embroidered saddle cloths—   365
as gifts for all the Teucrians in order.
Gold chains hang down their chests, their harnesses
are gold, and with their teeth they champ gold bits.
And for the Trojans' absent chief, he chooses
a chariot and a pair of stallions; born   370
of an ethereal seed, these horses breathed
fire from their nostrils; they were of the race
that cunning Circe, having stolen some
immortal stallions from her father, bred
as bastards from a mortal mare. Latinus   375
gives them these words and gifts; Aeneas' sons
return, high on their horses, bringing peace.

But even then the savage wife of Jove
was well embarked upon the air, returning
from Argos, city of Inachus; even   380
from Sicily's Pachynus, far away,
across the sky she spied the glad Aeneas
and all his Dardan fleet. She sees them building
their houses, settling on the land, deserting
their ships. Her grief is sharp; she cannot move.   385
She shakes her head; these words pour from her breast:
"O hated race, whose fates have crossed my fates!
For could I beat them on Sigean fields?
When captured, could they suffer capturing?
Could Troy in flames destroy them? They have found   390
a way across the armies and the fires.
Either my power is now worn out at last
or, having had my fill of hate, I rest.
Not so: for I have dared to follow them,
in exile from their land, across the waters;   395

I faced those fugitives on all the seas,
and every force of sky and wave was spent
against the Teucrians. What use were Syrtes'
quicksands, or Scylla, or the vast Charybdis?
They are moored along the Tiber's riverbed—   400
men careless of the seas, careless of me.
For Mars was able to destroy the giant
race of the Lapithae; Diana's anger
could take the land of ancient Calydon—
and even from the father of the gods: 405
and were the Lapithae so criminal,
did Calydon deserve such ravaging?
But I, great wife of Jove—who left no thing
undared, who tried all ways in wretchedness—
am beaten by Aeneas. If my power   410
is not enough, I shall not hesitate
to plead for more, from anywhere; if I
cannot bend High Ones, then I shall move hell.
I cannot keep him from the Latin kingdoms:
so be it, let Lavinia be his wife,   415
as fates have fixed. But I can still hold off
that moment and delay these great events,
can still strike down the nations of both kings.
Then let the son- and father-in-law pay
for peace with their own peoples' death. Virgin,   420
your dowry will be Latin blood and Trojan,
your bridal matron is to be Bellona.
For Cisseus' daughter, Hecuba, will not
have been the only one to bear a torch
and nuptial flames within her womb; for Venus'   425
own son will be the same—another Paris,
another brand to burn new Pergamus."

This said, her hideous presence heads for earth.
And from the home of the appalling Furies
and hellish darkness she calls up the dread   430
Allecto, in whose heart are gruesome wars
and violence and fraud and injuries:
a monster, hated even by her father,
Pluto, and by her own Tartarean sisters,
so many are the shapes that she takes on,   435
so fierce her forms, so thick her snakes that swarm
in blackness. Juno goads her with these words:

"You, virgin, born of Night, do me this service,
this fitting labor: do not let my honor
and fame be hurt or beaten; do not let   440
the Trojans have their way with King Latinus
by marriage or besiege Italian borders.
For you can arm for battle brothers, though
they feel at one, and ruin homes with hatred;
and you can carry firebrands and lashes   445
beneath their roofs; you have a thousand names,
a thousand ways of injuring; awake
your fertile breast and break this settled peace;
sow war and crime; let sudden quarrel spur
young men to want, demand, and seize the sword."   450

At once Allecto, steeped in Gorgon poison,
makes first for Latium and the high palace
of the Laurentian chieftain. There she sits
before the silent threshold of the queen,
Amata, who is kindled by a woman's   455
anxieties and anger, seething over
the Trojans' coming, Turnus' thwarted wedding.
Then from her blue-gray hair the goddess cast
a snake deep in Amata's secret breast,
that, maddened by the monster, she might set   460
at odds all of her household. And the serpent
glides on, between the queen's smooth breasts and dress,
and winds its way unnoticed; by deceit
it breathes its viper breath into her frenzy.
The giant snake becomes a twisted necklace   465
of gold, a long headband to bind her hair,
and slithers down her limbs. And while its first
infection, penetrating with damp poison,
has gripped her senses and entwined her bones
in fire, before her soul has felt the force   470
of flame throughout her breast, Amata speaks
softly, as is the way of mothers, weeping
over her daughter and the Phrygian wedding:
"O husband, shall Lavinia become
the wife of Trojan exiles? And have you   475
no pity for your daughter and yourself?
No pity, either, for her mother, whom
the faithless robber, with the first north wind,
will leave behind as he seeks out high seas

and steals away the virgin as his prey?   480
Did not the Phrygian shepherd use this plan
to enter Lacedaemon, taking Helen,
the daughter of Leda, to the towns of Troy?
What of your sacred pledge? Of your old love
for your own people? What of your right hand   485
you swore so often to your kinsman, Turnus?
And if the Latins are to seek a son
from foreign nations, and this must be done,
and father Faunus' orders hold you back,
then I maintain that every land is foreign   490
that lies apart and not beneath our rule,
and so the gods have said. For if you ask
the early origin of Turnus' house:
his ancestors were Inachus, Acrisius;
and his first home, the middle of Mycenae."   495

But when she has tried these useless words and sees
Latinus standing firm against her, when
the serpent's maddening mischief has slid deep
within her bowels and traveled all her body,
exciting her with monstrous fantasies,   500
the wretched queen, indeed hysterical,
rages throughout the city. Even as
a top that spins beneath a twisted whip
which boys, when bent on play, will drive across
the empty courtyards in a giant circle: 505
drawn by the thong, it whirls along in curving
spirals; the crowd of children, puzzled, bend
above that turning wood in their amazement;
and each lash gives it life—so, not more slowly,
the queen is driven on her course among   510
her cities and fierce peoples. She pretends
that Bacchus has her; racing to the forest,
Amata now tries greater scandal, spurs
to greater madness. She conceals her daughter
in leafy mountains, stealing from the Trojans   515
that marriage, holding off the wedding torches:
"Evoe Bacchus!" is her shriek and cry,
"For only you are worthy of the virgin;
for you she has taken up the supple thyrsus;
she circles you in dance, for you she saves   520
her sacred hair." The news flies on. Straightway

all of the matrons feel the same zeal, kindled
by Furies in their breasts, to seek new homes.
And they desert their houses, bare their necks
and hair before the wind. Still others crowd   525
the skies with quivering cries; dressed in fawn hides,
they carry vine-bound spears. And at the center
Amata lifts a blazing firebrand
of pine and, raging, sings the wedding song
of Turnus and her daughter as she rolls   530
her bloodshot eyes; her cry is savage, sudden:
"O Latin mothers, listen now, wherever
you are: if any love still lives within
your pious hearts for sad Amata, if
care for a mother's rights still gnaws at you,   535
then loose the headbands on your hair, take to
these orgies with me." So Allecto drives
the queen to every side with Bacchus' goads
among the woods, the wilderness of beasts.

But after she is satisfied that this   540
first frenzy now is sharp enough, that she
has turned awry Latinus' plans and all
his palace, the grim goddess flies at once
on her dark wings to daring Turnus' walls:
the city built by Danaë when, carried   545
upon the swift south wind, she founded it
as home for her Acrisian colonists.
Our fathers used to call it Ardea;
and Ardea is still a mighty name,
but its great days are done. There Turnus lay   550
asleep, beneath his high roof, in black night.
Allecto sets aside her savage features
and Fury's body; she transforms herself,
becoming an old woman, furrowing
her filthy brow with wrinkles, putting on   555
white hair and headband, then an olive bough;
she now is Calybe, the aged priestess
of Juno and her temple. And she shows
herself before the young man with these words:
"O Turnus, can you let all you have done   560
run down to uselessness, your scepter pass
to Dardan colonists? The king denies

your bride, the dowry you have won by blood.
He seeks a foreign son to take the kingdom.
Scorned one, set out to face ungrateful dangers;   565
go now to lay the Tuscan armies low,
to give the Latins peace beneath your shield.
This is the message that the very presence
of Saturn's mighty daughter ordered me
to bring you while you lay in tranquil night.   570
Rise up and gladly call your men to ready
their arms, to march beyond the gates to battle,
to burn the Phrygian chieftains who have settled
by this fair river and their painted fleet.
So does the urgent force of gods command.   575
If King Latinus does not grant the marriage,
does not hold fast to his old promise, let
him learn at last what Turnus is in arms."

At this, the young man mocks the prophetess:
"I am well aware that ships are in the Tiber—   580
no need to conjure up for me such terrors.
Queen Juno has not been forgetful of me.
But old age, mother, overcome by rust,
fruitless of truth, has made you waste your cares;
among the quarrels of kings, it plays on your   585
prophetic spirit with false fears. Your task:
to guard the shrines and images of gods.
Let men run war and peace: war is their work."

Allecto blazed in anger at his words.
But even as he spoke, a sudden trembling   590
clutched at the limbs of Turnus, his eyes stared:
the Fury hisses with so many serpents,
so monstrous is the face she shows. She turned
her flaming eyes and thrust him, faltering, back,
as he tried to say more. She lifted up   595
two vipers from her hair; her lash was loud;
with maddened lips she added this: "Then look
at me—undone by rust, fruitless of truth,
whom old age plays upon with cheating terrors
among the quarrels of kings! Just look at me!   600
I come here from the home of the dread Sisters,
and in my hand I carry death and wars."

   *   *   *

And saying this, she cast a torch at Turnus,
fixing the firebrand within his breast,
and there it smoked with murky light. Great fear   605
shatters his sleep, sweat bursts from all his body
and bathes his bones and limbs. Insane, he raves
for arms, he searches bed and halls for weapons.
Lust for the sword and war's damnable madness
are raging in him and—above all—anger: 610
just as when burning, loudly crackling twigs
are heaped beneath a seething caldron's ribs,
the liquid dances with the heat; within,
the water rages, violent, and pours
a stream of smoke and foam; it will not rest   615
but flies up with dense steam. He now commands
his captains to march out upon Latinus,
profane the peace, prepare for arms, protect
their Italy, and drive the enemy
beyond her boundaries; and he declares   620
himself a match for Trojans and for Latins.
When he has spoken and invoked the gods
in prayer, then his Rutulians encourage
each other eagerly to arms. And some
are moved by Turnus' handsome youth and form,   625
some by his royal ancestors, and some
by those bright deeds that his right hand has done.

While Turnus fills his warriors with daring,
Allecto lifts herself on Stygian wings
and flies off toward the Trojans. And with new   630
deceits she spies the beach where handsome Iülus
was hunting down wild beasts with snares and horses.
And here the hellish virgin casts a sudden
frenzy upon his dogs, touching their nostrils
with scent they know too well, inflaming them   635
to chase after a stag: this hunting was
the first cause of the troubles, and for this
the rustic minds of Latium were driven
to war. There was a splendid wide-horned stag—
a stag which, taken from its mother's dugs,   640
the sons of Tyrrhus nursed, and Tyrrhus, too,
who keeps the royal herds and far-off fields.
Their sister, Silvia, with every care
had dressed the stag, grown used to her commands,

with gentle garlands on his horns; she combed him   645
and bathed him in a clear spring, and her hand
did not disturb him, and he fed beside
his master's table, and he roved the forest
and then came home, however late the hour,
to his familiar threshold. But while he   650
was wandering far off, the maddened dogs
of hunter Iülus startled him, just as
he chanced to swim downstream to cool his heat
along the green banks. Now Ascanius
himself, inflamed with love of praise, had aimed   655
an arrow from his curving bow; some god
did not allow his faltering hand to fail;
the shaft was driven, hissing loud; it pierced
both flank and belly. And the animal,
wounded, fled back to his familiar roof;   660
moaning, he reached his stall and, suppliant
and bleeding, filled the house with his lament.
And Silvia, the sister, is the first
to beat her hands against her arms, to call
for help and gather in the sturdy farmers.   665
And—since the fiendish Fury lies concealed
within the silent wood—they suddenly
are here: one armed with a scorched firebrand,
another with a heavy-knotted club;
what each can find, his anger makes a weapon.   670
Then Tyrrhus calls his troops and, breathing rage,
he snatches up an ax; by chance he was
cleaving an oak in four with hammered wedges.

But when the ruthless goddess—from a tower—
has marked the moment that is made for mischief,   675
she flies off toward the high roof of the stable
and from that summit sounds the shepherd's signal
and strains her voice of hell through a bent horn.
And every grove, however far off, trembled;
the woods resounded to their depths; the distant   680
lake of Diana heard it, and the sulphurous
white waters of the Nar, Velinus' fountains;
and mothers clasped their infants to their breasts
in terror. At the blast with which the dreadful
trumpet sent off its signal, fearless farmers   685
are quick to gather from all sides with armor;

and from their open camps the youths of Troy
now stream out, too, to help Ascanius.
The lines are drawn; this is no country battle
with sturdy clubs or burned-out firebrands;   690
they fight with two-edged steel, a horrid harvest
of unsheathed swords that bristle far and wide,
and arms of brass that glisten when the sun
strikes and they fling their light beneath the clouds:
as when a wave, beneath the wind's first breath,   695
begins to whiten; slow by slow, the sea
will lift its combers higher until, at last,
it climbs to heaven from its lowest depths.
And here in the first rank the eldest son
of Tyrrhus, the young Almo, is struck down: 700
a hissing arrow caught him, and the wound
held fast beneath his throat; it choked with blood
the path of his soft voice and tender breath.
And many bodies lie around him—even
the old Galaesus, fallen as he pleaded   705
for peace and threw himself between the ranks:
he was the justest man of all and once
the richest in Ausonia's fields; for him
five flocks of bleating sheep, five herds of cattle
came back from pasture, and it took a hundred   710
plows to turn up the farmlands of Galaesus.

And while they carry on the equal struggle
across the plains, the goddess, having kept
her promise—having drenched with blood the battle
and sent death into that first contest—quits   715
Hesperia and, carried through the air,
reports to Juno as a conqueror
with high words: "See the discord I made ripe
for you in bitter war. Just let them try
to join in peace and friendship, now that I   720
have splashed the Trojans with Ausonian blood!
And if you wish, I shall do more: I shall
compel the neighboring towns to war by rumor,
inflame their minds with love of insane Mars,
that they assemble from all sides with aid;   725
and I shall scatter arms across the fields."
Then Juno answers her: "There is enough
of fear and fraud; the causes of the war

are firm; they now fight hand to hand; the weapons
that chance first brought are now stained with new
    blood.   730
Such are the marriages, the wedding rites
that King Latinus and the splendid son
of Venus celebrate. The lord of high
Olympus will not let you wander free
about the upper air. Be gone from here.   735
I can attend to all that now remains."
So Saturn's daughter spoke. And then Allecto
lifts up her wings that hiss with snakes, leaving
the heights to seek her dwelling in Cocytus.
Just at the heart of Italy, beneath   740
steep mountains, lies the Valley of Ampsanctus,
famous in many lands; on either side
the border of a grove, black with thick leaves,
has hemmed it in; along the middle runs,
tumultuous, a torrent echoing   745
across the rocks in twisting eddies. Here
a horrid cave—the breathing vents of Dis,
the savage one—appears; a huge abyss
where Acheron erupts here opens its
infectious jaws. In these the Fury hid   750
her hated power, freeing earth and sky.

Meanwhile the royal daughter of Saturn gives
a final touch to war. Now all the shepherds
are pouring toward the city, bringing back
the slain: young Almo and the mangled face   755
that was Galaesus. They implore the gods
and call on King Latinus. Turnus, too,
is there; and in the outcry at the slaughter,
among the fires of passion, he redoubles
the terror. He says Teucrians are called   760
to rule, that Phrygian blood is to be mingled
with Latin, that he is banished from the palace.
And then the kinsmen of those women who,
when driven wild by Bacchus, leaped across
the pathless groves in dances (and the name   765
of Queen Amata is not without effect)
join in from every side and cry "War! War!"
At once, despite the signs and oracles
of gods, through some perverted power all

ask for unholy war. In eagerness   770
they press around the palace of Latinus.
He, like a steady rock amid the sea,
resists—a rock that, when the breakers crash,
holds fast through its great mass while many waves
howl on against it; all around in vain   775
the crags and foaming sea cliffs roar; the seaweed,
dashed hard against its sides, is driven back.
But when no power is granted him to check
their blind resolve, when all moves at the will
of savage Juno, then—again, again—   780
father Latinus calls upon the gods
and on the empty air; he cries: "The fates
have crushed us, we are carried by the storm.
Unhappy men! The penalty for this
will yet be paid with your profaning blood.   785
O Turnus, vengeance, bitter punishment
for this unholy act will wait for you;
too late your prayers will venerate the gods.
My rest is near, my harbor is in view;
a happy burial is all I lose."   790
He said no more but shut himself within
the palace, let the reins of rule fall slack.

Within Hesperian Latium there was
a custom which the Alban cities held
as holy from that time and which now Rome,   795
the mistress of the world, still honors: when
they first incite Mars into battle, whether
preparing for a lamentable war
against Hyrcanians, Getae, Arabs, or
to march on India and to hunt the Dawn   800
and claim their standards back from Parthians—
there are twin Gates of War (so they are called)
made sacred by religion and the fear
of savage Mars; a hundred bolts of brass
and the eternal strength of iron hold them;   805
their keeper, Janus, never quits the threshold.
And when the elders' will is set on combat,
the consul, in the robe of Romulus
and Gabine girdle, with his own hand unlocks
the creaking portals, and he calls on battle   810
to issue out; the young take up his cry,
the brazen trumpets echo hoarse accord.

In this way, too, Latinus was commanded
to call for war against Aeneas' sons,
to unlock the gates of sorrow. But their king   815
and father would not touch the doors; he turned
and fled from that foul office, hid himself
among blind shadows. Then the queen of gods,
when she had glided from the heavens, forced
the slow gates; on their turning hinges Saturn's   820
daughter burst the iron doors of war.

Ausonia, once at rest, unmoved, is now
aflame. A part prepare to march on foot
across the plains; while others, mounted on
tall horses, charge in clouds of dust; all call   825
for arms with eagerness. Some burnish shields
to smoothness, brighten javelins with fat
tallow, or grind their axheads sharp on stone;
and they delight to bear their standards, hear
the clang of trumpets. So five mighty cities   830
set up their anvils and renew their weapons:
the strong Atina, Ardea, haughty Tibur,
Crustumium, and turreted Antemnae.
Some hollow trusted helmets for their heads
and, for their shields, weave frameworks out of willow; 835
while others hammer breastplates out of bronze
or mold their polished greaves in pliant silver.
The honor and the love that once was theirs
for plowshare and for sickle yield to this;
for this they forge anew their fathers' swords   840
in furnaces. The trumpets wail. The watchword
passes from man to man, the battle signal.
One snatches up a helmet from his house
in trembling haste; another yokes impatient
horses and buckles on his shield and mail   845
of three-ply gold, makes fast his faithful sword.

O goddesses, now open Helicon
and guide my song: what kings were spurred to war;
what squadrons filled the plains behind each chieftain;
what men graced lovely Italy even then;   850
what arms set her ablaze. For goddesses,
you can remember and retell; the slender
breath of that fame can scarcely reach to us.
         ❀   ❀   ❀

First, from the Tuscan coasts, Mezentius
the cruel, despiser of the gods, marches   855
to war and arms his men. His son is with him:
Lausus—no one more handsome marched, except
for Turnus; Lausus, tamer of wild horses,
a hunter and a victor over beasts,
who leads out of the city of Agylla   860
a thousand men who followed him for nothing;
one worthy to obey a better father—
a father who was not Mezentius.

And after these the handsome Aventinus,
a son of handsome Hercules, displays   865
along the grass his palm-crowned chariot
and his triumphant horses; on his shield
his father's emblem glows, a hundred snakes
and Hydra, girt with serpents: Aventinus,
brought to the boundaries of light by secret   870
birth in the woods upon the Aventine
hill by the priestess Rhea—a mortal woman
but mated to a god—after Tirynthius,
a victor over slaughtered Geryon,
had reached Laurentum's boundaries and bathed   875
his Spanish oxen in the Tuscan river.
The troops of Aventinus carry grim
pikes, javelins, tapering swords, and Sabine spits.
And he himself moves out on foot, swinging
a giant lion mane, uncombed; its bristles   880
are terrifying, and its gleaming teeth
are set upon the head of Aventinus.
So, rough, he stalks into the royal palace,
his shoulders in the clothes of Hercules.

And next, twin brothers leave the walls of Tibur   885
(their brother's name, Tiburtus, named their race)—
Catillus and brave Coras, youths of Argos.
They march in the front ranks to face the shower
of shafts: as when two Centaurs, born of clouds,
descending in their headlong course a high   890
hillside, leave Homole or snow-white Othrys;
the giant forest yields a passage to them,
the underbrush gives way with a loud roar.

  ✿   ✿   ✿

Nor was the founder of Praeneste absent:
King Caeculus, whom every age believed   895
to be the son of Vulcan, born among
the rural herds and found upon the hearth.
A country legion, drawn from far and wide,
now follows him: men come from high Praeneste,
from fields of Gabine Juno, from the Anio's   900
cold stream, and from the Hernicans' rock-bound
towns watered by these rivers—you, the rich
Anagnia; you, father Amasenus.
Not all of these have clanging arms or shields
or chariots: most of them shower pellets   905
of livid lead; some wield twin javelins,
with tawny caps of wolfskin as their headgear.
They wear their left foot naked as they march,
the other foot is shod in a rawhide boot.

Meanwhile Messapus, Neptune's son and tamer   910
of horses, whom no one can fell by fire
or steel, has quickly rallied all his people
long since at peace, his troops unused to battle,
and takes the sword again. His musters come
down from Soracte's heights, Flavinia's fields,   915
Aequi Falisci, and Fescennium,
Ciminius' lake and hill, Capena's forests.
They marched in time and sang their leader's praises:
just as the song of snow-white swans, among
the liquid clouds, when they return from pasture   920
and sing through their long throats in gracious measures;
the river Cayster and the Asian lake
struck by that far-off sound, in turn reecho.
One would not think that multitude was made
of brass-clad ranks, but of an airy cloud   925
of hoarse birds driven shoreward from the sea.

Here Clausus, of the ancient blood of Sabines,
leads on a mighty army, he himself
the equal of an army; and from him
the Claudian tribe and nation spread throughout   930
all Latium when Rome was shared in part
with Sabines. Amiternum's giant legion
marches together with him, and the ancient
Quirites, and all ranks that have come from

Eretum and Mutusca, rich in olives; 935
and those whose home is in Nomentum or
in Rosean fields near by Velinus or
on Tetrica's rough crags and Mount Severus,
in Foruli, Casperia, or along
Himella's waters; those who drink of Tiber 940
and Fabaris; those sent by frigid Nursia,
the Hortine squadrons, and the Latin nations;
and those the river Allia—unlucky
its name—divides as it flows on: as many
as waves that roll along the Libyan sea, 945
when harsh Orion sinks beneath the winter
waters; or just as thick as ears of corn
scorched by the eastern sun on Hermus' plains
or Lycia's yellow fields. Their shields are loud;
earth, startled, trembles at their tramping feet. 950

Next, one of Agamemnon's men, Halaesus,
who hates the name of Troy, has yoked his horses
and rides his chariot; in the cause of Turnus
he sweeps along a thousand savage tribes:
the men whose harrows turn the Massic plains, 955
fields rich with wine, and those sent down from high
hillsides and from the nearby Sidicine
farmlands by the Auruncan fathers; and
those come from Cales or the fields that border
that shallow stream, Volturnus; and the rough 960
Saticulans have come, and bands of Oscans.
Their arms are tapered clubs; but they are used
to fastening these with pliant thongs. A leather
shield serves as cover over their left arms;
for combat hand-to-hand they use hooked swords. 965

Nor shall you pass unnoticed in these verses,
you Oebalus, the son—they say—of Telon
when Telon mated with the nymph Sebethis
while, well along in years, he ruled the kingdom
of the Teleboans at Capreae. 970
But not content with what his father held,
the son had, even then, enlarged his realm
on all sides, to the tribes of the Sarrastes,
the plains the Sarnus waters, and those who
hold Rufrae, Batulum, Celemna's fields; 975

and those who make their home beneath the walls
of apple-rich Abella. Like the Teutons,
they hurled their studded clubs, and for their headgear
they stripped the bark of cork trees. And their shields
are glittering with bronze; with bronze, their swords.   980

Down from its mountains Nersae sent to battle
you, Ufens, marked by fame and blessed in war,
who rule a tribe more savage than all others—
the Aequi with their stony soil, men used
to hard hunts in the forest; armed, they till   985
the earth and always take delight in their
new plunder, in a life of violence.

And from the Marsians, sent by King Archippus,
there came a priest, the most courageous Umbro,
his helmet wreathed with fruitful olive leaves.   990
By spell and touch he scattered sleep on vipers
and pestilential hydras; by his art
he soothed their rage and cured their stings. And yet
he could not heal the hurt of Dardan steel;
neither sleep-giving charms nor herbs brought from   995
the Marsian hills could help him with those wounds.
For you Angitia's forest wept, the crystal
wave of the Fucinus, for you bright lakes.

And handsome Virbius also came to war:
son of Hippolytus, sent by his mother,   1000
Aricia, he was wearing splendid armor.
He had been raised along the marshy shores
within Egeria's grove, where—rich and peaceful—
the altar of Diana stands. They tell
how when he fell by his stepmother's guile   1005
and paid a father's vengeance with his blood,
torn into pieces by his panicked horses,
Hippolytus had risen toward the stars,
called back into the air of upper earth
by the Healer's herbs and by Diana's love.   1010
Then the all-able Father, in his anger
at any mortal's rising from infernal
shadows up to the light of life, cast down
the son of Phoebus, Aesculapius,

the finder of such medicines, such arts, 1015
into the Stygian waves. But generous
Diana hid Hippolytus in secret,
then sent him to the nymph Egeria,
the grove where all alone, unhonored, he
lived out his life among Italian forests 1020
and changed his name to Virbius. For this,
no horn-hoofed horse can ever trespass in
the sacred grove and temple of Diana;
because when they were panicked by sea monsters,
they spilled the youth and chariot on the shore. 1025
Nevertheless, along the level fields
his son was driving glowing stallions
and racing in his chariot to war.

The handsome-bodied Turnus is himself
among the vanguard, taller by a head 1030
than all. He grips a sword; and his high helmet
is crested with a triple plume and carries
Chimaera breathing from her jaws with flames
like Etna's; as the fighting grows more savage,
with flowing blood, she rages more, ferocious, 1035
with her grim fires. But on his burnished shield
were—chased in gold, her horns uplifted—Io,
shown as already shaggy, as already
a heifer (splendid emblem), and the virgin's
custodian, Argus; from a sculpted urn 1040
the river of her father, Inachus,
poured. After Turnus, like a cloud, the shielded
ranks of the infantry crowd all the fields:
the youths of Argos and Auruncan squadrons;
Rutulians; Sicanians, old settlers; 1045
Sacranians; and with their painted bucklers,
Labicians; and, Tiber, those who till
your valleys or Numicius' holy shores,
or plow Rutulian slopes or Circe's hill
or fields where Jupiter of Anxur rules 1050
together with Feronia, who delights
in her green grove; and those from Satura's
black marsh, where icy Ufens makes its way
through deep-cut valleys, then is lost at sea.

   *   *   *

With these, Camilla of the Volscian tribe   1055
leads on her band of horsemen, squadrons bright
with brazen armor. She is a warrior;
her woman's hands have never grown accustomed
to distaffs or the baskets of Minerva;
a virgin, she was trained to face hard battle   1060
and to outrace the wind with speeding feet.
Across the tallest blades of standing grain
she flies—and never mars the tender ears;
or poised upon the swelling wave, she skims
the sea—her swift soles never touch the water.   1065
And as Camilla passes, all the young
pour out from field and house; the matrons crowd
and marvel, staring, in astonishment
at how proud royal purple veils Camilla's
smooth shoulders, how a clasp of gold entwines   1070
her hair, at how she bears her Lycian quiver,
her shepherd's pike of myrtle tipped with steel.

VIII·307

BOOK VIII

W<small>HEN</small> T<small>URNUS AT</small> the fortress of Laurentum
lifted the flag of war and trumpets blasted,
raucous, when he aroused his eager stallions
and clashed his arms, at once all hearts were restless.
All Latium is leagued in startled tumult,   5
a savage spirit grips the hot young men.
Messapus, Ufens, and Mezentius,
despiser of the gods—the chief captains—
have mustered troops from every quarter, stripped
the broad fields of their farmers. Venulus   10
is sent to mighty Diomedes' city
of Arpi to ask help, to tell him that
the Teucrians have come to Latium—
Trojan Aeneas with his fleet, who brings
defeated household gods, declaring he   15
is called by fates to be a king; that many
nations now have joined the Dardan chieftain,
his name gains ground in Latium. What end
Aeneas means with these beginnings, wants
as outcome of the quarrel if fortune favors,   20
will surely be more clear to Diomedes
than to King Turnus or to King Latinus.

❖   ❖   ❖

And so it went through all of Latium;
and when the Trojan hero has seen this,
he wavers on a giant tide of troubles;   25
his racing mind is split; it shifts here, there,
and rushes on to many different plans,
turning to everything: even as when
the quivering light of water in bronze basins
reflected from the sun or from the moon's   30
glittering image glides across all things
and now darts skyward, strikes the roof's high ceiling.

Night. Over all the lands deep sleep held fast
the tired creatures, birds and herds. And father
Aeneas, restless over bitter war,   35
stretched out along the riverbank beneath
the cold, let late-come rest seep through his limbs.
The river god himself, old Tiberinus,
lord of that place and gentle stream, rising
from poplar leaves, then stood before Aeneas;   40
thin linen covered him with sea-green dress,
and shady reeds were covering for his head.
He spoke; his words exiled the Trojan's cares:

"O born of gods, you bring the Trojan city
back here to us from enemies and save   45
your Pergamus for ever—you, awaited
upon Laurentian soil and Latin fields—
for here your home and household gods are sure.
Do not draw back or panic at war's threats;
the rage and anger of the gods are done.   50
And now, lest you should think these are but empty
fictions sleep has feigned, you shall discover
a huge white sow stretched out upon the ground
along the banks beneath the branching ilex,
together with a new-delivered litter   55
of thirty suckling white pigs at her teats.
And this shall be the site set for your city,
and this the certain rest from all your toils.
And after thirty turning years, by this
omen, your son Ascanius will found   60
a city, Alba, of the sun-like name.
I do not speak of doubtful things. Now listen:
I tell you by what means you may accomplish

all that you are, as conqueror, to do.
Along these coasts Arcadians, a people   65
born out of Pallas, friends of King Evander,
and following his banners, chose a place
among the hills and built a city called—
for their ancestor, Pallas—Pallanteum.
They always are at war against the Latins.   70
Go take them in as allies to your camps
and join in treaty with them. I myself
shall guide your galleys straight upstream along
the banks, so that your oars may overcome
the countercurrent. Come now, goddess-born,   75
arise and, as the stars first set, be sure
to offer fitting prayers to Juno; let
your humble gifts defeat her threats and anger.
And when you are a victor, honor me.
I am the one you see touching the banks   80
with floods, dividing fat and well-tilled fields.
I am the blue-green Tiber, river most
beloved of the heavens. My great home
is here, and here the source of splendid cities."

The river god said this and then he sank   85
down into his deep stream, seeking the bottom.
Both night and sleep have left Aeneas now;
he rises and surveys the eastern rays
of heaven's sun and then in his cupped palms,
as due, lifts water from the river, pours   90
this prayer to the sky: "Laurentian nymphs,
the source of all these rivers, and you, father
Tiber, with all your sacred waves, receive
Aeneas, set him free at last from dangers.
For in whatever spring your pools contain you—   95
where you take pity on our trials—from
whatever fairest soil you flow, I shall
forever celebrate and worship you
with gifts, horned river, king of all the waters
within Hesperia; o be with me   100
and let your present power confirm your omens."
These are Aeneas' words; then from his fleet,
he picks two galleys fitted out with oars
and furnishes these chosen crews with weapons.

    *   *   *

But then a wonderful, a sudden sign: 105
within the wood, along the green shore, lay
a white sow, just as white as her white litter;
at this pious Aeneas offers up
to you, most mighty Juno, even to you
the sow and all her young before your altar.   110
And all night long, the Tiber soothed his swollen
waters and stayed his silent waves, smoothing
his flood until it seemed a gentle pool
or peaceful marsh, where oarsmen need not struggle.
The crewmen speed their voyage with glad shouts;   115
the ships, well smeared with pitch, glide on the waves;
the waters wonder at them; and the woods,
unused to such a sight, admire the shields
of men that glitter in the distance and
the painted keels that float along the river.   120

They tire out the night and day with rowing
and pass beyond the long and tedious windings
and sail beneath the shade of varied trees
and cleave green woods reflected in calm water.
The scorching sun has scaled the sky's midcircle   125
when they can see far off the citadel
and walls and scattered rooftops that today
the power of Rome has raised as high as heaven;
but then it was Evander's, a poor land.
They turn their prows quickly and near the city.   130

That very day the king of the Arcadians
happened to hold an anniversary feast
in honor of Amphytrion's great son
and all the other gods, within a grove
before the city. With Evander were   135
Pallas, his son, young chieftains, and his senate
(there was no wealth among them) offering incense;
the warm blood was still smoking on the altars.
They saw the tall ships gliding through dense woods,
the crewmen bending over silent oars;   140
and startled at the sudden sight, they all
rise up at once; the feast is interrupted.
But daring Pallas will not let them stop
the sacrifices; snatching up his sword,
he runs to meet the strangers; from a distant   145

mound, he calls out: "Young men, what urges you
to try these unknown ways? Where are you heading?
What is your tribe? Your home? Do you bring peace
or war?" And then from his tall galley, father
Aeneas answers; hand outstretched, he holds   150
a branch of peaceful olive: "Those you see
are sons of Troy, our weapons hate the Latins:
they have made us fugitives by war and outrage.
The king whom we are seeking is Evander.
Bring him my message, say that chosen Dardan   155
captains have come, asking for friendly arms."
A name so great as Troy's amazes Pallas.
"Whoever you may be," he cries, "come out
and speak before my father face to face,
and as our guest approach our household gods."   160
Then Pallas took Aeneas by the hand
and held it fast in welcome. And advancing,.
they leave the river, entering the grove.

And then with friendly words Aeneas turns
to King Evander: "You, the best of Greeks,   165
to whom my fortune wills that I appeal
and offer branches crowned with garlands, I
was not afraid because you were a Danaan
chieftain and an Arcadian, linked by blood
to the two sons of Atreus; my own worth,   170
the sacred oracles of gods, your fame
that now is known throughout the earth, and our
related ancestors join me to you;
and I obey my fate with willingness.
For Dardanus sailed to the Teucrians   175
to be the founder and father of Ilium:
and he—the Greeks relate—was born out of
Electra the Atlantean; mighty Atlas,
he who sustains the spheres of heaven on
his shoulders, was the father of Electra.   180
Your father is Mercury, to whom lovely Maia
gave birth upon Cyllene's icy summit;
but Maia—if we trust what we are told—
is also Atlas' daughter, that same Atlas
who props the stars. Then both our races branch   185
out of one blood. Trusting to this, I shunned
ambassadors or sly approaches; I

have brought myself—myself and my own life;
I come, a suppliant, before your doors.
For those same Daunians who torment you   190
with bitter war torment us, too: if they
succeed in driving us away, they will
stop at no thing; and all Hesperia
will fall beneath their sway, and both the seas,
the upper and the lower. Take and give   195
trust: for our breasts are brave for war, our spirits
are high, events have tried our warriors."

Aeneas stopped. But while he spoke, Evander
for long had scanned his face, his eyes, and all
his body. Then he answered in few words: 200
"How willingly I recognize, receive
you, bravest of the Teucrians! How I
recall the words, the voice, the face of great
Anchises! And I still remember Priam,
son of Laomedon, when he was traveling   205
toward Salamis; for on his way to see
the kingdom of Hesione, his sister,
he came as visitor to Arcadia's
cold boundaries. At that time early youth
had clothed my cheeks with down; I marveled at   210
the Trojan captains, and especially
at Laomedon's own son. But as he walked,
Anchises was the tallest of them all;
and with young love, I longed to speak to him,
to clasp his hand in mine; and I drew near   215
and, eager, guided him to Pheneos' walls.
Departing, he gave me a splendid quiver
and Lycian arrows and a mantle woven
with gold and then a pair of golden bits
my Pallas now has. Therefore, my right hand,   220
for which you ask, is joined in league with you;
and when the first light of tomorrow turns
back to the earth, I shall see that you leave
happy, with aid; I'll help you as I can.
Meanwhile, since you have come as friends, rejoice   225
with us and celebrate this annual
rite, which it would be sinful to put off;
and now the feast of comrades waits for you."
           *   *   *

This said, he orders all the food and drink,
which had been set aside, brought back again   230
and guides the guests to places on the grass;
and as a sign of honor for Aeneas,
invites him to a throne of maple and
a couch of shaggy lion skin. Then chosen
young men, together with the altar priest,   235
bring in—they rush in eagerness—roast flesh
of oxen; and they load the baskets with
the gifts that Ceres grants to human labor
and pour out wine. Aeneas and, with him,
his Trojan comrades feasted on the whole   240
chine of an ox and sacrificial entrails.

When hunger left—their need for food at last
at rest—then King Evander spoke: "It was
no empty superstition on our part
and not our ignorance of ancient gods   245
that laid these solemn rituals on us,
this customary feast, this altar sacred
to such a mighty presence. Trojan guest,
because we have been saved from savage dangers—
it is for this that we now sacrifice,   250
that we renew the honors due this worship.
But first, look at this cliff with hanging rocks,
with boulders scattered far about; the mountain
house now is desolate, its stones are fallen
into tremendous ruin. Here a cavern   255
was set back in a vast recess; the rays
of sun had never reached it; it was held
by the fierce shape of the half-human Cacus.
The ground was always warm with recent slaughter;
and fastened to the proud doorposts, the faces   260
of men hung pale with putrefaction. Vulcan
was father of this monster; those black fires
that Cacus belched—and his huge hulk—were Vulcan's.
At last, in answer to our prayers, time
brought help to us, the coming of a god.   265
For Hercules was here, the great avenger,
proud in the slaughter and the spoils of triple-
shaped Geryon; he drove his giant oxen
as conqueror; his cattle filled the valley

and riverbanks. But then the mind of Cacus   270
was driven wild with frenzy; lest he fail
to dare or try all ways of crime or fraud,
he stole from pasture four remarkable
bulls paired together with four splendid heifers.
He dragged them by the tail into his cavern—   275
so that, hoofprints reversed, they left no trace—
and hid them in dark rocks. No one could find
a sign of cattle going to the cave.
But meanwhile, when Amphytrion's son had led
his well-fed herd out of the pasture, ready   280
to move on elsewhere, as his cattle left,
the oxen bellowed, all the grove was filled
with their complaints; they moaned across the hills.
One heifer answered their outcry; she roared
from that vast cavern, even in her prison,   285
and cheated Cacus and his hopes. At this,
the wrath of Hercules was hot with black
gall and with grief; he snatches up his weapons
and massive, knotted club, makes for a hilltop.
That was the first time that our shepherds ever   290
saw Cacus terrified, fear in his eyes.
He flies more swiftly than the east wind, seeking
the cave; and to his feet, fear added wings.

"No sooner had he shut himself in, loosed
the iron chains that, by his father's art,   295
sustained the huge portcullis made of rock,
and slammed it down and pressed the doorposts tight,
which he then fastened by a bolt, than—look—
Tirinthyus was come in frenzied anger
and scanning every entry. Hercules,   300
gnashing his teeth, turned this way, that. He tramps
three times across the Aventine, in wrath;
three times he tries in vain the gates of stone;
three times he sinks, tired out, along the valley.
But from the cavern's roof there rose a sharp   305
flint cliff with sheer rock faces on all sides;
it towered high, a fitting home for nests
of birds of evil omen. As it leaned
to left and toward the river, Hercules
strained from the right-hand side against the rock,   310
wrenched out its deepest roots and broke it loose.

Then suddenly he hurled it down; the wide
air thunders at the thrust; the riverbanks
now leap apart; the stream recoils in fear.
The den of Cacus, his enormous palace,   315
lay bare and, deep inside, his shadowed caverns
were naked to the eye; as if the earth,
ripped open by some violence, unlocked
the house of hell and all its pallid kingdoms,
so hated by the gods, and one could see   320
deep down into that dread abyss, the Shades
trembling within as sunlight made its way.
On Cacus then, caught by the unexpected,
the sudden day, trapped in the hollow rock,
his bellowing inhuman, Hercules   325
now showers shafts from overhead, calling
on every kind of weapon, raining branches
and huge millstones. With no escape from danger,
the monster belches black smoke from his jaws—
amazingly—and overwhelms his dwelling   330
with blinding soot that rips sight from the eyes,
gathering fog and night within the cavern
and shadows that are mingled in with fire.
The rage of Hercules was past all patience:
he threw himself through flames; he leaped headlong   335
just where the smoke rolled in thick waves, a cloud
of darkness surging through the giant grotto.
And here, as Cacus vomits useless fires
within that black mist, Hercules grips him
as in a knot and, clinging, squeezes out   340
his strangled eyes, his throat run dry of blood.
At once the house of darkness is thrown open,
the doors torn off—the stolen oxen and
the perjured plunder plain before the heavens.
The shapeless corpse is dragged out by the feet.   345
We cannot get enough of watching Cacus:
his terrifying eyes, his face, the shaggy
and bristling chest of that half-beast, his jaws
with their extinguished fires. From that time on
the fame of Hercules is celebrated   350
and happy generations keep this day.
Potitius especially was founder
of this observance; the Pinarii
are keepers of the rites of Hercules.

For Hercules himself had first established   355
this altar in the grove; and we shall always
call it the Greatest Altar, it shall be
forever greatest. Therefore, young men, come:
in honor of such deeds bind up your hair
with leaves and, cups in hand, now call upon   360
our common good and freely offer wine."
His words were done. Then Hercules' own tree,
the two-hued poplar, covered King Evander's
hair with its shade, entwining him with leaves.
The sacred cup of wood filled his right hand.   365
And all are quick to pour their glad libations
upon the table and entreat the gods.

But meanwhile evening nears the downward slope
of heaven: now the priests—Potitius first—
all clad in skins as is their custom, make   370
their way, carrying torches; they renew
the feast; as welcome offering they bring
a second meal. They heap the altars high
with loaded platters. Then the Salii,
their temples bound with poplar branches, sing   375
around the kindled altars; one a choir
of youths, the other of old men, who chant
the praises and the deeds of Hercules:
how first he strangled in his infant grip
twin serpents, monsters sent by his stepmother;   380
then how, in war, he overcame great cities,
Oechalia and Troy; and how he bore
a thousand heavy labors by the sentence
of unjust Juno, under King Eurystheus.
"By your own hand, unconquered one, you killed   385
both Pholus and Hylaeus, double-limbed
sons of the clouds; you killed the Cretan monsters,
the giant lion under Nemea's rock.
For you the lakes of Styx have trembled and
the guardian of Orcus as he huddled   390
within his bloody cave on half-chewed bones.
No shape could panic you, not even tall
Typhoeus, bearing arms; the snake of Lerna,
its host of heads surrounding you, could not
rob you of reason. Hail, true son of Jove,   395
a glory added to the gods; be gracious,

draw near to us and this your sacred worship."
Such acts they celebrate in song; above all,
they sing of fire-breathing Cacus' cavern;
and all the grove resounds, the hills reecho.   400

The holy rites are ended; all return
into the city. But the king was heavy
with age; he kept Aeneas and his son
beside him as companions as he walked
while lightening the way with varied talk.   405
Aeneas marvels; eagerly he turns
his eyes on everything Evander notes:
he is so captivated by the place
that, glad, he seeks and, one by one, he learns
the chronicles that tell of men of old.   410

Then King Evander, founder of Rome's stronghold:
"These groves were once the home of fauns and nymphs
and of a race of men sprung from tree trunks
and sturdy oaks. They had no rule and no
refinements; for they could not yoke their bulls   415
or gather wealth or save what they had gained;
they fed on branches and harsh food of hunters.
Then Saturn came to them from high Olympus,
a fugitive from his lost kingdom, flying
from the attack of Jove. He made a nation   420
of those untamed and scattered in high mountains
and gave them laws. And he chose Latium
as name, because he had lain safely hidden
along these coasts. The golden age they tell of
was in the time of this king; for he ruled   425
his tribe in tranquil peace. But by degrees
an age depraved and duller took its place,
with war's insanity and love of gain.
Then came Ausonians, Sicanians;
the land of Saturn often changed its name.   430
And kings arose and giant, cruel Thybris,
from whose name we Italians called our river
the Tiber; ancient Albula lost her
true name. All-able fortune and my fate,
the inescapable, have driven me,   435
when banished from my country, across far seas
to settle here. The warnings of my mother,

the nymph Carmentis, and the urgings of
our patron god, Apollo, spurred us on."

His words were scarcely done when, moving on,   440
he points out both the altar and the gate
the Romans call Carmental, ancient tribute
in honor of the nymph Carmentis, fate-
foretelling prophetess, the first to sing
the greatness of Aeneas' sons and future   445
of noble Pallanteum. And Evander
then shows to him a spacious grove that, later,
brave Romulus made into an asylum;
and, underneath cold crags, the cavern called—
in the Arcadian manner—the Lupercal,   450
after Lycaean Pan; and then he shows him
the wood of sacred Argiletum, telling
how Argus, when he was Evander's guest,
died there. He leads him next to the Tarpeian
house and the Capitol, now golden, once   455
rough with thick underbrush. And even then
its holiness had filled the fearful farmers
with dread, and even then they shuddered at
the woods and rock. "This grove, this hill, tree-topped,
are some god's home," he says, "although we do   460
not know which god; Arcadians believe
that often they have seen Jupiter himself
as he woke storm clouds, shook his darkening
aegis in his right hand. And farther on
you see two towns with ruined walls, the relics   465
and the memorials of ancient men:
for father Janus built this city, that
was built by Saturn; and the name of one,
Janiculum; Saturnia, the other's."

With such talk to each other, they drew near   470
a poor man's house, the home of King Evander;
and here and there the cattle lowed along
what are today the elegant Carinae
and Roman Forum. When they reached his doorway
Evander said: "The victor Hercules   475
has stooped to cross these thresholds; even he
has found a welcome in this royal house:
my guest, dare to despise riches, and try—

as he did—to deserve divinity;
do not be sullen, seeing our poor things."   480
He spoke and then beneath his simple roof
he led the great Aeneas, making ready
a couch of scattered leaves, a Libyan bearskin.
Night rushes down; her dark wings wrap the earth.

But Venus, as a mother, takes alarm—   485
and not in vain—noting the harsh uprising
and threats of the Laurentians. And she turns
to Vulcan in their golden wedding chamber,
breathing celestial love into her words:
"While Argive kings were ravaging doomed Troy   490
and towers fell before the fires of hate,
I did not ask your help for my sad Trojans,
or weapons made by your own art and power.
I did not trouble you, my dearest husband,
or make you work in vain, however much   495
I owed to Priam's sons, however often
I wept at the hard trials of Aeneas.
But now, by Jove's command, he has landed on
the coasts of the Rutulians; therefore,
I, who before asked nothing of you, come   500
as suppliant, a mother for her son,
to beg arms of the god whom I adore.
The daughter of Nereus—she could sway you; and
so could Tithonus' wife; they both used tears.
Just see what nations join, what cities shut   505
their gates and sharpen swords for me and mine."

The goddess spoke; and as he hesitates,
with snow-white arms on this side and on that
she warms him in a soft embrace. At once
he caught the customary flame; familiar   510
heat reached into his marrow, riding through
his agitated bones—just as at times
a streak of fire will rip through flashing thunder
and race across the clouds with glittering light.
His wife, rejoicing in her craftiness   515
and conscious of her loveliness, sensed this.
Chained to her by undying love, her lord
says: "Why do you reach so far back for reasons?
Where, goddess, has your trust in me gone? If

you felt concern before, it would have been   520
quite right for me to arm the Teucrians.
For neither the all-able Father nor
the fates prevented Troy from standing or
King Priam from surviving ten years more.
And now if you prepare for battle, if   525
this war is what you want, then I can promise
whatever care is in my art, what can
be done by fire and steel, by bellows and
molten electrum. Now do not entreat
me anymore or put your powers in doubt."   530
This said, he gave her the embrace she wanted;
then, stretched across the breast of Venus, he
searched straight for tranquil sleep with all his body.

The hour when early rest drives sleep away,
when in the circle of the passing night   535
the housewife, her first task to sustain life
by weaving and Minerva's humble arts,
awakes the embers and the sleeping fires,
as she adds on the night to her day's work
and keeps her housemaids toiling on at some   540
long chore by lamplight, that her husband's bed
be chaste, and that she raise her children well:
just so, and just as eagerly, the Lord
of Fire rises up, at that same hour,
from his soft couch to labor at the forge.   545

Close by that side of Sicily where lies
Aeolian Lipare there rises high
an island steep with smoking rocks. Beneath it
a den with caves of Etna, hollowed out
by forges of the Cyclops, roars; and pounding   550
strokes echo, groaning, on those anvils; bars
of Chalyb steel hiss through the caverns; fire
pants in those furnaces: the house of Vulcan;
and that land's name, Vulcania. The Lord
of Fire from heaven's height descended here.   555

In that vast cave the Cyclops—Steropes,
Pyracmon, Brontes—naked, worked the forge.
They shaped a bolt of thunder of the kind
the Father often hurls from all of heaven

down to the earth: a part was polished, but   560
the rest was still unwrought. And they had added
three shafts of twisting hail to it, and three
of raining cloud, and three of ruddy lightning,
and three of the south wind. Now they mixed in
tremendous flashes, roarings, fear, and anger   565
with persecuting flames. And in another
corner of Vulcan's cavern they made ready
a work for Mars—the chariot and flying
wheels that he uses to wake men and cities;
and polished eagerly the terrifying   570
aegis, the weapon of the angry Pallas,
with serpents' scales and gold and intertwining
snakes—on the goddess' breastplate there is Gorgon
herself, her eyes turned toward her severed neck.
But Vulcan bawls at them: "Stop all, I say!   575
Cyclops of Etna, haul off everything
you are working on and turn your minds to this.
You must make weapons for a brave man; now
you need your strength, your swift hands, all your art.
And no delays." He said enough. At once   580
they set to work, in equal parts allot
the labor. Brass and gold ore pour in streams,
and wounding steel is melted in the vast
furnace. And now they shape a giant shield
to stand alone against all Latin shafts   585
and plate it seven-ply, circle on circle.
Some man the heaving bellows and its blasts,
while others dip the hissing brass in troughs.
The grotto groans beneath the mounted anvils.
With great force each in turn lifts up his arms   590
in cadence, wields the iron with gripping tongs.

And while along Aeolian coasts the lord
of Lemnos speeds this work, the gracious light
and morning songs of birds beneath his roof
awake Evander in his humble home.   595
The old man rises, wraps a tunic on,
and winds Tyrrhenian sandals on his feet;
with Tegean sword he girds his side and shoulders;
a panther's hide hangs loosely from his left.
A pair of watchdogs, too, accompany   600
their master as he makes his way, moving

across his high threshold. For he was seeking
the quiet quarters of his guest, Aeneas,
remembering the help he had promised him.
Aeneas, too, awoke this early. Pallas   605
walked on with one; the other had Achates.
They meet, clasp hands, and then sit down between
the houses, in the open air; at last
they can talk freely. And the king begins:

"Chief captain of the Teucrians—for while   610
you live, I can't admit that Troy and her
kingdom have been defeated—though our name
be great, we have but slender means to help
in war. On this side we are hemmed in by
the Tuscan Tiber; on the other press   615
Rutulians, who roar around our walls
with arms. But I am readying great tribes
and armies rich in kingdoms as your allies—
a safeguard unexpected chance has brought.
You come here at the call of fate. Not far   620
Agylla lies, a city built of ancient
stone, where a Lydian tribe, well known in war,
has long since made its home on Tuscan heights.
For many years that state was flourishing—
until Mezentius became its king;   625
his rule was arrogant, and cruel, his arms.
Why tell the tyrant's dreadful massacres?
And why his savagery? Gods keep such things
for his own head and his posterity!
For he would even link the living with   630
dead bodies, fitting hand to hand and face
to face—what savage torture!—and in that
obscene embrace, with dripping blood and poison
he massacred them by a lingering death.
But tired out at last, the citizens   635
surround the monstrous madman in his house;
they butcher his companions, burn the palace.
Yet he, amid that slaughter, slipped away
and fled to the Rutulians, where Turnus,
his host, defended him with shield and shelter.   640
So all Etruria rose up in just anger;
now, with impatient war, they ask to have
their king brought back to them for punishment.

Aeneas, I will make you chieftain of
these thousands, for their ships crowd all the coast,　　645
eager for battle; they would have their banners
march out, but their old augur holds them back,
foretelling fate: 'Maeonia's best sons,
the flower and the force of an old race,
a just resentment drives you into war,　　650
Mezentius kindles you with rage he merits;
but no Italian can command so proud
a nation; choose a stranger as your leader.'
At that the ranks of the Etruscans camp
along the nearby plain, in panic at　　655
the warning of the gods. Tarchon himself
has sent me envoys with the royal crown
and scepter, offering these emblems to me,
that I might join their camp and take the throne
of Tuscany. But I am held in check　　660
by age, made weak by time; its sluggish frost
begrudges me that kingdom; it is late
for bravery. I should urge on my son
to take it, were it not that he is mixed
in blood, for Pallas' mother was a Sabine;　　665
from her he has a share in Italy.
But you, whose years and blood are blessed by fate,
whom gods have called, take up your way: most brave
chieftain of both the Trojans and Italians.
But I shall join to you my hope and comfort,　　670
Pallas, my son: with you as master let
him learn to suffer war and Mars' hard labor,
to see your acts and take you as a model
from early years. I shall give him two hundred
Arcadian horsemen, our best youths; and Pallas　　675
will add as many more in his own name."

His words were scarcely done, and both Aeneas,
son of Anchises, and the true Achates,
intent, would long have brooded over many
hardships within their sad hearts had not Venus　　680
sent them a sign across the cloudless sky.
For sudden lightning shuddered through the air
with thunder; all things seemed to reel; a blast
of Tuscan trumpets pealed across the heavens.
They look up; and again, again, there roars　　685

tremendous thunder. In the sky's clear region,
within a cloud, they see a red-gold gleam
of weapons as they clash and clang. The rest
stood back, astounded, but the Trojan hero
had recognized the sound, his goddess-mother's   690
promise to him. He said: "My hosts, do not,
indeed, do not ask me what things these omens
are bringing; I am summoned by Olympus.
The goddess who gave birth to me foretold
that, if war were at hand, then through the air   695
she would bring Vulcan's weapons to my aid.
What slaughter menaces these sad Laurentians!
What penalties will Turnus pay to me!
What shields of men and helmets and brave breasts
will roll beneath your waves, o father Tiber!   700
Now let them ask for battle, break their treaties!"

This said, Aeneas rises up from his
high throne and first awakes the sleeping altars
with fire for Hercules. Then he approaches
the God of Hearths he had worshiped yesterday   705
and then the humble household gods. He offers,
as is the custom, chosen sheep, and King
Evander and the Trojans do the same.
This done, Aeneas goes down to the ships,
revisiting his comrades; from their number   710
he picks the bravest as his aides in war.
The others glide downriver with the current,
slowly, to carry word of what has happened
and of his father to Ascanius.
The Trojans making for the Tuscan fields   715
are given horses; and the one they choose
to lead out for Aeneas wears a tawny
lion skin that gleams with claws of gold.

The news runs suddenly through that small city;
the people hear that horsemen now are speeding   720
to seek the Tuscan king along his coasts.
Alarmed, the mothers tell their vows again,
again, for terror dogs the heels of danger,
Mars' image now seems larger. King Evander
takes up the hand of his departing son   725
and clings with endless tears and speaks these words:

"If Jupiter would only give me back
the years that passed, let me be as I was
when I cut down the foremost ranks beneath
Praeneste's very walls—when, as a victor,   730
I burned their heaped-up shields, with this right hand
sent down to Tartarus King Erulus
to whom at birth Feronia, his mother,
gave three lives and—how terrible to tell—
three sets of weapons for his use: three times   735
he had to be cut down by death; and yet
this right hand robbed him then of all his lives
and stripped him of as many suits of armor.
My son, were I but such again, no thing
could ever tear me from your dear embrace;   740
and then on this his neighbor's head the tyrant
Mezentius never would have heaped his insults
or dealt so many savage deaths by sword,
deprived his city of so many sons.
But you, o High Ones, and you, Jupiter,   745
the greatest ruler of the gods, I ask,
take pity on the king of the Arcadians
and hear a father's prayers: for if your power
or if the Fates keep Pallas safe for me,
if I still live to see him, still to meet him   750
again, then I do pray for life and I
can stand all trials. But Fortune, if you threaten
my son with the unspeakable, then now,
oh, now let me break off this cruel life,
while fear is still uncertain and my hope   755
cannot yet read the future, while I hold
you, my dear boy, my late and only joy,
lest sadder word should ever wound my ears."
The father poured these parting words; his servants
then carried him, fainting, into his house.   760

The horsemen now ride through the open gate;
among the first, Aeneas and Achates,
then other Trojan lords. Pallas himself
is at the center of his troops, set off
by cloak and ornamented arms: just as   765
the Morning Star, whom Venus loves above
the fire of any other star, when he,
bathed in the Ocean's wave, lifts up his sacred

head high in heaven and dissolves the darkness.
The mothers tremble, standing on the walls,   770
and watch the cloud of dust, the gleaming brass.
The armed troops cut across the underbrush.
A shout goes up; they form a line; the hoofs'
four-footed thunder shakes the crumbling plain.

Close by the cooling stream of Caere stands   775
a spacious grove, held sacred far and wide
in ancient reverence; and on all sides
the hills hem in the forest of dark firs.
The old Pelasgians—the story goes—
who long ago first held the Tuscan borders,   780
had consecrated to Silvanus, god
of fields and flocks, both grove and festive day.
Not far from here King Tarchon and the Tuscans
had pitched their camp on sheltered ground, and now
their tents stretched out across the wide fields. Father 785
Aeneas and his chosen men march here
and rest their horses and their tired bodies.

But Venus, the bright goddess, bearing gifts,
drew near in airy clouds; and when far off
she saw her son in a secluded valley,   790
withdrawn beside a cooling stream, then she
showed herself freely to him, saying this:
"You see, my son, these perfect offerings,
my husband's promised art; then do not doubt,
but dare brave Turnus and the proud Laurentians   795
to battle." These were Cytherea's words.
She sought her son's embraces, then set up
his glittering arms beneath a facing oak.
Aeneas cannot have enough; delighted
with these gifts of the goddess, this high honor,   800
his eyes rush on to everything, admiring;
with arm and hand he turns the helmet over,
tremendous with its crests and flood of flames,
the sword that deals out fate, the stiff brass corselet,
blood-red and huge as when a blue-gray cloud,   805
which rays of sun have kindled, glows far off;
the polished greaves made of electrum and
of gold, resmelted many times; the spear;
the shield, its texture indescribable.

❖   ❖   ❖

For there the Lord of Fire had wrought the story   810
of Italy, the Romans' victories,
since he was not unskilled in prophecy
or one who cannot tell the times to come.
There he had set the generations of
Ascanius, and all their wars, in order.   815
There, too, he made a mother-wolf, reclining
in Mars' green cavern; and at play beside her,
twin boys were hanging at her dugs; fearless,
they sucked their mother. She, at this, bent back
her tapered neck to lick them each in turn   820
and shape their bodies with her tongue. Not far
from this he set the Romans and the Sabine
women they carried off—against all law—
while in the crowded theater the great
Circensian games were under way; and sudden   825
war then broke out again between the Romans
and aged Tatius, king of austere Cures.
Next, Romulus and Tatius, these same kings,
their quarrels set to rest, stood at Jove's altar;
both, armed and cup in hand and having offered   830
a sow as sacrifice, swore league and friendship.
Not far from this, two chariots that rushed
in different directions tore apart
Mettus (but then you should have kept your word,
o man of Alba!); Tullus hauled the guts   835
of that conniving man into the forest;
the briers dripped with splattered blood. There, too,
Porsenna, asking Rome to readmit
the banished Tarquin, hemmed the city in
with strangling siege; Aeneas' sons rushed on   840
the sword for freedom's sake. You might have seen
Porsenna as one wild and menacing,
since Cocles dared tear down the Tiber's bridge,
and Cloelia broke her chains and swam the river.

Carved in the upper part was Manlius,   845
the guardian of the Tarpeian rock,
who stood before the temple gates, defender
of the high Capitol; the new-carved palace
was shaggy with the straw of Romulus.
And here a silver goose fluttered across   850
the gilded colonnades, signaling that

the Gauls were at the threshold. Through the brush
the Gauls crept toward the tower, under cover
of darkness and dense night. Their hair is golden;
and golden, too, their clothes, set-off by gleaming,   855
striped cloaks; their milk-white necks are bound in gold;
each brandishes two Alpine javelins
and, with an oblong shield, defends his body.
Here in relief were carved the nude Luperci
and dancing Salian priests, with woolen caps   860
and shields that fell from heaven; through the city
chaste matrons in their cushioned carriages
led sacred rites. Away from these scenes Vulcan
added the house of Tartarus, the high
doorways of Dis, the penalties of crime;   865
and Catiline, you hanging from a cliff
that threatens, trembling at the Furies' faces;
and, set apart, the pious who receive
their laws from Cato. Bordering these scenes,
he carved a golden image of the sea,   870
yet there were blue-gray waters and white foam
where dolphins bright with silver cut across
the tide and swept the waves with circling tails.

Across the center of the shield were shown
the ships of brass, the strife of Actium: 875
you might have seen all of Leucata's bay
teeming with war's array, waves glittering
with gold. On his high stern Augustus Caesar
is leading the Italians to battle,
together with the senate and the people,   880
the household gods and Great Gods; his bright brows
pour out a twin flame, and upon his head
his father's Julian star is glittering.
Elsewhere Agrippa towers on the stern;
with kindly winds and gods he leads his squadron;   885
around his temples, glowing bright, he wears
the naval crown, magnificent device,
with its ships' beaks. And facing them, just come
from conquering the peoples of the dawn,
from the red shores of the Erythraean Sea—   890
together with barbaric riches, varied
arms—is Antonius. He brings with him
Egypt and every power of the East

and farthest Bactria; and—shamefully—
behind him follows his Egyptian wife.   895
The squadrons close headlong; and all the waters
foam, torn by drawn-back oars and by the prows
with triple prongs. They seek the open seas;
you could believe the Cyclades, uprooted,
now swam upon the waters or steep mountains   900
had clashed with mountains as the crewmen thrust
in their great galleys at the towering sterns.
Torches of hemp and flying darts of steel
are flung by hand, and Neptune's fields are red
with strange bloodshed. Among all this the queen   905
calls to her squadrons with their native sistrum;
she has not yet looked back at the twin serpents
that swim behind her. Every kind of monster
god—and the barking god, Anubis, too—
stands ready to cast shafts against Minerva   910
and Venus and at Neptune. In the middle
of all the struggle, Mars, engraved in steel,
rages beside fierce Furies from the sky;
and Discord, joyous, strides in her rent robe;
Bellona follows with a bloodstained whip.   915
But Actian Apollo, overhead,
had seen these things; he stretched his bow; and all
of Egypt and of India, and all
the Arabs and Sabaeans, turned their backs
and fled before this terror. The queen herself   920
was seen to woo the winds, to spread her sails,
and now, yes now, let fall the slackened ropes.
The Lord of Fire had fashioned her within
the slaughter, driven on by wave and west wind,
pale with approaching death; but facing this,   925
he set the Nile, his giant body mourning,
opening wide his folds and all his robes,
inviting the defeated to his blue-gray
breast and his sheltering streams. But entering
the walls of Rome in triple triumph, Caesar   930
was dedicating his immortal gift
to the Italian gods: three hundred shrines
throughout the city. And the streets reechoed
with gladness, games, applause; in all the temples
were bands of matrons, and in all were altars;   935
and there, before these altars, slaughtered steers

were scattered on the ground. Caesar himself
is seated at bright Phoebus' snow-white porch,
and he reviews the spoils of nations and
he fastens them upon the proud doorposts.   940
The conquered nations march in long procession,
as varied in their armor and their dress
as in their languages. Here Mulciber
had modeled Nomad tribes and Africans,
loose-robed; the Carians; the Leleges;   945
Geloni armed with arrows. And he showed
Euphrates, moving now with humbler waves;
the most remote of men, the Morini;
the Rhine with double horns; the untamed Dahae;
and, river that resents its bridge, the Araxes.   950

Aeneas marvels at his mother's gift,
the scenes on Vulcan's shield; and he is glad
for all these images, though he does not
know what they mean. Upon his shoulder he
lifts up the fame and fate of his sons' sons.   955

IX · 443

1980

BOOK IX

A<small>ND</small> <small>WHILE</small> <small>FAR</small> off these things were happening,
Saturnian Juno down from heaven sent
Iris to daring Turnus. As it chanced,
he then was resting in a sacred glen,
the forest of his ancestor, Pilumnus.   5
The rose-lipped daughter of Thaumas spoke to him:

"Turnus, that which no god had dared to promise
in answer to your prayers, circling time
has brought unasked: Aeneas, leaving city
and friend and fleet, seeks out the Palatine,   10
Evander's palace. Nor is that enough;
he has made his way into the farthest towns
of Corythus; he musters troops among
the Lydian farmers. Then why hesitate?
Enough delays! Now is the time to call   15
for horse and chariot! Now lay hands upon
the panicked Trojan camp." Her words were done.
On level wings she rose to heaven, tracing
a great rainbow beneath the clouds. Young Turnus
had recognized her; stretching both hands starward,   20
he cried these words to Iris as she fled:
"O Iris, heavens' glory, who has sent you

down from the clouds to me on earth? From where
this storm of sudden brightness in the air?
I see the heavens' center opening   25
and stars that wander all about the pole.
I follow such an omen and whoever
it is who now has called me to take arms."
And as he spoke, he reached the riverbank,
scooped water from the swirling stream, and praying   30
long to the gods, loaded the air with vows.

And now Rutulian armies make their way
across the open plain, with many horses,
embroidered robes, and gold. Messapus marshals
the vanguard; Tyrrhus' sons take up the rear;   35
and at the center of the line is Turnus,
their captain—even as the silent Ganges
that rises high with seven tranquil streams,
or Nile when his rich flood ebbs from the fields
and he at last sinks back into his channel.   40
And here the Teucrians can see a sudden
cloudbank that gathers with black dust and darkness
that rises from the plains. And from a rampart
Caicus is the first to cry aloud:
"My countrymen, what rolling mass is this   45
of gloom and darkness? Quick, bring sword and lance;
the enemy is on us, mount the walls."
Through all the gates the Trojans, clamoring,
take cover, and they man the battlements—
for so Aeneas, best of warriors,   50
had ordered them to do on his departure:
were anything to happen in his absence,
they should not dare an open fight or chance
the field, but only guard the camp and walls,
secure behind their ramparts. And, therefore,   55
though shame and anger goad them into battle,
they bar the gates as they were told and, armed,
await the enemy within the towers.

Turnus, who had outstripped his tardy column,
with twenty chosen horsemen after him,   60
comes first upon the city, unobserved.
He is mounted on a piebald Thracian stallion,
his golden helmet has a crimson crest:

"Young men, who will be first to face these Trojans
together with me? Look!" he cries and casts   65
his javelin high in the air. The fight
begins. Bold Turnus rides across the fields.
His comrades take his shout up, follow him
with horrid din; they marvel at the coward
hearts of the Teucrians, at how they shun   70
the level plain and will not fight but hug
their camp. Fanatic Turnus scans the walls;
he rides from this side back to that, seeking
an entrance where there is none. Even as
a wolf who waits outside the full sheepfold   75
will howl beside the pens at midnight, facing
both wind and storm; beneath their dams the sheltered
lambs keep on bleating; fierce and desperate
with rage, the wolf is wild against his absent
prey; after such long famine now the frenzy   80
for food, his dry and bloodless jaws torment him:
just so, as he surveys the wall and camp,
is Turnus' anger kindled; indignation
is hot in his hard bones. How shall he test
their entrances? How can he drive the Trojans   85
from their defenses, pour them on the plain?
At last he launches an attack against
the fleet, where it lies hidden near the camp:
to one side, ramparts; on the other, river.
He calls for fire to his rejoicing comrades;   90
he snatches eagerly a blazing pine.
Now Turnus' presence spurs them; they all work
in earnest; all take up black firebrands.
They strip the hearths; the smoking torches cast
a glare of pitch; the Lord of Fire lifts   95
the mingled sparks and ashes to the stars.

What god, o Muses, fended off such fierce
fires from the Teucrians? Who saved their ships
from such a blazing conflagration? Tell me.
For that which makes us trust the tale is old,   100
and yet the story's fame is everlasting.

When he prepared to seek high seas, Aeneas
first built his fleet in Phrygian Ida; then
the Berecynthian herself, the mother

of gods, is said to have addressed these words   105
to mighty Jove: "My son, now you have won
Olympus, listen to my prayer, grant
what your dear mother asks. I had a forest
of pine, which I had loved for many years,
upon my mountain's summit, where men brought   110
their offerings to me; here, shadowed, stood
a grove of black pitch trees and trunks of maples.
I gave these gladly to the Dardan chief
when he had need to build a fleet. But anxious
fear now torments my troubled breast. Free me   115
of dread and answer this, a mother's prayer:
that in their journeying no wave or whirlwind
may ever tear these timbers; let it be
a help to them that they grew on my mountains."

Her son, who turns the constellations, answered: 120
"Why, Mother, have you called upon the Fates?
What are you asking for your favorites?
That hulls made by the hands of mortals should
have the immortals' privilege? And that
Aeneas may pass, sure, through unsure dangers?   125
What god commands such power? Nonetheless,
when they have fulfilled their tasks and reached their end
of journeying, the harbors of Ausonia,
then all that have escaped the waves and carried
the Dardan leader to Laurentum's lands   130
are saved: I shall strip off their mortal form;
I shall command those galleys to take on
the shapes of goddesses of the great waters,
even as are the Nereids, Galatea
and Doto, whose breasts cut the foaming sea."   135
He spoke and by his Stygian brother's waters,
by riverbanks that seethe with pitch, a black
and whirling vortex, nodded his assent,
and with his nod made all Olympus shudder.

The promised day was come, the time of fates   140
was full, when Turnus' outrage called the Mother
to drive the torches off her sacred ships.
And first upon all eyes a strange light glittered,
and from the east a giant storm cloud seemed
to race across the skies. Idaean choirs   145

were thundering; an awesome voice ran through
the air, filling the Trojan and Rutulian
armies with terror: "Teucrians, do not
take weapons in your hands, do not defend
my fleet; it is far easier for Turnus   150
to burn the seas that touch my sacred pines.
Go free, my ships: go, you sea goddesses;
the mother of the gods now gives this order."
And on the instant all the ships have ripped
their cables off the banks and with their beaks,   155
like dolphins, dived to seek the deep; and then
as many virgin shapes—amazing omen—
rise up to ride the sea as, just before,
were brazen prows lined up along the shore.

Now panic takes Rutulian hearts; even   160
Messapus is afraid, his stallions startled;
the hoarse flow of the river stops, for father
Tiber has turned his footsteps from the sea.
But daring Turnus still is confident.
He goads his comrades' courage with his words,   165
he even scolds with this reproach: "These signs
are aimed against the Trojans; Jupiter
himself has snatched away their usual help;
their ships did not await our lance or torch.
The Trojans have no way across the seas;   170
they have no hope of flight. Half of the world
is now denied to them; and for the rest,
the land is in our hands: so many thousands
now crowd armed Italy. I do not fear
the destined oracles of gods, of which   175
these Phrygians boast so much. It is enough
for fate and Venus that the Trojans touched
the fertile fields of Italy. And I
have my own fates to set against their own,
to whip this cursed nation with the sword.   180
They stole my wife from me; such injury
and hurt do not touch only Atreus' sons;
Mycenians are not the only ones
who war by right. The Trojans say, 'But one
destruction is enough.' But to have sinned   185
once was enough. By now these Trojans should
have shunned all women utterly and not

have followed Helen with Lavinia.
These men who take their courage from the thin
margin of battlement or ditch between   190
themselves and death: have they not seen the walls
of Troy, which Neptune's own hand built, sink down
in flames? But you, my chosen ones, who will
be first to join me with his sword, to cut
their ramparts down, to rush their panicked camp?   195
I have no need of Vulcan's arms nor any
need of a thousand keels against the Trojans.
And straight off they can take all of the Tuscans
as comrades. Here they need not fear the darkness,
the shameful theft of their Palladium,   200
the murder of the high tower's guardians.
The dark womb of a horse will not hide us.
In broad daylight, in sight of all, I mean
to gird their walls with fire. They will know
that what they face is not a quarrel with Danaans   205
or with Pelasgian boys whom Hector held
at bay ten years. But now, my men, since day's
best part is gone, for what is left of it,
refresh your bodies gladly; you did well;
be sure, we shall be ready for fresh battle."   210

Meanwhile Messapus is assigned the task
of posting pickets to blockade the gates
and circling all the walls with sentry fires.
Twice-seven men are chosen for patrols;
each has along with him a hundred soldiers   215
with purple plumes and glittering with gold.
They hurry off to take their posts by turns;
some watch, some stretch along the grass, enjoying
wine as they tilt bronze bowls. The fires burn bright;
the sentries game away the sleepless night.   220

All this the Trojans see from their stockade
where, armed, they hold the heights; in anxious fear
they test the gates and, sword in hand, link up
their battlements by bridges. Mnestheus and
the brave Serestus spur the work, whom father   225
Aeneas left to guide the warriors,
to take command in crisis, should there be
some menace in his absence. All the legion,

when they have cast their lots for posts of danger,
stand watch along the walls; each takes his turn,   230
patrolling at the place he must protect.

Nisus was guardian of a gate, the son
of Hyrtacus, tenacious warrior,
whom Ida, home of hunters, sent to serve
Aeneas with his racing javelin and   235
light arrows. Near him stood Euryalus,
his comrade; and no one who served Aeneas
or carried Trojan weapons was more handsome:
a boy whose face, unshaven, showed the first
down of his youth. Their minds and hearts were one;   240
in war they charged together; and now, too,
they shared a sentry station at one gate.
And Nisus says: "Euryalus, is it
the gods who put this fire in our minds,
or is it that each man's relentless longing   245
becomes a god to him? Long has my heart
been keen for battle or some mighty act;
it cannot be content with peace or rest.
You see how sure are those Rutulians:
a few lights glitter here and there; they lie   250
sprawled out and slack with sleep and wine; the night
is still. Hear what I have in mind. The people,
the elders—everyone now urges that
Aeneas be called back, that messengers
be sent to bring him tidings he can trust.   255
If they agree to give to you instead
the prize that I can claim for such a deed—
since for myself the glory is enough—
then close by that mound there I may have found
a path to reach the walls of Pallanteum."   260

Euryalus, amazed and struck by great
passion for praise, answers his fiery friend:
"But, Nisus, how can you deny me? Why
not let me join you now in this adventure?
Shall I send you alone against such dangers?   265
Opheltes, wise in ways of war, my father
who reared me through Troy's trials and Argive terrors,
had never taught me this; and this is not
the way I have served with you beneath great-hearted

Aeneas, facing all that fate could do.   270
Mine is a soul that scorns the light of life
and holds that honor for which you now strive
as cheaply bought if all its price is life."

And Nisus: "This is sure: I did not doubt you.
To do so would have been indecent; just   275
as surely may great Jupiter (or else
whatever name is fit for the High Father)
look down on me with kindness, bring me back
triumphantly to you. And yet if any
misfortune—often met in such attempts—   280
if any chance or god should sweep me on
into disaster, then I would that you
survive; your youth has better claim to life.
Let someone live to lay me in the ground,
to rescue or to ransom back my body   285
from war, or—if, as often happens, chance
denies this—to set up a cenotaph
and honor me, the absent one, with gifts.
My boy, I cannot take you with me, cannot
bring such a sorrow to your suffering mother—   290
she is the only one of many matrons
to dare this distant journey and not choose
to wait within Acestes' walls." But he:
"You weave these pretexts uselessly. My purpose
is set. I have not yielded. Let us hurry."   295
With that, he wakes new sentrymen. They come
to take their turns; and with the station left
in sure hands, he walks off as Nisus' comrade.
So, side by side, they go to seek the prince.

Across the earth all other creatures let   300
their cares fall slack in sleep; their hearts forget
their labors. But the Teucrians' chief captains
and chosen warriors were holding council
about their people's troubles: what to do,
and whom to send with tidings to Aeneas.   305
They lean on their long spears, hands resting on
their shields, around the center of their camp
and fields. Then Nisus and Euryalus
together ask to be let in at once:
their business is important, and they say   310

it will repay the interruption. Iülus
was first to welcome the impatient pair,
commanding Nisus to speak on. The son
of Hyrtacus said this: "Men of Aeneas,
listen with open minds and do not measure   315
our offer by our years. Now the Rutulians
lie still, deep in their sleep and wine. We have seen
a place to serve our stratagem, outside
the gate nearest the sea, where forked roads meet.
The watch fires of the enemy are spent;   320
their black smoke smolders toward the stars. If you
will let us use this chance, then we shall go
to Pallanteum; we shall find Aeneas,
and after slaughtering many, soon return
with plunder. And the way will not deceive us,   325
for we have seen the outskirts of the city
from shadowed valleys in our frequent hunting,
and both of us know all the river's course."

At this, Aletes, weary with his years
but ripe in reason: "O my country's gods,   330
beneath whose power Troy must always stay,
in spite of all you still do not intend
to cancel out the Trojans; you have brought us
young men so resolute and so audacious."
As he said this, tears flooding down his face   335
and cheeks, he clasped them both at hand and shoulder:
"Young men, what prize is possible for you,
what can match worth with such a daring deed?
Your first and fairest prize will come from gods
and out of your own conduct; then the pious   340
Aeneas will at once repay the rest;
and young Ascanius will not forget
such worthiness." Ascanius then adds:
"And I, whose only safety lies in my
dear father's coming back, beseech you both,   345
o Nisus, by my mighty household gods,
the God of Hearths dear to Assaracus,
and by the inner shrines of white-haired Vesta;
in you I now place all my hope and fortune;
recall my father, let me see Aeneas   350
again; with his return, all grief is gone.
And I shall give to you two silver bowls

skillfully wrought, embossed, both taken by
my father at the conquest of Arisba;
two tripods; two great golden talents; and   355
an ancient goblet, gift of Sidon's Dido.
And if as victors we take Italy
and win its scepter and assign its booty:
you both have seen the horse that Turnus rode,
his armor all of gold—and that same horse,   360
that shield and crimson crest, I shall exempt
from chance; even now, Nisus, they are yours.
To these my father will add twice-six women,
the choicest, as your slaves, and then male captives,
each with his armor; in addition, all   365
the fields that now are held by King Latinus.
And you, Euryalus—though young, revered—
to whom my years are so much nearer, I
embrace at once with all my heart as comrade
in every fortune. I shall seek no glory   370
in any thing without you; whether I —
find peace or war, always my final trust
for act and word shall be Euryalus."

And then Euryalus, who answered him:
"No day shall ever find me fallen short   375
of such adventuring, if fortune only
be kind to me and not an enemy.
But more than all your gifts I pray you this:
I have a mother, from the ancient line
of Priam, and she journeyed out with me;   380
no Trojan land nor King Acestes' city
could keep her back, poor woman. Now I leave
without farewell to her; she does not know
the risk I face, whatever it may be.
For night and your right hand are witness that   385
I could not stand against a parent's tears;
I pray you comfort her when she is in need,
support her loneliness. Let me have hope
from you, let me go bolder toward all trials."

The Dardans feel his words and weep—above all   390
the handsome Iülus, for this pious image,
a son's love for his parent, touches him.
And then he speaks: "Be sure that everything

will be deserving of your great attempt.
For she shall be a mother to me, lacking   395
only the name Creüsa. No small honor
awaits her now for bearing such a son.
Whatever be the outcome of your deed,
I swear by this, my head, as once my father
was used to swear, that all I promised you   400
in safe and prosperous return belongs
for ever to your mother and your house."
So Iülus speaks, in tears; and from his shoulder
he strips the gilded sword that had been forged
remarkably by Gnosian Lycaon   405
and neatly fitted with an ivory sheath.
To Nisus, Mnestheus gives this gift: a skin
stripped from a shaggy lion; true Aletes
exchanges helmets with him. Armed, the pair
start off at once; and all the band of chieftains,   410
both young and old, escort them to the gates
with prayers, as does the handsome Iülus, who
with a man's mind and cares beyond his years
then charges them with tidings for his father.
But winds will take and scatter all of these   415
and give them, useless offerings, to the clouds.

They cross the trenches as they leave and, through
the shadow of the night, make for the camp
that will bring death to them—though before that,
they will be the end of many. Everywhere   420
they can see bodies sprawling, deep in sleep
and drink, and tilted chariots on the shore,
men tangled in the harnesses and wheels,
and casks of wine and weapons all about.
And Nisus spoke out first: "Euryalus,   425
the right hand has to dare; the time invites;
our way is here. You guard and watch from far,
lest any band come at us from behind.
I will act here, to kill and cut a wide
pathway that you can follow." So he speaks,   430
then checks his voice and drives his sword at once
into the haughty Rhamnes, who by chance
was cushioned on a heap of rugs piled high
while snoring out his sleep from his wide chest:
himself a king, and one who served as King   435

Latinus' best-loved augur; and yet he
could not avert this end by augury.
He cuts down three attendants next to Rhamnes
as they lie sprawled at random around their lances,
and then the charioteer and armor-bearer   440
of Remus, whom he caught beneath the horses.
He hacks their drooping necks and then lops off
their master's head. He leaves the trunk to gurgle
as it spouts blood; the earth, the rugs are steeped
in warm black gore. Then he kills Lamyrus,   445
Lamus, and young Serranus, known for beauty,
who had gamed long that night, then lay, his limbs
undone by too much Bacchus; had he played on
and made that gaming last the night away,
until the light of day, he had been happy!   450
For even as a starving lion, raging
through crowded sheepfolds, urged by frenzied hunger,
who tears and drags the feeble flock made mute
by fear and roars with bloody mouth—so Nisus.

No less, the slaughter of Euryalus: 455
he, too, is kindled, wild, and falls upon
a vast and nameless rabble, catching Fadus,
Herbesus, Abaris—all three unconscious.
But Rhoetus was awake and saw it all,
for in his terror he had hid behind   460
a massive jar; and when he rose nearby,
then Nisus plunged his blade hilt-high in Rhoetus'
breast, and he drew it back, now drenched with death.
So Rhoetus vomits out his purple life
and, crying, throws up wine with mingled blood.   465
Euryalus is hot for secret slaughter.
He had drawn near the comrades of Messapus,
where he could see the last camp fires flicker
and tethered horses grazing on the grass,
when Nisus, with few words (for he could sense   470
his comrade was berserk with lust for carnage),
stopped him: "Now let us go; our enemy,
daylight, is near; we have had enough revenge;
we have cut a pathway through these Latin ranks."

They leave behind them many soldiers' weapons,   475
arms wrought in solid silver, drinking cups,

and handsome rugs. Euryalus takes up
the gear of Rhamnes and his golden-bossed
sword belt, the gifts that long ago the rich
King Caedicus sent Remulus of Tiber   480
as witness from afar of their full friendship;
and he, when dying, gave them to his grandson;
and with his death in battle, the Rutulians
had captured them as spoils. Euryalus
takes these and fits them to his sturdy shoulders—   485
but all for nothing. Then he sets Messapus'
own handsome-crested helmet on his head;
it fits well. They leave camp and make for safety.

But meanwhile horsemen rode up from a force
that hurried out from Latium to carry   490
an answer to Prince Turnus. While the rest
had halted, readying for battle, these
three hundred riders came ahead, and all
were under shield, with Volcens as their captain.
And as they neared the camp, approached the wall,   495
they saw the pair far off along a path
and heading left; the helmet of the heedless
Euryalus betrayed him, flashing back
moonlight across the shades of gleaming night.
That is enough to stop them. Volcens cries: 500
"Halt, man! What is this march? Who are you, armed?
Where are you headed?" But the pair do not
attempt to answer, only rushing on
their flight into the forest, trusting the night.
Upon all sides the riders block familiar   505
crossways; the sentries stand at every outlet.
And shaggy, wide, the forest stretched, with dark
ilex and thorny thickets; everywhere
the tangled briers massed, with here and there
a pathway glimmering among the hidden   510
tracks in the dense brushwood. Euryalus,
who is hampered by the shadowed branches, by
his heavy spoils, mistakes his way through fear.
But Nisus now is clear; he had escaped
the enemy and, still unthinking, passed   515
the place that later is to be called Alban
for Alba Longa—but then King Latinus
kept his tall cattle stalls there—when he halted,

looked back for his lost friend and could not find him.

"Where have I left you, poor Euryalus?   520
Where can I search for you, and how unravel
my tangled path through that deceptive forest?"
With this, he tracks and traces back his footsteps
and threads his way through silent thickets until
he hears hoofbeats and trampled brush and signals   525
of chase and, not long after, an outcry;
and sees Euryalus whom now, betrayed
by night and the terrain, bewildered by
the sudden tumult, all the troop are hauling
away as, overpowered, he thrashes, hopeless.   530
But what can Nisus do? What can he use,
what force or arms to dare his comrade's rescue?
Or should he rush to his sure end among
those troops and hurry with his wounds a seemly
death? Quickly then he draws his arm far back;   535
as he prepares his shaft, he gazes at
the steep moon, prays: "You goddess, guardian
of groves, and glory of the stars, o you,
Latona's daughter, now be with us, help
this labor. For if you were ever honored   540
by Hyrtacus, my father, when he brought
before your altar gifts on my behalf,
if I have ever added offerings
to you from my own hunting, hanging trophies
beneath your dome or nailing them upon   545
your gabled roof, then let me rout this troop;
you guide my spearhead through the air." He spoke,
then, straining all his body, hurled his steel.
Across the shadows of the night it flies,
then strikes the facing back of Sulmo; there   550
it snaps and, splintered, passes through his midriff.
As Sulmo tumbles over in chill death,
he vomits out a warm stream from his chest;
his long-drawn gasps heave heard against his ribs.
The Latins look around, at every angle.   555
While they still tremble, Nisus, even fiercer,
now poises a new shaft at his eartip.
The hissing spear drives straight through both the temples
of Tagus; warm, it stuck in his pierced brain.
Though Volcens rages, crazed, he cannot see   560

whoever was the sender of that shaft
or where he can attack in frenzy. "Yet
until we find him, you shall pay," he cried,
"the penalties of both with your warm blood."
He rushed with drawn sword at Euryalus.   565
Then, mad with terror, Nisus cries aloud—
he could not hide in darkness anymore
or stand so great a grief: "I did it—I:
your steel, Rutulians, is meant for me;
the crime is mine; he has not dared anything,   570
nor could he; heaven be my witness and
the knowing stars: he only loved too well
his luckless friend." So was he pleading when
the sword, thrust home with force, pierced through the ribs
and broke the white breast of Euryalus.   575
He tumbles into death, the blood flows down
his handsome limbs; his neck, collapsing, leans
against his shoulder: even as a purple
flower, severed by the plow, falls slack in death;
or poppies as, with weary necks, they bow   580
their heads when weighted down by sudden rain.
But Nisus rushes on among them all;
he is seeking only Volcens, only Volcens
can be the man he wants. The enemy
crowd him; on every side, their ranks would drive   585
him back, but Nisus presses on unchecked,
whirling his lightning sword until he plunged
it full into the Latin's howling mouth
and, dying, took away his foeman's life.
Then, pierced, he cast himself upon his lifeless   590
friend; there, at last, he found his rest in death.

Fortunate pair! If there be any power
within my poetry, no day shall ever
erase you from the memory of time;
not while Aeneas' children live beside   595
the Capitol's unchanging rock nor while
a Roman father still holds sovereignty.

The Latin victors, taking spoils and plunder
and weeping, carried lifeless Volcens back
to camp. But there the wailing was no less   600
when they found Rhamnes dead, together with

so many other chieftains butchered in
one slaughter—here Serranus, Numa here.
Around the bodies of the dead and dying
a mighty crowd has gathered, and the ground   605
is warm with recent killings, channels run
with foaming blood. They recognize the spoils,
the gleaming helmet of Messapus, all
his gear that was regained with so much sweat.

Now early Dawn had left Tithonus' saffron   610
bed, scattering new light upon the earth:
now sunrays streamed, now day made plain all things.
Turnus, himself in arms, calls up his men
to war; each Latin captain spurs his bronze-
clad company to battle, each one stirs   615
their anger with a different tale of horror.
They even fasten on uplifted pikes—
a miserable sight—the heads of Nisus
and of Euryalus and march behind them
with ringing shouts. Aeneas' sturdy sons   620
line up against them, ranged along the left-
side walls (the river keeps their right); they man
the massive trenches, and they stand in sadness
on their high towers. How much more sad—when they
can suddenly make out, impaled, held high,   625
the heads of men known much too well by their
unhappy comrades, heads that drip black gore.

Meanwhile winged Rumor, rushing, flies across
the frightened town with tidings; she glides toward
the mother of Euryalus and reaches   630
her ears. At once the warmth abandons her
poor bones; and from her hands the shuttle falls;
the skein unravels. Wretched, she runs out
and, with a woman's wailing, tearing her hair
and heedless of men's presence and the darts   635
and danger, mad, she races toward the walls'
front lines. Then she fills heaven with her cries:
"Euryalus, is this the way I see you?
You, evening peace of my last years, cruel son,
how could you leave me here alone? Sent out   640
on such a dangerous task, you did not even
let me, your mother, in my misery,

say last farewells. You lie in a strange land,
the prey of Latin dogs and birds. And I,
your mother, did not follow you—your corpse—   645
or close your eyes, or wash your wounds, or wrap
your body in the clothes that I was weaving—
I, hurrying by night and day to finish
before my death, consoling with the loom
the cares of an old woman. Where shall I   650
go now to find you? For what land now holds
your limbs, your severed loins, your mangled corpse?
My son, is there no more than this that you
can now bring back to me? Is it for this
I followed after you by land and sea?   655
If you have any tenderness, Rutulians,
then run me through, hurl all your shafts at me,
and let me be the first you kill! Great father
of gods, take pity; with your thunderbolt
cast down this hated head to Tartarus;   660
that is the only way I can cut short
this cruel life." Her wailing moved their minds;
a moan of sorrow passed through all; their force
is broken, numbed for war. As her grief kindles,
so Actor and Idaeus, at a word   665
from tearful Iülus and Ilioneus,
lift her and bear her homeward in their arms.

But from far off the trumpet rang its call
of dread, its song of brass. Then battle cries
reecho through the sky. The Volscians hurry   670
their march with their locked shields in even lines;
they are bent on filling up the trenches and
on tearing down the ramparts. Some seek out
an entrance, climbing up their scaling ladders
there where the line is thin, the ring of men   675
less dense and gleaming light can pass. Against them
the Teucrians, who have learned to guard their walls
by long warfare, pour down all kinds of weapons
and thrust with their tough poles. They also roll
down boulders big enough to kill, trying   680
to crack the cover of the Latins' shields.
Yet these, beneath the roof of their locked shields,
are able to withstand all things. But now
it is too hard; for where the troops are thickest

and menace most, the Trojans heave and cast
a giant mass that scatters the Rutulians
both wide and far, that cracks their armor cover.
But now the bold Rutulians no longer
care for their covered weapons; with their shafts
they try to clear the battlements. Elsewhere,   690
and terrible to see, Mezentius
is brandishing a torch of Tuscan pine
and whirling fire and smoke; while here Messapus—
horse tamer, son of Neptune—batters down
the ramparts, calls for ladders up the walls.   695

O you, Calliope, and all the Muses,
do you, I pray, inspire me: I must
sing of the slaughter and the deaths that Turnus
spread with his sword across the field of battle,
of those each fighting man sent down to hell;   700
unroll with me the mighty scroll of war.
You, goddesses, remember, you can tell.

In front, well placed, there stood a formidable
tower, with bridges running to the walls,
which all of the Italians tried to storm   705
with their full force, to overturn with every
strength that they had; and facing them, the Trojans,
defending it with stones and crowding close,
were showering their darts through hollow portholes.
First Turnus threw a blazing torch of hemp   710
and fastened fire along the tower's flank.
Fanned by the wind, the flame caught fast the planks
and gripped the gate posts as it burned. Inside,
men tremble, troubled, try in vain to find
escape from this disaster. While they huddle,   715
retreating where the fire has not yet taken
hold—there, beneath the sudden weight the tower
falls; all of heaven thunders at that crash.
And as the monstrous mass collapsed upon them,
they reached the ground, half-dead, pierced by their
     own   720
spear shafts, with splintered hardwood through their chests.
Almost the only ones to fall to safety
were Lycus and Helenor. Young Helenor,
whom a Licymnian slave had borne in secret

to the Maeonian king and then had sent   725
to serve at Troy with arms forbidden to him,
is lightly armed, with naked sword, his blank
shield bears no blazon. When he sees himself
hemmed in by Turnus' thousands, Latin troops
to this side and to that—then even as   730
a wild beast trapped by hunters in a dense
circle, who rages at their shafts and, not
unknowing, casts himself on death, and with
a leap, falls on their hunting spears: so he,
a youth prepared to die, now rushes out   735
among his enemies, and where the shower
of darts is thickest, there he makes his way.
But Lycus, faster-footed, gains the walls
by flight through enemies and through their missiles;
he clutches for the top of a tall buttress   740
to catch his comrades' outstretched hands. But Turnus,
who chases after him with foot and spear,
now as a victor taunts him: "Madman, where
did you hope to escape my hands?" With this,
he grabs at hanging Lycus, tears him down   745
together with a great chunk of the wall:
as when the eagle, armor-bearer of Jove,
while soaring toward his eyrie has swept up
some hare or snow-white swan in his hooked claws,
or when the wolf of Mars has snatched a lamb   750
out of the fold, its mother searching long,
with many bleatings. All about, the Latin
troops shout as they rush forward, heaping earth
to fill the trenches, others tossing blazing
torches up toward the roofs. Ilioneus   755
heaves down the great rock fragment of a mountain
and kills Lucetius as he nears the gateway
while bearing firebrands; and Liger kills
Emathion; Asilas, Corynaeus;
one skillful with the javelin, the other   760
with arrows that steal on, unseen, from far.
Then Caeneus kills Ortygius; Turnus then
kills Caeneus as he stands victorious,
and Itys, Clonius, and Dioxippus,
and Promolus, and Sagaris, and Idas—   765
this last was at his post on the high towers.
And Capys kills Privernus, whom before this

Themillas' spear had lightly grazed; Privernus,
mad, had thrown down his shield to touch the wound;
at this, a gliding arrow pinned his hand   770
to his left side and, penetrating, broke
with death's own wound the breathways of his life.

The son of Arcens, famed for handsomeness,
stood out upon the wall in splendid armor,
his short cloak wrought with needlework and bright   775
with steel-blue Spanish dye. He had been raised
within his mother's grove along the river
Symaethus, where the rich and gracious altar
built by Palicus stands; and then his father
had sent him out to serve under Aeneas.   780
Against this son of Arcens, as he stood,
Mezentius himself, spear set aside,
takes up a whizzing sling; three times he whirled
the thong around his head; with molten lead
he cracked the temples of his enemy   785
and stretched him headlong, sprawling on deep sand.

Now—for the first time in his life, it is said—
Ascanius, who until then had only
been used to scaring fleeing beasts of quarry,
aimed his swift shaft in battle, laying low   790
by his own hand the valiant Numanus—
his surname Remulus—who had but lately
wed Turnus' younger sister. For Numanus
had stalked before the front lines, shouting things
both worthy and unworthy to be spoken,   795
his heart puffed up with his new link to kings,
and boasting as he swaggered, bellowing:

"Twice-conquered Phrygians, are you not ashamed
to be hemmed in again by siege and ramparts,
to set up walls between yourselves and death?   800
Look, those who want to take our brides by battle!
What god brought you to Italy or what
insanity? Do not expect to find
the sons of Atreus here or fable-babbling
Ulysses, but a race from sturdy stock.   805
For first we bear our infants to the river
and harden them by cruel frost and water;

and then our boys grow keen in hunting, ranging
the forests; and their sports are breaking horses
and aiming arrows from their bows. As youths   810
they learn frugality and patient labor
and tame the earth with harrows or compel
defiant towns to tremble. All our life
is spent with steel; we goad the backs of bullocks
with our inverted spears, and even slow   815
old age can never sap our force of spirit
or body's vigor. We clamp down gray hairs
beneath a helmet, always take delight
in our new plunder, in a violent life.
But you wear robes of saffron, ornamented   820
and gleaming purple; you like laziness,
and you delight in dances; and your tunics
have sleeves, your bonnets, ribbons. You indeed
are Phrygian women—hardly Phrygian men:
now go, prance through high Dindyma, there where   825
the twin-mouthed pipes delight familiar ears!
The timbrel and the Berecynthian flute
of Ida's mother summon you to revels;
leave arms to men, you have had enough of swords."

These bragging words and warnings were too much.   830
Ascanius drew back his horse-gut bowstring,
his arrow, stretched his arms apart, and pausing,
prayed first, a suppliant, with vows to Jove:
"All-able Jupiter, be kind to my
audacious try! For I myself shall bring   835
my yearly offerings into your temple;
before your altars I shall set a dazzling
white bullock with gilt brow, tall as his mother,
and old enough to butt with horns, his pawing
hoofs scattering the sand." The Father heard,   840
and from a cloudless part of heaven he
then thundered on the left. That very instant
the fatal bowstring twangs. The arrow, taut,
speeds on with dreadful hissing, driving through
the head of Remulus and, with its steel,   845
pierces his hollow temples. "Go now, mock
our bravery with words that taunt! This is
the answer sent by twice-defeated Phrygians
back to Rutulians." He said no more.

The Trojans, glad, applaud Ascanius;   850
their shouting lifts their spirits to the stars.

It happened then that, from the upper air,
while seated on a cloud, long-haired Apollo
was looking down upon the Trojan city
and on the army of Ausonia.   855
He speaks to the triumphant Iülus: "Grow
in your new courage, child; o son of gods
and ancestor of gods, this is the way
to scale the stars. All fated, future wars
shall end in peace beneath Assaracus'   860
house; for the walls of Troy cannot contain you."
And saying this, he flashes from steep heaven
and parts the panting winds and seeks Iülus;
but first he takes the shape of aged Butes:
once he was armor-bearer to Anchises   865
and trusted keeper of his gate, but later
the father of Ascanius had made him
the boy's companion. As he walked, Apollo
in every way was like the old man: voice
and coloring, white hairs, and clanging weapons.   870
He calms excited Iülus with these words:

"It is already much, son of Aeneas,
that by your shafts you have laid low Numanus,
yourself unharmed. The great Apollo grants
the glory of this first success; and he   875
does not begrudge your matching him in arms:
but after this, my boy, enough of war."
This said, Apollo, even as he spoke,
put off his mortal form and vanished far
from sight into thin air. The Dardan chieftains   880
had recognized the god and his divine
arrows; they heard his quiver rattle as
he flew away. And so, because of Phoebus'
word and his will, they curb Ascanius,
still anxious for fresh battle; they themselves   885
rush out again to fight, to risk their lives
in open perils. All around the walls
a roar runs through the bulwarks as they bend
their bitter bows and whirl their slings. The ground
is littered far and wide with missiles; shields   890

and hollow helmets clash and clang; the battle
grows ever bloodier: just as a gale
that, born beneath the stormy Hyades,
will rush out from the west and flail the ground;
or hail that whips the shoals when Jupiter,   895
rough with his turning south winds, twists the squall
of water, cracks the heavens' hollow clouds.

Then two sons of Alcanor, Pandarus
and Bitias, raised in the wood of Jove
on Ida by the nymph Iaera, two   900
young men the match of their own native firs
and mountains, held the gate assigned to them
by order of their chieftains. But relying
on arms alone, they freely open this,
invite their enemies inside the walls.   905
And they themselves take posts inside the entrance,
before the towers to the right and left;
they are armed with swords, their tall heads glittering
with plumes: even as twin oak trees that rise
high in the air, along clear streams, beside   910
the riverbanks of Padus or nearby
kind Athesis, when they lift up their shaggy
heads unto heaven, nodding their steep crowns.
When they can see the entrance free, the Latins
burst in. But straightway Quercens, reckless Tmarus,   915
Aquicolus, most handsome in his armor,
and Haemon, son of Mars, are beaten off
with all their men and turn their backs in flight
or lose their lives upon the very threshold.
Now anger grows more fierce in minds that hate;   920
the Trojans rally to the gateway, daring
to battle hand to hand; they sally out.

Turnus is raging elsewhere in the attack,
bringing confusion to his foes; but then
he hears the news that, hot with their new kill,   925
the enemy have opened wide their gates.
He drops what he began; moved by tremendous
wrath, he now rushes toward the Dardan entrance
and those proud brothers. And the first he kills,
casting his javelin, is Antiphates—   930
a bastard son of great Sarpedon, born

out of a Theban mother—as he stands
foremost. For the Italian shaft of dogwood
flies through thin air; it drives into his belly
and then twists upward into his deep chest;   935
the wound's dark mouth pours out a wave of foam,
the steel tip warms itself in his pierced lungs.
He next kills Meropes and Erymas,
Aphidnus, and then Bitias himself,
for all his glaring eyes and raging mind—   940
not with a javelin, for that could never
take Bitias' life away, but with a whirling   ˙
Saguntine pike that raced with mighty hissing,
one driven like a bolt of thunder; neither
his shield with two bull's hides nor the twin row   945
of golden scales upon his trusty corselet
could stand against it. His tremendous limbs
collapse and fall; earth groans; his giant shield
comes crashing down upon him. Even so
along the coast of Baiae near to Cumae   950
at times a stony pier, built to great size,
which then is set into the sea, will fall;
and as it tumbles, trails just such destruction,
dashing to rest beneath the shoals; the seas
are in a turmoil and the black sands heave;   955
and Prochyta's steep island trembles at
that roar; Inarime's stone bed, laid down
by Jove's command, above Typhoeus, shudders.

At this, Mars, god of arms, gave to the Latins
new force and heart. He spurred their breasts with   960
   sharp
goads, but he set black Fear and Flight among
the Teucrians. From every side the Latins
now rally, taking every chance to fight;
the warrior god glides deep into their minds.
But Pandarus, who sees the fallen body   965
of Bitias, his brother, who can tell
how fortune stands, what chance is ruling things,
heaves hard with his great shoulders, straining much,
and twists the gate back on its swinging hinges.
And he leaves many comrades shut outside   970
the walls in bitter battle; many others—
those quick to rush inside with him—he welcomes.

Madman! Among the troops that hurried in
he had not seen Prince Turnus; heedless, he
had locked him in the city like some monstrous   975
tiger among the helpless flocks. At once
a new light glittered in the eyes of Turnus,
his arms clanged horridly; his bloody crests
are quivering on his helmet; gleaming lightnings
flash from his shield. Aeneas' men, in panic,   980
have recognized his hated face and massive
frame. Giant Pandarus makes straight for him
and, hot with anger for his brother's death,
cries: "This is not Amata's dowry palace;
this is not Ardea, your native place.   985
You see a hostile camp, with no escape."
Untroubled, Turnus smiles at him and says:
"Throw first, if there is courage in your heart,
then try my right hand; you shall say to Priam
that here, too, an Achilles can be found."   990
He stopped. Then Pandarus called all his force
and whirled his knotted spear of still-green oak.
The winds received the wound; Saturnian
Juno had parried it; the spearhead sticks
fast in the gate. "But you will not escape   995
this weapon wielded by my strong right hand;
this wound and weapon are another man's—
not his who held your shaft." So Turnus says;
stretching, he raises high his sword; the steel
slices the brow of Pandarus between   1000
the temples, severing his beardless cheeks
with one enormous wound. A thud: earth quakes
beneath his great weight. Dying, on the ground,
his fainting limbs are sprawled, his armor splashed
with brains; his head is dangling in equal halves   1005
from either shoulder, to this side and that.

The Trojans turn and run in fear and trembling;
and if the victor then had taken care
to smash the bolts, to let his comrades pour
inside the gates, that day had been the last   1010
day of the war and of the Trojan nation;
but rage and an insane desire for slaughter
drove Turnus on against his enemies.
And first he catches Phaleris, and then

he catches Gyges, whom he hamstrings; seizing   1015
their spears, he hurls them at the fleeing crowd
as Juno helps him on with force and heart.
To keep them company, he next sends off
both Phegeus—piercing through his shield—and Halys.
And then—as, unaware, they stand upon   1020
the walls, inciting war with those outside—
these four are slaughtered next: Alcander, Noemon,
and Halius and Prytanis. Then Lynceus
draws near and calls upon his Trojan comrades;
but Turnus, sweeping toward the rampart on   1025
his right, hacks Lynceus down with gleaming sword;
his head, sliced by one blow, fell far away,
together with his helmet. Turnus next
kills these: first Amycus, who hunted down
wild beasts—no hand had been more skillful in   1030
anointing shafts and arming steel with poison;
then Clytius, the son of Aeolus;
and after him falls Cretheus, the companion
of Muses: Cretheus, Muses' comrade, one
who always took delight in lyre and song   1035
and setting measured music on the strings;
he always sang of horses, warriors, wars.

At last the Trojan captains—brave Serestus
and Mnestheus—hearing of the slaughter, meet;
they see their comrades wandering about,   1040
the enemy within the gates. And Mnestheus
cries out: "And where are you retreating to?
What other walls, what ramparts lie beyond?
My countrymen, will you let one lone man,
hemmed in by your own bulwarks on all sides,   1045
still carry on such killing in your city
and go scot free? Shall he send down so many
of our best youths to Orcus? Cowards, are you
not moved by shame and pity for your luckless
homeland, your ancient gods, for great Aeneas?"   1050

Excited by these words, they steady, stand
in compact ranks. And gradually Turnus
moves back from battle, making for the river,
for that side of the camp along the banks.
At this the Teucrians push on more fiercely,   1055

shouting and massing, just as when a crowd
will press a cruel lion with hating spears:
in fear, yet bold and glaring, he gives ground;
his wrath and courage will not let him flee;
and yet, though this is what he wants, he cannot   1060
charge on against so many men and weapons.
And even so is Turnus, hesitant,
as he moves backward with slow steps; his spirit
boils up with rage. But even then he twice
rushed out against the center of their ranks,   1065
twice turned them, in disorder, into flight
along the walls. But quickly all the troops
pile out in one mass from the camp; nor can
Saturnian Juno dare to give him strength
against them; for from heaven, Jupiter   1070
sent Iris through the air as messenger
with orders—they were hardly gentle—for
his wife-and-sister, warning her that Turnus
now has to quit the Trojans' battlements.
And so the soldier cannot stand much longer   1075
with either shield or sword; he is overwhelmed
by shafts from every side. His helmet never
stops clanging, dizzying his hollow temples;
his horsehair crest is dashed from off his head;
his shield-boss cannot take so many blows.   1080
The Trojans—and among them, thunderous
Mnestheus himself—redouble their attack
with spears. Then sweat runs down all Turnus' body,
a stream like pitch; he cannot breathe; his limbs,
exhausted, shake with painful panting. Then   1085
he leaps at last and gives himself headlong,
together with his weapons, to the river.
The Tiber's yellow stream welcomed his coming;
it lifted him on soft waves, washed away
his blood, and sent him back, glad, to his comrades.   1090

X·1142

1980

BOOK X

Meanwhile the palace of Olympus opens;
the father of the gods and king of men
within his house of stars has called a council;
there, high upon his throne, he watches all
the lands, the Dardan camps, the Latin peoples.   5
The gods take up their seats within a hall
flanked east and west by portals. Jove begins:

"Great sons of heaven, why this shift in plan,
this bickering with such belligerence?
I ordered Italy to leave the Trojans   10
untouched; why quarrel, then, against my will?
What fear persuaded one side or the other
to take the way of war, provoke the sword?
The fitting time for battle will yet come
(and soon enough without your hurrying)   15
when savage Carthage will unleash its hate
and ruin on the towers of Rome, unlock
the Alps against them: then it will be right
to rage and fight and ravage everything.
Now it is time to stop, to give your glad   20
assent to what I want: a league of peace."
      ❖   ❖   ❖

So Jupiter in few words, but a few
are not enough when golden Venus answers:
"O Father, o eternal king of men
and things—what higher force can I beseech?—   25
you see how arrogant are these Rutulians—
how Turnus, with his handsome horses, rides
across the ranks; how, puffed with pride, he charges,
the favorite of Mars. Even their barred
ramparts are not enough to shield the Trojans;   30
they fight within the gates, along the bulwarks
and walls; they flood the trenches with their blood.
Aeneas is away and does not know.
And will you never let the Teucrians
be free from siege? Again the walls of Troy,   35
newborn, are menaced by an enemy,
another army, and again a son
of Tydeus marches out against them, from
Aetolian Arpi. And I think more wounds
are still to come to me; I, your own daughter,   40
must still await the weapon of a mortal.
For if the Trojans have reached Italy
without your leave, against your will, then let
them suffer for their crime, do not bring help.
But if they followed oracles of High Ones,   45
of gods above and gods below, then why
can anyone annul what you command
or make new fates for them? Must I recall
their galleys burned along the coast of Eryx?
Or raging winds the king of tempests wakened   50
out of Aeolia? Or the descent
of Iris from the clouds? Now Juno even
stirs up the Shades (no one before disturbed
that region of the world); and suddenly
Allecto is set loose on upper earth,   55
raving throughout the towns of Italy.
I do not care at all for empire, though
such was my hope when fortune favored; now
let those be victors whom you choose to be.
And if there is no country your cruel wife   60
will let the Trojans have—then, Father, I
beseech you by the smoking remnants of
my fallen Troy to let me send away
Ascanius, unharmed, from battle: let
my grandson live. Aeneas may be cast,   65

just as you will, on unknown waves and follow
whatever pathway fortune finds for him;
but let me shield Ascanius and take him
far from this dreadful war. I have high Paphos,
Cythera, Amathus, Idalia's temple;   70
then let Ascanius live unhonored there,
his weapons set aside. Have Carthage crush
all of Ausonia in her hard grip;
Ascanius will not stand in the way
of Tyre. What use is it to have escaped   75
the plague of war, to flee through Argive fires,
to try out every risk of sea and vast
lands, if the Trojans still are searching for
their Latium, their newborn Pergamus?
And would it not have been far better for them   80
if they had settled on the final ashes
of their homeland, on soil that once was Troy?
I pray you, Father, to give back the Xanthus
and Simois to these poor men; let them
live through the trials of Troy a second time."   85

Then royal Juno, urged by bitter anger:
"Why are you forcing me to break my deep
silence, to publish my most secret grief?
Did any god or man compel Aeneas
to take the way of war, to let himself   90
be used as enemy of King Latinus?
'The fates have led him into Italy':
oh, yes—the prophecies of mad Cassandra!
Did I press him to leave his camp, to trust
his fortune to the winds? To place a child   95
in charge of his defenses? Or to tamper
with Tuscan loyalties, the peace of nations?
What god, what ruthless power of mine drove him
to crime? Does Juno have to do with this,
or Iris sent from clouds? You say it is   100
disgraceful for Italians to surround
the newborn Troy with torches and for Turnus
to take a stand upon his native ground—
Turnus, who has as ancestor Pilumnus,
whose mother is Venilia, the goddess.   105
But what have you to say when Trojan force
is used to fling black torches at the Latins?
Or crushes foreign fields beneath their yoke

and carries off their plunder? When they pick
at will whatever daughters they would wed   110
and snatch pledged brides away from proper lovers?
Or beg for peace but dress their ships in armor?
You have the power to pluck Aeneas from
the hands of the Achaeans, giving them
the mist and empty winds instead of him,   115
to change Troy's ships into as many nymphs:
then is it terrible if we in turn
have given the Rutulians some help?
'Aeneas is away and does not know'—
indeed, let him not know and be away!   120
You say that Paphos, high Cythera, and
Idalium are yours: why meddle, then,
with towns that teem with war and bitterness?
For is it I who try to tear away
your tottering Troy from its foundations? I?   125
Or is it not that wanton one who laid
the wretched Trojans open to the Greeks?
Was it not he who caused both Europe and
Asia to rise in arms, whose treachery
first violated ties of peace? Did I   130
lead on the Teucrian adulterer
to plunder Sparta? Did I furnish him
with weapons or use lust to foster war?
That was the time to care about your friends.
But now, too late, you rise with your complaints,   135
unjustly casting pointless taunts at me."

This was the plea of Juno. All the sons
of heaven murmured their assent to her
or else to Venus: even as a tempest's
first sighs, when trapped within the forest, rustle   140
and struggle back and forth with muffled roar
that warns seafarers of high winds to come.
Then the all-able Father, as chief lord
of every thing, speaks out; and with his words
the high home of the gods is hushed; the earth   145
is made to tremble down to its deep base;
steep air is silent and the west winds still;
the deep seas stay their waters, and they rest.

"Then listen, set these words fast in your minds:
since Teucrian and Latin cannot join   150
in treaty and your quarrel cannot find
an end, I shall allow no difference
between the Trojans and Rutulians;
whatever fortune each may find today,
what hope each side may follow, I shall not   155
care if the Trojans are besieged because
of the Italians' destiny or for
their own mistakes or their misguided omens.
Nor shall I be of help to the Rutulians.
What each man does will shape his trial and fortune.   160
For Jupiter is king of all alike;
the Fates will find their way." He sealed his word;
he nodded by his Stygian brother's rivers,
by banks that flood with pitch and dark whirlpools,
and shook all of Olympus with his nod.   165
The speeches now were ended. Jupiter
rose from his golden throne; and heaven's sons,
surrounding him, escort him to his threshold.

Meanwhile at all the gates the Latins strive
to cut the Trojans down, to gird the walls   170
with flame. The men Aeneas leads are still
trapped inside their stockade, without escape.
Aimless and sad, they stand upon the towers
and man the ramparts in a meager ring.
And Asius, the son of Imbrasus;   175
the pair who bear Assaracus' own name;
Thymoetes, son of Hicetaon; and
both Castor and old Thymbris—these are foremost;
beside them stand Sarpedon's brothers, Clarus
and Thaemon, who have come from hilly Lycia.   180
And he who strains with all his body, carries
a massive rock, huge fragment of a mountain,
is Acmon of Lyrnesus, just as huge
as is his father Clytius or his brother
Menestheus. And some try defense with lances   185
and some with stones, and some cast firebrands
or fit bowstrings with arrows. In the thick
the Dardan boy himself, the favored one
of Venus, handsome head uncovered, glitters

just as a jewel set in tawny gold
as an adornment for the neck or head,
or gleaming ivory inlaid with skill
in boxwood or Orician terebinth.
His milk-white neck receives his flowing hair
encircled by a clasp of pliant gold.   195
And Ismarus, you, too, were seen by your
great-hearted tribesmen from Maeonia,
where rich wheat fields are tilled by men and then
bathed by the golden flood of the Pactolus:
son of a noble house, you took your aim   200
to wound, anointing shafts of reed with poison.
And Mnestheus, too, was there, whom yesterday's
triumph—his thrusting Turnus from the high
ramparts—exalts in glory; Capys, too,
whose name is now a city in Campania.   205

And so they fought a stubborn, cruel fight;
meanwhile Aeneas cut the waves at midnight.
For when he left Evander he had entered
the Tuscan camp and there approached King Tarchon.
He tells the king his name and race, declares   210
what help he needs, what help he brings the Tuscans,
informing him of what Mezentius
would muster and of Turnus' violence
and of what faith to put in human things,
and with his warnings mingles in entreaties.   215
No time is lost: King Tarchon joins his forces;
their pact is made. And then the Lydian nation,
free now from fate's restraint, at last beneath
a foreign leader by the gods' command,
takes ship. First in the fleet: Aeneas' galley;   220
beneath its beak are Phrygian lions, and
above them, towering, the mount of Ida,
a scene most welcome to the exiled Trojans.
Here great Aeneas sits, considering
the many and inconstant ways of war;   225
and Pallas, at his left, clings close and asks
about the stars and how they chart a path
for us across the darkened night, and what
trials had Aeneas faced on land and sea.

Now open Helicon, you goddesses,   230
and while they sail, awake your song and tell

what forces from the Tuscan shores are with
Aeneas, man the ships, and ride the sea.

First Massicus, their captain, cuts the waters
in "Tiger," ship with beak of bronze; he brings   235
a thousand young men in a band come from
the walls of Clusium and town of Cosae,
with arrows and light quivers on their shoulders
and deadly bows. Beside him sails grim Abas,
all of his men in splendid arms, a gilded   240
Apollo gleaming on his stern. Six hundred
young men, expert in war, were given him
by Populonia, the mother city;
and Ilva, with her inexhaustible,
rich island mines of Chalybean metal,   245
sent out three hundred. Third in line, Asilas,
interpreter between the gods and men—
whom cattle entrails and the stars of heaven
and languages of birds and lightning flashes
of prophesying thunder all obey—   250
has brought with him a thousand, close arrayed;
their spears are bristling. All are sons of Pisa,
a city set on Tuscan soil and yet
Alphean in its origin. And next
most handsome Astyr follows: Astyr, who   255
trusts in his horse and many-colored weapons.
Three hundred more, but all with one will, come
from Caere, Minio's farms, and ancient Pyrgi
and from Graviscae, the unhealthy city.

Nor shall I overlook you, Cinyras,   260
bravest in war of all Ligurians,
nor you, Cupavo, though your troops were few.
The feathers of a swan rise from your crest
(as a reproach to Love and to Love's mother),
the emblem of your father's transformation.   265
For it is said of Cycnus that—while he
was grieving over Phaethon, consoling
his melancholy love with music, singing
beneath the poplar leaves of his dead love's
sisters—he altered; covered with soft feathers   270
like white old age, he soared away from earth
and, singing still, made for the stars. His son
Cupavo, with his troops young as himself,

drives on with oars his giant ship, the "Centaur."
Its emblem towers above the waters: bold,   275
it menaces the waves with a huge rock
and furrows the deep seas with its long keel.

There, too, another chieftain comes who from
his native coasts has mustered squadrons: Ocnus,
the son of prophesying Manto and   280
the Tuscan river; Mantua, he gave you
walls and his mother's name—o Mantua,
so rich in ancestors and yet not all
of one race; for you are the capital
of peoples rising from three races, each   285
the rulers of four towns; but you yourself
have drawn your chief strength from your Tuscan blood.
And here Mezentius' city sends five hundred
men out against him, led across the seas
in pine warships; upon their prows is Mincius,   290
the river god and son of Lake Benacus;
he is crowned with gray-green reeds. And next Aulestes,
lashing the waters, comes on heavily;
he rises to the stroke with a full hundred
oars of tree trunks; the waters foam, the sea   295
is overturned. He is carried by a prow
that bears a giant Triton, one whose shell
frightens the blue-gray seas; for as he swims,
his hairy chest is human to the waist,
but then his belly ends in fish; beneath   300
the breast of this half-beast, waves churn and foam.

So many were the chosen chiefs who sailed
in three-times-ten ships to the aid of Troy
and plowed the plains of brine with prows of bronze.

Now day had left the sky; and gracious Phoebe,   305
in her night-wandering chariot, was trampling
through mid-Olympus. At the helm Aeneas
himself both steers and tends the sails; his cares
have stripped his limbs of calm and rest. Then—look!—
across the middle of the seaway came   310
a band of his own squadron; for the nymphs,
whom Cybele had made sea goddesses

when she changed them from ships to nymphs, swam on
together, cutting through the waves, as many
as once were brazen prows along the coast.   315
They recognize Aeneas from far off
and, dancing, circle him: Cymodoce,
most skilled at speaking, follows in his wake
and grips the stern with her right hand, lifting
her back above the surface; with her left   320
she rows across the soundless waves below.
And then she turns to the astonished king:

"Aeneas, son of gods, are you awake?
Be up and ease the cords! Set free the sails!
We are the pines of Ida's sacred summit,   325
your ships that now are water nymphs. As Turnus,
the traitor, harried us with flame and sword,
reluctantly we broke your ropes and then
went off in search of you across the seas.
The mother of the gods was merciful;   330
she gave us this new form as goddesses,
to spend our life beneath the waters. But
your son Ascanius is trapped by trenches
and walls, hemmed in by spears and war-mad Latins.
Arcadian horsemen, joined by bold Etruscans,   335
are ready at their stations; and yet Turnus
is set to head them off with his men, lest
they join your camp. Enough; be up; and as
Dawn comes, command your comrades to take arms
early; and take the shield, invincible,   340
with golden borders, you were given by
the Lord of Fire. For tomorrow's light—
if you believe my words are not for nothing—
shall see great heaps of slain Rutulians."
She ended and, at parting, shoved the tall   345
ship forward, using her right hand and just
the needed force; it flies across the waters
faster than javelin and wind-swift arrow.
And all the other ships drive on more quickly.

Anchises' Trojan son is mystified   350
and marvels, yet this omen lifts his heart;
and he prays briefly toward the high curved sky:

"Generous goddess of Ida, you, mother
of gods, who take delight in Dindyma
and towered towns and lions yoked in pairs,   355
now guide me in this coming battle; goddess,
make this sign favorable, stride beside
the Phrygian squadrons with your gracious step."
He said no more. Meanwhile returning day
rushed on with its ripe light and banished night.   360

He first instructs his comrades how to follow
the standards, to prepare their hearts for battle,
to set their ranks in order for the fight.
Now, standing on the high stern, he can see
his Trojans and his camp. At once he lifts   365
the glowing shield in his right hand. The Dardans
raise high a starward shout up from the ramparts;
new hope has kindled rage; they shower darts—
even as the Strymonian cranes will signal
beneath dark clouds their coming; clamorous,   370
they skim across the skies, fleeing before
the south winds with glad cries. But this astounded
the chieftains of Ausonia and the prince
of the Rutulians, until they looked
backward and saw the sterns turned toward the shore 375
and all the waves alive with gliding ships.
Aeneas' helmet tip glows on his head
as it pours fire down from his towering crest;
his golden shield boss spouts tremendous flames:
just as a bloody comet when it glares,   380
sinister, on some clear night; or as
the blazing Dog Star, bringer of diseases
and drought to tired mortals, when it rises
with light and menace, saddening the skies.

Yet there was no despair in daring Turnus: 385
he meant to take the landing beach before them,
to drive them off while they were disembarking.
Straightway he spurs his men with words. He goads:
"What you have prayed for, you can do now: break them;
Mars is himself within your hands. Let each   390
remember wife and home, recall the bright
acts and the glories of his ancestors.
Now let us meet them at the water's edge

at once, while they are trembling still, with their
first footsteps tottering to land; for fortune 395
helps those who dare." So Turnus says and then
considers whom to lead against them, whom
to leave in charge of war against the walls.

Meanwhile Aeneas, from his tall ships, lands
his crewmen down the gangways. Many watch 400
the languid surf for ebbing waves, then trust
themselves to shallows with a leap, and others
slide down on oars. But Tarchon scans the shores
where no waves breathe, no breakers murmur, only
the inoffensive sea glides with its swell, 405
and suddenly he turns his prows, urging
his comrades: "Now, my chosen ones, press hard
on your tough oars; drive high the ships; let this
land of the enemy feel beaks that cleave,
and let the keel itself dig out a trough. 410
So long as we have gained our ground, I do not
care if our fleet shipwrecks on such a beach."
At Tarchon's words the crews rise on their oars
and bear the galleys up on Latin shores.
The beaks have gripped dry land, and all the keels 415
can settle down, unharmed. But, Tarchon, not
your own ship, for she strikes the shoals and hangs
on an uneven, hard sandbank; she is held
for long in balance, beating at the waves,
until she smashes, tossing out her men 420
among the breakers. And the sailors tangle
with drifting rowing benches, broken oars,
and waves that ebb and suck make going hard.

No lazy lingering keeps Turnus back;
fierce, he attacks the Trojans with full force 425
and plants his ranks against them on the shore.
The trumpets blare. Aeneas is the first
to fall upon the farmer troops—a good
beginning—as he lays the Latins low.
First he kills Theron, tallest man of all, 430
who dared to seek a duel with Aeneas.
Well driven through the bronze joints of his shield
and through his tunic rough with scales of gold,
the Dardan's blade drinks blood from his split side.

Aeneas next kills Lichas, who had been   435
cut out of his dead mother's womb and then
made sacred, Phoebus, unto you, because
you let his infant life escape that knife.
Then, not far off, Aeneas cast huge Gyas
and sturdy Cisseus to their death as they   440
were battering the Trojan troops with clubs.
The arms of Hercules were useless to them;
their tough hands did not help, nor did their father,
Melampus—once the comrade of Alcides
for all the while that earth gave him hard trials.   445
And then, while Pharos bragged with empty words,
Aeneas hurled a javelin that struck him
full in his bawling mouth. You, too, sad Cydon,
while you were following your latest darling—
your Clytius, his cheeks blond with first down—   450
would then have fallen headlong by the Dardan's
right hand and lain, a miserable corpse,
forgetful of the boyish loves that always
were dear to you, had not your seven brothers
assailed the enemy with compact ranks: 455
the seven sons of Phorcus with their seven
lances against Aeneas. Some bound off
his shield and helmet pointlessly; but some
are turned aside by kindly Venus, and
they only graze his flesh. But then Aeneas   460
asks this of true Achates: "Give me those
spearheads that once were fixed within the bodies
of Greeks upon the plains of Ilium;
my right hand shall not hurl them now for nothing
against Rutulians." With that, he takes   465
a giant shaft and flings it; as it flies,
it crashes through the brazen shield of Maeon
and cracks at once his breastplate and his chest.
Alcanor, Maeon's brother, runs to hold him,
collapsing, with his right hand, but the rushing   470
spearhead holds fast its bloody course; Alcanor's
right arm is run right through; dying, it hung
down from Alcanor's shoulders by the tendons.
Then Numitor plucked from his brother's body
that very shaft and aimed it at Aeneas;   475
but he was not allowed to strike him straight—
it only grazed the thigh of great Achates.

                    ❖   ❖   ❖

Now, confident in his young body, Clausus
of Cures comes to face the landing party:
from far he casts his stiff lance, striking Dryops   480
with full force underneath the chin, piercing
his throat: he robs him, even as he speaks,
of life and voice; and Dryops' forehead hits
the earth; he vomits thick gore from his mouth.
Three Thracians, too, born of the noble blood   485
of Boreas, and three their father, Idas,
had sent from Ismarus, their home—Clausus
of Cures kills each Trojan differently.
Halaesus rushes up to join him first
and then Auruncan soldiers and Messapus,   490
the son of Neptune, with his splendid horses.
They strain to thrust the landing parties back,
fighting along Ausonia's very border.
As in high air the striving winds do battle
with equal force and spirit; and no wind   495
gives way to wind, no cloud to cloud, no wave
to wave; the fight is long, uncertain; each
against the other, obstinate: just so
the troops of Troy and Latium now clash;
foot presses against foot; man crowds on man.   500

But elsewhere in the battle, where a torrent
had hurtled rolling boulders far and wide
and torn up trees along its banks, there Pallas
saw his Arcadians, unused to charge
on foot, as they went fleeing from the Latins—   505
the rough terrain had lured them to send back
their horses. He has only one response
at such a crisis; now with pleas and now
with bitter words he calls upon their courage:
"Where are you running, comrades? By your valor   510
and by the name of your own King Evander,
by victories you have won and by my hope
that now would match my father's fame, you cannot
trust to your feet. The sword must hack a passage
through Latin ranks. And where their mass is thickest,   515
there, there is where your noble homeland asks
that you and your chief, Pallas, find a path.
There are no gods against us: mortals, we
are driven back by mortal enemies;

we have as many hands and lives as they.   520
Just see, the waters hem us in with their
great sea wall; there is no retreat by land.
Then shall we seek the deep or Troy's new camp?"
This said, he charged against the crowding Latins.

Lagus, led on by his uneven fates,   525
is first to face him. For while Lagus hauls
a heavy boulder, Pallas hurls a lance
that stabs him through the middle of his back,
just where the spine divides the ribs; and Pallas
stoops down to tug the shaft from Lagus' bones.   530
Then Hisbo hacks at Pallas from above,
hoping to take him by surprise, but fails:
while Hisbo charges, reckless and gone wild
because he saw his comrade dying, Pallas
strikes Hisbo first, piercing his swollen lung.   535
The next to be cut down is Sthenius
and then Anchemolus, descended from
the ancient line of Rhoetus: he was one
who dared defile his own stepmother's bed.
Two more—twin brothers, Thymber and Larides,   540
the sons of Daucus—fell on Latin fields;
so like each other, indistinguishable,
that even their own parents made sweet errors.
But Pallas drew a cruel difference
between them: he lopped off the head of Thymber;   545
from you, Larides, he chopped off the hand;
now severed, it seeks out its master, and
its dying fingers twitch and try again,
again to clutch the sword. The Arcadians,
excited by the warning shouts of Pallas,   550
and seeing what he has done so splendidly,
are armed by mingled shame and indignation
to face the enemy. Then Pallas pierces
Rhoeteus, racing past upon his chariot.
His dying gave delay and time to Ilus: 555
for Pallas had cast his tough lance from far
at Ilus; but the one it struck was Rhoeteus,
who intercepted it as he took flight
from you, brave Teuthras, and your brother, Tyres.
And Rhoeteus tumbles, half-dead, from his chariot;   560
and with his heels he spurns the Latin fields.

Just as, in summer, when the winds he wished for
awake at last, a shepherd scatters fires
across the forests; suddenly the space
between the kindled woods takes fire, too;   565
the bristling and unbroken battle line
of Vulcan spreads across wide plains; the shepherd,
a victor, watches the delirious flames:
not unlike this, all of your comrades' courage
now rallies to one point—to help you, Pallas.   570

But now Halaesus, valiant in battle,
has gathered all his strength behind his shield
and marches out against the Arcadians.
He kills Demodocus, then Ladon, Pheres;
with gleaming sword he rips Strymonius'   575
right hand—raised high against Halaesus' throat;
he strikes the face of Thoas with a rock
and scatters both his bones and brains about.
His father, who foresaw his fate, had hidden
Halaesus in the forests. And yet when   580
the old man's whitened eyes fell slack in death,
the Fates had laid their hands upon his son,
assigned Halaesus to Evander's lance.
Now Pallas heads for him, but first he prays:
"O father Tiber, give the steel I poise   585
good fortune, passage through Halaesus' chest;
this done, an oak made sacred to you will
have all his weapons and his warrior's spoils."
The god heard Pallas' words. For while Halaesus
uses his shield in sheltering Imaon,   590
all unprotected, he himself presents
his luckless breast to the Arcadian lance.

But Lausus, such a bulwark in that battle,
will not let his troops panic at the slaughter
that Pallas dealt. And first he cuts down Abas,   595
tough knot and stay in combat. The Etruscans
are fallen and Arcadia's young men
and Trojans, you whom Greeks could not destroy.
The armies clash in close melee, their might
and captains matched. The rear ranks crowd against   600
the vans; the crush is such they cannot move
their hands or weapons. Pallas spurs and urges;

against him, Lausus—both close in their years,
and both most handsome; both denied by fortune
return to their homelands. Nevertheless,   605
the king of high Olympus did not let
them duel; soon enough their fates await them,
each fate beneath another, greater hand.

But meanwhile Turnus' gracious sister warns him
that Lausus needs his help. He cuts across   610
the intervening ranks in his swift chariot.
And when he sees his comrades, Turnus shouts:
"You have had enough of battle. I alone
meet Pallas; he is owed to me, my own;
I could have wished his father here to watch."   615
This said, his comrades left the field as ordered.
But when they have gone off, the youth, amazed
at Turnus' arrogance, admires him;
he runs his eyes across that giant frame
and from a distance, grim, scans everything,   620
then casts these words against the prince's words:
"Soon I shall win my glory, either by
the spoils I carry off from a commander
or by a splendid death. My father can
stand up to either fate. Enough of threats."   625
With this he takes the middle of the field.
Blood gathers, cold, in the Arcadians' hearts.
And Turnus leaped down from his chariot,
going on foot to meet him hand to hand.
Even as when, from some high point, a lion   630
who sees a bull far off along the plains,
preparing for a battle, rushes on:
just so is Turnus' image as he comes.
But Pallas, when he thought him close enough
for spear cast, is the first to move ahead,   635
to see if chance can help his daring try—
his powers are overmatched—and so he cries
out to the giant heavens: "Hercules,
I pray you by my father's welcome to you,
the board that you, a stranger, shared with him,   640
to help my great attempt! Let dying Turnus
see me strip off his bloody weapons, let
his dying eyes see me a conqueror."
        ❋   ❋   ❋

And Hercules heard Pallas; he pressed back
a great groan deep within his chest; he shed   645
tears that were useless. Father Jupiter
then spoke kind words to Hercules, his son:
"Each has his day; there is, for all, a short,
irreparable time of life; the task
of courage: to prolong one's fame by acts.   650
For under Troy's high walls so many sons
of gods have fallen; even great Sarpedon,
my own child, lost his life together with them.
And Turnus, too, is called by his own fates;
he has reached the border given to his years."   655
He speaks, then turns his eyes from Latin fields.

But Pallas casts his spear with massive force
and tears his bright sword from its hollow scabbard.
The spearhead flies and strikes just where the armor
of Turnus rises to the shoulders, tugs   660
its way straight through the shield edge, and at last
it even grazes his tremendous body.
Then Turnus, poising long his lance of oak,
one tipped with pointed steel, aims it at Pallas
and cries: "Now see if my shaft pierces more."   665
So Turnus spoke. The lance head shudders through
the very center of the shield, across
so many plates of iron, plates of bronze,
so many layers of bulls' hides, driving through
the corselet and enormous chest of Pallas.   670
Hopeless, he plucks the warm tip from the wound;
his blood and life flow out by one same path.
He falls upon his wound; his armor clangs
above him; as he dies, his bloody mouth
strikes on the hostile ground. Then Turnus stands   675
above him, crying: "O Arcadians,
remember, take my words back to Evander:
just as he has deserved, I send him Pallas!
Whatever comfort lies in burial
I freely give. His welcome to Aeneas   680
will not have cost your King Evander little."
This said, his left foot pressed upon the body,
and he ripped off the ponderous belt of Pallas,
on which a scene of horror was engraved:

a band of fifty bridegrooms, foully slaughtered   685
one wedding night, and bloodied marriage chambers.
This had been carved in lavish gold by Clonus,
the son of Eurytus; now Turnus revels
and glories in his taking of the plunder.
O mind of man that does not know the end   690
or future fates, nor how to keep the measure
when we are fat with pride at things that prosper!
A time will come to Turnus when he will long
to purchase at great price an untouched Pallas,
when he will hate this trophy and this day.   695
But crowding comrades carry Pallas back,
laid out upon his shield, with many moans
and tears. O with what grief and what great honor
you make your homeward journey to your father!
This day first gave you up to war and this   700
same day is that which carries you away,
and yet you leave behind vast heaps of Latins!

Now not mere rumor of the slaughter, but
a messenger more certain brings Aeneas
word that his comrades stand beside death's danger;   705
the routed Teucrians now need his help.
His sword hacks down whoever stands most close
as, hot, he cuts a broad path through the Latins
with steel; for Turnus, he is seeking you—
you, insolent with your fresh killing. Pallas . . .   710
Evander . . . all are now before his eyes . . .
the tables he first came to as a stranger,
the pledged right hands. He grabs four youths alive,
four sons of Sulmo, then four raised by Ufens,
to offer up as victims to the Shade   715
of Pallas, to pour out as captive blood
upon the funeral pyre. Next from far
Aeneas casts his hostile lance at Magus;
but Magus is adroit enough to stoop,
and quivering, the lance flies over him.   720
He grips Aeneas' knees and, suppliant,
he begs him: "By your father's Shade and by
your hopes in rising Iülus, I entreat,
do spare this life for my own son and father.
I have a splendid house; there, hidden deep,   725
are many talents of chased silver; I

have heaps of wrought and unwrought gold; the victory
of Trojans cannot turn on me; one life
will not make such a difference"—so Magus.
Aeneas answered him: "Those heaps of talents, 730
the gold and silver that you tell of, Magus,
save them for your own sons; such bargaining
in war was set aside by Turnus first,
just now when he killed Pallas. This is what
Anchises' Shade decides, and so says Iülus." 735
With this he grips the Latin's helmet crest
in his left hand; his right drives on the sword
hilt-high into that bent, beseeching neck.

Not too far off was Haemon's son, the priest
of Phoebus and Diana, with his temples 740
encircled by his headband's holy wreath;
he glittered in his robe and splendid armor.
Aeneas comes upon him, driving him
across the battlefield and, when he stumbles,
stands over Haemon's son and slaughters him 745
and wraps him in the giant shade of death.
Serestus gathers up the arms as booty
and bears them on his shoulders as a trophy
he meant for you, King Mars, who stride in battle.

But then the Latin ranks are knit again 750
by Umbro, priest come from the Marsian mountains,
and Caeculus, of Vulcan's race. The Dardan
storms straight at them. His iron sword had just
hacked Anxur's left arm off and, with it, all
the circle of his shield (Anxur was bragging 755
and, thinking force would follow words, perhaps
had puffed his soul to heaven, promising
white hairs and many long years to himself),
when right across Aeneas' blazing path
came Tarquitus, who swaggered in bright armor— 760
he was the son of Dryope, the nymph,
and Faunus, who was keeper of the forests.
Aeneas draws his lance, pins Tarquitus'
cuirass and ponderous shield; as Tarquitus
prays helplessly, wanting to say so much, 765
Aeneas strikes his head to earth and kicks
the warm trunk over, cries with hating heart:

"Lie there, you dreaded one; no gracious mother
will bury you in earth or weight a native
tomb with your limbs. You will be left to savage   770
birds; or the waves will bear you, sunk below
the sea, where famished fish will suck your wounds."

This done, Aeneas races toward Antaeus
and Lucas, Turnus' foremost warriors,
and sturdy Numa and the tawny Camers,   775
born of great-hearted Volcens; Camers, richest
in land of all Ausonians, who ruled
in silent Amyclae. Just as Aegaeon,
who had a hundred arms and hands—they say—
and fire burning from his fifty mouths   780
and chests, when he clanged at Jove's thunderbolts
with fifty shields, each one just like the other,
and drew as many swords: so does Aeneas
rage on, victorious, across the field
once blood has warmed his blade. Now see! He
        charges   785
against the four-horsed chariot of Niphaeus.
But when the team from far off see Aeneas
striding at them, and raging dreadfully,
they rear, rush backward, spill their driver, whirl
the chariot of Niphaeus toward the shore.   790

Meanwhile, as they race with their team of two
white horses down the center of the ranks,
the brothers Lucagus and Liger wheel
about: fierce Lucagus whirls high his sword;
his brother holds the reins. Aeneas could   795
not stand their angry charging; he rushed up,
tremendous, facing them with javelin.
And Liger: "This is not Achilles' chariot
nor Diomedes' horses that you see,
and not the plain of Phrygia; now and here,   800
upon our land, you end your life and warfare."
Mad Liger scatters words like these. And yet
the Trojan hero does not ready words
against his enemy; instead he hurls
his javelin. As Lucagus leans out   805
to lash his team, goading the horses with
his sword tip, with his left foot forward, ready

for battle, then the javelin cuts through
the lower border of his gleaming shield
and pierces his left groin. Thrown from his chariot,   810
and dying, he is rolled across the plain.
With bitter words, pious Aeneas taunts him:
"O Lucagus, no panicked flight of horses,
no empty shadows have betrayed your chariot
or turned them from the enemy; but you   815
yourself desert them, leaping from the wheels."
This said, he seized the horses. Tumbling down
from that same chariot, the luckless brother,
Liger, stretched out his helpless hands and pleaded:
"O Trojan hero, by yourself and by   820
the parents who have brought to birth so great
a son, spare me my life; with pity hear
my prayer." There had been more; Aeneas cut
him off: "These words were not your words before.
Die; do not leave your brother all alone."   825
Then with his sword, he opened Liger's breast,
in which the spirit has its hiding place.

Such were the deaths dealt by the Dardan chieftain
across the plains while he raged like a torrent
or black whirlwind. The boy Ascanius   830
and all the warriors break out at last
and quit their camp site; now the siege is pointless.

And meanwhile Jupiter speaks first to Juno:
"Both wife and sister to me, and much loved,
as you supposed (your judgment is not wrong),   835
the power of Troy has been sustained by Venus,
not by their fighting men's keen hands in battle,
not by their stubborn souls, patient in trials."
And Juno answered humbly: "Handsomest
husband, why trouble me? I am sick with worry   840
and so afraid of your severe commands.
If I still had the force in love that I
once had and that should last for ever, then
indeed, all-able Father, you would not
deny me this: that I might draw Prince Turnus   845
away from war and send him back, unharmed,
to his dear father Daunus. As it is,
now let him die and with his pious blood

pay for the vengeance of the Teucrians!
Yet he receives his name from our own kind;   850
his great-grandfather's father is Pilumnus;
and he has often weighted down your altars
with open hands, with many gracious gifts."

The king of high Olympus answered briefly:
"If you ask respite from impending death,   855
a breathing space for that doomed youth, and you
will understand that I have meant it so,
then let your Turnus flee, and snatch him from
the fate that threatens him. This much I can
indulge. But if beneath your pleas is hidden   860
some other favor and you think that all
the war, with this that I now grant, is shifted
or altered, then you feed on empty hopes."

Then Juno, weeping, answered: "And what if
your mind should grant me what your voice denies,   865
and Turnus' life continue after all?
For as things are, a heavy death awaits him
though he is guiltless—or I am brought far
from truth. But I should rather be deluded
by empty terrors if you would improve   870
what you have planned for him—you can do that."

This said, she cast herself, cloaked in a cloud
and driving storms, down from high heaven, seeking
the troops of Ilium, Laurentian camps.
Then out of insubstantial mist the goddess   875
fashions a phantom, thin and powerless,
that has Aeneas' shape (astounding sight)
and wears the Dardan's arms: she imitates
the shield and helmet of his godly head
and gives it empty words and sound that has   880
no meaning, and she counterfeits his gait;
like forms that—it is said—hover when death
has passed, or dreams that cheat the sleeping senses.
That image swaggers, glad, before the first
line of the warriors, provoking Turnus   885
with words and weapons. Turnus charges toward it
and hurls his hissing spear from far; the phantom
then wheels around and shows its heels. When Turnus

thought that Aeneas had lost heart in flight,
his mind, bewildered, drank in empty hope: 890
"Where are you off to, Trojan? Don't abandon
your promised bride; this right hand will provide
the land that you have sought across the seas."
So shouting, Turnus chases after it
and brandishes his naked blade; he does 895
not see that winds bear off his victory.

Chance had it that a ship was anchored there,
along a ledge of high rock, ladders set
and gangways at the ready; it had just
borne King Osinius from Clusian shores. 900
And here the anxious phantom of Aeneas,
escaping, dashes to conceal itself;
but Turnus, just as quickly, rushes on
and leaps across the ladders and high bridge.
Yet he had hardly touched the prow when Juno 905
slices the cable, sweeps the severed galley
across the ebbing waters. While Aeneas
searches for vanished Turnus to do battle
and sends down many warriors to death,
and that thin phantom tries to hide no longer 910
but flies on high and mingles with black clouds,
a stiff wind carries Turnus on the waters.
Not knowing what is happening, ungrateful
for his escape, he looks around, then lifts
his hands and voice starward: "All-able Father, 915
have you thought me so guilty? Would you have me
pay such a penalty? Where am I carried?
Where have I come from? What can bring me back?
And how? And shall I once again look on
Laurentum's walls and camp? What will they say— 920
the warriors who followed me and my
arms, all whom I have left behind (a shameful
crime) to unutterable death? And now
I see them scattered; I can hear the groans
of those who fall. What shall I do? What land 925
could now gape deep enough to take me? Winds,
have pity; for I, Turnus, pray you: drive
my ship against the reefs, the rocks, or dash
it on the savage shallows of some sandbank,
where neither the Rutulians nor Rumor, 930

who knows what I have done, can find me out."
As he says this, his mind is torn in two:
whether, because of his disgrace, he should
insanely fall upon his sword and drive
the brutal blade into his ribs; or plunge   935
among the waves and, swimming, reach the curving
coastline, and so return to face the Trojans.
Three times he tried each way, three times great Juno
held Turnus back; with pity she restrained him.
He glides ahead; with favoring wave and tide   940
he cuts across the sea; and he is carried
down to his father Daunus' ancient city.

Meanwhile, spurred on by Jupiter, Mezentius
takes up the fight; ferocious, he attacks
the Teucrians, who are wild with their success.   945
The Tuscan troops charge on together, pressing
toward him alone, at him alone they cast
all of their hates and shafts. Just like a rock
that juts into a waste of waters, bare
to maddened winds and naked to the breakers,   950
taking the force and menace both of heaven
and of the seas, while it persists, unmoved:
such is Mezentius. He lays low the son
of Dolichaon, Hebrus; Latagus;
and Palmus as he runs off. Latagus   955
attempts to strike him; but Mezentius meets
him first, full in the face, and with a rock—
a mountain fragment—smashes in his mouth;
while he leaves Palmus hamstrung, powerless,
to writhe about. And he lets Lausus have   960
both Palmus' plumes and armor for his crest
and shoulders. Then Mezentius kills Evanthes
and Mimas, one who was a friend of Paris
and of the same age: for Theano brought him
to light, the son of Amycus, the very   965
same night that—pregnant with a firebrand—
the daughter of Cisseus, Hecuba, bore Paris.
Now Paris lies within his native city;
Mimas lies unknown on Latin shores.

Just as a boar that, for long years, found shelter   970
within Mount Vesulus' pine forests or

among the marshlands of Laurentum, where
he pastured on rich reeds, when driven down
from his high hills by gnashing dogs and caught
by rings of netting, halts and fiercely roars   975
and bristles up his shoulders; not one hunter
has heart enough to show his anger or
move in against him; but far off and safe
they hound and harry him with shafts and shouts:
then, even so, no one, however just   980
his indignation, dares to meet Mezentius
with drawn sword; they provoke him from a distance
with missiles and loud shouts. He hesitates
from side to side; but unafraid, gnashing
his teeth, he shakes their lances from his shield.   985

Now from the ancient lands of Corythus
Acron, a Greek, had come and, in his rush,
had left behind an uncompleted wedding.
And when Mezentius saw him from far off
as he dashed through the ranks with crimson plumes   990
and purple robe, the gift of his betrothed—
even as, often, if a starving lion,
when ranging deep within the forest, driven
by his mad hunger, sees, by chance, a racing
goat or a great-horned stag, then he rejoices;   995
his mouth gapes monstrously; he rears his mane
and clings, crouching, above the carcass' guts,
his cruel jaws bathed by black blood: just so
Mezentius rushed on, keen, against the crowd
of enemies. Poor Acron is cut down;   1000
he hammers at the black ground with his heels
and, dying, stains his broken spear with blood.
That same arm did not condescend to kill
Orodes as he fled, to wound him from
behind with hurled spearhead; Mezentius moved   1005
about and met him face to face, to win
by force of arms and not by stealthiness.
Then, with his foot upon Orodes' body,
pressing, and tugging at his shaft to wrench
it free, to throw the dead man off, Mezentius: 1010
"My men, one who was great in war lies here,
the high Orodes!" All his comrades join;
they all take up their chieftain's joyful paean.

But with his dying breath Orodes cries:
"Whoever you may be, o victor, I   1015
shall not go unavenged, you will not shout
for long with joy; the same end waits for you;
you, too, shall soon be stretched on these same fields."
To this, Mezentius, smiling in his anger:
"Now die. And let the father of the gods   1020
and king of men look after me." This said,
he wrenched the spear out of Orodes' body.
Then brutal quiet, iron sleep press down
his eyes; their light is locked in endless night.

Caedicus kills Alcathoüs; Sacrator,   1025
Hydaspes; Rapo kills Parthenius
and hardy Orses; and Messapus kills
both Clonius and Ericetes, son
born of Lycaon—one as he lay on
the ground, thrown by his rearing horse; the other 1030
on foot, in hand-to-hand combat. And Agis
the Lycian rode up, too; but Valerus,
one worthy of his tough ancestors, kills him.
Then Thronius is slain by Salius,
and Salius is slaughtered by Nealces,   1035
he famous for his javelin and for
far-ranging arrows that come on by stealth.

And now the heavy hand of Mars gave grief
and death to both alike; the armies were,
both conquerors and conquered, each in turn   1040
killing and being killed. And neither side
knew what was flight. The gods inside Jove's palace
take pity on both armies' pointless anger;
they sorrow at the trials of mortal men.
Here Venus watches; there, against her, Juno;   1045
and pale Tisiphone storms through those thousands.

But now Mezentius wheels across the field,
a whirlwind, brandishing his giant shaft.
Even as great Orion when he strides
on foot, cutting a path across the sea's   1050
great deeps, his shoulder taller than the waves;
or when, while carrying an aged ash
from some high mountain, he advances on

the ground, head hidden in the clouds: such was
Mezentius marching in his mammoth armor. 1055

But when Aeneas sees him down the long
line of attack, he hurries on to meet him.
The massive body of Mezentius stands,
unfrightened, steady, and awaiting his
great-hearted enemy; his eyes take measure 1060
of how much space is needed for his spear:
"My own right hand, which is my god, and this
my shaft that I now poise to cast, be gracious:
I vow that you yourself, Lausus, my son,
shall be the living trophy of Aeneas, 1065
dressed in the spoils stripped from that robber's body."
He spoke and hurled his hissing spear from far;
it flies but glances off Aeneas' shield
and strikes, nearby—between the groin and side—
the great Antores, friend of Hercules, 1070
who, sent from Argos, stayed with King Evander
and settled down in an Italian city.
Luckless, he has been laid low by a wound
not meant for him; he looks up at the sky
and, dying, calls to mind his gentle Argos. 1075
And now pious Aeneas casts his lance;
and through the hollow shield of triple brass,
the layers of linen, and the woven work
of three bulls' hides it passed and sank to rest
low in Mezentius' groin; and yet by then 1080
its strength was spent. Aeneas, glad to see
the Tuscan's blood, snatches his sword quickly;
he lifts it from his thigh, and raging, he
now races toward his trembling enemy.
But Lausus, for the love of his dear father, 1085
groaned deep as he saw this; his tears were many.

And here I surely shall not leave untold—
for such a deed can be more readily
believed because it was done long ago—
the trial of your harsh death and gallant acts 1090
and you yourself, young man to be remembered.

Mezentius—helpless, hampered—lumbered off;
the bitter lance trailed from his shield. But Lausus

rushed from the ranks into the press of weapons;
and even as Aeneas raised his right hand   1095
and aimed a blow, he slipped beneath the blade,
deflected it, delayed him. Lausus' comrades
with loud shouts follow him, until his father,
beneath the shelter of his son's shield, can
retreat; they shower shafts, try to drive back   1100
the enemy with lances cast from far.
Aeneas, furious, must still take cover.
Just as, at times, when storm clouds pound with hailstones,
then every plowman, every farmer flees
the fields, and travelers hide in safe retreats   1105
along the riverbanks or else beneath
the cleft of some high rock until the rain
is done and, with the sun returned, they can
complete their day's work: even so Aeneas,
beneath a shower of shafts on every side,   1110
endures the cloud of war until its thunder
is past; and he taunts Lausus, menacing:
"Why are you rushing to sure death? Why dare
things that are past your strength? Your loyalty
has tricked you into recklessness." And yet   1115
the youth is wild and will not stop; at this,
harsh anger rises in the Dardan chief;
the Fates draw the last thread of Lausus' life.
Right through the belly of the youth Aeneas
now plunges his tough sword until it hides   1120
hilt-high. The blade passed through the shield, too thin
for one who was so threatening, and through
the tunic Lausus' mother spun for him
of supple gold. His chest was filled with blood;
across the air his melancholy life   1125
passed on into the Shades and left his body.
But when he saw the look and face of dying
Lausus—he was mysteriously pale—
Anchises' son sighed heavily with pity
and stretched out his right hand; the image of   1130
his love for his own father touched his mind.
"Poor boy, for such an act what can the pious
Aeneas give to match so bright a nature?
Keep as your own the arms that made you glad;
and to the Shades and ashes of your parents   1135
I give you back—if Shades still care for that.

But, luckless, you can be consoled by this:
You fall beneath the hand of great Aeneas."
He even calls the hesitating comrades
of Lausus, and he lifts the body off   1140
the ground, where blood defiled the handsome hair.

Meanwhile, along the Tiber's banks, Mezentius
had stanched his wounds with water while he rested,
his body propped against a tree. Nearby
his brazen helmet dangles from the branches,   1145
his heavy armor lies along the grass.
His chosen youths surround him; sick and panting,
he eases back his neck; his flowing beard
spreads out across his chest. He often asks
for Lausus, sending messengers again,   1150
again to fetch him, bring him the commands
of his sad father. But the tearful comrades
of Lausus then were carrying him, lifeless,
upon his shield, a giant corpse undone
by giant wounds. And yet Mezentius' mind,   1155
foreknowing, recognized their moans from far.
He fouls his white hair with the filth of dust
and stretches both his hands to heaven, then,
as he clings to the corpse, cries out: "My son,
was I held fast by such delight in life   1160
that I let my own seed—instead of me—
give way before an enemy's right hand?
Am I, a father, saved by these your wounds?
Do I live by your death? For now at last
I understand the misery of exile,   1165
and now at last my wound is driven deep.
More, I myself have stained your name, my son,
with sins; for I was banished—hated—from
the throne and royal power of my fathers.
I owed my homeland and my angry people   1170
their right revenge; I should have given up
this guilty life to death from every side.
But I still live, have still not left the light
of day, the land of men. But I shall leave them."
With this, he rises on his crippled thigh,   1175
and though that deep wound slows his force, Mezentius,
unshaken, asks them to lead out his horse.
This was his pride and comfort; from all wars

it carried him away, victorious.
He turns to that sad beast. These are his words: 1180
"Rhoebus, we have lived long, if anything
that mortals have is long. This day you will
return, a victor, with Aeneas' head
and bloody spoils and take revenge with me
for Lausus' sufferings; or if no power   1185
will let us take that way, then you will fall
together with me—I do not believe
that you, brave beast, would ever stand a stranger's
commands, or take a Trojan as your master."
This said, he mounted Rhoebus; and he settled   1190
his limbs in that familiar saddle, loaded
each hand with a sharp javelin; his head
was gleaming with his brazen helmet and
was shaggy with a horsehair crest. And thus
he made his swift way back into the battle.   1195
In that one heart there burn at once Mezentius'
tremendous shame and madness mixed with sorrow.

And now he called three times upon Aeneas
with his great voice. Aeneas recognizes
the challenge, and he prays with joy: "So may   1200
the father of the gods allow it, so
may high Apollo! You be first to strike!"
This said, the Trojan moves against Mezentius
with lance and menace. But Mezentius answers:
"You, savage one, why try to frighten me   1205
now that my son is torn away? That was
the only way to ruin me. For I
do not fear death or care for any god.
Enough; I come to die. But first I bring
these gifts to you." He spoke, then cast a shaft   1210
and then another and another, wheeling
around the battlefield in a great ring;
Aeneas' golden shield deflects them all.
Three times Mezentius, riding to his left,
has hurled his javelins, circling around Aeneas,   1215
who stands in readiness. Three times the Trojan
hero has turned with him; upon his shield
of bronze he bears a giant grove of shafts.
Then, tired of long delays and tired of tearing
the javelins from his shield, and very pressed   1220

by such unequal contest—now at last,
Aeneas, having thought of many ways,
breaks out; he springs and hurls his spear between
the hollow temples of the warrior horse.
The beast rears bolt upright; he flails the air   1225
with his forehoofs, then topples down upon
the fallen rider and entangles him;
then crumples forward, shoulder out of joint.
The Trojans and the Latins with their shouts
set fire to the skies. Aeneas rushes,   1230
draws out his sword, and cries this over him:
"Where now is brave Mezentius, and where is
his ruthless force of mind?" The Tuscan drank
the air and watched the sky and came to life
and then replied: "My bitter enemy,   1235
why do you taunt and threaten me? There is
no crime in killing me; I did not come
to war with any thought of quarter, nor
did Lausus ever draw such terms with you.
I ask you only this: if any grace   1240
is given to the vanquished, let my body
be laid in earth. I know my people's harsh
hatred that hems me in. I beg of you
to save me from their fury, let me be
companion to my son within the tomb."   1245
So says Mezentius; then, with full awareness,
he gives his throat up to the sword and pours
his life in waves of blood across his armor.

XI·116

BOOK XI

MEANWHILE AURORA ROSE; she left the Ocean.
Aeneas—anxious though he is to give
his comrades rapid burial, and though
his mind is much distressed by Pallas' death—
first pays the gods a victor's vows beneath   5
the morning star. He hacks the branches off
a massive oak, around all sides, then plants it
upon a mound of earth; this tree he dresses
in glittering arms, the spoils of chief Mezentius—
a trophy meant for you, great God of War.   10
To this Aeneas fastens helmet crests
dripping with blood, the warrior's shattered shafts,
the breastplate smashed and pierced through twice-six times;
upon the left he ties the shield of brass
and hangs the ivory scabbard from the neck.   15
Then he spurs on triumphant comrades, all
the crowding company of his commanders:

"Men, we have done great things; for what is left,
away with fear! These are the spoils, first fruits
of war, from a proud king; here is Mezentius,   20
made by my hands. And now our way lies toward
the Latin king and walls. Prepare your weapons

with good hearts, look with hope to battle, so
that when the High Ones let us lift our standards
and march our legions out from camp, there be   25
no fear to make us falter in our purpose
and no delay to take us by surprise.
Meanwhile let us entrust to earth our comrades'
unburied bodies: this, the only glory
deep Acheron can know." And then he adds: 30
"Go honor with our final tribute those
bright souls who, with their blood, have won for us
this homeland. First let Pallas be sent back
to the sad city of Evander: one
whose courage was not wanting, whom the black   35
day swept away and plunged in bitter death."

These words Aeneas says and weeps, then turns
back toward his threshold, where the lifeless body
of Pallas is watched over by the old
Acoetes: he was once the armor-bearer   40
of King Evander, in Arcadian days;
now he had come, assigned as a companion
to Pallas, his beloved foster son,
beneath less happy auspices. And all
were gathered around the body, both the band   45
of servants and the Trojan crowd, together
with mourning Ilian women, hair disheveled
as was their custom. When Aeneas entered
the high doorway, they beat their breasts and raised
a great groan to the stars; the royal tent   50
was loud with lamentation. When he saw
the pillowed head of Pallas, his white face,
and the Ausonian spearhead's yawning wound
in his smooth chest, Aeneas speaks with tears:
"Poor boy, when Fortune came with happiness,   55
was she so envious as to grudge me this:
not let you live to see my kingdom or
return in triumph to your father's city?
For this was not the promise that I gave
Evander when I left with his embrace,   60
when he sent me to win a mighty empire,
when he warned me, in fear, that I should meet
men harsh in battle and a sturdy race.
And even now, beguiled by empty hopes,

perhaps Evander makes his vows and heaps   65
his gifts upon the altar stone; while we,
grieving, accompany the lifeless youth
who now owes nothing to the gods, although
we pay him useless honors. Luckless father,
you are to see your own son's funeral.   70
Is this our coming back, the victory
that we expected? This, the solemn trust
Evander placed in me? Yet you will not
see your own son cut down by coward's wounds
or, as a father, call for death because   75
your Pallas had been saved disgracefully.
Ausonia, what a great shield you have lost,
and, Iülus, what a great defender is gone!"
So he lamented; then he orders them
to carry off the sad corpse, and he sends   80
a thousand men, chosen from all the ranks,
as presences at the last rites, to share
a father's tears: small consolation for
so vast a grief, yet owed to poor Evander.
And others quickly wrap the pliant bier   85
of wickerwork in shoots of wild arbutus
and twigs of oak; they shade the high-piled couch
beneath a canopy of leaves. They set
the soldier high upon his rustic bed:
just as a flower of gentle violet   90
or drooping hyacinth a girl has gathered;
its brightness and its form have not yet passed,
but mother earth no longer feeds it or
supplies its strength. And then Aeneas brought
twin tunics, stiff with gold and purple, which   95
Sidonian Dido, glad in that task, had
once made for him with her own hands, weaving
thin gold into the web. Sadly he wraps
one of these tunics around the youth, his last
honor; with it Aeneas veils the hair   100
soon to be burned. Beside it he piles up
great trophies of the encounter with the Latins
and orders spoils brought out in long array,
then adds the horses and the lances Pallas
had stripped from enemies. Aeneas had   105
the hands of captives bound behind their backs,
to send them down as offerings to the Shades,

to sprinkle altar flames with slaughtered blood.
He has the chiefs themselves bring tree trunks dressed
in Latin arms; to each trunk is attached   110
an enemy's name. The sad Acoetes, worn
by years, is led along, disfiguring
his chest with fists, his face with nails; and as
he goes, he throws himself to earth headlong.
They lead out chariots bathed in Latin blood.   115
Next, Aethon, Pallas' warhorse, weeping, comes,
his trappings laid aside, his muzzle wet
with heavy tears. And others carry Pallas'
spear and his helmet; Turnus, in his triumph,
has kept the other arms. The mourning band   120
of Teucrian and Tuscan captains and
Arcadians, with arms inverted, follow.
When that long file of comrades had advanced,
Aeneas halted; sighing deeply, he said:
"The same black fate of war calls me from this   125
to other griefs. I hail you now forever,
great Pallas; and forever, my farewell."
Aeneas said no more; but turning toward
the high walls, made his way back to the camp.

Now from the Latin city envoys came,   130
shaded with olive branches, asking grace:
they beg Aeneas for the bodies scattered
by sword across the plain, to bury them
in mounds of earth. One cannot war, they plead,
against the dead or the defeated; let him   135
spare men who once had welcomed him, the kinsmen
of his own bride-to-be. And good Aeneas—
to those who ask what cannot be denied—
replies with kindness, and he adds these words:
"Latins, what shameful fate so tangled you   140
in such a war that now you fly from us,
who are your friends? You seek peace for the dead
and those cut down beneath the chance of battle?
But I would give that to the living, too.
I should not be here if the fates had not   145
made this my home and place. I do not war
against your nation. But your king abandoned
our friendship; he preferred to trust himself
to Turnus' sword. It would have been more just

had Turnus risked the death that took your comrades.   150
If he intends to end this war by force—
to drive the Trojans out—why, then, he should
have faced me here with arms. One of us would
have lived: that one to whom the gods or else
his own right hand had given life. Now go,   155
light fires beneath your luckless countrymen."

So said Aeneas; and they stood amazed
and silent, searching out each other's eyes.
But then the aged Drances, one who hated
young Turnus with a festering bitterness,   160
replies: "O Trojan, great in glory but
far greater still in battle, how can my
words praise you heaven-high? Shall I admire
your justice first, or else your work in war?
But, grateful, we shall carry what you have said   165
back to our native city; and if fortune
helps us, then we shall join you to Latinus.
Let Turnus seek out treaties for himself.
And more, we even shall be glad to raise
your massive walls decreed by fate, to carry   170
the stones of Ilium upon our shoulders."
All murmured their assent as with one voice.
They settled on a truce of twice-six days;
and with that peace between them, Teucrians
and Latins roamed together, safe, across   175
the mountain forests. Tall ash trees ring out
beneath the pounding of the two-edged ax;
pines high as stars are toppled; wedges split,
without a stop, the oak and scented cedar;
the hauling wagons groan with funeral timbers.   180

Now Rumor, first to tell of such a sorrow,
races to King Evander, filling all
his house and city—she who, just before,
had told of Pallas' triumphs in the war.
As was their ancient custom, the Arcadians   185
snatch up their funeral firebrands and rush
beyond the city gates. The roadway gleams
with a long line of flames that, on each side,
light up the fields. As they approach, the Phrygian
troops join the mourning crowd. And when the matrons 190

can see them drawing near their homes, their wailing
sets fire to that sad city. But no one
can keep Evander back; he hurries on
into the middle of the throng. The bier
set down, he falls on Pallas, clinging and   195
weeping and keening; he can hardly force
a passage through his sorrow for his voice:

"O Pallas, this was not the pledge you gave
your father, to commit yourself with more
caution to cruel Mars. I might have known   200
how much new fame in arms can do, how very
sweet is the glory of the first encounter.
O sad first fruits of youth, harsh rudiments
of war that was so near! No god would hear
my vows and prayers! And you, most holy wife,   205
were happy in your death, and not spared for
this pain. But I, in living, have undone
the fate of fathers: I survive my son.
Would I had joined the troops of Troy, had been
crushed by the Latin shafts. I would have given   210
my life: this pomp would then bring me, not Pallas,
home. But I cannot blame you, Trojans, or
our treaties or the right hands we have joined
in friendship, for this was the chance assigned
to my old age. But if untimely death   215
was waiting for my son, then I am glad
he fell while leading on the Teucrians
to Latium, and only after he
had cut down thousands of the Volscians' army.
No, Pallas, I could never honor you   220
with greater funerals than have the pious
Aeneas and the mighty Phrygians and
the Tuscan chieftains, all the Tuscan squadrons.
They carry splendid trophies: those who took
their death from you. You, Turnus, also would   225
have stood now as a giant trunk in arms,
had you been of the same age as my son,
had his same force of years! But why do I,
unhappy, keep the Teucrians from battle?
Go, and be sure to give your king this message: 230
that if I drag along my hated life
though Pallas now is dead, it is because

of your right hand—which, as you see, still owes
Turnus to father and to son. This is
the only thing that still is left undone   235
by your own worth and fortune. I do not
implore this joy of you for my own life—
that would be wrong—but that I may yet carry
these tidings to my son in the deep Shades."

Meanwhile Aurora showed her gracious light   240
to miserable mortals, bringing back
their work and tasks. And now father Aeneas,
now Tarchon, raised the pyres for funerals
along the winding shore. There Trojans, Tuscans,
Arcadians—each following his fathers'   245
old customs—brought their dead; the dark fires set,
the black smoke hides steep skies. Three times they marched
around the burning pyres in gleaming armor;
three times the horsemen circled death's sad fires,
their voices wailing. Tears stream on the ground,   250
tears stream across their weapons. Cries of men,
the blasts of trumpets climb as high as heaven.
Now some of them fling spoils into the flames,
stripped from the slaughtered Latins—helmets, bridles,
and handsome swords and glowing chariot wheels;   255
and then the gifts of these familiar arms—
the dead men's own, their shields and luckless shafts.
And many bullocks' bodies lie about
in sacrifice to death; and bristling swine
and sheep are seized from all the countryside   260
and butchered on those fires. Down that long beach
men watch their comrades burning and keep guard
beside the smoldering piles; they cannot tear
themselves away until the damp night wheels
through heavens studded with the glittering stars.   265

Elsewhere, and no less zealous, the sad Latins
raised high their countless pyres. Though many bodies
are buried on the spot and some sent off
to neighboring towns and some into the city,
the rest are burned, a giant heap of tangled   270
butchery without number, without honor;
and all of that wide countryside is bright
with rival, crowded fires. And when the third

morning had exiled cold shadows from heaven,
the Latins sadly swept into a heap   275
the bones and ashes mingled in the remnants
of fire and piled on earth still warm with embers.
But now the loudest keening, greatest grief
are in the houses, in the city of
the rich Latinus. Here the mothers and   280
their sons' poor wives, the loving breasts of sisters
in mourning, boys deprived of fathers curse
the dreadful war, the wedding rites of Turnus.
They cry that he himself, and only he,
should risk the war's result by arms and sword,   285
since it is he who asks for Italy's
kingdom and for first honors for himself.
Ferocious Drances weights his accusations;
he testifies that Turnus is the only
one whom Aeneas calls upon, the only   290
one whom he wants to battle. But against him
are many who speak up in different ways
for Turnus; he is sheltered by the queen's
great name, his fame, the trophies he has won.

But in the middle of this heated brawl,   295
this angry fracas, the ambassadors
come back from Diomedes' city; sadly
they carry this reply: that all their work
has gone for nothing; gifts were of no help,
nor gold, nor their entreaties; Latium   300
must seek out other arms or else must sue
the Trojan chief for peace. And even King
Latinus sinks beneath his grief. The anger
of gods, the newmade graves that he can see—
all these serve as a warning that Aeneas   305
is called by fate, the will of gods is clear.
Therefore Latinus calls a solemn council
of chiefs, who are to meet in his high palace.
And there they all converge through crowded streets.
Latinus, eldest and the first in power,   310
sits at the center; now he asks the envoys
who have just returned from the Aetolian city
to tell their tidings, setting out the answers
that Diomedes sent, complete, in order.
Then every tongue is still. As King Latinus   315

has asked, so Venulus reports to him:

"O citizens, we have seen Diomedes
and his Greek settlement, have made our way
through every trial, have touched the hand by which
the land of Ilium fell. We saw him building   320
a city called, after his father's race,
Argyripa, set near Garganus' hills,
among Iapygian fields that he had conquered.
When we had entered and received his leave
to speak, we offered first our gifts, announced   325
our name and country, told him who had come
to war against us, what brought us to Arpi.
He heard, and then he answered us serenely:

" 'O happy people, sons of Saturn's kingdom
and old Ausonia, what fortune stirs   330
your quiet state, what lures you to incite
uncertain war? All we who violated
the fields of Ilium by sword—I do not
speak of the suffering that ground us down
in fighting under those high walls, the men   335
whom Simois swept up—we have endured
tortures across the globe, such penalties
of crime as never can be told; even
Priam might well take pity on our band.
Minerva's evil star; Euboean cliffs;   340
Caphereus, the avenger—they know this.
For driven from that war to other shores,
the son of Atreus, Menelaus, went
as far as Proteus' pillars in his exile;
Ulysses set his eyes upon the Cyclops   345
of Etna! Shall I tell you of the kingdoms
of Neoptolemus? Of household gods
lost by Idomeneus? Of Locrians
on Libya's coast? And even the Mycenean,
the leader of the great Achaeans, was   350
cut down, and just beyond his threshold, by
the right hand of his execrable wife;
after he had conquered Asia, an adulterer
still lay in wait for him. And for myself,
surely the gods need not have grudged me this: 355
return to my own homeland's altars, my

beloved wife and lovely Calydon!
And even now dark omens hunt me down:
I see my lost companions seek the air
on wings or wandering about the streams   360
as birds—a fearful torment for my comrades;
they fill the crags with tearful cries. And this,
this is the fate that waits for me since when,
insane, I raised my sword against the bodies
of gods and violated with a wound   365
the hand of Venus. No, do not, do not
provoke me into such a battle! More:
since Troy is fallen now, I have no quarrel
with Teucrians; and I do not recall
with joy the old trials of that war. Take back   370
the gifts you bring me from your native shores
and give them to Aeneas. We have stood
against his cruel lances, we have fought
against his troops. Listen to me, believe
one who has tried him: how he lifts his shield   375
and how he casts his lance just like a whirlwind.
Had Ida's land borne two more just like him,
the Trojans would have even reached the towns
of Inachus; her fates reversed, Greece would
have mourned. In all that long delay before   380
Troy's sturdy walls it was Aeneas' hand,
and Hector's, that kept back the Greeks, that checked
their victory until nine years had passed.
Both were remarkable for courage, both
excelled in arms; but first in piety,   385
Aeneas. Join your hands to him in treaty
as best you can. Beware of setting arms
against his arms.' Best king of kings, Latinus,
you have heard what Diomedes answered, what
advice he gave to us on our great war."   390

No sooner were the envoys done than murmurs,
conflicting, ran along the anxious lips
of the Ausonians: just as, when boulders
have slowed a racing river, then the stifled
flood roars, the pounding waters sound against   395
the neighboring banks. But when their spirits calmed,
their troubled tongues fell still, the king first called
upon the gods, then from his high throne said:

"O Latins, how I wish we could have settled
this mighty matter earlier: that would   400
have been far better than debating now
with Trojans at our walls. My citizens,
we wage a luckless war against a nation
of gods, unconquered men; no battle can
exhaust them; if defeated, they do not   405
give up the sword. If you had any hope
of help from the Aetolians, forget it:
each must be his own hope, but now you know
how poor a thing that is. And for the rest,
you all can see and touch what has destroyed us.   410
I am not blaming you: whatever courage
could do, is done; we have fought with all the force
our kingdom has. Now listen; in few words
I shall reveal, if you will pause, what course
seems justified in my uncertain mind.   415
I have an ancient territory near
the Tuscan river, stretching westward even
beyond the bounds of the Sicanians.
Auruncans and Rutulians now till
those fields; their plowshares work the stubborn hills;   420
they use the harshest slopes for pasturing.
Let all this region, with its mountain ridges
of pines, pass to the Teucrians in friendship;
and let us strike an equal treaty with them,
invite them as allies to share our kingdom.   425
And they can settle there, if that is what
they think worthwhile, and build their towns. But if
they long for other boundaries, another
nation, if they are free to leave our soil,
then let us build out of Italian oak   430
twice-ten ships for the Trojans—even more,
if they can fill them. All the wood we need
now lies, already hewn, along the shore;
and they can tell us both the size and number
of galleys they require; and we shall furnish   435
the brass and labor and their naval gear.
And in addition I should have this message
brought to them by a hundred Latin envoys,
men chosen from our nobles, to confirm
this treaty. They must carry with them gifts   440
of ivory, golden talents, and my chair

and robe—the emblems of my sovereignty.
Now counsel frankly, help our troubled state."

Then Drances, just as spiteful as before,
spurred by the stings of his insidious envy   445
of Turnus' glory; Drances, who was lavish
with wealth and even more with words (his hands
too cold for war); Drances, a mighty counselor
and man of faction, on his mother's side
of noble birth, but low-born on his father's—   450
rises and, taunting, heaps resentment high:
"Good king, you ask for counsel about things
that are not hid from anyone, that need
no words of ours. For all confess they know
the way our people's fortune has to go,   455
and yet they hesitate to speak aloud.
Just let him grant us liberty to speak,
relax his arrogance; his stubborn ways
and his unhappy auspices (yes, I
shall speak, although he menace me with arms   460
and death) have led to ruin for so many
bright chieftains, a whole city sunk in mourning,
while he, when sure of flight, provokes the Trojans'
camp, frightening the heavens with his weapons.
Add one more thing, o best of kings, just one   465
to those great gifts that you would send the Trojans:
do not let violence by any man
prevent you, as a father can, from giving
your daughter to a famous son-in-law
in worthy wedding that would seal this peace   470
by an eternal pact. But if our minds
and our hearts are so afraid, let us beseech
Turnus, and beg his favor, that he may
give way, forego his own right for the sake
of king and homeland. Why have you so often   475
driven your luckless countrymen to open
dangers: you who are source and cause of all
these trials of Latium? There is no safety
in war. What all of us are asking you,
Turnus, is peace—peace and the only thing   480
that is the inviolable pledge of peace.
Look, I shall be the first to ask you this
(I whom you hold to be your enemy;

that does not matter to me): pity us,
your fellow citizens; put off your pride   485
and, beaten, leave the field. We have seen enough
of death in our defeat, enough broad lands
stripped of their husbandmen. Or if you are moved
by glory and your heart is stout enough
or you are set upon a dowry palace,   490
then dare and, in your confidence, commit
your breast against the enemy. That Turnus
may find his royal bride, shall we, sad souls,
lie headlong on the battlefield, a rabble
unburied and unwept? Now you: if any   495
force is in you, or any of your fathers'
old fight, go out to face your challenger!"

At this the violence of Turnus blazes;
he groans; this voice explodes from his deep chest:
"O Drances, you are always rich in words,   500
even when war has asked for swords; and when
the elders are assembled, you are first.
There is no need to fill the senate house
with speeches, all the blustering that you
let fly in safety, while the enemy   505
is still beyond the battlements and no
blood floods our trenches. Therefore, Drances, thunder
eloquently—as you always do—
accusing me of fear, since your right hand
has made so many heaps of slaughtered Trojans,   510
and everywhere your trophies mark the fields.
Now you can try what lively courage can;
you need not seek our enemies far off,
for they surround us on all sides. Shall we
go out to meet them? Why do you draw back?   515
Will Mars be always in your windy tongue
and in your flying feet? Have I been beaten?
Will anyone, you faithless liar, rightly
call me defeated, who can see the swollen
Tiber rising with the blood of Ilium   520
and all Evander's house and race in ruin
and his Arcadians stripped of arms? Not so
did Bitias and giant Pandarus
know me, not so the thousand men whom I—
a victor—sent to Tartarus in just   525

one day, though I was shut within their ramparts,
hemmed in by hostile walls. 'There is no safety
in war.' Madman, you tell that to the Dardan
chieftain and to yourself! But go ahead,
confusing everything with panic, praising   530
the strength of those who are twice-beaten, while
you hold Latinus' arms in check. To hear you,
even the captains of the Myrmidons
now shudder at the Phrygians' weapons, even
the son of Tydeus, even the Larissan   535
Achilles; and the flow of Aufidus
flies backward from the Adriatic's waves.
Just hear his sneaking cunning when he feigns
himself as trembling at my menaces,
embittering his calumny with terror.   540
But do not be afraid: a life like yours
will not be taken by me; it is yours,
and let it keep its home within your breast.

"And now, my father, I return to you
and to the crucial matters of this council.   545
If you have lost all hope in Latin arms,
if we are so abandoned—so undone
by one repulse—that fortune cannot change,
then let us plead for peace, stretch out our hands,
defenseless. But if something still remains   550
of our old courage, then I should consider
him happy in his trials and best of souls
who—to avoid the sight of such a peace—
would fall in death and gnaw the dust once and
for all. But if, instead, our wealth and youth   555
are yet intact, if Latin towns and peoples
can still support us, if the Trojans bought
their glory with much blood (they, too, have their
own deaths; the storm of war swept all alike),
why falter in dishonor at the threshold?   560
Why, then, this terror at the trumpet's blast?
Time and the varied work of turning years
have mended many things; for transient fortune
has first mocked many men but, come again,
has then restored them to the solid ground.   565
The Aetolian and his Arpi will not help us;

we have Messapus and Tolumnius,
the lucky augur, and the captains sent
by many peoples; no small glory follows
the chosen warriors of Laurentian fields   570
and Latium; there is Camilla, come
from the illustrious Volscians, with her horsemen
and squadrons glittering with brass. But if
the Trojans call for me in single combat,
and that is what you want, and only I   575
impede the good of all, then victory
has not fled from my hands or hated them
so much that I should turn away from any
trial offering such hope. I shall go bold
against Aeneas, even though he be   580
tremendous as Achilles, though he wear
like armor, made for him by Vulcan's hands.
To you, the Latin elders and Latinus,
the father of my bride, I, Turnus, second
to no one of our ancestors in courage,   585
have dedicated this my life. They say
Aeneas calls on me alone; I pray
that he may call. Do not let Drances fight
instead of me, if either heaven's wrath
is turned against us and demands a death   590
or there is glory to be gained by courage."

This was their quarrel at that time of crisis.
Meanwhile Aeneas marched his troops from camp
into the field. A racing messenger
now clatters through the royal palace, setting   595
the city in alarm, announcing troops
of Troy and Tuscany descending from
the Tiber's banks across the plains. At once
confusion takes the Latins, all the crowd
is stung, their anger spurred by provocations   600
that are not trivial. They quickly ask
for arms: the young men clamoring for weapons,
the fathers, sad and mournful, muttering.
And now dissension riots through the air
from every side: even as when a flock   605
of birds has settled down in some high grove
or when, along Padusa thronged with fish,

hoarse swans are loud among loquacious pools.

And Turnus takes advantage of this moment.
"Yes, citizens, by all means call a council   610
and sit here praising peace while they take arms
against our kingdom." He had had enough
of words and quickly left the high-roofed palace.
"You, Volusus," he calls out, "you command
the Volscian bands to arm, bring the Rutulians!   615
Messapus, you, and Coras, with your brother,
see that armed horsemen spread across the plains.
Some reinforce the city guards, some watch
the towers, and the rest shall follow me."

Now all the city hurries to the walls   620
straightway. Dismayed by that disaster, father
Latinus leaves the council. He postpones
his formidable plans; he blames himself
again, again, because he had not welcomed
Dardan Aeneas, taken him as son   625
into the city. Some of them dig trenches
before the gates or heave up stones and stakes;
the raucous trumpet sounds the bloody signal
for battle. Boys and women, in a motley
circle, are ranged along the walls, the final   630
crisis calls all. And Queen Amata, too,
with many women, bearing gifts, is carried
into the citadel, Minerva's temple
upon the heights; at her side walks the girl
Lavinia, the cause of all that trouble,   635
her lovely eyes held low. The women follow;
and they perfume the altars with the smoke
of incense, and their voices of lament
pour from the shrine's high threshold: "Powerful
in battle, Queen of War, Tritonian virgin,   640
let your hands crack the Trojan robber's shafts;
cast him headlong beneath our tall gateways."

Turnus, as quick as any, girds himself
for battle; he puts on his red-gold breastplate
and bristles with its scales of brass; he wraps   645
his legs in greaves of gold. His temples still
are bare, his sword is fastened to his side;

gleaming with gold, he hurries from the high
fortress. He is delirious with courage,
his hope already tears the enemy: 650
just as a stallion when he snaps his tether
and flies off from the stables, free at last
to lord the open plains, will either make
for meadows and the herds of mares or else
leap from the stream where he is used to bathing   655
and, wanton, happy, neigh, his head raised high,
while his mane sweeps across his neck and shoulders.

Camilla, with her Volscians, rode to meet him.
The queen leaped from her horse beside the gates;
and just as she did, all her troops dismounted,   660
gliding to earth. Then she says: "Turnus, if
the brave deserve to trust in their own selves,
why, then I dare and promise to oppose
Aeneas' squadrons, to ride out alone
against the Tuscan horse. Let me try war's   665
first dangers; Turnus, you can man the walls
with infantry and shield the city." He,
with eyes set on the awesome girl: "O virgin,
you, pride of Italy, what thanks can I
prepare in word or act; but since you are   670
above all praise or prize, then share the trial
with me. Our scouts confirm this rumor: shameless
Aeneas has sent on his light-armed horse
to shake the plains while he makes for the city
across the rugged mountain wilderness.   675
But I shall lay this stratagem along
a sloping path within the woods; I shall
besiege him from both jaws of the defile.
And meanwhile you shall meet the Tuscan horsemen
head on; together with you, I assign   680
Messapus, Latin troops, Tiburtus' squadron,
and you shall be their chieftain." After this,
and with like words, Turnus encourages
Messapus and the other allied captains;
then he himself moves out to face Aeneas.   685

There is a winding valley that is just
fit for the traps and the deceits of war,
confined by dark, dense leaves on either side.

It can be reached along a narrow path,
a tight gorge, and a scanty entryway.   690
Among the lookouts on the mountaintop
above lie secret plains and safe retreats;
from these, from left or right, one can rush down
against the enemy or stand upon
the ridge and roll great boulders at him. Here   695
young Turnus follows a familiar road;
he sets an ambush in the dangerous wood.

Meanwhile in heaven's house the melancholy
Diana, daughter of Latona, turned
to one of her companion virgins, swift   700
Opis, a member of her holy band:
"O nymph, Camilla goes to cruel war
and wears in vain our armor—she who is
more dear to me than any other, for
the love Diana feels for her is not   705
new; I have not been touched by sudden fondness.
Years since, because his people hated him
for his arrogant tyranny, King Metabus
was driven from his kingdom and Privernum's
old city; as he hurried from the battle,   710
in flight he took his infant daughter with him
as comrade in his exile; and he called her
Camilla for her mother's name, Casmilla,
but slightly altered. And he carried her
clutched to his breast while traveling across   715
long ridges, through the solitary forest;
on all sides savage lances pressed against him;
far-ranging Volscian soldiers hemmed him in.
And as he fled, the river Amasenus
in flood had foamed across its highest banks—   720
so fierce a storm had burst out of the clouds.
As Metabus prepares to swim across,
his fondness for his daughter holds him back,
his fears for that dear burden. Suddenly,
and yet reluctantly, he came to this   725
resolve: he happened then to have a giant
lance in his sturdy hand, well knotted, tough,
of seasoned oak; to this he binds his daughter,
well wrapped in cork-tree bark, and fastens her
neatly around the middle of the shaft.   730

Then poising it in his enormous hand,
he cries to heaven so: 'O generous
Diana, virgin daughter of Latona,
who make your home in groves, I dedicate
this child as your attendant—I, her father: 735
for through the air, a suppliant, she flees
the enemy; and this first weapon she
holds fast is yours. I pray you, goddess, take
her as your own whom I must now entrust
to the uncertain winds.' This said, with arm   740
drawn back, he casts the twisting shaft; although
waves thunder, his Camilla flies across
the racing river on the hissing lance.
Then Metabus, as many troops draw near,
plunges into the torrent; and in triumph,   745
now safe upon the other shore, he plucks
his lance and daughter, offerings to Diana,
up from the grassy turf. No cities took him
within their walls, their houses; he was much
too wild to yield to city ways. He lived   750
the life of shepherds in the lonely mountains.
Here Metabus, among the underbrush
and bristling dens of beasts, would nurse his daughter,
feeding her wild milk from a brood mare's teats;
into her tender lips he squeezed the udder.   755
As she took her first steps, he placed a pointed
lance head within her hand, and from that little
girl's shoulder he made bow and quiver hang.
In place of golden hairbands and long robes,
a tiger skin hangs from her head and down   760
her back. And even then her tender hand
would hurl her childish shafts and whirl about
her head a sling with its smooth thongs and bring
to earth Strymonian cranes or snow-white swans.
And there were many mothers in the towns   765
of Tuscany who wanted her, in vain,
as daughter-in-law. But she is happy with
Diana; intact, she cherishes an endless
love of her arms and of virginity.
I wish this war had not swept her away   770
and tempted her to try the Teucrians;
so would she still be dear to me and one
of my companions. But, since bitter fates

are set on her untimely death—come, nymph,
glide down from heaven, find the Latin boundaries,   775
where this sad fight is fought with luckless omens.
And take my weapons; from my quiver draw
a shaft of vengeance. And whoever would
defile her sacred body with a wound,
whether a Trojan or Italian, let   780
him pay the penalty of blood with this.
Then I will carry in a hollow cloud
the body of the sad Camilla and
her still unplundered weapons, lay her in
a tomb upon her native ground." Diana   785
said this; her quiver clattering, Opis sped
through heaven's light air, wrapped in a black whirlwind.

Meanwhile the Trojan ranks approached the city,
the Tuscan chiefs and all the cavalry
arrayed in companies. Across the plains   790
the prancing horses neigh, fret at the stay
of reins, and swerve to every side; the field
is bristling far and wide with steel of spears
and glittering with arms held high. Against them
Messapus and the dexterous Latins and   795
Coras together with his brother and
virgin Camilla's squadron take the field;
their hands are drawn far back; they couch their lances
and brandish javelins; the rush of men,
the horses' breath grow hot. The armies halted   800
now, each within a spear cast of the other;
but then with sudden shouts they burst ahead,
spurring their eager stallions, showering
on every side their shafts as thick as snow;
the sky is covered by a shadow. At once   805
Tyrrhenus and the fierce Aconteus dash
against each other with their leveled lances;
they are the first to fall with a huge crash;
their chargers race and shatter breast to breast.
Aconteus, hurtled like a thunderbolt   810
or like a stone an engine catapults,
falls far; his life is scattered through the air.

At this the lines are broken; and the Latins,
now routed, sling their shields around and turn

their horses toward the city. But the Trojans,   815
led by Asilas, gallop after them;
and they were almost at the gates when once
again the Latins raise a shout and slew
around their stallions' supple necks. The Trojans
flee; and as they retreat, their reins fall slack: 820
as when, with thrust and tug of surf, the sea
now charges at the land and, foaming, casts
its breakers at the crags and bathes the farthest
sands with its winding waves; now, swift, recedes
and sucks the churning stones within its surge   825
and leaves the beach, glides back across the shoals.
Twice had the Tuscans turned the Latins toward
the walls; and twice, repulsed, the Tuscans look
back as they sling their covering shields around.
But in the third encounter all the troops   830
are tangled with each other, man to man;
and then indeed the groans of dying ones,
of wounded horses, butchered men rise up;
the bodies, weapons mingle in deep blood;
the fight is brutal. There Orsilochus   835
let fly a lance against the charger ridden
by Remulus (Orsilochus did not
dare to face Remulus himself); he left
his steel beneath its ear. And, furious
at this, the stallion reared, kicked high its legs,   840
impatient of the wound; it thrust its chest
back, casting Remulus flat on the ground.
Catillus kills Iollas and Herminius—
he, giant-hearted and a giant in
his body and his weapons; tawny hair   845
flows down his bare head, and his shoulders, too,
are bare; he has no fear of wounds; so much
of him is naked to the enemy.
The lance head shudders through his massive arms
and, as it pierces, doubles him with pain.   850
On every side the black blood pours; they fight,
and each of them gives death by steel and seeks
the wounds that will bring honorable death.

But at the center of the struggle, like
an Amazon, one breast laid bare for battle,   855
Camilla with her quiver charges, wild;

and now she showers stout spearheads, and now
untiring, she takes up a two-edged ax;
the golden bow and arrows of Diana
clang, loud upon her shoulders. Even when　　　　860
she has been driven back, she turns to cast
her flying shafts; she is ringed by chosen comrades—
virgin Larina, Tulla, and Tarpeia,
who brandishes a brazen ax, all three,
Italian girls, whom the divine Camilla　　　　865
herself had picked to serve as guard of honor
and true attendants in both peace and war:
a band just like the Thracian Amazons
when they ride hard upon Thermodon's shores
and fight in gilded armor, whether around　　　　870
Hippolyte, or when Penthesilea,
Mars' daughter, in her chariot, returns,
a victor, and with shrill and shrieking clamor
her women troops run wild with half-moon shields.

Who was the first and who the last to fall,　　　　875
fierce virgin, by your shaft? How many bodies
did you stretch, dying, headlong on the ground?
The first: Euneus, son of Clytius,
whose bare chest, as he faced her, she impaled
on her long fir-wood lance. He vomits streams　　　　880
of blood and, falling, bites the gory ground
and, dying, writhes in pain upon his wound.
Then she cuts Liris down and Pagasus
above him: for while one, thrown off, tugs at
the reins of his stabbed horse, the other runs　　　　885
to stay his fall; they tumble over, headlong,
together. And to these she adds Amastrus,
the son of Hippotas, and throws herself
forward, as she aims far at Tereus and
Harpalycus, Demophoön and Chromis;　　　　890
and just as many shafts as she sent twisting
out of her virgin hand, so many were
the Phrygians who fell then. Not too far off
the hunter Ornytus rides up on his
Apulian horse; he is unused to armor;　　　　895
a bullock's hide is draped on his broad shoulders
for battle, and his helmet is a huge
wolf's head with gaping mouth and white-fanged jaws;

his hand holds fast a rustic javelin;
as he rides with the troops' main force, he towers   900
above them by a full head. When Camilla
has overtaken him—done easily,
for he is tangled in that rout—she stabs
him through; her hating heart cries out above him:
"O Tuscan, did you think that you were hunting   905
wild beasts within the woods? The day has come
that, with a woman's weapons, will refute
your nation's threats. Yet this is no small glory
you carry to your fathers' Shades: to have
fallen beneath the spearhead of Camilla."   910

And next she kills Orsilochus and Butes,
enormous-bodied Teucrians. She spears
the mounted Butes in the back, just there,
between his corselet and his helmet, where
his neck is gleaming and upon his left   915
his shield hangs down. She flees Orsilochus
until, pursued in a wide circle, she
has lured him on into a smaller ring,
pursuing her pursuer; rising up,
again, again she drives her stout axhead   920
straight through his armor and his bones, though he
now begs and prays for mercy. Through that cleft
the warm brains splatter down his face. And next
she comes upon the warrior son of Aunus,
who had ridden from the Apennines, one not   925
the least of the Ligurians so long
as fates allow him still to cheat. He halts;
he is amazed to see her suddenly.
And when he knows he cannot flee the fight
or turn the charging queen against another,   930
he tries deception with these cunning words:
"What is so splendid, though you are a woman,
in trusting your brave horse? Let us send off
our means of flight; meet me on even ground
in hand-to-hand combat, if you are certain;   935
make ready for a fight on foot, and soon
you will find out to whom such blustering brings
defeat." He spoke; and furious, burning
with bitterness, she gives up her warhorse
to one of her companions. Now on foot   940

she stands with equal arms, unterrified,
with naked sword and shield without device.
The youth, supposing he has won by fraud,
does not delay but starts to ride away
and turns his bridle back and rushes, goading   945
his swift horse with steel spurs. "Ligurian fool,
puffed up with meaningless presumption, all
your native wiles and guile are pointless; no
deception can restore you now unharmed
to cheating Aunus." So the virgin cries   950
and, hot, with racing feet, outstrips his horse.
She grips his reins and, facing him, she takes
her payment from his hated blood: just as
easily as a hawk, the sacred bird
of Mars, from his steep rock can overtake   955
in flight, high in a cloud, a dove, and then
can clutch her fast within his crooked claws
and disembowel her; from the upper air
her blood and her torn plumage flutter down.

But seated on his throne in high Olympus,   960
the lord of men and gods does not look down
with heedless eyes. The Father rouses Tarchon
the Tuscan to the cruel battle, sharpens
his anger with no gentle goad. And so,
among the slaughter and retreating squadrons,   965
Tarchon rides out and urges on the horsemen;
he calls on each by name, with many shouts,
and rallies beaten ranks to fight: "You Tuscans,
incapable of shame, and always laggard,
what fear, what utter cowardice has taken   970
your hearts? And can a woman drive you off
and smash your ranks? Then what good is the sword?
Why bother brandishing these useless weapons?
But when it comes to love and night-time battles,
or when the curving flute proclaims the dances   975
of Bacchus, then you are not lazy. No:
to wait for feasts and cups upon abundant
tables—yes, that is what you love and live for,
until the augur graciously announces
the sacrifice, until the fattened victim   980
invites you to the deep groves." Saying this,
Tarchon himself, ready to die, spurs his

horse straight into the melee; like a whirlwind
he charges Venulus, an enemy,
and tears him from his charger, grips him fast   985
in his right hand, and tugs him to his breast;
then, riding hard, he bears off Venulus.
A shout goes up to heaven; all the Latins
have turned their eyes to watch as lightning Tarchon
races across the plains with man and weapons.   990
And next he breaks the tip of Venulus'
lance head; he searches out unguarded flesh,
to strike the wound of death. But Venulus
would wrestle with him, forcing Tarchon's grip
back from his throat; he thwarts that violence   995
with violence. As when a tawny eagle,
while flying high, bears off a serpent and,
with feet entwined, his talons clutch; but in
its winding coils the wounded serpent writhes,
its bristling scales grow stiff and, rising up,   1000
it hisses with its mouth; nevertheless,
with his hooked beak, wings beating on the air,
the eagle mauls his thrashing prey: just so
triumphant Tarchon hauls away his victim;
he lugs him from the line of the Tiburtines.   1005

The Tuscans, seeing what their chief has done,
then follow his example, charging on.
And Arruns, fated, stalks around the swift
Camilla with his javelin, trying
to find an easy opening; with cunning,   1010
anticipating all her moves. Wherever
the raging virgin dashes toward the ranks,
there he will track her silently. Wherever
she rides back from the enemy, a victor,
just there he turns his quick reins furtively.   1015
For now he studies this approach, now that,
and circles all the field relentlessly,
his lance, inevitable, quivering.

Chance had it then that in the distance Chloreus,
one dear to Cybele and once her priest,   1020
stood out because of his bright Phrygian armor
while he spurred on his foaming horse: and it
was mantled by a cloth that golden buckles

held fast to scales of brass, a covering
like plumage. He himself was gleaming with   1025
rich foreign purple; from his Lycian bow
he cast Gortynian arrows; on his shoulders
he held a golden quiver, and the seer's
helmet was golden, too; his saffron cloak,
with rustling linen folds, was gathered up   1030
into a knot by yellow gold; his tunic
and oriental leggings had gold thread.
The virgin singled him out in the battle;
and whether she had wanted to hang up
the Trojan arms of Chloreus in the temple   1035
or just to dress herself in captive gold,
she hurried after him, blind to all else,
a huntress. Fearless, with a female's love
of plunder and of spoils, she raged through all
the army. Arruns sees and takes his chance;   1040
from ambush he awakes his lance, and thus
he calls upon the High Ones with his voice:

"Highest of gods, Apollo, guard of sacred
Soracte, whose chief worshipers we are,
for whom we feed the pinewood's burning pile;   1045
for whom, as votaries, we walk upon
so many embers through the fire, trusting
our piety—all-able Father, now
let this disgrace be canceled by our arms.
I do not ask for spoils, nor for a trophy;   1050
I want no booty from the beaten virgin;
for other deeds may win me praise: if only
my blow can fell this brutal plague, I shall
go back to my own city without glory."

Phoebus had heard, and in his heart he answered   1055
half of that prayer; the other half he scattered
to the swift winds. He granted this: that Arruns
should strike Camilla down with sudden death;
but did not grant him safe return to his
illustrious homeland. This last request   1060
the tempests carried to the south winds. Thus,
as Arruns' lance hissed from his hand, all Volscians
turned anxious eyes and minds upon the queen.
But she herself was heedless of the sound,

the rush of wind, the weapon from the air,   1065
until the shaft drove in below her breast,
held fast and drank deep of her virgin blood.
Her comrades, panicked, rush about her, catch
their mistress as she falls. Arruns, above all
astonished and with mingled joy and fear,   1070
flies off. He dares not try his lance again,
or face the virgin's weapons. Even as
a wolf, when he has killed a shepherd or
a giant bullock, will steal off at once,
before the hating shafts can hunt him down,   1075
to hide in the high hills; aware of what
he dared to do, he lets his quivering tail
fall slack and tucks it back beneath his belly
as he makes for the woods; even so Arruns,
uneasy, sneaks away; glad to escape,   1080
he mingles in the mob of troops. Dying,
Camilla tries to tug the lance out with
her hand; but its steel head holds fast her bones
within the ribs in that deep wound. She falls,
bloodless; her eyes are faltering, chill in death;   1085
her color, once so bright, has left her face.
As her breath fails, she turns to Acca—one
true to Camilla more than to all else,
the equal of Camilla in her years
and only sharer of Camilla's cares—   1090
and says: "My sister Acca, until this
I still could fight; but now the bitter wound
has ruined me; all things around are black
with shadows. Go and bear my last commands
to Turnus; let him take my place and drive   1095
the Trojans from the city gates; farewell."
She dropped the reins; she crumpled, helpless, limp,
along the ground. Then just as she grew chill,
she slowly freed herself from all her body;
her neck relaxed, her head was overcome   1100
by death, her weapons fell, and with a moan,
her life, resentful, fled to Shades below.
At this an overwhelming clamor rose
and beat against the golden stars. Camilla
cut down, the fight grows fiercer. In a crowd   1105
they rush together—all the forces of
the Teucrians, the Tuscan captains, and

Evander's horsemen, the Arcadians.

Yet Opis, as Diana's sentinel,
had long been seated on a mountaintop,   1110
on high, where, undismayed, she watched the battle.
But when she saw, far off, Camilla done
to death among the shouts of raging young
soldiers, she groaned and, from her deepest breast,
cried out these words: "O, virgin, you have suffered   1115
too cruel a torment—yes, too cruel for
daring to face the Teucrians in war!
The way you served Diana while you were
lonely among the wilds has been no help,
nor were our quivers, carried on your shoulder.   1120
But now your queen will not leave you dishonored
in your last hour; neither will your death
go now without its glory through the nations;
men will not say that you were unavenged;
whoever has defiled your body with   1125
a wound will pay that debt with his own death."

Beneath that summit, sheltered by a thick
ilex, there stood a mound of earth, the massive
tomb of Dercennus, one of the Laurentians'
most ancient kings. Here first the lovely goddess   1130
descends with speed; then, halting, she spies Arruns
from that high barrow. As she saw him, bright
in armor and puffed up with pointless pride,
she cries: "Why are you running off? Come here,
come here to claim your death, to take the prize   1135
we owe you for Camilla! Shall one like
you, even you, die by Diana's arrows?"
At this the Thracian virgin drew a swift
shaft from her gilded quiver; and she stretched
her leveled bow, long, taut, drawing it back   1140
until the curved points met; with even hands
she pulled the bow until her left could touch
the arrow's iron tip, until her right
could feel the bowstring and her breast. At once
he heard the hissing shaft, the whirring air;   1145
and in that very instant iron drove
deep in his chest. But Arruns' heedless comrades
desert him as he gasps, groans out his last

along the battlefield's unknowing dust.
And Opis wings her way to high Olympus.   1150

The first to fly—their mistress lost—Camilla's
own light-armed horse; the Latins, routed, run;
daring Atinas flees. Their captains scattered,
forsaken companies seek safety; turning,
they gallop to the walls. No one is able   1155
to stay with spears or stand against the press
of Trojans bringing death. And now the Latins
haul off slack bows on their exhausted shoulders;
four-footed hoofbeats shake the crumbling plain.
The dust that whirls in cloud and darkness rolls   1160
back to the city; as they beat their breasts,
the mothers on the watchtowers raise laments,
the cries of women, high as heaven's stars.
The first to gallop through the open gates
full speed still find the enemy entangled   1165
within their ranks; the fugitives cannot
escape sad death; the Trojan shafts still thrust;
within their native walls, upon their threshold,
within the very shelter of their houses
the Latins gasp their last. Some shut the gates;   1170
they do not dare to open them for their
own comrades and are deaf to any prayers.
And then, a wretched butchery: some guard
the gates with swords; their own companions charge
against them. Some, shut out, are rolled headlong   1175
into the trenches, driven by the rout,
before the eyes, the very presence of
their weeping parents; some, with loosened reins,
blind, spur ahead and batter at the gates,
the tough and bolted doors. Even the mothers   1180
along the walls, remembering Camilla,
are rivals in their eagerness to cast
their shafts with anxious hands; true love of homeland
points out the way; they rush to imitate
steel with their sturdy oak clubs and charred stakes;   1185
each burns to die first for her city's sake.

Meanwhile, within the woods, the bitter word
finds Turnus. Acca brings the warrior
news of confusion: Volscian squadrons ruined,

Camilla fallen, and the enemy   1190
advancing, Mars behind him, sweeping every
thing, panic reaching to the very walls.
Raging, he quits his ambush in the hills,
deserts the rugged groves—so Jove's harsh will
demands. He has just marched from sight and gained   1195
the plain when father Aeneas, entering
on the unguarded pass, across the ridge,
moves out from the dense forest. Rapidly
and in full force the two make for the city;
there is little space between them. When Aeneas   1200
made out, far off, the plain that smoked with dust,
the Latin ranks—at that same moment Turnus
caught sight of fierce Aeneas in his armor
and heard the tramp of men, the panting horses.
They would at once have faced the test of battle,   1205
but now the crimson Phoebus bathes his weary
horses within the Spanish sea, restoring
the night as day retreats. Before the city
they pitch their camps and fortify their earthworks.

XII · 1268

BOOK XII

WHEN TURNUS SEES the Latins faltering
and broken by the countercourse of battle,
and sees all eyes are turned to him, demanding
that now he keep his pledge—implacable
and keen, he burns to fight, his heat is high.   5
And as a lion on the Punic plains,
when hunters wound him gravely in the chest,
at last awakes to battle and is glad,
and shakes the hairy mane along his neck,
and, fearless, snaps the hunter's shaft and roars   10
with bloody jaws: just so did violence
urge on fanatic Turnus. Hectic, he
cries out to King Latinus with these words:

"Turnus will not delay; the coward Trojans
need not retract their words, take back their promise.   15
I go to meet him. Father, have the holy
rites readied, draw the treaty: either I
send down this Dardan, Asia's renegade,
to hell with my right hand—while Latins sit
and watch—and by my single sword blot out   20
the slur that stains us all; or we are beaten
and held by him, he takes Lavinia."
   ❀   ❀   ❀

Latinus answered him with quiet heart:
"Young man remarkable for spirit, just
as you excel in unrelenting courage,   25
so much the more must I with care consider
and weigh with fear the outcome of this duel.
You have the kingdoms of your father, Daunus,
and many towns your arms have won; Latinus
also has gold and generosity.   30
In Latium and in Laurentum's lands
other unmarried girls are waiting—born
of not unseemly stock. Let me say these
ungentle things frankly, without deceit,
and let your spirit pay them close attention.   .   35
It was not right for me to give my daughter
to any of her former suitors; all—
both gods and men—had told us this. And yet,
too overcome by love for you, by our
related blood, and by my sad wife's tears,   40
I broke all of these curbs; I snatched my daughter
back from her promised husband; I took up
unholy arms. For Turnus, you see what
disasters hunt me down from that day on,
what evils you, above all, had to suffer.   45
Twice-beaten in great battles, we can hardly
keep Italy's hopes safe within our city;
and even now our blood still warms the Tiber;
the giant plains are still white with our bones.
Why have I drifted back so often, what   50
new madness shifts my purpose? If, with Turnus'
death, I am ready to accept the Trojans,
to take them in as allies, then why not
stop this war now, with Turnus still untouched?
For what will our Rutulian kinsmen say,   55
and what the rest of Italy, if I
betray to death—may fate refute my words—
you, who have sought my daughter's hand? Think back
on all the chance and change of battle; pity
your aged father: even now his native   60
Ardea holds him far from us, in sadness."

Words cannot check the violence of Turnus:
the healing only aggravates his sickness;
his fury flares. As soon as he is able

to speak, he still insists: "Most gracious king,   65
I pray you: set aside your care for me
and for my safety; let me barter death
for glory. For I, too, can cast a lance;
the steel my right hand uses is not feeble;
my father, blood flows from the wounds I deal.   70
The Trojan's goddess-mother will be too
far off to shelter her retreating son,
to hide him, as a woman would, within
the same deceiving cloud that covers her."

But frightened by the terms of this new duel,   75
the queen, weeping, prepared to die, held fast
her raging son-in-law: "Turnus, by these
tears and by any reverence you still
feel for Amata—you, the only hope
and quiet left my sad last years: the honor   80
and power of Latinus is with you,
this house in peril stands or falls with you;
I beg one thing: you must not meet the Trojans.
For in this duel that you so wish to enter,
whatever waits for you waits for me, too;   85
together with you, I shall leave this hated
light; for I will not be a captive, see
Aeneas as my son-in-law." Lavinia's
hot cheeks were bathed in tears; she heard her mother's
words; and her blush, a kindled fire, crossed   90
her burning face. And just as when a craftsman
stains Indian ivory with blood-red purple,
or when white lilies, mixed with many roses,
blush: even such, the colors of the virgin.
His love drives Turnus wild; he stares at his   95
Lavinia; even keener now for battle,
he answers Queen Amata with few words:

"I pray you, Mother, as I go to face
so hard a duel, do not send me off
with weeping, with such dreary omens. Turnus   100
cannot delay his death, if it must come.
You, Idmon, be my messenger and carry
these words—which will not please him—to the Phrygian
tyrant: that when tomorrow's dawn first rides
on crimson wheels and reddens in the sky,   105

let him not lead the Teucrians against
the Latins; let their weapons rest; the war
will be decided by our blood; the bride
Lavinia will be won upon that field."

This said, he hurries back into the palace,   110
calls for his horses, and on seeing them
as they neigh there before him, he rejoices:
for Orithyia herself once gave these stallions
as offerings in his honor to Pilumnus,
whiter than snow and faster than the wind.   115
Keen charioteers surround the chargers, striking
their sounding chests with hollow palms and combing
their shaggy manes. Then Turnus wraps his corselet,
made stiff with gold and gleaming orichalcum,
about his shoulders; sets in place his sword   120
and shield, the sockets of his crimson crest—
the sword the Lord of Fire himself had forged
for Turnus' father Daunus, dipping it,
while glowing hot, into the wave of Styx.
And then he clutches hard his hefty lance,   125
that stood just at the center of the hall,
propped up against a giant pillar—spoil
taken from the Auruncan Actor; Turnus
shakes this until it quivers as he cries:
"Now, lance that never failed my call, your time   130
is come. The mighty Actor bore you once,
you now belong to Turnus; grant me this:
to lay his body low, to tear his corselet,
ripped by my right hand, from the Phrygian half-man,
and to defile his hair with dust—that hair   135
he curls with heated irons, drenching it
with myrrh." Turnus is driven by the Furies;
he glows with sparks; his fierce eyes flame with fire:
as when a bull, preparing to do battle,
awakes tremendous bellowings; trying   140
to hurl his rage into his horns, before
the fight, he butts against a tree trunk and
he beats the wind with blows and paws the sand.

Meanwhile Aeneas, no less keen for battle
and ruthless in the arms his mother gave him,   145
calls up his indignation, happy that

the war is to be settled by this compact.
He comforts his companions, stays the fears
of sad Ascanius; he teaches them
the ways of fate. Then he commands his men   150
to carry his firm answer back to King
Latinus, and he dictates terms of peace.

The new day was just wakened, scattering
the tallest peaks with light—the hour in which
the horses of the Sun first rise up from   155
the deep surge, breathing rays from lifted nostrils—
when Trojans and Rutulians made ready
the measured field for dueling beneath
the walls of the great city. In the middle
they set their braziers and their grassy altars   160
for offerings to the gods that they both worship;
while others, dressed in priestly aprons, foreheads
bound in verbena garlands, brought spring water
and fire. Ausonia's legions now march out;
tight-columned squadrons pour through crowded
     gates.   165
To this side all the Trojan troops and Tuscans
are hurrying with mingled armor, wearing
their steel even as if the bitter battle
of Mars had called on each of them. No less,
the captains race among the thousands, bright   170
with gold and purple: Mnestheus, who was born
out of Assaracus, and bold Asilas
and—born of Neptune's seed—Messapus, tamer
of horses. At a given signal each
draws back to his allotted space and plants   175
his lance upon the ground and rests his shield.
At this the matrons and the unarmed crowd
and weak old men are eager to pour out;
and they press toward the rooftops and the towers
while others stand upon the tall gateways.   180

But Juno, from the hilltop now called Alban—
the mountain then had neither name nor fame
nor honor—saw the battlefield and both
the ranks of Troy and of Laurentum and
the city of Latinus. Then, straightway,   185
a goddess to a goddess, she addressed

the sister of Turnus, mistress of the pools
and roaring rivers (Jupiter, the high
king of the upper air, had given this,
a sacred honor, to her for his theft   190
of her virginity): "You, nymph, the glory
of rivers and most dear to me, you know
how more than all the Latin girls that mounted
upon great-hearted Jove's ungrateful bed
it was yourself I held the highest, giving   195
to you, and willingly, a place in heaven.
Juturna, learn your sorrow, lest you blame me.
Wherever Fortune left me leeway, where
the Fates let Latium succeed at all,
there I watched over Turnus and your city.   200
But now I see him face unequal Fates;
the day of doom, of bitter force draws near;
I cannot bear to see this battle or
this treaty; if you can dare something more
to help your brother, do so; that is proper.   205
Perhaps some gladness still awaits the sad."

As soon as Juno stopped, Juturna wept;
three and four times she beat her lovely breast.
"This is no time for tears," Saturnian Juno
cries out to her. "Be quick; snatch back your brother 210
from death if there is any way, or else
incite them all to arms and smash the treaty.
It is myself who order you to dare."
And with this counsel Juno left Juturna
in doubt, restless, the harsh wound in her mind.   215

Meanwhile the kings advance: Latinus rides
upon his massive four-horse chariot;
and twice-six golden rays—an emblem of
the Sun, his ancestor—surround his temples;
a pair of milk-white horses carry Turnus;   220
two broad-tipped javelins quiver in his grip.
Against them from the camp site marches out
the founder of the Roman race, father
Aeneas, blazing with his star-bright shield
and heaven-given arms; Ascanius,   225
the second hope of mighty Rome, is near him.
A priest in spotless tunic leads the young

born of a bristling boar, and an unshorn
sheep, two years old; he sets these animals
before the burning shrines. Both warriors,   230
turning their eyes to face the rising sun,
now scatter salted meal before them, mark
the foreheads of the victims with a sword,
and from their cups pour offerings on the altars.
Then, with drawn blade, pious Aeneas prays: 235

"Now may the Sun be witness to my prayer,
together with this Earth, for whom I have
endured such trials; to you, all-able Father,
and you, Saturnia, his wife—o goddess
at last more generous—to you I pray;   240
you, famous Mars, the father in whose power
lies every war; you, fountains, and you, rivers—
you, too, I call upon, together with
whatever should be feared in the high air,
whatever powers keep the blue-gray waters.   245
For if by chance the victory should fall
to Turnus the Ausonian, then we,
defeated, must leave for Evander's city;
and Iülus shall give up these fields; Aeneas'
sons never are to carry arms against you   250
or menace Latin kingdoms with the sword.
But if the war is settled in our favor
by victory (as I should rather judge,
and may the gods confirm this with their will),
then I shall not subject Italians   255
to Teucrians, ask kingdoms for myself:
both nations, undefeated, shall accept
the equal laws of an eternal compact:
their sacred rites, their gods, shall be intact,
Latinus, as my father, keep his sword   260
and, as my father, hold his lawful rule.
For me, the Teucrians shall build a city;
Lavinia shall give those walls her name."

So says Aeneas, first to speak; Latinus,
looking to heaven, follows after him,   265
stretching his right hand to the stars: "Aeneas,
I swear by these same powers: earth and sea
and stars, and by the twin seed of Latona,

the Sun and Moon, by two-faced Janus and
the power of the lower gods, the dwelling   270
place of the savage Dis; and may the Father
who sanctifies our treaties, striking those
who perjure with his thunderbolt, hear me.
I touch these altars and I call to witness
this fire and these gods that stand between us: 275
however things may fall, no day shall break
this peace and pact for Italy; no force
shall turn me from this pledge, not even if
it overwhelms the earth, confounding all
in waves and deluge, heaven into hell: 280
as surely as this scepter"—for he carried
his scepter in his right hand—"never shall
blossom with tender leaves as branch or shade,
now that, cut from its lower stem within
the forest, it has lost its mother tree,   285
laid low its leaf and branch before the ax;
for once it was a bough, but now the hand
of artisans has covered it with seemly
bronze, ready to be borne by Latin elders."
With such words, while the chieftains watched,
    Aeneas   290
and King Latinus swore their treaty; duly
they slaughter sacred victims in the fire,
and tear the living entrails out of beasts,
and heap the altars high with loaded platters.

But the Rutulians had long since felt   295
this duel was unequal; they are puzzled;
conflicting feelings move their hearts; more so
when they can see the fighters poorly matched.
And Turnus adds to their uncertainty:
he paces silently and, suppliant,   300
he worships at the shrine with lowered eyes,
with wasted cheeks, and with his pale young body.
And just as soon as she saw this and felt
the crowd was doubtful in its heart, Juturna,
his sister, threw herself into the ranks,   305
miming the shape of Camers (one who had
great ancestors, a father famed for valor,
and was himself a most tenacious fighter);
then, skillfully, she scatters many rumors:

"O Latins, are you not ashamed to let   310
this giant army stake all on one life?
For are we not their match in numbers, strength?
Why, take the lot of them: the Trojans and
Arcadians and the Etrurians,
the fate-manipulated, those who hate   315
our Turnus; even if but half of us
do battle, there are not enough of them
to face us. He indeed will climb by fame
up to the High Ones, at whose altars he
has vowed his life; he will live on men's lips.   320
But we, our homeland lost, shall be compelled
to yield before insulting masters—we
who sit today as laggards on these fields."

Her words only inflame the warriors more
and more; a murmur glides from man to man.   325
And both the Latin ranks and the Laurentians,
who just before had hoped for rest from war
and for security, are changed; they now
want weapons, pray the pact can be unmade;
they pity Turnus' unfair fate. Juturna   330
then adds to this: she shows in the high heavens
a sign that could confound Italian minds
and lead them on with its prodigiousness
far more than any other omen could.
For as the golden bird of Jove was flying   335
across the crimson sky, pursuing fowl
that flock along the shore in loud winged ranks,
he swoops low on the waters suddenly
and, brutal, snatches up in his hooked talons
a handsome swan. This startles the Italians   340
when—wonderful to see—all of those birds
wheel right around and, as they clamor, darken
the air with wings; against their enemy
they press, a compact mass, across the skies,
until their force and weight defeat him; he   345
gives way and casts his prey down from his claws
into the river, flees to far-off clouds.

At this indeed the Latins greet the omen
with shouts and set their hands for war; the augur
Tolumnius becomes the first to cry: 350

"This was the portent I have often prayed for;
I follow it; I recognize the gods;
I am your leader; now take up your swords,
o Latins, whom this wanton foreigner
has terrified by war, as if you were   355
but helpless birds—he devastates your shores.
But he, too, shall take flight; across the waters
he shall yet sail far off. As with one mind,
close tight your ranks; defend in this encounter
the king who has been stolen from your side."   360
This said, he rushed ahead and hurled his lance
against his enemies. The hissing shaft
of cornel wood is shrill; it cuts the air
with certainty. At once a piercing roar
leaps high; a frenzy takes them all; their hearts   365
are hot, tumultuous. And as the lance
flew off, it chanced nine handsome brothers stood
across its path—so many brothers, yet
all born to the Arcadian Gylippus
by his own faithful Tuscan wife. It pierces   370
right through the ribs of one of these young men,
remarkable for beauty and bright armor,
along his waistline where the stitched belt rubs
against the belly and the buckle gnaws
against rib ends. He falls on yellow sands.   375
But of his brothers—a courageous band,
inflamed by grief—part draw their swords, part seize
their shafts of flying steel and rush ahead
blindly. And the Laurentians charge against them;
but here again the compact ranks of Trojans   380
pour out—together with Agyllines and
Arcadians with ornamented armor.
They all have just one passion: for the sword
to settle this dispute. They strip the altars
for firebrands; across the skies a dense   385
tempest of shafts, a rain of iron falls.
Within that storm some of the Latins carry
libation cups and braziers toward the city.
And King Latinus, bearing back his beaten
gods and the broken treaty, now retreats.   390
The others draw their chariot reins or mount
their horses, riding up with naked swords.
　　　❋　　　　❋　　　　❋

Messapus, anxious to destroy the truce,
charges on horseback toward a Tuscan prince,
Aulestes, wearer of a royal emblem.   395
Aulestes, luckless in retreating, stumbles
and tumbles over on his head and shoulders
against the altars at his back. But fierce
Messapus rushes with his lance; from high
upon his horse, with his tremendous shaft   400
he strikes Aulestes heavily, although
he pleads so much. Messapus cries: "He has it;
I give to the great gods a better victim."
The Latins crowd around; they strip Aulestes'
warm limbs. But as they move in, Corynaeus   405
snatches a charred torch from the altar, and
as Ebysus strides close and aims a blow,
he smashes fire in his face; the stench
of singeing rises; Ebysus' great beard
bursts into flame. And Corynaeus follows   410
close on the stroke; he grips the hair of his
stunned enemy; he pins him down with thrusting
bent knee, and stabs his side with rigid sword.
Another Trojan, Podalirius,
who charges with drawn sword, towers above   415
the shepherd Alsus even as he rushes
just where the fight is hottest. But the Latin
draws back his ax, and Podalirius
has his head split from forehead down to chin;
his splattered blood drenches the arms of Alsus.   420
Then cruel quiet, iron sleep press down
his eyes; their light is locked in endless night.

But stretching out his unarmed hand, the pious
Aeneas, with bare head, cries to his comrades:
"Where are you rushing? Why this sudden tempest?   425
Hold back your anger! Now the truce is set,
its terms are fixed, I am the only one
who has the right to battle; let me fight,
and set your fears aside. With my right arm
I shall maintain our treaty. Sacred rites   430
make Turnus mine." Yet as he pleaded, cried,
a hissing arrow glided on its wings,
shaft aimed and driven, whirling, home by hand

that is unknown; and whether it was chance
or was a god who gained so great a glory   435
for the Rutulians, the fame is hidden;
no soldier boasted of Aeneas' wounding.

When Turnus sees Aeneas quit the ranks
and sees the captains in dismay, he burns
with sudden hope; at once he calls for horse   440
and weapons; proud, he mounts his chariot
and takes the reins. Racing, he gives to death
so many bodies of brave men; he topples
so many, half-dead; as he wheels ahead,
he tramples over troops; he snatches spear   445
on spear and flings them at the fugitives.
Even as bloody Mars in breakneck course
along the riverbanks of Hebrus clangs
his shield and calls to war and gives loose rein
to his wild horses; they fly off across   450
the open plain, outstripping south and west winds;
and farthest Thracia groans beneath their pounding
hoofs, and around him, as his retinue,
black Fear and Anger race, and Stratagem:
just so the eager Turnus lashes at   455
his horses as they sweat and foam; he tramples
his enemies, miserably cut down.
The quick hoofs splash their way through gory spray;
they beat upon the mingled blood and sand.
Now he has given Stheneleus and Pholus   460
and Thamyris to death: two in close combat,
and Stheneleus from far. From far he catches
Glaucus and Lades, sons of Imbrasus,
whom Imbrasus himself had raised in Lycia
and furnished—each of them—with the same armor,   465
fit both for dueling hand to hand or else
for riding, faster than the winds, on horseback.

Elsewhere Eumedes rides into the melee;
he is descended from old Dolon, famed
in war; and he renewed the name of his   470
grandfather and his father's heart and hand;
his father once spied on the Danaan camp,
then dared to ask as his reward Achilles'
chariot; for such daring Diomedes

had punished him with other payment; now   475
he hopes no longer for Achilles' horses.
When Turnus sees Eumedes far away,
across the open plain, he first casts his
light javelin; then he checks his team of horses,
leaps from his chariot, and overtakes   480
Eumedes, fallen, half-dead. Turnus digs
his foot into Eumedes' neck; he plucks
Eumedes' glowing sword from his right hand;
he dips it deep into his throat and adds:
"Trojan, lie there and measure out these lands,   485
the Italy you tried to win by war:
this is the prize of those who try to tempt me
to battle; so do they establish walls."
And then, to keep Eumedes company,
his lance sends down Asbytes to the Shades,   490
and Chloreus, Sybaris, Thersilochus,
and Dares, and Thymoetes, fallen from
the neck of his uneasy horse. Just as
the blast of the Edonian Boreas
echoes across the deep Aegean sea,   495
and chases breakers in to shore; and winds
sweep and the clouds retreat across the sky:
so, too, wherever Turnus cuts his way,
there do the ranks recede, then, routed, run;
his very speed propels him on; the wind   500
against his chariot shakes his flying crest.
But Phegeus could not stand his urgency,
his raging anger; and he blocked the way
of Turnus' chariot; with his right hand
he gripped the bits of those excited horses   505
that foamed across their reins. And while they drag
off Phegeus, hanging from their harness, Turnus'
broad lance head reaches his defenseless side;
set fast, it breaks his double-plated coat
of mail; it grazes Phegeus with a flesh wound.   510
Yet Phegeus whirled around, and with his shield
he faced his enemy: he sought the aid
of his drawn blade; but then the wheel and axle,
as they rolled on, hurled him headlong and sprawling
across the ground. With this, Turnus hacked off   515
the head of Phegeus with a sword: a stroke
between the upper border of his breastplate

and helmet's lower edge; and then he left
the trunk of Phegeus lying on the sand.

While Turnus triumphs, dealing death across   520
the plains, the true Achates, Mnestheus, and
Ascanius as comrade bring the bleeding
Aeneas into camp; he limps along,
supporting every other step with his
long spear. And in his rage he tries to wrench   525
the arrow by its broken shaft; he calls
for any ready way to help: to cut
the wound out with a broad sword and to lay
naked the arrow's deepest hiding place,
to send him back to battle. Now Iapyx,   530
the son of Iasus, drew near; he was
dearest above all other men to Phoebus;
to him Apollo, struck by piercing love,
once wished to give his arts, his gifts: his power
of augury, his lyre, and his swift arrows.   535
Iapyx, to delay his dying father's
fate, chose to know instead the powers of herbs,
the ways of healing, and to practice these,
the silent arts, unhonored. Wild and bitter,
Aeneas, propped upon his giant spear,   540
stood near that crowd of warriors, beside
the mourning Iülus, but unmoved by tears.
And old Iapyx, sleeves rolled back, dressed in
the manner of physicians, with his healing
hand and the potent herbs of Phoebus, tries   545
again, again, in vain; in vain, he tugs
the dart and grips the steel with grasping tongs.
Good fortune does not guide his path; his teacher
Apollo does not help him. More and more
the savage horror is loud upon the plain,   550
disaster draws much nearer. Now the sky
seems like a wall of dust; the riders rush,
the shower of shafts is thick upon the camp.
The wretched cry of warriors climbs the air,
of men who fall beneath tenacious Mars.   555

But then Aeneas' pain, unmerited,
distresses Venus; with a mother's care
she plucks—from Cretan Ida—dittany,

a stalk with leaves luxuriant and shaggy
and purple flower, a plant not unfamiliar   560
to wild goats when they are wounded by winged arrows.
This, Venus, with black mist to hide her face,
now carries down; with this she medicates,
in secret, waters poured in gleaming vats;
she steeps the plant and sprinkles healing juices   565
of scented panacea and ambrosia.
And old Iapyx, unaware of this,
then bathes Aeneas' wound with that same liquid.
And suddenly all pain fled from his body,
and all the blood held fast in that deep wound;   570
and following Iapyx' hand, the arrow,
unforced, fell out; fresh strength returned to him.
"Quick! Bring his weapons! Why do you delay?"
Iapyx shouts, the first to stir their spirits
against the Latins. "This is not the work   575
of mortal hands or skillful art; my craft
has not saved you, Aeneas: here there is
a greater one—a god—who sends you back
to greater labors." He is hot for combat;
he sheathes his legs on this side and on that   580
with golden greaves; he hates to linger here
and brandishes his spear. Then to his flank
his shield is fitted; to his back, his corselet;
and dressed in mail, he hugs Ascanius
and through his helmet gently kisses him: 585
"From me, my son, learn valor and true labor;
from others learn of fortune. Now my arm
will win security for you in battle
and lead you toward a great reward: only
remember, when your years are ripe, your people's   590
example; let your father and your uncle—
both Hector and Aeneas—urge you on."

This said, he marched out through the gates, a giant;
a great shaft quivers in his hand; and Antheus
and Mnestheus also hurry out at once,   595
and all the Trojan crowd abandons camp.
Then blinding dust confounds the plains; the earth
is panicked by their pounding feet and shudders.
Turnus could see them from a facing mound;
the Latins saw; cold trembling took their bones.   600

The first of the Ausonians to hear,
Juturna; and she recognized the sound
and fled in terror. He, Aeneas, races
and drives his dark band on the open plain.
Even as, when a sudden squall has fallen,   605
a storm cloud moves to land from open seas,
and luckless farmers, seeing it far off,
shudder within their hearts, for it will bring
destruction to their orchards, kill their crops,
and cut down every planting; and the winds   610
fly fast before it, roaring toward the shore:
just so the Trojan chieftain drives his troops
straight at his enemies; his soldiers muster
around him, thickly, all in compact ranks.
Thymbraeus strikes the huge Osiris with   615
his sword; and Mnestheus kills Arcetius;
Achates, Epulo; and Gyas, Ufens;
Tolumnius the augur also falls—
he was the first to break the truce, to cast
his shaft against the enemy. A shout   620
mounts to the sky; wheeling about, the Latins
in turn now give their backs, clouded with dust,
to flight across the fields. Aeneas does
not deign to strike down fugitives to death;
he does not charge at those who meet him now   625
on foot or horse or flinging darts; he only
wants Turnus; through that dark cloud, he seeks out
Turnus; he calls on him alone to battle.

Then, terrified, Juturna, warrior maiden,
flings out Metiscus, Turnus' charioteer,   630
from in between the reins; she pushes him
far from the pole; he falls; and she takes up
his place; her hands hold fast the rippling reins;
in everything she counterfeits Metiscus—
his voice and body and his armor. Even   635
as a black swallow, when it flies across
some wealthy lord's vast villa, hovers, circling
the high halls on its wings; it scavenges
for scanty crumbs and food for its loud fledglings;
and now it calls through empty porticoes   640
and now around the damp cisterns: just so
Juturna is carried by her chargers through

the enemies in her swift chariot;
while racing, she scans everything; and now
here and now there displays her victor brother　　　645
but will not let him set his hand to battle
Aeneas; deviously, she flies far.
Nevertheless, Aeneas tracks the winding
course; he is seeking Turnus, and he shouts
aloud for Turnus through the routed troops.　　　650
As often as Aeneas catches sight
of him and races toward the winged-foot horses,
so often does Juturna wheel about
and turn her chariot. What can Aeneas
do now? In vain he wavers on the shifting　　　655
surge of his feeling; his conflicting cares
invite his mind to try this plan, then that.
But now Messapus, dexterous, moves against him;
with a sure blow he hurls the first of those
two pliant steel-tipped javelins he carried.　　　660
Aeneas stopped; he drew himself together
behind his shield; he bent down on one knee;
but even so, the hurtled shaft took off
his helmet crest and shook his highest plumes.
At this indeed Aeneas' anger seethes;　　　665
excited by the treachery of Turnus,
whose chariot and horses have been carried
far off, and having often pleaded with
Jove and the altars of the shattered treaty,
at last Aeneas charges into battle;　　　670
and terrible, with Mars behind him, he
awakens brutal, indiscriminate
slaughter, he lets his violence run free.

What god can now unfold for me in song
all of the bitterness and butchery　　　675
and deaths of chieftains—driven now by Turnus,
now by the Trojan hero, each in turn
throughout that field? O Jupiter, was it
your will that nations destined to eternal
peace should have clashed in such tremendous
　　turmoil?　　　680

Aeneas comes upon Rutulian Sucro—
this combat was the first to check the Trojans'

rush—but without delaying much, he plunges
his naked sword there where the end is quickest:
right through the ribs, the grating of the chest.   685
Diores and his brother Amycus
are thrown by Turnus from their horses, then
on foot he charges at them, striking one
before he had reached Turnus, with his long
lance; and he stabs the other with his sword;   690
he lets two severed heads hang from his chariot
and carries off the pair, both damp with blood.
Aeneas sends the tough Cethegus, Talon,
and Tanais to death—the three in one
attack—and sad Onites: he is Theban;   695
his mother, Peridia. Turnus kills
the brothers from Apollo's fields and Lycia,
and young Menoetes of Arcadia,
one who detested warfare, but in vain:
he worked as fisherman and had his poor   700
home near the pools of Lerna, never knowing
the thresholds of the great; his father sowed
on rented soil. Even as fire set loose
from different sides upon dry woods and shrubs
of rustling laurel; or as foaming streams   705
that hurtle from high mountains, roaring, rushing
to sea, each laying waste its own pathway;
just so do Turnus and Aeneas, no
less eagerly rush on to fight; now, now
wrath is a storm in them; their breasts do not   710
know what defeat is; they are bursting; now,
with all their force, they plunge ahead toward wounds.

Murranus—as he brags of his forefathers,
the names of all his ancient ancestors,
his race of Latin kings—is toppled by   715
Aeneas with a rock and whirling stone,
headlong upon the ground. Beneath his chariot's
yoke and his reins the wheels rolled on; the hoofs
of horses, heedless of their master, pound
again, again, upon Murranus. Turnus,   720
as Hyllus charges with enormous wrath,
encounters him and hurls his lance against
his forehead with its gold headband; the shaft
pierces his helmet, then the tip holds fast

within his brains. And Cretheus, bravest Greek,   725
your right hand could not snatch you free from Turnus.
Nor was the priest Cupencus saved by his
own gods against Aeneas' charge; he gave
his breast to meet the blade, and the delay
of brazen shield was of no profit to him.   730
Laurentian plains saw you, too, Aeolus,
collapse, your broad back sprawling on the ground:
you fall, whom Argive troops could never topple,
nor he who cut down Priam's lands, Achilles.
For here you found the boundary of death;   735
you had a handsome home beneath Mount Ida,
your handsome home was at Lyrnesus; yet
your tomb is on Laurentian soil. Now all
the troops rush back into the struggle—all
the Latins, all the Dardans: Mnestheus and   740
the brave Serestus, and Messapus, tamer
of horses, tough Asilas, and the Tuscans,
and the Arcadian squadrons of Evander—
each gives his all; they strive with total force,
no lingering, no rest, in that vast contest.   745

But then Aeneas' lovely mother set
his mind to this: to march against the city,
to sweep his army quickly toward the ramparts,
confound the Latins by a sudden slaughter.
As he looked here and there, searching for Turnus,   750
scanning the varied ranks, he saw the city
free from the stress of war, intact, at rest.
Straightway the image of a greater struggle
has kindled him; he calls his captains—Mnestheus,
Sergestus, and Serestus; then he climbs   755
a mound where other Trojans crowd around him;
but they do not put by their spears or shields.
There, standing at the center, he speaks out:

"Let there be no delay in what I ask,
for Jupiter is with us; let no one   760
still linger just because this plan is sudden.
This day—unless they yield, accept our rule,
submit to us—I shall annihilate
that city, cause of war, the capital
of King Latinus; I shall level all   765

their smoking rooftops. For, indeed, am I
to wait on Turnus' pleasure to do battle?
Is he, already beaten, still to meet me?
This, citizens, this is the head, the sum
of this accursed war. Be quick, bring torches;   770
the time has come to ask our treaty back
with flames." He is done; his men are keen; they form
a wedge; they march—a dense mass—toward the walls.
In no time, ladders, sudden fires appear.
Some hurry to the gateways, hacking down   775
the first guards they encounter; others cast
their steel; the sky is dark with shafts. Aeneas
himself is in the vanguard, stretching out
his hand beneath the ramparts; and he shouts
his accusations at Latinus, calls   780
the gods to witness that he had been forced
to battle; twice the Latins have become
his enemies; twice they have broken treaties.
Dissension takes the panicked citizens:
some say the city is to be unlocked,   785
the gates thrown open to the Dardans; they
would drag the king himself up to the ramparts;
while others carry arms, rush to defend:
as when some shepherd tracks a swarm of bees
that shelter in a porous cliff, and fills   790
their hive with bitter smoke; they rush about
their waxen camp in panic; buzzing loud,
they whet their wrath; across their cells the black
stench rolls; rocks echo with the stifled murmurs;
smoke trickles up into the empty air.   795

Then new calamity fell on the weary
Latins; and all the city shook with grief
to its foundations. When the queen can see
from her high palace roof the enemy
approaching, charging at the walls, the fires   800
climbing as high as housetops, with the army
of the Rutulians nowhere, and no troops
of Turnus to be seen—then, wretched, she
believes her warrior has been killed in combat;
dismayed by sudden sorrow, she cries out   805
that she herself is guilty, is the source

of their misfortunes; mad, she utters many
wild things in moaning frenzy; she is ready
to die and tears her purple robe and fastens
a noose of ugly death from a high beam.   810
As soon as the unhappy Latin women
have heard of this affliction, first Lavinia
rages; she tears at her bright hair and cheeks
of rose; then all the crowd around her raves;
the wailing fills the palace's wide halls.   815
The sad report goes out across the city.
Now hearts sink down; Latinus, in torn garments,
dazed by his wife's fate and his city's ruin,
defiles his aged hairs with filthy dust.

Meanwhile, along the border of the field,   820
the warring Turnus slows his pace; now less
and less excited by his horses' triumphs,
he chases a few stragglers. But the wind
brought him the capital's confusing clamor;
the joyless murmur struck his straining ears;   825
in that far sound were mingled his blind fears.
"What sorrow so disturbs our walls, what is
this roar that races from the distant city?"
This said, he grabs the reins and, frantic, halts.
But in Metiscus' shape, his sister—who   830
had guided chariot, reins, and horses—cries:
"Here, Turnus, let us hunt the sons of Troy;
here victory first showed the way to us;
the others can defend our home. Aeneas
attacks the Latins, joining battle; let   835
us, too, send cruel death—to Teucrians.
When you are done, your score of killings and
your glory will match his." But Turnus says:
"O sister, I knew you long since, both when
you first disturbed our pact by craftiness   840
and plunged into these wars; and when you tried—
in vain—to trick me, hiding your godhead.
But who has willed that you be sent from high
Olympus to endure such trials? Was it
to see your luckless brother's brutal death?   845
What can I do now? Or what fortune can
promise me safety? I have seen Murranus—
no one more dear to me is left alive—

fallen before my very eyes as he
called out to me—and he a giant man,   850
defeated by a giant wound. Sad Ufens
has died that he might not see my disgrace;
the Trojans own his body and his weapons.
And shall I let the Latins' homes be leveled—
the only shame my fate has yet to face—   855
not let my sword refute the words of Drances?
Shall I retreat? Shall this land see me fleeing?
And after all, is death so sad a thing?
May you, o Shades, be kind to me now that
the will of High Ones turns against me. Stainless   860
in soul, and ignorant of cowardice—
the sin you scorn—I shall descend to you,
never unworthy of my great ancestors."

As Turnus finished, Saces rushes up,
a Latin riding on a foaming horse   865
and flying through the ranks of enemies;
his face had been struck head on by an arrow;
he calls for Turnus, calls his name: "O Turnus,
our final safety is in you; take pity
upon your comrades. For Aeneas thunders   870
in arms; and now he threatens to cast down
the tallest towers of Italy, giving them
to ruin; firebrands fly to the roofs.
The Latins call on you, they turn their eyes
to you—for even King Latinus mutters   875
in doubt: whom should he call his son-in-law
or to what treaties should he bind himself.
And more, the queen herself, devoted to you,
has fallen by her own right hand; in panic
she fled the light. Messapus and the valiant   880
Atinas, all alone, keep up the fight
before the gates. The crowding squadrons stand
and circle them; the Trojans' iron harvest
of swords drawn out of scabbards bristles; yet
you turn your chariot toward deserted grass."   885

Confused by all these shifting images
of ruin, Turnus stood astounded, staring
and silent. In his deepest heart there surge
tremendous shame and madness mixed with sorrow

and love whipped on by frenzy and a courage　　　890
aware of its own worth. As soon as shadows
were scattered and his mind saw light again,
in turmoil then, he turned his burning eyes
upon the walls and, from his chariot, looked
back to that splendid city. There a whirlwind　　　895
of flames was rolling on, storey by storey,
skyward, and gripping fast a tower—one
that he himself had built, of tight-packed timbers;
beneath it wheels were set; above it, tall
drawbridges. "Sister, fate has won; do not　　　900
delay me; let us follow where both god
and cruel fortune call; I am set to face
Aeneas, set to suffer death in all
its bitterness; sister, no longer will
you see me in disgrace. I beg you, let　　　905
me rage this madness out before I die."
So Turnus; then he left his chariot, leaped
down to the field; charging through enemies,
through shafts, he quits his grieving sister; swift,
he crashes through the center of the ranks.　　　910
Just as a rock when, from a mountaintop,
it hurtles headlong, having been torn up
by wind or washed away by a wheeling storm
or loosened by the long lapse of the years;
the mass, enormous, with a mighty thrust　　　915
drives down the slope and bounds upon the earth,
rolls woods and herds and men along its course:
so Turnus rushes through the scattered bands
up to the city walls, there where the ground
is soaked in shed blood and the air is shrill　　　920
with shafts. He signals with his hand, then shouts
aloud: "Rutulians, stop now; and you,
Italians, stay your steel; whatever chance
is here belongs to me; it is more just
for me alone to pay this covenant,　　　925
decide this war by sword." And then they all
drew back and left the center free for combat.

But when he hears the name of Turnus, father
Aeneas leaves the ramparts and tall towers;
he casts aside delay, breaks off the siege;　　　930
and now, exultant, joyous, and tremendous,

he pounds upon his shield—as huge as Athos,
as Eryx, or as father Apenninus
himself when, roaring, with his trembling oaks
he lifts his snow-topped summit skyward, glad.   935
Now all—Rutulians, Trojans, and Italians—
turned eagerly to look: both those who manned
high battlements and those below, who ran
a battering ram against the walls; they slung
their weapons off their shoulders. King Latinus   940
himself is wonderstruck to see such giant
men—born within such distant, different lands—
now come together for this trial by steel.
And they, as soon as space was cleared for them
along the open plain, first fling their spears   945
from far, then swiftly rush to fight; they dash
the brass of clanging shields together. Earth
groans, and their frequent sword blows double; chance
and courage mingle into one. Just as,
on giant Sila or on tall Taburnus,   950
when two bulls charge together into battle
with butting brows, the herdsmen fall back; all
the flock is mute with fear; the heifers wonder
who is to rule the forest, whom the herds
must follow; and the bulls with massive force   955
trade wounds; they gore with struggling horns; they bathe
their necks and shoulders in a stream of blood;
their groans and bellows echo through the grove:
so did the Daunian hero and the Trojan
Aeneas clash their shields; their violence   960
fills all the air. There Jupiter himself
holds up two scales in equal balance, then
he adds two different fates, one on each hand:
whom this trial dooms, what weight sinks down to death.

Now Turnus, thinking he is safe, springs out: 965
he rises up to his full height; with sword
upraised, he strikes. The Trojans and the anxious
Italians shout: the tension takes both ranks.
But, treacherous, that blade breaks off, deserts
fanatic Turnus at his blow's midstroke   970
had flight not helped him then. As soon as he
sees that strange hilt in his defenseless hand,

he runs away, swifter than the east wind.
They say that in his first wild dash to battle,
when mounting on his chariot, he had left   975
his father's sword behind and, rushing, snatched
the weapon of his charioteer, Metiscus;
so long as routed Trojans turned their backs,
that sword had served him well, but when it met
the armor that the God of Fire had forged,   980
the mortal blade, like brittle ice, had splintered;
the fragments glitter on the yellow sand.
So Turnus madly flees across the field;
now here, then there, he wheels in wayward circles.
The Trojans in a dense ring press against him;   985
to one side lies the vast Laurentian marsh,
and on the other, high walls hem him in.

And though the arrow wound within his knees
stays and delays him, nonetheless Aeneas
runs after Turnus. Keen, he presses on   990
against his trembling enemy, foot to foot:
even as, when a hunting dog has found
a stag hemmed in beside a stream or hedged
by fear before the netting's crimson feathers,
he chases, barking, pressing near; the stag,   995
in terror of the snare and of the river's
high banks, wheels back and forth a thousand ways;
and yet the lively Umbrian hound hangs close
to him with gaping mouth; at every instant
he grasps, he grinds his jaws but, baffled, bites   1000
on nothing. Then indeed the shouting rises;
the shores and lakes resound; confusion takes
the skies. But Turnus, even as he flies
away, rebukes all his Rutulian ranks;
he calls on each by name, he shouts for his   1005
familiar blade. And for his part, Aeneas
now menaces with death and instant ruin
the head of anyone who dares draw near;
he threatens to tear down the city and
he terrifies the shuddering Italians;   1010
though wounded, he keeps on. Five times they circle
the field and, just as many times, weave back,
this way and that. They seek no trifling prize:

what they strive for is Turnus' blood and life.

Just here, by chance, had stood a bitter-leaved   1015
wild olive tree, sacred to Faunus; sailors
had long since venerated it; when saved
from waves, they fastened here their offerings
to the Laurentians' god; here they would hang
their votive garments. Heedless of this custom,   1020
the Teucrians had carried off the sacred
tree trunk to clear the field, to lay it bare
for battle. Here the shaft Aeneas first
had cast at Turnus stood; its impetus
had carried it and held it fast in that   1025
tenacious root. The Dardan bent, wanting
to wrench his shaft free, then with spear, to catch
the warrior whom he could not overtake
on foot. And Turnus, wild with terror, cries:
"I pray you, Faunus, pity me; and you,   1030
most gracious Earth, hold fast that steel if I
have ever kept your rites—those that Aeneas'
men have profaned by war." He spoke, invoked
the help of gods with prayers that were not useless;
for though Aeneas struggled long and lingered   1035
above the gripping root, no force of his
could loose the spearhead from that tough wood's bite.
While, fierce, he wrenches, tugs, the Daunian
goddess, Juturna, once again takes on
the form of Turnus' charioteer, Metiscus;   1040
she runs and gives his blade back to her brother.
But Venus, furious that this was granted
the daring nymph, drew near; and then she tore
Aeneas' spearhead free from that deep root.
Both men are high in heart; they face each other,   1045
their arms and courage fresh again—one trusts
his sword; the other, tall and fierce, his shaft—
Aeneas, Turnus, breathless for Mars' contest.

Meanwhile Olympus' king calls out to Juno
as from a golden cloud she scans the battle: 1050
"Wife, how can this day end? What is there left
for you to do? You know, and say you know,
that, as a deity, Aeneas is owed
to heaven, that the fates will carry him

high as the stars. What is your plan? What is   1055
the hope that keeps you lingering in these
chill clouds? And was it seemly for a god
to be profaned by a human wound? Or for
a sword that had been lost to be restored
to Turnus (without you, Juturna could   1060
do nothing)? Was it right to give fresh force
to those who are defeated? Stop at last;
give way to what I now ask: do not let
so great a sorrow gnaw at you in silence;
do not let your sweet lips so often press   1065
your bitter cares on me. This is the end.
You have harassed the Trojans over land
and wave, have kindled brutal war, outraged
Latinus' home, and mingled grief and marriage:
you cannot pass beyond this point." So, Jove;   1070
the goddess, Saturn's daughter, yielding, answered:

"Great Jupiter, it was indeed for this—
my knowing what you wish—that I have left
both Turnus and the earth, unwillingly.
Were it not so, you would not see me now   1075
alone upon my airy throne, enduring
everything; but girt with flames, I should
be standing on the battlefield itself,
to drag the Trojans toward the war they hate.
I do confess that I urged on Juturna   1080
to help her luckless brother; I approved
her daring greater things to save his life;
yet not to aim an arrow, not to stretch
her bow. I swear this by the pitiless
high fountainhead of Styx, the only pledge   1085
that fills the upper gods with dread. And now
I yield; detesting wars, I give them up.
And only this—which fates do not forbid—
I beg of you, for Latium, for your
own father's greatness, for the race of Saturn: 1090
when with their happy wedding rites they reach
a peace—so be it—when they both unite
in laws and treaties, do not let the native-
born Latins lose their ancient name, become
Trojans, or be called Teucrians; do not   1095
make such men change their language or their dress.

Let Latium still be, let Alban kings
still rule for ages; let the sons of Rome
be powerful in their Italian courage.
Troy now is fallen; let her name fall, too."   1100

And Jupiter smiled at her then; the maker
of men and things said: "Surely you are sister
to Jove, a second child of Saturn, for
deep in your breast there surge such tides of anger.
But come, give up this useless madness: I   1105
now grant your wish and willingly, vanquished,
submit. For the Ausonians will keep
their homeland's words and ways; their name will stay;
the body of the Teucrians will merge
with Latins, and their name will fall away.   1110
But I shall add their rituals and customs
to the Ausonians', and make them all—
and with one language—Latins. You will see
a race arise from this that, mingled with
the blood of the Ausonians, will be   1115
past men, even past gods, in piety;
no other nation will pay you such honor."
Juno agreed to this; with gladness she
then changed her mind. She quit the skies, her cloud.

This done, the Father, left alone, ponders   1120
another plan: to have Juturna driven
far from her brother. It is said there are
two fiends who bear the name of Furies; they
were born in one same birth with hell's Megaera
out of untimely Night, who wrapped all three   1125
in equal serpents' folds and added wings
that take the wind. These wait before the throne
of Jove, the threshold of the cruel king,
and spur the fears of feeble mortals when
it happens that the king of gods flings down   1130
dread sorrow and diseases or when he
sends war to terrify unrighteous cities.
And quickly Jupiter sends one of these
from heaven's height, commanding her to meet
Juturna as an evil emissary.   1135
She flies off; cloaked in whirlwinds, she is carried

to earth. Just as an arrow that is driven
from bowstring through a cloud, an arrow tipped
in gall and venom, an incurable shaft,
shot by some Parthian—a Parthian   1140
or a Cydonian; as it hurtles, hissing,
it passes through swift shadows, seen by no one:
so did the child of Night rush on; she sought
the earth. As soon as she can see the Trojan
ranks and the troops of Turnus, suddenly   1145
she shrinks into the shape of that small bird
which sometimes sits by night on tombs and lonely
rooftops, where it chants late, among the shadows,
its song of evil omen; so transformed,
the foul one howls before the face of Turnus,   1150
flies back and forth; her wings beat at his shield.
Strange stiffness, terror, took the limbs of Turnus;
his hair stood up; his jaws held fast his voice.

But when, far off, Juturna recognized
the shrill wings of the Fury, luckless, she   1155
tears at her flowing hair, defiles her face
with nails, her breast with fists. "Turnus, how can
your sister help you now? And what is left
for all my struggle? By what art can I
draw out your daylight? Can I stand against   1160
such prodigies? Now I must leave the field.
You, filthy birds, do not excite my fears;
I know the beating of your wings, your fatal
shrieking; I know these are the harsh commands
of that great-hearted Jove. Is this how he   1165
requites me now for my virginity?
Did he give me eternal life for this?
For this have I have been made exempt from death?
I surely would be done with such a sorrow
and go as my sad brother's comrade through   1170
the Shadows. I immortal? But can any
thing that is mine be sweet to me without
you, brother? For what lands are deep enough
to gape before me, to send me, a goddess,
into the lowest Shades?" And saying this,   1175
Juturna placed a gray veil on her head;
moaning, she plunged into the river's depths.
           ❋   ❋   ❋

And now Aeneas charges straight at Turnus.
He brandishes a shaft huge as a tree,
and from his savage breast he shouts: "Now what   1180
delay is there? Why, Turnus, do you still
draw back from battle? It is not for us
to race against each other, but to meet
with cruel weapons, hand to hand. Go, change
yourself into all shapes; by courage and   1185
by craft collect whatever help you can;
take wing, if you so would, toward the steep stars
or hide yourself within the hollow earth."
But Turnus shakes his head: "Your burning words,
ferocious Trojan, do not frighten me;   1190
it is the gods alone who terrify me,
and Jupiter, my enemy." He says
no more, but as he looks about he sees
a giant stone, an ancient giant stone
that lay at hand, by chance, upon the plain,   1195
set there as boundary mark between the fields
to keep the farmers free from border quarrels.
And twice-six chosen men with bodies such
as earth produces now could scarcely lift
that stone upon their shoulders. But the hero,   1200
anxious and running headlong, snatched the boulder;
reaching full height, he hurled it at the Trojan.
But Turnus does not know if it is he
himself who runs or goes or lifts or throws
that massive rock; his knees are weak; his blood   1205
congeals with cold. The stone itself whirls through
the empty void but does not cross all of
the space between; it does not strike a blow.
Just as in dreams of night, when languid rest
has closed our eyes, we seem in vain to wish   1210
to press on down a path, but as we strain,
we falter, weak; our tongues can say nothing,
the body loses its familiar force,
no voice, no word, can follow: so whatever
courage he calls upon to find a way,   1215
the cursed goddess keeps success from Turnus.
Then shifting feelings overtake his heart;
he looks in longing at the Latin ranks
and at the city, and he hesitates,
afraid; he trembles at the coming spear.   1220

He does not know how he can save himself,
what power he has to charge his enemy;
he cannot see his chariot anywhere;
he cannot see the charioteer, his sister.

In Turnus' wavering Aeneas sees   1225
his fortune; he holds high the fatal shaft;
he hurls it far with all his body's force.
No boulder ever catapulted from
siege engine sounded so, no thunderbolt
had ever burst with such a roar. The spear   1230
flies on like a black whirlwind, carrying
its dread destruction, ripping through the border
of Turnus' corselet and the outer rim
of Turnus' seven-plated shield; hissing,
it penetrates his thigh. The giant Turnus,   1235
struck, falls to earth; his knees bend under him.
All the Rutulians leap up with a groan,
and all the mountain slopes around reecho;
tall forests, far and near, return that voice.
Then humble, suppliant, he lifts his eyes   1240
and, stretching out his hand, entreating, cries:
"I have indeed deserved this; I do not
appeal against it; use your chance. But if
there is a thought of a dear parent's grief
that now can touch you, then I beg you, pity   1245
old Daunus—in Anchises you had such
a father—send me back or, if you wish,
send back my lifeless body to my kin.
For you have won, and the Ausonians
have seen me, beaten, stretch my hands; Lavinia   1250
is yours; then do not press your hatred further."

Aeneas stood, ferocious in his armor;
his eyes were restless and he stayed his hand;
and as he hesitated, Turnus' words
began to move him more and more—until   1255
high on the Latin's shoulder he made out
the luckless belt of Pallas, of the boy
whom Turnus had defeated, wounded, stretched
upon the battlefield, from whom he took
this fatal sign to wear upon his back,   1260
this girdle glittering with familiar studs.

And when his eyes drank in this plunder, this
memorial of brutal grief, Aeneas,
aflame with rage—his wrath was terrible—
cried: "How can you who wear the spoils of my   1265
dear comrade now escape me? It is Pallas
who strikes, who sacrifices you, who takes
this payment from your shameless blood." Relentless,
he sinks his sword into the chest of Turnus.
His limbs fell slack with chill; and with a moan   1270
his life, resentful, fled to Shades below.

GODS, HALF-GODS, MORTALS, PEOPLES, PLACES:

A GLOSSARY

The references at the end of each entry in this glossary are to the *first* occurrence of the proper name, with line numbers referring to the English lines of this translation. For a rough gauge of the Latin line number to which the English line corresponds, see the Latin line numbers given at the top of each page in the translation.

Cross-references in the body of an entry are indicated by capitals and small capitals. Only the most useful of them have been so marked.

The following note on this glossary will be needless for some readers. But for those to whom the accentuation and syllabification of Latin proper names are not familiar, I urge a careful reading of this note before consulting the glossary. Poets are devoted to naming and names and, especially, to proper names. To mangle a name in reading is to mangle a line, and some lines —in catalogue passages, battle scenes—are made up mostly of names. The shape of these lines will not be lost for those who have gone through the following with a little patience.

Two marks are used in this glossary: the accent mark and the diaeresis. These are supplemented by the hyphen in the few instances where, without a hyphen, syllabification might be unclear.

The accent mark is used to indicate the principal—and, most

often, only—stress in a word; it appears *after* the syllable receiving that stress.

The diaeresis is used for two purposes: 1) to indicate that a terminal **e** preceded by a consonant or consonants forms part of a syllable to be pronounced separately (**Andro'machë, Cymo'docë**); 2) to separate vowels that cluster together but are to be pronounced as, or in, separate syllables *when the vowels are not already separated by an accent* (thus, there will be a diaeresis in **Hippo'coön, Pasi'phaë, Creü'sa**; there will not be one in **I'o**).

Vowel clusters may involve:

1. Two vowels that are to be pronounced as, or in, separate syllables. As already indicated, they will either be separated by an accent (**Aene'as, Alphe'us, I'o**) or, if they are not separated by an accent, the second vowel will be marked by a diaeresis (**A'niö, Andro'geös**).

2. Two vowels that are to be considered and sounded as one: the Latin diphthongs **ae** (**Ae'olus**), **au** (**Lau'sus**), **oe** (**Oe'balus**), and **eu** (**Or'pheus**). Please remember that **ae, au, oe,** and **eu** are not *necessarily* diphthongs; they are diphthongs only if not separated by an accent or marked by a diaeresis. Thus the **ae** of **Pasi'phaë**, the **au** of **Menela'us**, the **oe** of **Be'roë**, the second **eu** of **Eune'us**, are not diphthongs. The diphthongs may be pronounced in a variety of ways:

a) **ae** like **y** in **by** in the classical method, and like **a** in **late** in the ecclesiastical or Italian method: **Thymbrae'us**. Anglicized as **e** of **less** or **ee** of **see** in the familiar **Dae'dalus** and **i** of **trip** in the familiar **Chimae'ra**.

b) **au** like **ow** in **now** in both the classical and ecclesiastical methods: **Lau'sus, Cerau'nia**. Anglicized **au** of **caution** will also do.

c) **oe** like **oi** in **oil** in the classical method and like **a** in **late** in the ecclesiastical or Italian method: **Coroe'bus**. Anglicized **ea** of **easy** will also do.

d) **eu** like **eu** in **feud** in the classical method and like **eu** of Italian **neutro** in the ecclesiastical method: **Salmo'neus, An'theus**.

3. Combinations involving more than two vowels. These take five forms in this translation: diphthong followed by a vowel, a vowel followed by a diphthong, three vowels, two diphthongs, two vowels followed by a diphthong. In the four cases where the accent and the diaeresis are not enough to make the separate syllables clear for the reader, hyphens have been used between vowel elements, as in **Ae-ae'an**, where the hyphen

separates two diphthongs. A number of words in this class also carry separate notes to add to clarity.

With the above in hand, the reader can easily apply the rule that *a Latin word has as many syllables as it has vowels and diphthongs,* needing only two supplementary guides to help him with dividing a word into syllables:

1. A single consonant between two vowels goes with the second vowel: the l of **Pi-lum′nus.**

2. When two or more consonants stand between two vowels, the last consonant goes with the second vowel: **Cas-mil′la.** The exceptions to this are **p, b, t, d, c, g** plus **l** or **r;** these pairs go with the second vowel: the **cl** of **Co′cles,** the **dr** of **An-tan′dros. Ch, ph, th,** and **qu** also count as single consonants and go with the second vowel: **ch** of **A-chae-me′ni-des; ph** of **O-phel′tes; th** of **A′ma-thus; qu** of **A-qui′co-lus.** (Exception: **Vol′scian** and **Vol′scians,** Anglicized forms in this translation, have also been Anglicized in their syllable divisions in the glossary.)

The *only* points of uncertainty in relation to vowel clusters and number of syllables will occur with two vowel pairs, ia and iu, *when neither vowel bears a principal stress.* The **ia** of **Lavi′nia** and the **iu** of **Mezen′tius** are examples (whereas the **u** of **Iü′lus,** which does bear stress, will be marked). These vowel pairs, **ia** and **iu,** are not marked by diaereses in this translation—though they would definitely count as, or in, separate syllables in Latin—for this reason: In my English text there are indeed times where they *must* be read as belonging to two syllables as they would in Latin ("First, from the Tuscan coasts, Mezentius," VII, 854). But in other metrical contexts, I have elided these pairs. (There are many terminological variants for the phenomenon referred to here. Robert Bridges speaks of the "midword synaloepha common to our speech"; elsewhere synizesis, syneresis, or—as I should prefer—the use of couples in one metrical position covers what I am talking about. But elision, though less precise, is by far the most familiar term.) Elision *can* also affect pairs that *are* marked by diaereses under the indications given earlier; that is, it can affect *any* situation where two vowels appear together. But elision is more likely to affect **ia** and **iu** than other vowel pairs; and I have, therefore, left them more flexible and unmarked. In general—with reference to all vowel pairs, with or without diaeresis—elision will be more likely where both vowels are free of principal stress, less likely where one of the vowels does bear principal stress.

A'baris: one of the Rutulians besieging the Trojans' camp in the absence of Aeneas. IX, 458.

A'bas:

1. one of the captains of Aeneas' fleet; his ship suffers in the storm. I, 173.
2. a Greek warrior killed at Troy whose arms Aeneas dedicates at Actium. Conington discounts the coincidence of his name with that of an early king of Argos. III, 370.
3. an Etruscan who comes to the aid of Aeneas from Populonia. X, 239.

Abel'la: a city in Campania known for its orchards. VII, 977.

A'camas: a Greek—son of Theseus and brother of Demophoön —concealed in the wooden horse. II, 363.

Acar'nian: of Acarnia, a mountainous region in western Greece. V, 394.

Ac'ca: a comrade in arms of Camilla. XI, 1087.

Aces'ta: a city in western Sicily, originally named after Acestes, then called Egesta and, later still, Segesta. V, 947.

Aces'tes: King of Sicily, of Trojan lineage. I, 271.

Achae'an: Greek. I, 691.

Achaeme'nides: a Greek, crewman of Ulysses. He is rescued by the Trojans from the CYCLOPS. III, 796.

Acha'tes: faithful companion of Aeneas. I, 173.

A'cheron: "River of Grief" in the lower world or, in general, a name for the lower world. V, 137.

Achil'les: son of Peleus, the king of Phthia, and of the goddess Thetis (whom Jupiter had wooed but abandoned when he learned she would bear "a son destined to be greater than his father"). He was the greatest warrior in the Greek army at Troy. His quarrel with Agamemnon, his commanding officer, is central to Homer's *Iliad*. For his chivalrous treatment of the aged Priam, who had come to him as a suppliant for the return of his son Hector's body, see *Iliad*, XXIV. I, 47.

Ac'mon: a Trojan, son of Clytius and brother of Menestheus; he came from Lyrnesus. X, 183.

Acoe'tes: an Arcadian, armor-bearer of Evander, sent to war as attendant of PALLAS. XI, 40.

Acon'teus: a Latin. XI, 806.

A'cragas: Greek name for a coastal city of southwestern Sicily; in Latin, Agrigentum, modern Agrigento. III, 910.

Acri'sian: of the Argives; see Acrisius. VII, 547.

Acri'sius: king of Argos and father of Danae. VII, 494.

A'cron: a Greek ally of Aeneas. X, 987.

Ac'tian: of ACTIUM. VIII, 916.

Ac'tium: a headland on the northwestern Greek coast and site of a temple to Apollo. Here Aeneas makes a landfall;

here Octavian, later called Augustus, defeated Antony and Cleopatra on September 2, 31 B.C. III, 361.

Ac'tor: one of those defending the Trojan camp in the absence of Aeneas. IX, 665.

Adamas'tus: father of ACHAEMENIDES. III, 797.

Adras'tus: King of Argos, one of the Seven against Thebes, and the only one to return alive. VI, 632.

Adria'tic: the modern Adriatic, sea bordering Italy on the east. XI, 537.

Ae'acus: father of Peleus and grandfather of Achilles, ancestor of the Macedonian kings. VI, 1116.

Ae-ae'an: of Aeaea, an island where Circe had her home. III, 502.

Aegae'on: hundred-headed giant who warred against the gods; he is sometimes identified with Briareus. X, 778.

Aege'an: adjective used with reference to the sea between Greece and Asia; also applied to Neptune. III, 97.

Ae'gis: see GORGON.

Aemi'lius Pau'lus: (died 160 B.C.), Roman general who conquered the Macedonian king Perseus (a reputed descendant of Achilles) in 168 B.C. VI, 1114.

Aene'adae: a settlement founded by Aeneas on the coast of Thrace. III, 26.

Aene'as: hero of the *Aeneid*. The son of Anchises and Venus and a member of the royal family of Troy, he was a secondary figure in the *Iliad*, which yet notes that "his might shall reign among the Trojans." There was an early tradition that he escaped when Troy fell and went to some place in Italy. I, 131.

Aeö'lia: a group of islands off the coast of Sicily, thought to include the domain of Aeolus and the home of the winds. I, 76.

Aeö'lian: of Aeolia. VIII, 547.

Ae'olus:
1. god of the winds. I, 78.
2. father of Misenus. VI, 227. This Aeolus may be a Trojan (perhaps, as Heyne suggests, the Trojan who was killed in XII, 731) or the god of the winds.
3. a king of Thessaly; according to post-Homeric legend, the father of Sisyphus and grandfather of Ulysses. VI, 700.
4. father of CLYTIUS (1), IX, 1032.
5. see AEOLUS (2). XII, 731.

Ae'qui: Italian mountain tribe inhabiting the valleys of the upper Anio, Tolenus, and Himella in central Italy. VII, 984.

Ae'qui Falis'ci: an Etrurian town near Fescennium. VII, 915.

Aescula'pius: son of Apollo, renowned as a healer. When Aesculapius restored Hippolytus to life, Jupiter was angered

at his interference and killed Aesculapius with his thunder-
bolt. VII, 1014.

Ae'thon: the warhorse of Pallas. (In the *Iliad,* VIII, 185, the
name is given to one of Hector's horses.) XI, 116.

Aeto'lian: of Aetolia, a district in northwestern Greece, birth-
place of Diomedes; hence applied to ARPI. X, 39.

Af'rica: used here for the country around Carthage. IV, 47.

Af'ricus: the southwest wind. I, 122.

Agamem'non: king of Mycenae, brother of Menelaus and
commander in chief of the Greeks before Troy. He had
sacrificed his daughter, Iphigenia, to obtain favorable winds
for the Greek fleet; on his return from the war he was
murdered by his wife Clytemnestra. At Apollo's order, their
son Orestes killed his mother to avenge his father. IV, 650.

Agathyr'si: a people of Scythia who practiced tattooing. IV,
194.

Age'nor: an ancient king of Phoenicia. I, 478.

A'gis: a Lycian. X, 1031.

Agrip'pa, Mar'cus Vipsa'nius: (ca. 63 B.C.–12 B.C.) friend of
Augustus and commander of the fleet at ACTIUM. Earlier
he had been decorated with the naval crown—which bore
representations of the prows of ships—for his victory over
Sextus, son of Pompey the Great. VIII, 884.

Agyl'la: old name for CAERE. VII, 860.

Agyl'lines: people of AGYLLA. XII, 381.

A'jax: son of Oileus; a Greek warrior. (He is not to be con-
fused with "the greater Ajax," son of Telamon.) During
the sack of Troy Ajax violated Cassandra, who had fled for
sanctuary to the altar of Minerva's temple. For this crime
Minerva punished him. I, 63.

Al'ba: a city in Italy destined to be founded by Ascanius,
son of Aeneas; from it came the mother of Romulus and
Remus, founders of Rome. I, 12. Also Alba Longa. I, 379.

Al'bans: people of ALBA. V, 789.

Al'bula: ancient name for the TIBER. VIII, 433.

Albu'neä: site of a grove and sulphur spring, variously sup-
posed to be near Tibur, near Ardea, or near Lavinium; a
place of prophecy taking its name from the nymph
Albunea. For a full discussion of the difficulties in defining
and locating Albunea, see Conington on this passage. VII,
105.

Alcan'der: a Trojan defending Aeneas' camp against the
Rutulian attack. He is killed by Turnus. IX, 1022.

Alca'nor:
1. Trojan, father of Pandarus and Bitias. IX, 1022.
2. son of Phorcus, brother of Maeon. He fought for
Turnus. X, 469.

Alca'thoüs: a Trojan. X, 1025.

Alci'des: "a descendant of Alcaeus," used especially for Hercules. The name is based on Alcaeus, son of Perseus, who was the father of Amphitryon and grandfather of Hercules. v, 547.

Ale'tes: a Trojan, comrade of Aeneas, whose ship is damaged in the storm; in Book IX he is present at the council in Aeneas' camp. I, 174.

Allec'to: one of the FURIES. (Her "Gorgon poison" may be an allusion to the serpents which grew from her head instead of hair, as did the snakes of the GORGONS.) VII, 431.

Al'lia: a river, tributary of the Tiber, on whose banks the Romans were disastrously defeated by the Gauls under Brennus on July 16, 390 B.C. The anniversary of this defeat was ever afterward a day of evil omen. VII, 943.

Al'mo: eldest son of Tyrrhus, killed at the outbreak of hostilities between Trojans and Latins. VII, 700.

Alo'eus: a giant whose sons Otus and Ephiates warred against the gods and were therefore punished in Tartarus. VI, 772.

Alphe'an: of the River ALPHEUS, which flows by the city of Pisa in Elis (part of the Peloponnesus in Greece); the similar names gave rise to a belief that emigrants from this Greek city had established Pisa in Etruria. X, 254.

Alphe'us: a river (and river god) in southern Greece, part of whose channel lay underground; the ancients believed that the god had thus forced a passage undersea to reach the nymph ARETHUSA. III, 898.

Al'pine: of the Alps or its inhabitants. VII, 857.

Alps: modern Alps. VI, 1101.

Al'sus: a Latin. XII, 416.

Al'tars: name given to certain reefs between Sicily and Africa. I, 156.

Amase'nus: a river in Latium east of the Pontine marshes. (Virgil addresses it as a god.) VII, 903.

Amas'trus: a Trojan, victim of Camilla. XI, 887.

Ama'ta: wife of Latinus, mother of Lavinia. VII, 455.

A'mathus: a city on the southern coast of Cyprus, site of a temple of Venus. X, 69.

Amazo'nian: of the AMAZONS. V, 411.

A'mazons: a race of women warriors living near the Black Sea. "Amazon" in Greek means "breastless"; they were said to remove their right breasts to handle their bows better. They were allies of the Trojans against the Greeks; their queen PENTHESILEA was killed by Achilles. I, 694.

Amiter'num: city of the Sabines in Italy, now San Vittorino. VII, 932.

Amphi'tryön (four syllables; the "y" counts as a vowel): husband of Alcmene, who was, by Jupiter, the mother of Hercules, VIII, 133.

Ampsanc'tus: a lake and its valley, east of Naples, said to be one of the entrances to the lower world. VII, 742.

Amy'clae: a coastal town of Latium between Caieta and Anxur supposed to have been settled by Greeks from the town of the same name in Laconia, southeast of Sparta. The epithet "silent" is explained by deriving it from the Laconian Amyclae, whose people were proverbially taciturn, "laconic," or by the legend that after many false alarms a law was enacted under which no one in Amyclae might ever announce the enemy's approach. When the real enemy came, the city fell by silence. X, 778.

A'mycus:

1. a Trojan, comrade of Aeneas, reported missing among the survivors who land with Aeneas at Libya. I, 310.
2. ruler of Bebrycia in Bithynia, Asia Minor. Renowned as a boxer, he was killed by Pollux. V, 493.
3. a Trojan follower of Aeneas, defender of the Trojan camp against the Rutulian attack; killed by Turnus. IX, 1029.
4. father of Mimas by Theano. X, 965.
5. brother of DIORES (2); perhaps identical with Amycus (1) according to Conington. XII, 686.

Anag'nia: town in Latium. VII, 903.

Anche'molus: a Marsian who had incestuous relations with his stepmother and fled to Turnus' side. X, 537.

Anchi'ses: member of the younger branch of the royal family of Troy; grandson of Assaracus, son of Capys, and father of Aeneas by Venus. I, 866.

An'cus (Mar'tius): fourth king of Rome, according to tradition. VI, 1081.

Andro'geös:

1. Greek warrior at Troy. II, 499.
2. son of King Minos of Crete; he was killed by the Athenians, for which deed each year they had to deliver to the Minotaur seven youths and seven maidens as expiatory victims until the monster was slain by Theseus. VI, 28.

Andro'machë: wife, then widow of Hector, mother of Astyanax. At the fall of Troy she, together with Helenus—son of Priam—was assigned to Achilles' son Pyrrhus (or Neoptolemus) as a spoil of war. After the murder of Pyrrhus by Orestes, Helenus and Andromache—now married—succeeded to his realm. II, 610.

Angi'tia: a goddess whose name may be connected with or derived from *anguis,* "snake." She was worshiped by the Marsi and had a sacred grove on the lake of Fucinus. A city of the Marsi, on the lake of Fucinus, takes its name from her. VII, 997.

A'niö: a river in the Sabine region of Italy on the border of Latium. VII, 900.

A'nius: a king of Delos and priest of Apollo. III, 105.

An'na: sister and confidante of Dido. IV, 10.

Antae'us: a soldier of Turnus. X, 773.

Antan'dros: a town of Asia Minor, near Troy. III, 8.

Antem'nae: ancient Italian town not far from Rome. It belonged to the Sabines and stood where the Anio flowed into the Tiber. It was conquered by Romulus. VII, 833.

Ante'nor: nephew of Priam. He escaped the fall of Troy and reached Italy before Aeneas. There he founded Padua. I, 338.

An'theus: a Trojan. He was a comrade of Aeneas. I, 254.

Anti'phates: son of Sarpedon who fights alongside the Trojans in Italy. IX, 930.

Anto'nius: Mark Antony (ca. 82 B.C.–30 B.C.). He was designated by the Second Triumvirate to rule the East. His love for Cleopatra was a factor in his war with Rome, in which he was defeated at Actium. He and Cleopatra committed suicide. VIII, 892.

Anto'res: companion of Hercules, adherent of Evander, ally of Aeneas. X, 1070.

Anu'bis: an Egyptian god usually represented by a human body and the head of a dog or jackal. VIII. 909.

An'xur:

1. a coastal town of the Volscians in Latium, site of a cult of Jupiter. It was later called Terracina. VII, 1050.

2. a soldier of Turnus. X, 754.

Aör'nos: "birdless"; Greek name for AVERNUS. VI, 323.

Ap'ennines: principal mountain range of central Italy. XI, 690.

Apenni'nus: the APENNINES personified as "father." XII, 933.

Aphid'nus: a Trojan defending the camp in Italy during Aeneas' absence. IX, 939.

Apol'lo: son of Jupiter and Latona, brother of Diana, god of the sun, inspirer of prophecy, patron of music, he was born at DELOS. I, 465.

Apu'lian: used in this translation as variant for IAPYGIAN. XI, 895.

Aqui'colus: a Rutulian, one of those who attack the Trojans' cam in Aeneas' absence. IX, 916.

A'rab: inhabitant of the country of Arabia, in southwest Asia, but loosely applied to any nomadic tribesmen akin to the Arabs. VII, 799.

Ara'xes: a river in modern Armenia. Alexander had a bridge built over it, but it was swept away. VIII, 950.

Arca'dia: a mountainous district of Greece in the Peloponnesus, home of rustic simplicity and innocence, birthplace of Evander. VIII, 208.

Arca′dian: of Arcadia. v, 395.

Ar′cens: father of an unnamed auxiliary of Aeneas. ix, 773.

Arce′tius: a Rutulian. xii, 616.

Ar′cher God: APOLLO. iii, 98.

Archip′pus: king of the Marsi who sends troops to aid Turnus. vii, 988.

Arctu′rus: brightest star of the constellation Bootes, which rises in stormy weather. i, 1038.

Ar′deä: a town in Italy, south of Rome, capital of the Rutulians; it is the birthplace of Turnus. vii, 548.

Arethu′sa: a nymph with whom ALPHEUS fell in love when she bathed in his river. She fled from him as far as Syracuse in Sicily where she was transformed by Artemis into a fountain. But Alpheus flowed undersea and rejoined Arethusa. iii, 900.

Argile′tum: a district of Rome near the Forum. The name is derived from *argilla* "clay." Virgil, following the popular etymology, says that one Argus, Evander's guest, was put to death here (*letum*) for treachery. In later times the booksellers established themselves in this district. viii, 452.

Ar′give: (noun) Greek. i, 60.

Ar′give: (adj.) Greek. i, 338.

Ar′gos: a city in Greece loved by Juno; also used for Greece as a whole; thus the name Argives for the Greeks. i, 38.

Ar′gus:
  1.   a monster with a hundred eyes sent by Juno to guard Io after her transformation into a heifer; when at Jupiter's request Mercury killed Argus, Juno set the eyes of the slain Argus into the tail feathers of her bird, the peacock, and sent a gadfly to torment Io. vii, 1040.
  2.   a guest of Evander, killed at ARGILETUM. viii, 453.

Argy′ripa: Arpi; since Diomedes, its founder, was Aetolian by birth, this Italian city is called "Greek" or "Aetolian." xi, 322.

Ariäd′në: daughter of Minos. She fell in love with THESEUS and, aided by Daedalus, helped Theseus find his way through a labyrinth by means of a guiding thread. vi, 40.

Ari′cia: a nymph, consort of HIPPOLYTUS-Virbius after his resurrection and mother by him of VIRBIUS (2). The town of Aricia—a city in Latium south of Alba Longa, famous as a site of Diana's worship—is named for her. vii, 1101.

Aris′ba: a city in the Troad near Abydos; according to Homer (*Iliad*, ii, 836), it sent auxiliary forces to Troy. ix, 354.

Ar′pi: a city of Apulia (now Puglia) in Italy founded by Diomedes after the Trojan war. Its other name was ARGYRIPA; the similarity of this name to Argos may have prompted the legend of its founding. viii, 12.

Ar′pis: the people of ARPI. xi, 566.

Ar'runs: an Etruscan on Aeneas' side. XI, 1008.

Asby'tes: a Trojan. XII, 490.

Asca'nius: son of Aeneas by Creüsa. He was destined to inherit the Italian realm on his father's "translation." While Troy stood, he was called Ilus—supposedly from Ilium—and as the Trojans fared toward Italy, he was called Iülus as the ancestor of the *gens Iulia,* from which came Julius Caesar and Augustus. I, 373.

A'sia: Asia Minor or its western coast; name used originally for a town of Lydia. I, 547.

A'sian: of Asia. VII, 922.

Asi'las:

　1. a Trojan. IX, 759.

　2. Etruscan chief and seer from Pisa. He came to the aid of Aeneas. X, 246.

A'sius: a Trojan. X, 175.

Assa'racus:

　1. an early king of Troy, son of Tros and brother of Ilus and Ganymede. He was the father of Capys and the grandfather of Anchises. This Capys is not to be confused with the two of the same name mentioned in the *Aeneid.* I, 398.

　2. name of two soldiers of Aeneas. X, 176.

Asty'anax: the little son of Hector and Andromache. The Greeks threw him down from the walls so that he could not grow up to avenge his city. II, 613.

As'tyr: an ally of Aeneas. X, 255.

A'thesis: the Adige, a river of northern Italy. IX, 912.

A'thos: mountain in Macedonia at the end of the peninsula of Chalcidice. XII, 932.

A'tian: of the *gens* Atia; see ATYS. V, 747.

Ati'na: Italian town near Arpinus; its people were Volscians. VII, 832.

Ati'nas: a Rutulian leader. XI, 1153.

Atlante'an: descending from Atlas. VIII, 178.

At'las:

　1. the mighty being who supported the sky on his shoulders. He was the father of the Pleiades, and he was skillful in astronomy. I, 1034.

　2. mountain in north-west Africa, supposed to be the sky-bearer Atlas, metamorphosed. IV, 330.

At'reus: son of Pelops, king of Mycenae, father of Agamemnon and Menelaus. I, 649.

A'tys: a Trojan boy, a special friend of Iulus. He was said by Virgil to be the ancestor of the *gens Atia,* from which came the mother of Augustus. Virgil is thus prefiguring the adoption of Augustus (then Octavianus), from the *gens Atia,* by Julius Caesar of the *gens Iulia.* V. 747.

Au'fidus: a river in the Apulian territory of Diomedes now called the Ofanto; it flows into the Adriatic. XI, 536.

Augus'tus Cae'sar: C. Octavius, grandnephew of Julius Caesar, who adopted him. He was then known as C. Julius Caesar Octavianus. He was the first Roman emperor, his rule extending from 27 B.C. to 14 A.D. Augustus was used as his title to avoid a monarchial ring. VI, 1049.

Aules'tes: Etruscan chief, ally of Aeneas. X, 292.

Au'lis: port of embarkation for the Greek forces against Troy. IV, 584.

Au'nus: a Ligurian, whose son is killed by Camilla. XI, 924.

Auro'ra: goddess of the dawn, mother of Memnon. I, 1046.

Aurun'ca: an old town in Campania. VII, 273.

Aurun'can: of the Aurunci, a central Italian people, the oldest inhabitants of Italy, who lived near the coast and the rivers Liris and Ufens. VII, 958.

Auso'nia: Italy (from which the adjective Ausonian). III, 226.

Auso'nian: of Ausonia. IV, 316.

Auto'medon: charioteer and armor bearer of Achilles; in some versions Achilles' charioteer and armor bearer of Pyrrhus. II, 627.

A'ventine: see AVENTINUS. VII, 871.

Aventi'nus: son of Hercules by a priestess, Rhea. He was born on the Aventine, one of the seven hills of Rome, which became the plebian quarter and a place of worship for "strange gods." VII, 864.

Aver'nus: a lake and its woods near Cumae. Its fumes were thought fatal to birds passing over it (see AORNOS); close by, there was said to be an entrance to the lower world. III, 577.

Bacchan'tes (always a trisyllable in this translation): women worshippers of Bacchus who held wild rites in his honor in forests and on mountain tops. III, 168.

Bac'chus: god of wine. He is also known as Lyaeus, Liber, and Dionysus. I, 888.

Bac'tria: an oriental kingdom near India. It had been conquered by Alexander. VIII, 894.

Ba'iae (bisyllable; the "i" does not count as a vowel): a resort on the Campanian coast near Naples and Cumae with hot springs and baths. Wealthy Romans had villas there, built out onto the sea. Virgil may have had the opportunity to watch construction of the *portus Bulius* at Baiae. IX, 950.

Barcae'an: of a North African tribe whose city was Barca. IV, 156.

Bar'cë: the nurse of Sychaeus. IV, 872.

Ba'tulum: a city in Campania built by the Samnites. VII, 975.

Bears: the Big and Little Dipper. I, 1039.

Bebry'cian: of Bebrycia, a region of Bithynia in Asia Minor. V, 493.

Bello'na: goddess of war. VII, 422.

Be'lus:

    1. father of Dido. I, 870.

    2. father of the Tyrian dynasty. I, 1016.

    3. father of Palamedes. II, 114.

Bena'cus: a lake in the region of Verona, now called Lago di Garda, from which the Mincius rises. X, 291.

Berecyn'thian: of Berecynthus, a mountain in Phrygia sacred to Cybele. VI, 1039.

Be'roë: an old Trojan woman; Iris takes on her form. V, 817.

Bi'tias:

    1. a courtier of Dido. I, 1030.

    2. a Trojan, son of Alcanor and Iaera, brother of Pandarus. He is among the defenders of Aeneas' camp in Aeneas' absence. IX, 899.

Bo'la: town in Latium. VI, 1024.

Bo'reäs: god of the north wind. He may be imagined as coming out of Thrace. X, 486.

Bri'areus: a hundred-handed giant who warred against the gods; he is also known as Aegaeon. VI, 379.

Bron'tes: CYCLOPS (2). VIII, 557.

Bru'tus: in the *Aeneid* the name refers to Lucius Junius Brutus, who drove out TARQUIN in 510 B.C. and founded the Roman republic. He executed his sons for plotting the restoration of the Tarquins. VI, 1084.

Bu'tes:

    1. a famous boxer who had been defeated by Dares. V, 492.

    2. the old armor bearer of Anchises to whom Aeneas entrusts Ascanius. IX, 864.

    3. a Trojan. XI, 911.

Buthro'tum: a port in Epirus, now Butrinto in Albania. III, 379.

Byr'sa: "the Hide," a Greek corruption of the Phoenician Bosra, the citadel of Carthage. From this corruption, there arose the legend of the Phoenician colonists buying from the Libyans a stretch of land as large as could be encompassed by a bull's hide. By the ingenious stratagem of cutting the hide into thin strips, the Phoenicians were able to enclose and obtain a large tract of land. I, 519.

Ca'cus: "the Bad"; fire-breathing giant, son of Vulcan. He terrorized the country around Pallanteum until he was slain by Hercules. VIII, 258.

Cae'culus: founder of Praeneste, son of Vulcan, ally of

Turnus. His mother is said to have conceived him from a spark which flew up from the hearth. VII, 894.

Cae'dicus:
 1. an Italian, a friend and guest of Remulus. IX, 480.
 2. an Etruscan in the ranks of Mezentius. X, 1025.

Cae'neus:
 1. The male name of the nymph Caenis, who had been transformed into a man by Neptune. IV, 591.
 2. a Trojan, one of those defending Aeneas' camp in his absence. IX, 762.

Cae'rë: Etruscan city previously called Agylla; now Cervetri. A center of religious worship, located on the coast northwest of Rome, it furnished the levies commanded by Lausus. VIII, 775.

Cae'sar: see JULIUS. I, 401.

Caï'cus: a Trojan, comrade of Aeneas. I, 255.

Caie'ta (trisyllable; the "i" does not count as a vowel, but as a consonantal "y"): nurse of Aeneas who, like Palinurus and Misenus, gave her name to her burial place, a harbor and headland on the western coast of Italy; modern Gaeta. VI, 1202.

Cal'chas: a Greek priest and seer who is with the army at Troy. II, 173.

Ca'les: a city located in Campania, a region south of Latium. It was the site of a cult of Juno. VII, 959.

Calli'opë: muse of epic poetry. IX, 696.

Ca'lybë: aged priestess of Juno at Juno's Rutulian temple; her form is assumed by Allecto when Allecto visits Turnus. VII, 557.

Ca'lydon: a city of Aetolia whose king, Oeneus, angered Diana. She sent a wild boar to devastate the region; it was hunted by a company of heroes and finally killed by Meleager, who awarded the trophies of the chase to Atalanta. Calydon was also the birthplace of Diomedes. VII, 404.

Camari'na: a coastal city of southern Sicily and a marsh of the same name. It was the marsh which "the Fates forbade to be dislodged"; when it was drained, the enemy was able to capture the city. III, 906.

Ca'mers: son of Volcens, comrade of Turnus. X, 775.

Camil'la: a Volscian warrior maiden, ally of Turnus. VII, 1055.

Camil'lus, Mar'cus Fu'rius: victor over the Gauls who had captured Rome in 390 B.C. He rescued the Roman standards, which had fallen to the Gauls after an earlier Roman defeat. VI, 1094.

Cape'na: city in Etruria, north of Rome. VII, 917.

Caphe'reus: a promontory on the eastern coast of Euboea, where the Greeks were shipwrecked when homeward bound from Troy. It was also said that the father of PALAMEDES hung out false beacons here to cause the shipwreck. XI, 341.

Ca'pitol: a reference to the summit of the Capitoline Hill and to the magnificent temple of Jupiter Optimus Maximus, or Jupiter Capitolinus, which stood there in historic times and was the center of the Roman state religion. VI, 1113.

Ca'pre-ae: modern Capri. VII, 970.

Ca'pys:
  1. a Trojan, comrade of Aeneas. I, 255. Mentioned as eponymous founder of Capua in X, 204.
  2. a king of Alba Longa whom Anchises shows to Aeneas in the line of their descendants. VI, 1014.

Ca'rians: a people living in western Asia Minor on the Aegean Sea. VIII, 945.

Cari'nae: the fashionable quarter in Rome from the last years of the Republic on. Cicero, Pompey, and Mark Antony were among its residents. VIII, 473.

Carmen'tal gate: one of the city gates of Rome, named in honor of CARMENTIS and standing near an altar to her. VIII, 442.

Carmen'tis: mother of Evander. She was a nymph gifted with prophetic powers; Ovid (*Fasti*, I, 467) derives her name from *carmen,* "prophetic song." VIII, 338.

Carpa'thian: a name for the stretch of the Aegean Sea between Crete and Rhodes, from an island located there. V, 782.

Car'thage: city in North Africa, for centuries the inveterate rival of Rome. Dido, fleeing with a band of Tyrian refugees from the atrocities of her brother, is its legendary founder. Its tutelary goddess is Juno. I, 19.

Carthagi'nians: people of CARTHAGE. VI, 1145.

Casmil'la: wife of METABUS, mother of CAMILLA. XI, 713.

Caspe'ria: a town of the Sabines. VII, 939.

Cas'pia: the region around the Caspian Sea. VI, 1058.

Cassan'dra: Trojan princess, daughter of Priam and Hecuba. She was loved by Apollo, who gave her the gift of prophecy; but when she rejected him, he added the curse that her prophecies would never be believed. II, 341.

Cas'tor: a Trojan who held the first line of defense at Aeneas' camp. X, 178.

Cas'trum I'nuï: a town in Latium; *Castrum* means a military camp. VI, 1023.

Ca'tiline, Lu'cius Ser'gius: Roman extremist who, in the last years of the republic, attempted to seize power by a coup d'état. His conspiracy was thwarted by Cicero. Declared an outlaw, he fled Rome and fell in battle with government troops in 62 B.C. VIII, 866.

Catil'lus: brother of Tiburtus and twin brother of Coras. A

founder of Tibur, he came to join Turnus in war against Aeneas. VII, 887.

Ca'to (the Elder): 234–149 B.C., Roman statesman, conservative in politics, severe in morals, embodiment of Roman gravity, an advocate of destruction for Carthage. VI, 1120.

Cau'casus: mountain near the Caspian Sea where Prometheus was chained. IV, 499.

Cau'lon: city of southern Italy. III, 720.

Cays'ter: a river of Lydia in Asia Minor. VII, 922.

Celae'no: chief of the HARPIES. III, 278.

Celem'na: a city in Campania. VII, 975.

Cen'taurs: a race of beings who are half-man, half-horse, said to have been begotten by Ixion, who, in his lust for Juno, was deceived by a cloud shaped like her. See LAPITHAE. VI, 378.

Cerau'nia: Greek for "thunder-headlands." Headlands in northwestern Epirus, dangerous to ships. III, 661.

Cer'berus: the three-headed dog who guarded the gates of Hades. VI, 551.

Ce'res: goddess of agriculture, especially of grain (therefore, English "cereal"), she was the daughter of Saturn, sister of Jupiter, and mother of Proserpina. I, 248.

Cethe'gus: a Rutulian. XII, 693.

Chal'cis: city of Euboea of which Cumae was a colony. VI, 24.

Cha'lyb: of the Chalybes, a people on the south coast of the Black Sea. They were legendary for their skill in ironwork and were sometimes considered the inventors of this craft. VIII, 552.

Chalybe'an: variant for CHALYB. X, 245.

Chaö'nia: district of Epirus. III, 378.

Chaö'nian: of CHAONIA. III, 345.

Cha'os: deity and personification of the primal state in which earth, sea, and sky were all mingled in confusion. In Virgil, he is the father of Erebus and Nox (Night). IV, 707.

Cha'ron: son of Erebus and Nox (Night); the ferryman who transports across the Styx those dead who have received the proper rites of burial (which often included the placing of a coin between the lips of the dead to pay the fare) or who, lacking these rites, have worked out their time by waiting 100 years on the near shore. VI, 394.

Charyb'dis: the monster whirlpool on the Sicilian side of the Straits of Messina. Together with SCYLLA, it represents a danger to ships.

Chimae'ra:
1. a monster, one of the guardians of the underworld. Part lion, part goat, part serpent, it breathed fire. In V, 162 its name is used for a ship. VI, 381.

2. a miraculous representation of the monster on the helmet of Turnus. VII, 1033.

Chlo'reus:
1. a Phrygian priest of Cybele. XI, 1019.
2. a Trojan, XII, 491.

Chro'mis: a Trojan, killed by Camilla. XI, 890.

Cimi'nius or Ci'minus: mountain and lake (now Lago di Ronciglione). VII, 917.

Ciny'ras: a Liguran ally of Aeneas, supposedly the brother of Cupavo and the son of CYCNUS. X, 260.

Cir'cë: an enchantress who changed Ulysses' men into swine. III, 502.

Circen'sian: (adj.) of or celebrated in the Roman Circus. VIII, 825.

Cis'seus:
1. ruler of Thrace, father of Hecuba, father-in-law of Priam. V, 704.
2. son of MELAMPUS, fighting for Turnus. X, 440.

Cithae'ron: a mountain in Greece on which the rites of Bacchus were celebrated. IV, 407.

Cla'rus: brother of SARPEDON. X, 179.

Clau'dian: see CLAUSUS. VII, 930.

Clau'sus: a Sabine chieftain from whom the prominent Claudian family in Rome was descended. VII, 927.

Cloän'thus: a Trojan, comrade of Aeneas, founder of the Roman house of Cluentius. I, 311.

Cloe'lia: a Roman girl, one of the several hostages given to Lars PORSENNA; she escaped with her companions, swam the Tiber, and returned to Rome. The Romans sent all the hostages back to Porsenna who, according to tradition, was moved by admiration, not anger, at Cloelia's bravery (Livy, II, 13). VIII, 844.

Clo'nius:
1. a Trojan. IX, 764.
2. another Trojan. X, 1028.

Clo'nus: son of Eurytus, skilled worker in metals, decorator of the belt of Pallas (son of Evander). X, 687.

Cluën'tius: patrician family of Rome. V, 168.

Clu'sian: of CLUSIUM. X, 900.

Clu'sium: one of the twelve chief cities of Etruria (modern Chiusi), situated on the river Clanis, which flows into the Tiber. X, 236.

Cly'tius:
1. son of Aeolus. IX, 1032.
2. father of Acmon and Menestheus of Lyrnesus. X, 184.
3. a beautiful Rutulian youth, beloved of Cydon, who fights for Turnus. X, 450.

4. father of EUNEUS, perhaps identical with CLYTIUS (2). XI, 878.

Cnos'sus: capital of Crete, and site of the palace of Minos and the Labyrinth. III, 155.

Co'cles, Pu'blius Hora'tius: famous Roman who held the Etruscans (under Lars PORSENNA) at bay until the Pons Sublicius, a wooden bridge over the Tiber, could be cut down by Cocles' companions, leaving the enemy on the far bank with no access to the city. Then Cocles, in full armor, jumped into the river and swam back to the city. VIII, 843.

Cocy'tus: river in the underworld. VI, 184.

Coe'us: son of Earth, one of the Titans. IV, 237.

Colla'tia: town of the Sabines near Rome. VI, 1022.

Co'ra: Volscian town of Latium. VI, 1024.

Co'ras: brother of Tiburtus and twin brother of Catillus. He was founder of Tibur and an ally of Turnus against Aeneas. VII, 887.

Co'rinth: a city in central Greece, on the isthmus of the same name. In 146 B.C. Mummius captured and destroyed it. VI, 1112.

Coroe'bus: an ally of Priam. He is in love with Cassandra and fights alongside Aeneas in the last battle of Troy. II, 464.

Coryban'tes: priests who honored CYBELE with loud music and wild dances. III, 148.

Corynae'us:
1. a Trojan priest, first mentioned as taking part in the funeral rites for Misenus, then (IX, 759) as one who is killed by Asilas. VI, 305.
2. another Trojan. XII, 405.

Co'rythus:
1. father of Dardanus. He was said to have founded the city of Corythus in Italy. III, 226.
2. ancient town of the Etruscans, reputed birthplace of Dardanus. X, 986.

Co'sae: an old Etruscan city. X, 237.

Cos'sus, Au'lus Corne'lius: one of the three Roman generals ever to win the "chieftain's spoils" (spolia opima) by killing the enemy commander and taking his armor in single combat. (The other two were ROMULUS and MARCELLUS.) Cossus won his spoils of honor by slaying Tolumnius the Etruscan king in 437 B.C. VI, 1120.

Cre'tans: people of Crete. IV, 193.

Crete: island in the Aegean Sea. III, 138.

Cre'theus:
1. a Trojan warrior-lord who took part in the defense of Aeneas' camp against the Rutulians. IX, 1033.
2. a Greek. XII, 725.

Creü'sa: daughter of Priam, first wife of Aeneas, mother of Ascanius. Her fate is left in question; on the night of Troy's fall she is perhaps "translated" into an attendant of CYBELE. II, 756.

Crini'sus: Sicilian river god. In some texts, Crimisus. V, 51.

Crustu'mium: ancient Italian town of the Sabines near Rome. III, 576.

Cu'mae: an Italian city, not far from Naples, first settled by the Greeks. It was the home of the Sibyl and was located near an entrance to the lower world. III, 576.

Cupa'vo: son of CYCNUS and ally of Aeneas. X, 262.

Cupen'cus: a Rutulian priest. XII, 727.

Cu'pid: son of Venus, god of love. I, 919.

Cu'res: capital of the Sabines near Rome; TATIUS was its king; and from Cures also came Numa Pompilius, second king of Rome, its legendary lawgiver and religious teacher. VI, 1075.

Cure'tes: early inhabitants of Crete, later known as dancing priests of Jupiter. Like the Corybantes, with whom they have been identified, they were said to have protected the baby Jupiter, hidden on Crete from his father Saturn, who sought to destroy him, by drowning out his cries with the clashing of their cymbals. III, 176.

Cy'belë:
  1. also called Rhea, sister and consort of Saturn or Cronos, mother of the gods. The worship of this goddess is thought to have reached Troy from Crete. She is represented as riding in a chariot drawn by lions; her priests were the Corybantes, eunuchs who worshiped her with clashing cymbals, ecstatic dances, and orgiastic rites. X, 312.
  2. a mountain in Phrygia, sacred to Cybele. III, 147. In XI, 1020, where the Latin has "Cybelus" for Mount Cybele, the translation simplifies to Cybele, the goddess rather than the mountain.

Cy'clades: an island cluster in the Aegean forming a circle around Delos. III, 170.

Cy'clops (normally "Cyclo'pes" in the plural, but out of my distaste for the sound of that, I have used "Cyclops" as both singular and plural in this translation, for which the OED provided some warrant):
  1. a race of giants inhabiting Sicily. They had an eye in the center of their foreheads and they fed on human flesh. I, 281.
  2. the superhuman workers of Vulcan's forge. Their names: Steropes, "Lightener"; Pyracmon, "Fire-anvil"; and Brontes, "Thunderer." VII, 556.

Cyc'nus: mythical king of Liguria, father of Cupavo, friend of Phaethon. While grieving over the death of Phaethon, he was changed into a swan. x, 266.

Cy'don: a soldier in the army of Turnus. x, 448.

Cydo'nian: of Cydonia in Crete, used for Cretan. xii, 1141.

Cylle'në: mountain in Arcadia, birthplace of Mercury. iv, 337.

Cymo'docë: a sea nymph, daughter of Nereus. v, 1092.

Cymo'thoë: a sea nymph. i, 203.

Cyn'thus: a mountain of Delos, birthplace of Apollo and Diana. i, 703.

Cy'prus: one of the homes of Venus; same as modern Cyprus. i, 871.

Cythe'ra: an island off the southeastern coast of Greece near which Venus was said to have been "born" of the sea foam (see Botticelli's painting "Primavera"). The island (modern Serigo) was a center of her worship. i, 952.

Cythere'a: another name for Venus, derived from the name of CYTHERA. i, 358.

Cythere'an: native of Cythera: Appellation of Venus. i, 918.

Dae'dalus: the fabulous craftsman who built the labyrinth to contain the Minotaur for King Minos of Crete. When imprisoned there with his son ICARUS, Daedalus contrived an escape by fashioning wings of feathers held by wax on wooden frames. Daedalus' flight ended at Cumae, vi, 19.

Da'hae: a nomadic tribe east of the Caspian Sea. viii, 949.

Da'naäns: the Greeks; derived from Danaus, ancient king of Argos. i, 136.

Da'naë: daughter of Acrisius. Her father imprisoned her because of a prophecy that said he would die by the hand of his daughter's son; but Jupiter visited her and she bore him a son, Perseus. Acrisius caused both mother and baby to be placed in a wooden chest which was set adrift upon the sea. According to Virgil, the waves carried it to Italy, where Danae founded Ardea. vii, 545.

Dar'dan: (noun and adj.) See DARDANUS. i, 698.

Dar'dans: see DARDANUS. i, 846.

Dar'danus: son of Zeus and of Electra, the daughter of Atlas. He was the mythical founder of Troy and first ancestor of Priam. From him the Trojans are sometimes called Dardanians or Dardans. i, 790.

Da'res:
    1.   a Trojan contender in the boxing match. v, 488.
    2.   another Trojan. xii, 492.

Dau'cus: father of the twins THYMBER and LARIDES. x, 541.

Dau'nian: one of the DAUNIANS. xii, 959.

Dau'nians: the people of Turnus; Rutulians. viii, 190.

Dau'nus: legendary king of Apulia, father of Turnus. x, 847.

De'cii: a Roman family of which two members, father and

son, both named Publius Decius Mus, reputedly gave up their lives in battle in order to obtain Roman victories. The father sacrificed himself at the time of the Latin War in 340 B.C. at the battle of Veseris, and the son at the battle of Sentinum in 295 B.C., fighting against the Samnites. VI, 1093.

De-i-o-pe′a: one of Juno's nymphs (perhaps a "divinity of honor," just as mortal queens have "maids of honor") whom Juno offers as bribe to Aeolus for routing Aeneas with a storm. I, 105.

Deï′phobë: daughter of Glaucus; the Cumaean Sibyl. VI, 50.

Deï′phobus: a son of Priam who married Helen after the death of Paris. In the fall of Troy, Helen betrayed Deiphobus to the Greeks; he was killed and mutilated. II, 423.

De′lian: of Delos. III, 215.

De′los: a holy isle in the Aegean Sea. It was said that when Latona, pregnant by Jupiter, felt her time approaching, she knew that no spot on earth would give her shelter because of Juno's jealousy—except for Delos, which was then a floating island. There Apollo and Diana were born. In gratitude, Apollo secured the island so that it no longer floated, and it became a center of his worship. Delos is also called Ortygia. III, 166.

Demo′docus: a soldier of Aeneas. X, 574.

Demo′leös: a Greek vanquished by Aeneas. V, 344.

Demo′phoön: a Trojan killed by Camilla. XI, 890.

Dercen′nus: an ancient king of the Laurentians. XI, 1129.

Dia′na: daughter of Jupiter and Latona; twin sister of Apollo; virgin goddess of the woods and the hunt. Diana is also goddess of the moon and, as Hecate, goddess of the lower world, of magic, and of crossways. Hence she is sometimes spoken of as Trivia, "triple-shaped" and "three-faced." I, 703.

Dic′të: a mountain in Crete. Here the infant Jupiter was hidden from his father Saturn. III, 227.

Di′do: Tyrian princess, also called Elissa. She founded Carthage when she fled with her followers from her murderous brother. I, 422.

Didyma′on: an artist in metal-relief work. V, 475.

Din′dyma: Phrygian mountain sacred to Cybele. IX, 825.

Diome′des: son of Tydeus; one of the most important Greek chieftains at Troy. The *Iliad* tells how he wounded Ares and Aphrodite. He captured the famous swift horses of Aeneas and drove off the horses of Rhesus before they could feed on Trojan pasture or drink of Trojan streams, thus preventing the fulfillment of the oracle that if these horses were to feed and drink of Troy, the city could never be taken. After the Trojan war, he settled Apulia, founding ARPI. I, 136.

Diö'në: mother of Venus. III, 29.

Diö'res:

1. a Trojan of Priam's family; comrade of Aeneas. V, 392.
2. brother of Amycus. XII, 686. Heyne identifies him with Diores (1), but Conington disagrees.

Diöxip'pus: a Trojan. IX, 764.

Dis: Pluto. IV, 968.

Dodo'na: town in Epirus, famous for its oracular oak tree sacred to Jupiter and for its brass caldrons. III, 610.

Dolicha'on: father of HEBRUS (2). X, 954.

Do'lon: a Trojan spy caught in the Greek camp and killed by Diomedes (*Iliad*, x, 299 ff.). XII, 469.

Dolo'pian: of or pertaining to a Greek people of Thessaly. II, 9.

Dony'sa: an Aegean island. III, 169.

Do'ric: of the Dorians, a Greek people. II, 39.

Do'ryclus: a man of Epirus, husband of Beroë. V, 818.

Do'to: a Nereid. IX, 135.

Dran'ces: an elderly Latin antagonistic to Turnus. XI, 588.

Dre'panum: coastal city of western Sicily; now Trapani. III, 915.

Dru'si: a Roman family from which came Livia, second wife of Augustus. VI, 1093.

Dry'opë: a nymph. Mother of Tarquitus by Faunus. X, 761.

Dryo'pians: a people of Greece. IV, 194.

Dry'ops: a warrior of Aeneas. X, 483.

Duli'chium: an island in the Ionian Sea not far from Ithaca. III, 350.

Dy'mas: a Trojan who fights alongside Aeneas in the last battle of Troy. II, 463.

Earth: the earth as a goddess. IV, 235.

E'bysus: a Latin. XII, 407.

Edo'nian: of the Edoni, a Thracian people on the Strymon. XII, 494.

Ege'ria: a nymph who, with Diana, sheltered HIPPOLYTUS. VII, 1003.

E'gypt: sometimes reckoned by the ancients as belonging to Asia. VIII, 893.

Elec'tra: a daughter of Atlas. One of the Pleiades, she was the mother of Dardanus by Jupiter. (Electra, daughter of Agamemnon and Clytemnestra, has no part in the *Aeneid*.) VIII, 178.

E'lis: a region and city of the Peloponnesus in Greece. III, 898.

Elis'sa: another name of DIDO. IV, 452.

Ely'sium: the region of the lower world reserved for those who had been righteous in life. V, 967.

Ema'thion: a Trojan killed by LIGER. IX, 759.

Ence'ladus: son of Earth, a Giant. After the attempt of the Giants to dethrone Jupiter, he was punished by being buried under Mount Etna. III, 752.

Entel'lus: Sicilian boxing champion. V, 513.

Epe'os: builder of the wooden horse and one of the troop concealed in it. II, 365.

Epi'rus: a coastal region of northwestern Greece. III, 377.

E'pulo: a Rutulian. XII, 617.

Epyti'des: guardian and companion of Ascanius. V, 717.

E'pytus: a Trojan. He fights alongside Aeneas at the fall of Troy. II, 461.

E'rato: a Muse whose principal association is with love poetry. It has been suggested that she is involved in Book VII because the war in Italy was kindled by the love of Lavinia's suitors. VII, 45.

E'rebus: primeval darkness. The offspring of Chaos, he is the father, by his sister Night, of Day; a name for the lower world. IV, 32.

Ere'tum: ancient city of the Sabines on the Tiber. VII, 935.

Erice'tes: a Trojan, son of LYCAON (2). X, 1028.

Eri'danus: a river which, flowing underground for part of its course, was thought to have its source in the lower world. It is sometimes identified with the Po. VI, 872.

Eriphy'lë: wife of Amphiaraus, king of Argos. In the war of the Seven against Thebes, she sent her husband to his death. For this act she herself was killed by her son Alcmaeon. VI, 587.

E'rulus: superhuman son of the goddess Feronia. He was killed by the youthful Evander. VIII, 732.

Eryman'thus: a mountain in Arcadia in southern Greece. Hercules killed a giant boar that lived thére. V, 595.

E'rymas: a Trojan, one of those defending the camp in Italy while Aeneas is absent. IX, 938.

Erythrae'an Sea: the Indian Ocean. VIII, 890.

E'ryx:
1. a mountain and city of the same name on the northwestern coast of Sicily, with a temple of Venus. I, 802.
2. a King in Sicily, son of Venus and thus stepbrother of Aeneas. Renowned as a boxer, he was nevertheless killed by Hercules in a boxing match. V, 32.

Ethiö'pia: country south of Egypt. IV, 663.

Et'na: a volcano in Sicily. III, 742.

Etne'an: of Etna. III, 876.

Etru'ria: a region of Italy settled by the people called Etruscan or Tuscan, who were believed to have come from Lydia in Asia Minor. VIII, 641.

Etru'rian: of Etruria. XII, 314.

Etrus'can: Tuscan. VIII, 654.

Euboe'an: of Euboea, a large Aegean island just east of Greece. Cumae, an Italian colony of the Euboean city of Chalcis, is called "Euboean." VI, 3.

Eume'des: a Trojan. XII, 468.

Eume'lus: a Trojan companion of Aeneas. He gives the alarm when the women set fire to the ships. V, 875.

Eune'us: a Trojan, son of CLYTIUS (4), killed by Camilla. XI, 878.

Euphra'tes: river of the Fertile Crescent, later fixed as the easternmost boundary of the Roman Empire. VIII, 947.

Eu'rope: continent of Europe, name said to have derived from Europa, daughter of Agenor, king of Phoenicia, mother of Sarpedon and Minos by Jupiter who, in the form of a bull, had carried her off to Crete. I, 547.

Euro'tas: the river on which Sparta stood. I, 702.

Eu'rus: the southeast wind. I, 121.

Eury'alus: a Trojan companion of Aeneas, friend of Nisus; a contestant in the foot race. V, 388.

Eury'pylus: a Greek, one of the host before Troy. II, 161.

Eurys'theus: the Greek king for whom Hercules performed his twelve labors. VIII, 384.

Eury'tiön: of Lycia, an ally of Troy, brother of Pandarus. He is a participant in the archery contest. V, 653.

Eu'rytus: father of CLONUS. X, 688.

Evad'në: wife of Capaneus, one of the Seven against Thebes. When he was killed, Evadne threw herself on his funeral pyre. VI, 590.

Evan'der: "Goodly man," son of Mercury by the nymph Carmentis and mythical king of Arcadia. Long before the fall of Troy, he founded Pallanteum, a colony of his exiled countrymen, on the banks of the Tiber. His son, Pallas, fights beside Aeneas. VIII, 66.

Evan'thes: a soldier of Aeneas. X, 962.

Fa'baris: a river of the Sabine region, affluent of the Tiber. Modern Farfa. VII, 941.

Fa'bii: a Roman family whose most famous member was Quintus Fabius Maximus (died in 203 B.C.) called Cunctator ("Delayer") because, with his policy of "Fabian gradualism," he wore down Hannibal by attrition —avoiding pitched battle, which the forces at his disposal could not have sustained. VI, 1125.

Fabri'cius: Roman consul and general in the early part of the third century B.C. Adversary of Pyrrhus the Macedonian, he was famous for his incorruptibility. VI, 1123.

Fa'dus: a Rutulian, one of those besieging the men of Aeneas in their leader's absence. IX, 457.

Fates: the Parcae, three goddesses who wrought the destinies of men: Clotho spun the thread of each mortal's life; Lachesis measured it; Atropos cut it. They also held power over the gods, as various deities themselves acknowledge directly or indirectly (Jupiter, Juno). The precise relation between Jupiter's sway over gods and men and the Fates' power is not made clear. In the *Aeneid* mortals address their prayers to the gods and goddesses, not to the Fates. I, 29.

Fau'nus: Italian rural deity or deified king; in the *Aeneid* he is represented as the son of Picus, grandson of Saturn, father of Latinus and (x, 543) of Tarquitus. VII, 58.

Fero'nia: ancient Italian goddess (one site of her worship was near Anxur) sometimes thought to be the wife of Jupiter of Anxur. She was a goddess of fertility to whom flowers and fruits were offered; also, the goddess of emancipation from slavery—the newly freed put on the cap of liberty at her shrine near Anxur. Her son was ERULUS. VII, 1051.

Fescen'nium or **Fescen'nia:** town in Etruria. VII, 915.

Fide'na: town in Latium near Rome. VI, 1021.

Flavi'nia: an Etruscan city. VII, 916.

Fo'ruli: a town in the Sabine region. Now called Civita Tommasa. VII, 939.

Fo'rum: the center of the political, commercial, and religious life of Rome. VIII, 474.

Fu'cinus: a lake in the Apennines east of Rome on which stood Marruvium, capital of the Marsi, and ANGITIA. VII, 998.

Fu'ries: the Dirae, Eumenides, or Avenging Goddesses, bearers of frenzy and madness; their names are Megaera, Allecto, and Tisiphone. Used by Virgil of the Harpies as well. III, 328.

Ga'bii: see GABINE. VI, 1021.

Ga'bine: relating to the people of Gabii, an ancient Latin town near Rome, a site of Juno's worship. The Gabines were said to have been attacked by an enemy force while they were offering sacrifice but to have resisted and defeated this enemy while in their ritual attire. This attire consisted of a toga wound around the body—hence, the Gabine girdle—a form of dress apparently retained for sacred and ceremonial occasions. VII, 809.

Gaetu'lia: see GAETULIANS. V, 69.

Gaetu'lians: a warlike tribe of Gaetulia in North Africa. IV, 52.

Galae'sus: an old Italian noted for his righteousness and his wealth. He is killed in the first fighting between Latins and Trojans while trying to make peace. VII, 705.

Galate'a: a Nereid. IX, 134.

Gan'ges: a river of India. IX, 37.

Ga'nymede: a beautiful youth, son of a Trojan king (Lao-medon or Tros); he was carried to Olympus by Jupiter's eagle to be the god's cup bearer, replacing—or displacing—Hebe, Juno's daughter. I, 44.

Garaman'tes: a tribe of the interior of Africa, to the south-east of the GAETULIANS. VI, 1052.

Garaman'tia: the land of the GARAMANTES. IV, 263.

Garga'nus: a mountain promontory on the coast of Apulia. XI, 322.

Gaul: home of Celtic tribes in France and northern Italy (also used with wider geographical range). Around 390 B.C. these tribes captured Rome. Though expelled then, the following centuries saw them a constant menace to Rome. By 222 B.C. they were substantially pacified, but not finally conquered until 191 B.C. VI, 1146.

Gauls: see GAUL. VIII, 852.

Ge'la: a coastal city of southern Sicily, situated on a river of the same name. III, 908.

Gelo'ni: a Scythian people whose land was in southern Russia. VIII, 946.

Ge'ryön (trisyllable; the "y" is a vowel): a giant with three bodies, killed by Hercules. VI, 382.

Ge'tae: a tribe that lived along the Danube. VII, 799.

Glau'cus:
  1. a sea deity. V, 1087.
  2. father of the Sibyl; perhaps identical with Glaucus (1). VI, 52.
  3. a Trojan warrior, son of Antenor, whose shade Aeneas encounters in the lower world. VI, 636.
  4. a Trojan, son of Imbrasus. XII, 463.

Gno'sian: Cretan. V, 404.

Gor'gon: (n. and adj.) one of three mythical sisters (Stheno, Euryale, and Medusa), with snakes for hair; anyone who looked at a Gorgon was turned to stone. Medusa, the only one of the three who was mortal, had her head cut off by Perseus; it was then given to Minerva, who fixed it to her shield, the aegis. VI, 381.

Gorty'nian: of Gortyna, a city in Crete. XI, 1027.

Grac'chi: a prominent Roman family whose best known members, the brothers Tiberius (died 133 B.C.) and Gaius Sempronius (died 121 B.C.), paid with their lives for their efforts to reform the Roman constitution. VI, 1121.

Gravis'cae: Etrurian port city, north of Rome. The name is related to *gravis*, "heavy" or "oppressive," apparently because the region had an unhealthy climate. X, 259.

Gryne'an: of Grynium, a town in Asia Minor that had a temple and an oracle of Apollo. IV, 467.

Gy'aros: a small Aegean island. Virgil represents it as one of the "anchors" of DELOS. III, 100.

Gy'as:

1. a Trojan, comrade of Aeneas. I, 311.
2. son of Melampus, fighting for Turnus against Aeneas. X, 439.

Gy'ges: one of the Trojans defending Aeneas' camp against the onslaught of Turnus. IX, 1015.

Gylip'pus: an Arcadian. XII, 369.

Hae'mon:

1. a Rutulian, participating in the attack on the Trojans' camp during the absence of Aeneas. IX, 917.
2. an Italian whose son, priest of Apollo and Diana, was a soldier of Turnus. X, 739.

Halae'sus: an ally of Turnus, chief of the Aurunci. His origin is Greek. VII, 951.

Ha'lius: a Trojan defending Aeneas' camp against the Rutulian attack. He is killed by Turnus. IX, 1023.

Ha'lys: a Trojan defending Aeneas' camp against the Rutulian attack. He is killed by Turnus. IX, 1019.

Ham'mon or Am'mon: a Lybian god whom the Greeks identified with Zeus, and the Romans with Jupiter. IARBAS boasted of his descent from Hammon and introduced the worship of his parent-god among his countrymen. IV, 262.

Harpa'lycë: a legendary Thracian princess renowned in war and in the hunt. I, 448.

Harpa'lycus: a Trojan, killed by Camilla. XI, 890.

Har'pies: monsters with women's faces and the bodies of birds. III, 279.

He'brus:

1. a river of Thrace. I, 450.
2. a soldier of Aeneas. X, 954.

He'catë or Tri'via: an aspect of DIANA, and goddess of the lower world and of witchcraft. She was worshiped at crossways. IV, 707.

Hec'tor: prince of Troy, son of Priam and Hecuba, husband of Andromache, father of Astyanax. He slew Patroclus; Achilles, in revenge, killed Hector and then dragged his body three times around the walls of Troy. Priam went as suppliant to Achilles' camp to plead for the body (see ACHILLES). I, 139.

He'cuba: Priam's queen. II, 671.

He'len: daughter of Leda and Jupiter (who visited Leda in the guise of a swan), though she is sometimes spoken of as the daughter of Tyndareos, Leda's mortal husband. Helen, the most beautiful of all the women in the world, was wooed by suitors from the whole of Greece. When she finally chose Menelaus, he made all the other suitors pledge that they would come to his aid against anyone who should try to take her from him. After Helen's flight with Paris, Menelaus invoked this pledge to raise the Greek army against Troy. I, 908.

Hele'nor: a defender of the Trojans' camp, said to be the son of the Lydian king by a Licymnian slave. IX, 723.

He'lenus: a son of Priam. He was a prophet. At the fall of Troy, he was taken by Pyrrhus, son of Achilles, to his domain in Epirus. After the murder of Pyrrhus, Helenus—now married to Andromache—succeeded to the kingdom. III, 381.

He'licon: a mountain of Boeotia, haunt of the Muses. VII, 847.

Helo'rus: a river in southeastern Sicily with wide marshes near its mouth. III, 903.

He'lymus: a Sicilian of the court of Acestes, contestant in the foot race. V, 396.

Herbe'sus: a Rutulian, one of those besieging Aeneas' camp. IX, 458.

Her'cules: son of Jupiter and Alcmena, celebrated for his strength and his completion of the "Labors," the twelve tasks imposed on him by Hera. Heyne supposes Virgil had some authority in a story, now lost, for associating Hercules with the foundation of Tarentum. III, 718.

Hermi'nius: an Etruscan. XI, 843.

Hermi'onë: daughter of Menelaus and Helen and grand-daughter of Leda. She was sought in marriage by ORESTES and by PYRRHUS. III, 426.

Her'mus: a river of Asia Minor. VII, 948.

Her'nicans: a warlike tribe of Latium whose home was in the Trerus valley in a mountainous region. VII, 901.

Hesi'onë: daughter of Laomedon, sister of Priam. When Laomedon withheld from Apollo and Neptune the payment due them for their having built the walls of Troy, Neptune retaliated by sending a sea monster to which Hesione was exposed. Hercules rescued her and killed the monster. Hesione married Telamon, King of Salamis. VIII, 207.

Hespe'ria: the Land of the Evening or the Western Land; a name for Italy, since for one starting out from Troy, Italy lay far to the west. I, 748.

Hespe'rides: nymphs, daughters of Hesperus, the Evening Star. They kept a garden in the West where golden apples, guarded by the dragon Ladon, grew. IV, 669.

Hiceta'on: father of THYMOETES (2). X, 177.

Himel'la: a river of the Sabines, affluent of the Tiber. VII, 940.

Hippo'coön: a Trojan taking part in the archery contest. V, 649.

Hippo'lytë: a queen of the Amazons, wife of THESEUS. XI, 871.

Hippo'lytus: son of HIPPOLYTE and THESEUS and faithful worshiper of Diana. His stepmother Phaedra fell in love with him and made advances to him; when he repulsed her, she accused him falsely to his father. Neptune, invoked by Theseus, sent a bull from the sea who maddened the horses of Hippolytus so that they dragged him to death. Virgil has it that AESCULAPIUS, son of Apollo, restored Hippolytus to life, that Jupiter was displeased at this resurrection, and that Diana sheltered her votary in her Italian precinct, where he went by the name of VIRBIUS. He married ARICIA and had a son, also named Virbius. VII, 1000.

Hip'potas: a Trojan, killed by Camilla. XI, 888.

His'bo: a Rutulian in the army of Turnus. X, 531.

Ho'molë: a mountain of Thessaly in Greece, reputed haunt of the CENTAURS. VII, 891.

Hor'tine: of Horta, an ancient town on the Tiber. According to Pliny, it "perished without a trace." VII, 942.

House'hold Gods: used in this translation for the Penates, household or family deities, or gods of the state considered as a household. The singular *Lar* is usually translated here as "the god of the hearth." I, 100.

Hy'ades: constellation which rises in the stormy season. I, 1039.

Hydas'pes: a Trojan. X, 1026.

Hy'dra: one of various water monsters usually represented as serpentine and many-headed.
1. the fifty-headed beast of Tartarus. VI, 559.
2. the seven-headed Lernean Hydra killed by Hercules. Since the heads grew back as fast as they were cut off, Hercules finally killed the monster by cauterizing each decapitated neck with a brand of fire. The monster has been seen as representing malarial fever and its death as the draining of the marsh. VII, 869.

Hylae'us: a Centaur. VIII, 386.

Hyl'lus: a Trojan. XII, 721.

Hy'panis: a Trojan who fights beside Aeneas in Troy's last battle. II, 463.

Hyrca'nian: of Hyrcania, on the shores of the Caspian Sea. IV, 500.

Hyr'tacus:
1. father of HIPPOCOÖN. V, 650.
2. a Trojan, father of NISUS. IX, 233.

I-ae'ra: nymph of Phrygian Ida; mother, by Alcanor, of Pandarus and Bitias. IX, 900.

Iäpy'gian: of Iapygia, the region of Apulia in southeastern Italy. So named from Iapyx, a son of Daedalus. XI, 323.

Iä'pyx:
1. see IAPYGIAN.
2. Apollo's pupil, physician to Aeneas. XII, 530.

Iär'bas: African ruler, rejected suitor of Dido, one who claims descent from Hammon or Jupiter. IV, 262.

Iä'sius: son of Jupiter and Electra, brother of Dardanus. III, 222.

I'asus:
1. father of PALINURUS. V, 1113.
2. father of IAPYX (2). XII, 531.

I'carus: son of DAEDALUS and imprisoned with him in the labyrinth. When his father constructed wings for their escape, he warned Icarus not to fly too close to the sun, lest its heat melt the wax holding the feathers in place. Icarus disregarded the warning and fell to his death. VI, 44.

I'da:
1. a mountain near Troy. II, 944.
2. a nymph, mother of Nisus, according to some. I have followed Conington and other editors in taking Ida (2) to be identical with Ida (1). IX, 234.
3. a mountain on Crete. III, 139.

Idae'an: of Ida (1). IX, 145.

Idae'us:
1. Priam's charioteer, whose shade Aeneas encounters in the lower world. VI, 638.
2. a Trojan, one of those defending Aeneas' camp in his absence. IX, 665.

Ida'lia: variant for IDALIUM. X, 70.

Ida'lium: both a mountain and forest of Cyprus sacred to Venus and a town of Cyprus, center of her worship. I, 952.

I'das: a Thracian whose sons were warriors of Aeneas. IX, 765.

Id'mon: a Rutulian. XII, 102.

Ido'meneus: king of Crete, one of the commanders against Troy, he made a vow to the gods that on his homecoming he would immolate the first living thing he encountered. He was met by his son and fulfilled his promise by offering up the boy. The gods, in anger, sent a pestilence, and the people of Crete drove Idomeneus into banishment. III, 162.

I'lia: also known as Rhea Silvia; a priestess of Vesta, daughter of King Numitor, who had been deposed by a usurper. She was the mother by Mars of Romulus and Remus, the founders of Rome. I, 382.

I'lian: of Ilium—that is, of Troy. I, 138.

Ili'onë: princess of Troy, eldest daughter of Priam and Hecuba. I, 913.

Ili'oneus: a Trojan comrade of Aeneas. He was usually delegated spokesman when Aeneas himself was absent. I, 172.

I'lium: TROY; derived from ILUS (2). I, 100.

Illy'rian: of Illyria, a land on the coast of the Adriatic Sea. Navigation along its shores was proverbially dangerous. I, 339.

I'lus:

1. another name for ASCANIUS. I, 376.
2. son of Tros, father of Laomedon, and founder of Troy, from whom it takes the name Ilium. VI, 860.
3. a Rutulian soldier of Turnus. X, 555.

Il'va: Elba. X, 244.

Ima'on: a soldier of Turnus. X, 590.

Im'brasus:

1. father of Asius (one of Aeneas' soldiers). X, 175.
2. a Lycian, father of Glaucus and Lades. XII, 463.

I'nachus: first king of Argos and father of Io. Son of Oceanus, he is sometimes imagined as a river-god and is so represented on the shield of Turnus. VII, 380.

Ina'rimë: a volcanic island in the Tyrrhenian Sea, between the promontory of Misenum and Prochyta—modern Ischia. The name represents Virgil's misunderstanding or imperfect recollection of a line in the *Iliad* (II, 783) containing the phrase *ein Arimois,* "among the Arimoi"; here the two words have fused to form the name of the island. IX, 957.

In'dia: region extending from the Indus to China. VII, 800.

In'dians: inhabitants of India. VI, 1053.

I'no: a sea goddess. V, 1088.

I'o: daughter of INACHUS and princess of Argos beloved by Jupiter. Transformed into a heifer, she was vindictively tormented by Juno but ultimately regained human form. Her appearance on the shield of Turnus emphasizes his relation to Argos, traditional enemy of Troy. VII, 1037.

Iöl'las: a Trojan. XI, 843.

Iö'nian: of Ionia, maritime region of Asia Minor. III, 277.

Iö'pas: bard at the court of Dido. I, 1033.

I'phitus: a Trojan. He fights beside Aeneas at the fall of Troy. II, 585.

I'ris: goddess of the rainbow, Juno's messenger. IV, 964.

Is'marus:

1. a warrior of Lydian extraction, one of the defenders of Aeneas' camp. X, 196.
2. a city in Thrace. X, 487.

I'thaca: island in the Ionian sea off the west coast of Greece. It was the home of Ulysses. III, 352.

Ita'lians: people of Italy. I, 156.

I'talus: ancient hero—and eponymous ancestor—of the Italians. VII, 236.

I'taly: I, 4.

I'tys: a Trojan. IX, 764.

Iü'lus: another name for ASCANIUS. I, 374.

Ixi'on: King of the LAPITHAE, father of PIRITHOUS. He was punished in Tartarus for his attempt upon the chastity of Juno. VI, 797.

Jani'culum: a hill across the Tiber from Rome where, according to the account of Evander, Janus had established a city. VIII, 469.

Ja'nus: ancient Italian deity who presided over gateways and over beginnings, as of the day and the year. He was represented as facing both forward and backward. VII, 239.

Jove: JUPITER. I, 64.

Ju'lian: see JULIUS. VIII, 883.

Ju'lius: family name of Julius Caesar, who was supposed to be a descendant of Iülus (Ascanius). Octavian, his grand-nephew, later AUGUSTUS, took on this Julian name when he was adopted by Caesar. I, 405.

Ju'no: daughter of Saturn, sister and wife of Jupiter, queen of the gods, patron deity of Carthage, goddess of marriage. Juno's enmity to the Trojans derives from the judgment of PARIS and from the seduction by Paris of HELEN. I, 7.

Ju'piter: chief of the gods for the Romans, corresponding to the Greek Zeus: son of Saturn, whom he dethroned; husband and brother of Juno. I, 312.

Jutur'na: nymph of Italian lakes and springs, sister of Turnus. XII, 197.

Labi'cians: inhabitants of Labicum, a town in Latium. VII, 1047.

Lacedae'mon: SPARTA. VII, 482.

Laci'nian: of Lacinium, a promontory in southern Italy, where a temple to Juno stood. III, 179.

Laco'nian: Spartan. The "Laconian woman" is Helen. II, 812.

La'des: a Lycian, son of Imbrasus (2). XII, 463.

La'don: an Arcadian ally of Aeneas. X, 574.

Laër'tes: father of Ulysses. III, 352.

La'gus: a soldier of Turnus. X, 525.

La'mus: a Rutulian with the troops besieging Aeneas' camp. IX, 446.

La'myrus: a Rutulian with the troops besieging Aeneas' camp. IX, 445.

Laö'coön: Trojan priest of Neptune. II, 56.

Laödami'a: wife of Protesilaus, the first Greek to land at Troy. He sacrificed himself for the success of the expedition, but her grief was so deep that the gods allowed him to return for three hours. When he left her again, she committed suicide to join him in the world of the dead. VI, 590.

Laö'medon: king of Troy, father of Priam. He was a notorious cheat and trickster. Neptune and Apollo built the walls of Troy for him, but he refused to pay the agreed price. III, 321.

La'pithae: a Thessalian people. At the wedding of their ruler Pirithous they fought a battle with the CENTAURS, defeating them. VI, 798.

Lari'des: a Rutulian, son of Daucus and twin brother of Thymber. He is with the army of Turnus. X, 540.

Lari'na: an Italian comrade of Camilla. XI, 863.

Laris'sa: a town in Thessaly, ACHILLES' native region. II, 280.

Laris'san: of Larissa. XI, 535.

La'tagus: soldier of Aeneas. X, 954.

La'tin: as a noun, a member of the people of Latium; as adj., of LATIUM or the Latins. I, 11.

Lati'nus: son of Faunus, husband of Amata, father of Lavinia, destined father-in-law of Aeneas. His realm was LATIUM. VI, 1189.

La'tium: the Trojans' promised land in Italy, supposedly so named because Saturn was hidden—i.e. latent—there. I, 10.

Lato'na: a goddess whom Jupiter loved; mother by him of Apollo and Diana. I, 703.

Lauren'tian: of Laurentum. Used in this translation as variant for "Laurentine." VII, 58.

Lauren'tians: people of Laurentum. VI, 1189.

Lauren'tine: of Laurentum. V, 1052.

Lauren'tum: city of LATIUM. VIII, 1.

Lau'sus: son of MEZENTIUS, handsome, brave and full of promise. He fights alongside his father on behalf of Turnus. VII, 857.

Lavi'nia: daughter and only surviving child of Latinus and Amata. Beloved of Turnus, she is the destined bride of Aeneas. VI, 1009.

Lavi'nian: of LAVINIUM; an adjective describing the coasts of Latium because Aeneas was to found there the city of Lavinium. I, 4.

Lavi'nium: the city of Latium which it was Aeneas' mission to found in Italy; named in honor of his wife, LAVINIA. I, 360.

Le'da: wife of Tyndareos, king of Sparta. By Jupiter, who approached her in the form of a swan, she bore two eggs: according to some accounts one contained HELEN, the other Castor and Pollux. She was also the mother of Clytemnestra. I, 911.

Le'leges: an ancient people of Asia Minor, mentioned by Homer. Virgil seems to use the name for its archaic qualities. VIII, 945.

Lem'nos: an Aegean island upon which Vulcan fell when Jupiter hurled him from heaven. It was consequently held sacred to him and became an important site of his worship. VIII, 593.

Lenae'an: Bacchic, of wine; from Greek *lenaios*, "wine vat." IV, 276.

Ler'na: a marsh in Greece, home of the HYDRA (2). VI, 380.

Le'thë: the river of forgetfulness in the lower world. V, 1139.

Leucas'pis: a Trojan. VI, 437.

Leuca'ta: promontory on the island of Leucas in the Ionian sea. It was the site of a temple to Apollo. III, 355.

Libur'nians: inhabitants of the northeastern shore of the Adriatic, a region famous for its swift ships. I, 340.

Li'bya: northern Africa, west of the Nile. I, 34.

Li'byan: of LIBYA. I, 425.

Li'chas: an Italian warrior born by Caesarian section and therefore sacred to Phoebus as the god of healing. An adversary of Aeneas. X, 435.

Licym'nian: of Licymnia, a town in Argolis. IX, 724.

Li'ger: brother of Lucagus, soldier of Turnus. IX, 758.

Ligu'rians: people of Liguria, a region north of Etruria around the gulf of Genoa. The land was part of Gaul-south-of-the-Alps (Gallia Cisalpina); and the people held out against Rome until the end of the Second Punic War. X, 261.

Lilybae'um: a promontory at the western tip of Sicily. III, 913.

Li'parë: one of the island group off the coast of Sicily that is called Aeolian or, because of the islands' volcanic activity, Vulcanian. VIII, 547.

Li'ris: an Etruscan (according to Heyne) killed by Camilla. XI, 883.

Lo'crians: a people of northern Greece, some of whom settled in the toe of Italy, founding Naryx. Their leader had been AJAX, son of Oileus. III, 519.

Love: see CUPID. I, 926.

Lu'cagus: brother of Liger, soldier of Turnus. X, 793.

Lu'cas: an Italian, soldier of Turnus. X, 774.

Luce'tius: a warrior in the force attacking Aeneas' camp. IX, 757.

Luper'cal (the "proper" accent is on the second syllable, but "Lu'percal" is so established in English that the translation allows the latter accenting if an epic caesura is read in the line): a cavern at the foot of the Palatine Hill, originally sacred to an Italian god who protected the flocks against wolves; this deity was later identified with the Greek god

Pan of Mount Lycaeus because of the supposed connection between the word Lycaeus and the Greek word for wolf *lykos*. Here the she-wolf is supposed to have nursed Romulus and Remus. VIII, 450.

Luper'ci: priests of Lupercus, god of the LUPERCAL; each year they performed the rites of the Lupercalia, which included purification and fertility magic. VIII, 860.

Lycae'an: belonging to the Arcadian mountain of Lycaeus sacred to Jupiter and Pan. VIII, 451.

Lyca'on:
1. an artist of Gnossus in Crete. IX, 405.
2. father of Ericetes, a Trojan. X, 1029.

Ly'cia: a district of Asia Minor, between Caria and Pamphylia, famous for its fertile soil. IV, 191.

Ly'cian: of or belonging to a people of Lycia in Asia Minor who were allies of the Trojans. I, 164.

Lyc'tos: a town in Crete. III, 520.

Lycur'gus: a king of Thrace, enemy of Bacchus. III, 20.

Ly'cus: a Trojan, comrade of Aeneas. I, 310.

Ly'dian: of Lydia, a region in Asia Minor from which the Etruscans were traditionally supposed to have come. Hence Virgil uses the epithet interchangeably for Etrurian, Tuscan, Tyrrhenian. II, 1054.

Lyn'ceus: one of the Trojans defending Aeneas' camp against the Rutulian attack. IX, 1023.

Lyrne'sus: a town in the Troad. X, 183.

Macha'on: a Greek concealed inside the Trojan horse. Homer represents him as a physician. II, 365.

Mae'on: one of the seven brothers of Cydon, fighting for Turnus. X, 469.

Maeö'nia:
1. a region of Lydia in Asia Minor. Because it was adjacent to Phrygia, the word can connote Phrygia or Troy. IV, 289.
2. because the Etruscans were thought to have come from Lydia, the word can connote Etruria. VIII, 648.

Maeö'nian: of MAEONIA (1). IX, 725.

Maeö'tis, Lake: the modern Sea of Azov, in region inhabited by the fierce Scythians. VI, 1058.

Ma'gus: an Italian in the army of Turnus. X, 718.

Ma'ia (2 syllables; the "i" can be written as "j" and does not count as a vowel): daughter of Atlas, one of the Pleiades, mother by Jupiter of Mercury. I, 419.

Ma'leä: promontory at the southeastern tip of Greece. It was dangerous to navigation. V, 255.

Man'lius: Marcus Manlius Torquatus Capitolinus. When the Gauls invaded Rome around 390 B.C., he successfully defended the citadel where the temple of Jupiter and the house of Romulus stood, since he was warned by the cackling of the sacred geese as the Gauls approached for a night attack. Livy states that afterward the nobles grew jealous of his popularity and threw him from the Tarpeian rock. VIII, 845.

Man'to: seeress, prophetess, daughter of Tiresias. At the fall of Thebes she was taken prisoner and given to Apollo. According to legend, she served as oracular priestess at Delphi and Claros before coming to Italy, where she married Tiberinus and bore Ocnus, who named his city Mantua in her honor. X, 280.

Man'tuä: city on the Mincius, north of the Po. Virgil was born in a small village nearby. Virgil represents Mantua as the capital of the Etruscan alliance of twelve cities; Cato and Pliny say otherwise. The three races of Mantua were variously said to be Greek, Etruscan, and Umbrian, or Etruscan, Venetian, and Gaulish. X, 281.

Marcel'lus:

1. died 208 B.C.; Roman general who fought against the Gauls and in the Second Punic War; in 222 B.C., he was the third—and last—Roman commander ever to win the "chieftain's spoils" (see Cossus). VI, 1140.

2. (43–23 B.C.); a namesake and descendant of the former, nephew and son-in-law of Augustus. He showed great promise but died young. VI, 1178.

Mari'ca: a nymph of the environs of Minturnae, near the river Marica. She was the wife of Faunus and the mother of King Latinus. VII, 58.

Marpes'san: from the mountain of Marpessus, in the island of Paros, which contained white marble quarries. VI, 619.

Mars: god of war, son of Jupiter. I, 383.

Mar'sian: of the MARSIANS. VII, 996.

Mar'sians: a tribe, famous as magicians, whose territory lay to the east of Rome around the lake of Fucinus. VII, 988.

Mas'sic: from Massica, a hill between Campania and Latium, famous for its wine. VII, 955.

Mas'sicus: an Etruscan ally of Aeneas. X, 234.

Massy'lian: belonging to the MASSYLIANS. IV, 176.

Massy'lians: a Numidian tribe of North Africa. IV, 668.

Ma'ximus: see FABII. VI, 1127.

Me'don: a Trojan, son of Antenor, whose shade Aeneas encounters in the lower world. VI, 636.

Megae'ra: one of the FURIES. XII, 1124.

Me'gara: coastal town of Eastern Sicily. III, 891.

Melam'pus: faithful companion of Hercules, father of the Italian warriors GYAS and CISSAEUS. X, 444.

Meliboe'an: of Meliboea, a Greek city in Thessaly. III, 523.

Me'litë: a sea nymph, one of the Nereids. v, 1090.

Mem'mians: a patrician Roman family name. v, 161.

Mem'non: son of Aurora and Tithonus, King of Ethiopia, ally of the Trojans. He was slain by Achilles. I, 692.

Menela'us: son of Atreus, brother of Agamemnon, ruler of Sparta, husband of HELEN. He and the many rejected suitors of Helen made a pact that, should any of them try to take her from him, all the others would come to his aid. When Helen eloped with Paris, this pact was invoked and the Trojan War began. II, 365.

Menes'theus: son of CLYTIUS (2) and brother of Acmon. x, 185.

Menoe'tes:

1. pilot of GYAS in the boat race. v, 215.
2. Arcadian fisherman. XII, 698.

Mer'cury: the Greek Hermes, son of Jupiter and Maia, messenger of the gods and guide of the souls of the dead to the underworld. IV, 297.

Me'ropes: a Trojan defending Aeneas' camp during the attack by Turnus. IX, 938.

Messa'pus: son of Neptune, ruler in Italy, ally of Turnus. VII, 910.

Me'tabus: king of the Volscians, father of Camilla. XI, 708.

Metis'cus: a Rutulian, charioteer of Turnus, whose form is assumed by JUTURNA in battle. XII, 630.

Met'tus (Fufe'tius): a Latin chieftain of Alba Longa. For his treachery against Tullus Hostilius, third king of Rome, the latter had him torn to pieces by two chariots moving in opposite directions (Livy I, 23). VIII, 834.

Mezen'tius: Etruscan king dethroned and driven into exile by his people. He is the father of Lausus and an ally of Turnus; a "scorner of the gods." VII, 854.

Mi'mas: a soldier of Aeneas from Troy. x, 963.

Min'cius: a river and river god of northern Italy rising from Lake BENACUS and flowing to the Po. It forms a lake around Mantua. x, 290.

Miner'va: Roman goddess identified with the Greek Pallas Athene, the maiden goddess of wisdom, who sprang fully armed from the brow of Jupiter. She is also the goddess of battle and the only other being Jupiter allows to wield his thunderbolt. In her more peaceful aspect she is patroness of such arts as spinning and weaving. To the Greeks she was the tutelary deity of Athens; Homer represents her as a guide and guardian of Odysseus. II, 22.

Miner'va's Height: Castrum Minervae or Arce Minervae, near the harbor of Portus Veneris; modern Castro, in Calabria. III, 692.

Mi'niö: a river in Etruria north of Rome. x, 258.

Mi′nos: King of Crete. His wife Pasiphae gave birth to the Minotaur by a bull, and Minos commissioned DAEDALUS to build the labyrinth as a place of confinement for the monster. Minos' daughter Ariadne aided the Greek prince Theseus in killing the Minotaur and in escaping from Crete. After his death Minos became a judge in the lower world. VI, 20.

Mi′notaur: see MINOS. VI, 36.

Mise′nus: the Trojans' trumpeter, son of AEOLUS (2). III, 312.

Mnes′theus: a Trojan, comrade of Aeneas, founder of the Memmian house. IV, 384.

Monoe′cus: "solitary dweller" in Greek; an epithet for Hercules, from his spending some time in seclusion. The site of a temple to him under this name is now called Monaco. VI, 1102.

Moor′ish: of or pertaining to the inhabitants of Mauritania, region in northern Africa. IV, 274.

Mo′rini: a tribe of Gauls living near the North Sea; their land is now part of Belgium. VIII, 948.

Mo′ther God′dess: CYBELE. III, 147.

Mul′ciber: VULCAN. VIII, 943.

Mum′mius: a Roman general who conquered and destroyed Corinth in 146 B.C. VI, 1110.

Murra′nus: a Rutulian. XII, 720.

Musae′us: legendary poet of Thrace, disciple of Orpheus. VI, 883.

Muse: one of the nine goddesses, daughters of Memory, whose domain was the fine arts and to whom, therefore, creative artists turned for inspiration. I, 13.

Mutus′ca: a city of the Sabines. VII, 935.

Myce′nae: a city of Greece ruled by Agamemnon. I, 399.

Myce′neän, the: AGAMEMNON. XI, 349.

Myce′neäns: people of MYCENAE. IX, 183.

My′conos: a small Aegean island. Virgil represents it as one of the "anchors" of Delos. III, 100.

Myg′don: father of COROEBUS. II, 464.

Myr′midon: one of a Greek people of Thessaly. Achilles was their lord. II, 9.

Nar: a tributary of the Tiber, swiftly flowing, foaming. Its waters contain sulphur. VII, 682.

Nary′cian: of Naryx, a city of the Locrians whose ruler was AJAX, son of Oileus. III, 519.

Nau′tes: companion of Aeneas. He was a seer, taught by Minerva. V, 928.

Na′xos: an Aegean island, largest of the Cyclades. It was noted for the worship of Bacchus. III, 167.

Neäl'ces: a Trojan. x, 1035.

Ne'meä: city of Greece near which Hercules—as the first of his twelve labors—killed a lion. VIII, 388.

Neöpto'lemus: "young warrior" in Greek; another name for PYRRHUS, son of Achilles. He was given this epithet because he came late to the war. (In its early stages he would have been too young for soldiering.) II, 364.

Nep'tune: Greek Poseidon, the god of the sea, Jupiter's brother. He had helped LAOMEDON build the walls of Troy, but became an enemy of Troy when Laomedon refused to pay him his reward. He nevertheless befriended Aeneas. I, 177.

Ne'reïds: sea nymphs, daughters of Nereus and Doris. III, 97.

Ne'reus: a sea god. His daughters, sea nymphs, are the Nereids. II, 562.

Ne'ritos: an island in the Ionian sea near Ithaca. III, 351.

Ner'sae: a city of the Aequi in Latium. VII, 981.

Nesae'a or **Nesae'e:** a sea nymph, daughter of Nereus. V, 1091.

Nile: river of Egypt whose outlet was a delta (hence the reference to its "seven mouths"). VI, 1060.

Niphae'us: a soldier of Turnus. X, 790.

Ni'sus: Trojan companion of Aeneas, friend of Euryalus. In Book V he is a contender in the foot race; in Book IX he is cited for conspicuous devotion in the face of the enemy. V, 388.

Noe'mon: a Trojan defending Aeneas' camp against the Rutulian attack. He is killed by Turnus. IX, 1022.

No'mad: of the NUMIDIANS. IV, 430.

Nomen'tum: an Italian town belonging to the Sabines. VI, 1021.

No'tus: the south wind. I, 121.

Nu'ma:
1. Numa Pompilius. See CURES. Referred to in VI, 1078.
2. a Rutulian among those slain during the sortie of Nisus and Euryalus. IX, 603.
3. a soldier of Turnus. X, 775.

Numa'nus (**Re'mulus**): brother-in-law of Turnus; a boaster. IX, 791.

Numi'cian: of NUMICIUS. VII, 318.

Numi'cius or **Numi'cus:** a holy stream in Latium between Ardea and Lavinium. VII, 194.

Numi'dians or **No'mads:** a tribe of North Africans who rode horseback without bridles. IV, 54.

Nu'mitor:
1. king of Alba Longa, father of Ilia, grandfather of Romulus and Remus. VI, 1014.
2. a Rutulian fighting for Turnus. X, 474.

Nur'sia: old Sabine city in the Apennines. VII, 941.

Nymphs: female deities—but inferior to the Olympians—who made their homes in forests, hills, and fountains. I, 236.

Ny'sa: city and mountain in India where Bacchus is supposed to have been born and/or brought up. VI, 1068.

O'cean: an imaginary river, believed to encircle the earth; the personification thereof. I, 402.

Oc'nus: Italian chieftain, ally of Aeneas, son of Manto and Tiberinus, founder of Mantua. X, 279.

Oe'balus: an ally of Turnus; the son of Telon and Sebethis. His father was king of Capri, and he himself had made extensive conquests on the mainland. VII, 967.

Oecha'lia: a city of Greece which Hercules destroyed when its king, Eurytus, rejected his suit for the princess Iole. VIII, 382.

Oeno'tria: ancient name for southern Italy. VII, 108.

Oeno'trians: people of OENOTRIA. I, 750.

Oï'leus: father of Ajax. I, 63.

Ole'aros: Isle of Olives, an Aegean island. III, 169.

Olym'pus: the mountain in Greece, on the border of Macedonia and Thessaly, on whose summit—veiled by clouds from mortal sight—the chief gods and goddesses had their home. I, 529.

Oni'tes: a Rutulian. XII, 595.

Ophel'tes: father of Euryalus. IX, 266.

O'pis: a nymph attending Diana. XI, 701.

Or'cus: god of the lower world, identifiable with Pluto, brother of Jupiter. By extension the world of the dead is sometimes called Orcus. II, 536.

Ores'tes: son of Agamemnon and Clytemnestra, brother of Iphigenia and Electra. At Apollo's command he slew his mother and her lover, Aegisthus, to avenge the betrayal and murder of his father: for this act he was haunted by the Furies until he was formally vindicated by Minerva. He also slew PYRRHUS, his rival for the hand of Hermione, who had been Orestes' betrothed. III, 429.

Ori'cian: of Oricus, a coastal city of Epirus. X, 193.

Ori'on: a legendary giant hunter. After his death he was translated to the skies as a constellation whose rising and setting marked stormy weather. I, 754.

Orithyi'a (four syllables, the "y" not counting as a vowel): daughter of Erechtheus, king of Athens; wife of Boreas, the north wind. (Boreas had been the father of the royal horses of Troy. Virgil is thought to have invented the friendship between Onthyia and PILUMNUS. XII, 113.

Or'nytus: a Tuscan, killed by Camilla. XI, 894.

Oro'des: a soldier of Aeneas. X, 1004.

Oron'tes: a comrade of Aeneas, in command of the Lycians. I, 164.

Or'pheus: mythical poet of Thrace, husband of Eurydice. When she died from a snakebite, he gained entrance to the underworld by the charm of his music and persuaded PROSERPINA to let Eurydice return to life with him on condition that he not look back at his wife as she followed him. When they neared the upper world, Orpheus, forgetting the condition, looked back, and Eurydice vanished forever. The Thracian Maenads later tore him to pieces, either for interfering with their worship or because he shunned all women after his loss of Eurydice. VI, 165.

Or'ses: a Trojan. X, 1027.

Orsi'lochus: a Trojan. XI, 835.

Orty'gia:
1. another name for DELOS. III, 193.
2. the name of an island district of Syracuse, Sicily. The name means "region of quails." III, 897.

Orty'gius: one of the Italians in the force attacking Aeneas' camp. IX, 762.

Os'cans: a Campanian tribe. Their language, of which fragmentary texts survive, was related to Latin. They fought under HALAESUS for Turnus. VII, 961.

Osi'nius: leader from Clusium in Etruria, on the side of Turnus. X, 900.

Osi'ris: a Latin. XII, 615.

Oth'rys:
1. father of PANTHUS. II, 435.
2. a mountain in Thessaly. VII, 891.

Pachy'nus: promontory at the southeastern tip of Sicily. III, 561.

Pacto'lus: a Lydian river which was said to carry gold dust after King Midas washed off his golden touch in its waters. X, 199.

Pa'duä: Patavium, founded by ANTENOR; a city in the north of Italy near Venice. I, 345.

Pa'dus: the modern Po. IX, 911.

Padu'sa: one of the seven mouths of the Po. XI, 445.

Pa'gasus: an Etruscan (according to Heyne) killed by Camilla. XI, 883.

Palae'mon: a lesser sea deity, the son of Ino. V, 1088.

Palame'des: a Greek hero. He had discovered the stratagem by which Ulysses hoped to evade service in the Trojan war. While the war was in progress, Ulysses instigated a trumped-up charge of treason against Palamedes, who was condemned and executed. Also see CAPHEREUS. II, 113.

Pa'latine: one of the seven hills of Rome. See PALLANTEUM. IX, 10.

Pali'cus: primitive Sicilian divinity, son of Jupiter by a nymph; his shrine was near the river Symaethus. IX, 779.

Palinu'rus: pilot of Aeneas' fleet. III, 264.

Palla'dium: an image of the goddess Minerva (Pallas), believed to have descended from heaven, upon which the safety of Troy depended. It was stolen from the temple of Pallas by Ulysses and Diomedes. II, 235.

Pallante'um: belonging to Pallas (see MINERVA); first a city in Arcadia, EVANDER's original home, then the city founded by Evander in Italy on the Palatine Hill at the site which was to be that of Rome. VIII, 69.

Pal'las:

1. a Greek name for MINERVA. I, 59.
2. an Arcadian hero, ancestor of Evander. VIII, 66.
3. the young son of Evander who fights on the side of Aeneas. VIII, 136.

Pal'mus: a soldier of Aeneas. X, 955.

Pan: Arcadian god of woods and shepherds; he is goat-footed and satyr-faced. VIII, 451.

Pan'darus:

1. a Trojan soldier, son of Lycaon (in the *Iliad*) and brother of Eurytion. He broke the truce between the Trojans and the Greeks by shooting an arrow at Menelaus. V, 654.
2. a Trojan, son of Alcanor (1), and brother of Bitias. IX, 898.

Panope'a: a Nereid. V, 1091.

Pa'nopes: a Sicilian, contender in the foot race. V, 397.

Panta'gias: river of Sicily. III, 890.

Pan'thus: a Trojan. He was a priest of Apollo. II, 434.

Pa'phos: a city of Cyprus. It was famous as a center of the worship of Venus. I, 591.

Pa'rian: of PAROS. I, 833.

Pa'ris: son of King Priam of Troy and his queen Hecuba; brother of Hector, Polites, Polydorus, Helenus, and Deiphobus. Before his birth, Hecuba dreamed that she was delivered of a firebrand that consumed the city. The baby was exposed but saved and brought up by a kindly shepherd. Grown to manhood, he returned to Troy, was recognized, and restored to his place in the royal family. When Eris (Strife) threw down a golden apple marked "For the Fairest," Venus, Juno, and Minerva all claimed the apple as prize, and Paris, the handsomest of mortal men, was asked to arbitrate the dispute. Each goddess tried to bribe him; he decided in favor of Venus and accepted her bribe—Helen, wife of Menelaus, most beautiful of women. This act precipitated the Trojan War. I, 42.

Pa'ros: an Aegean island famous for its white (Parian) marble. III, 170.

Parthe'nius: a Trojan. X, 1026.

Parthenopae'us: king of Argos and one of the Seven against Thebes. VI, 631.

Par'thians: a Middle Eastern people, famous for their archers who sent their "Parthian shots" even when in full retreat from a pursuing enemy. In 53 B.C., they defeated a Roman army at Carrhae in Mesopotamia and captured the Roman standards, which Augustus later recovered by treaty. VII, 801.

Pasi'phaë: wife of MINOS and queen of Crete, mother of Minotaur by a bull. VI, 34.

Pa'tron: a companion of Aeneas, contender in the foot race. V, 393.

Pelas'gians: an extremely ancient, perhaps aboriginal, people of Greece and, according to certain traditions, of Italy. VIII, 779.

Pe'leus: husband of Thetis, father of ACHILLES. II, 364.

Pe'lias: a Trojan who fights beside Aeneas at the fall of Troy. II, 585.

Pe'lops: an early king in Greece, from whom the Peloponnesus takes its name; an ancestor of Agamemnon and Menelaus. II, 274.

Pelo'rus: a promontory on the northeastern tip of Sicily. It marks the western side of the Straits of Messina. III, 536.

Pene'leüs: a Greek warrior. II, 571.

Penthesile'a: Queen of the AMAZONS, women warriors, ally of Troy. She was slain by Achilles. I, 693.

Pen'theus: king of Thebes who opposed the worship of Bacchus. He was driven mad by the god and torn to pieces by his own mother while she was in a state of Bacchic frenzy. Virgil is alluding to Euripides' *Bacchae.* IV, 647.

Per'gamum: the name given by Aeneas to his city in Crete. III, 178.

Per'gamus: the citadel of Troy; thus, generally, Troy. I, 660.

Peridi'a: mother of Onites. XII, 696.

Pe'riphas: a Greek who is a companion of Pyrrhus at the fall of Troy. II, 636.

Pete'lia: a town of Lucania in southern Italy, founded by Philoctetes. III, 522.

Phaeä'cians: a (mythical) people living off the western coast of Greece at Corcyra (Scheria in the *Odyssey*)—perhaps what is now Corfu. In the *Odyssey* they receive Ulysses with hospitality. III, 376.

Phae'dra: daughter of Minos, King of Crete; second wife of

THESEUS. She fell in love with her stepson HIPPOLYTUS, and when he rejected her accused him falsely, causing his death. She committed suicide. VI, 587.

Pha'ethon: son of Helios, the god of the sun, and Clymene. He tried to drive the sun chariot across the skies but lost control of the fiery horses. As the chariot plunged earthward, threatening worldwide conflagration, Jupiter struck Phaethon dead with his thunderbolt. The sisters of Phaethon, grieving for him, were turned into poplars. V, 144.

Pha'leris: a Trojan defending Aeneas' camp agains the Rutulian attack. IX, 1014.

Pha'ros: an Italian, adversary of Aeneas. X, 446.

Phe'geus:
  1. a servant of Aeneas. V, 346.
  2. a Trojan defending Aeneas' camp against the attack of Turnus. IX, 1019.
  3. another Trojan. XII, 502.

Phe'neös: a city in Arcadia, VIII, 216.

Phe'res: a soldier of Aeneas. X, 574.

Philocte'tes: A Greek chieftain who fought against Troy and, after the Trojan war, settled in Italy where he founded Petelia. III, 522.

Phi'neus: king of Thrace. Having unjustly blinded his sons, he was himself blinded by the gods, who also sent the Harpies to torment him. III, 280.

Phle'gethon: the river of fire in the lower world. VI, 351.

Phle'gyas: ruler of the Lapithae, father of Ixion, he was punished in Tartarus for setting fire to Apollo's temple at Delphi. VI, 821.

Phoe'bë: DIANA as a moon goddess. X, 305.

Phoe'bus: a Greek word meaning bright or radiant; title or epithet of APOLLO. II, 162.

Phoeni'cia: country on the coast of Syria that included the towns of Tyre and Sidon. I, 485.

Phoeni'cian: of PHOENICIA. I, 936.

Phoeni'cians: a great trading people from the Eastern Mediterranean. The Tyrians and hence the Carthaginians were of Phoenician stock. I, 426.

Phoe'nix: a Greek chieftain. He was the preceptor of Achilles. II, 1029.

Pho'loë: Cretan slave girl given by Aeneas as a prize to Sergestus after the boat race. V, 375.

Pho'lus:
  1. a Centaur. VIII, 386.
  2. a Trojan. XII, 460.

Phor'bas: a Trojan, companion of Aeneas. Sleep, lulling Palinurus, takes on Phorbas' shape. V, 1112.

Phor'cus:
1. a sea deity, son of Pontus and Gaea. v, 1089.
2. father of Cydon and his seven brothers who fight against Aeneas. x, 456.

Phry'gian: (adj. and noun) of the place and inhabitants of Phrygia, a region of Asia Minor east of the Troad. Sometimes applied pejoratively to the Trojans, for the Phrygians were noted for their sloth and effeminacy. I, 254.

Phthi'a: a city of Greece, home of Achilles. I, 399.

Pi'cus: Italian god of agriculture, grandfather of Latinus, father of Faunus, son of Saturn, first king of Latium. Circe changed him into a woodpecker after he spurned her love; his name means "woodpecker" in Latin. VII, 60.

Pilum'nus: an old Italian god whom Virgil makes the ancestor of Turnus on his mother's side. IX, 5.

Pina'rii: members of the gens Pinaria, one of the two clans responsible for conducting the rites of Hercules at Rome (cf. Livy, I, 7). Also see Potitius. VIII, 353.

Piri'thoüs: son of Ixion and a friend of Theseus. He helped Theseus in his attempt to carry off Proserpina from the lower world. As punishment, he was placed in chains forever. VI, 518.

Pi'sa: an Etruscan city thought to have been founded by colonists from the city of Pisa in Elis, Greece, which stood on the River ALPHEUS. x, 252.

Plemy'rium: Sicilian promontory near Syracuse. III, 896.

Plu'to: ruler of the lower world, also called Orcus, Dis, and Hades. VII, 434.

Podali'rius: a Trojan. XII, 414.

Poli'tes: young son of Priam. He is slain by PYRRHUS. II, 707.

Pol'lux: son of Jupiter by LEDA. He and his twin brother, Castor, are called the Dioscuri ("sons of Zeus"). When Castor's time came to die, Pollux interceded for him, and it was granted that each brother should spend his days alternately in the lower world and in the world above. VI, 168.

Polyboe'tes: Trojan priest of Ceres, whose shade is met by Aeneas in the lower world. VI, 637.

Polydo'rus: son of Priam treacherously murdered by the king of Thrace. III, 58.

Polyphe'mus: a CYCLOPS whom Ulysses blinded. III, 817.

Pome'tia: Volscian town of Latium. VI, 1023.

Pom'pey (the Great): 106–48 B.C., illustrious Roman general, ally of Julius Caesar and wed to Caesar's daughter Julia; after Julia's death in 54 B.C., opponent of Caesar in the Civil Wars. Defeated by Caesar at Pharsalia, then murdered in Egypt. VI, 1102.

Populo'nia: a seaport and source of Etruscan arms, located near Elba. x, 243.

Porsen'na: "Lars Porsenna of Clusium," an Etruscan king who made war on Rome to reestablish the rule of TARQUIN, who had been dethroned and banished by the Romans. VIII, 838.

Portu'nus: the god of harbors. v, 318.

Poti'tius: eponymous ancestor of the *gens Potitia*, one of two family groups which were responsible, in historic times, for conducting rites of Hercules at Rome (cf. LIVY, I, 7). Also see PINARII. VIII, 352.

Praenes'të: ancient city of Latium, modern Palestrina. VII, 894.

Pri'am:
1. son of Laomedon and king of Troy. I, 649.
2. son of Polites and grandson of Priam (1). v, 741.

Priver'num: city of the Volscians in Latium, birthplace of Camilla (cf. Livy VIII, 1). XI, 709.

Priver'nus: a Rutulian. IX, 767.

Pro'cas: a king of Alba Longa, shown to Aeneas by Anchises in Elysium. VI, 1013.

Pro'chyta: a small island just off the Campanian coast near the promontory of Misenum. Modern Procida. IX, 956.

Pro'cris: wife of Cephalus. To reassure herself of her husband's fidelity, she followed him when he went hunting. He heard a rustling in the covert where she was hidden and launched his javelin at what he supposed to be game; she was mortally wounded. VI, 587.

Pro'molus: a Trojan. IX, 765.

Proser'pina: Greek Persephone, daughter of Ceres, the goddess of grain; she was the wife of Pluto. IV, 961.

Pro'teus: a sea deity with prophetic powers, able to assume various shapes. Menelaus, returning with Helen after the Trojan war, was driven by storm to the island of Pharos, on the Egyptian coast, where he encountered Proteus (*Odyssey*, IV, 81 ff.). Virgil imagines the pillars of Proteus at the eastern end of the Mediterranean, near Egypt, like the pillars of Hercules at the western end. XI, 344.

Pry'tanis: a Trojan defending Aeneas' camp against the Rutulian attack. He is killed by Turnus. IX, 1023.

Pu'nic: Phoenician; and thus, also, Carthaginian. I, 477.

Pygma'lion: Dido's brother, murderer of her husband, Sychaeus. I, 489.

Pyrac'mon: see CYCLOPS. VIII, 557.

Pyr'gi: a city in Etruria which sent troops to Aeneas. x, 258.

Pyr'go: nurse in Priam's household. v, 850.

Pyr'rhus: son of Achilles (also called NEOPTOLEMUS). On the last night of Troy he killed Polites, young son of Priam and Hecuba, before their very eyes; then he killed Priam himself at his own altar. He carried off Andromache—Hector's widow—and Helenus—another son of Priam—as prizes. Pyrrhus married Hermione, the daughter of Helen and Menelaus, and the betrothed of Orestes. For this, Pyrrhus was slain by ORESTES. II, 627.

Quer'cens: a Rutulian, one of the force attacking Aeneas' camp. IX, 915.

Quiri'nal: see QUIRINUS. VII, 247.

Quiri'nus: ancient Italian deity, later identified with the deified ROMULUS. His name may mean "the spear bearer." That which relates to Quirinus or Romulus is called "Quirinal" or "Quirine." VI, 1147.

Quiri'tes: inhabitants of CURES, a Sabine town, birthplace of Numa. In historical times, as opposed to the legendary ones when the action of the *Aeneid* takes place, "Quirites" is the designation of Roman citizens. VII, 934.

Ra'po: an Etruscan. X, 1026.

Re'mulus:
1. a warrior from Tibur, guest and friend of Caedicus. IX, 480.
2. surname of NUMANUS. IX, 792.
3. a Rutulian. XI, 837.

Re'mus:
1. son of Mars and ILIA (or Rhea Silvia), brother of ROMULUS. After Romulus had received the favorable omen of the gods, designating him to found the city that would be Rome, Remus leaped derisively over his brother's newly begun city wall. Incensed, Romulus killed him. I, 412.
2. a Rutulian, one of the force surrounding Aeneas' camp. IX, 441.

Rhadaman'thus: brother of MINOS. In life he was a ruler of Crete and famed for justice; after death he became a judge in the lower world. VI, 749.

Rham'nes: a Rutulian chief and augur of Turnus, one of the force besieging Aeneas' camp. IX, 432.

Rhe'a: a priestess who became the mother of AVENTINUS by Hercules. VII, 872.

Rhe'sus: an ally of Troy who came from Thrace to give aid against the Greeks but was slain by Diomedes on the very night of his arrival. It was believed that Troy could not be taken if the horses of Rhesus tasted the grass or drank the water of Troy. These horses were therefore carried off by Diomedes and Ulysses before they could feed. I, 665.

Rhine: identical with the modern river. VIII, 949.

Rhoe'bus or **Rhae'bus:**   the war-horse of MEZENTIUS. X, 1181.

Rhoete'an: of Rhoeteum, near Troy; by extension, Trojan.
III, 143.

Rhoe'teus: a soldier of Turnus. X, 554.

Rhoe'tus:
1.   a Rutulian, one of the troop before the Trojans' camp.
IX, 464.
2.   a Marsian, forebear of Anchemolus. X, 538.

Ri'pheus: a Trojan. He fights at the side of Aeneas during
Troy's last night. II, 462.

Ro'man: adj. and noun for the people of Rome. I, 388.

Rome: chief city of Latium and the Roman empire, founded
in 754 or 753 B.C. I, 12.

Ro'mulus: mythical founder of Rome in 754 or 753 B.C., son
of Mars by ILIA (Rhea Silvia). According to legend he
and his brother REMUS were nursed by a she-wolf. See
TATIUS for Romulus' joint rulership with him. Romulus
subsequently disappeared in a thunderstorm. For his iden-
tification with QUIRINUS, see that entry. I, 385.

Ro'seän: of Rosea, a district in Sabine territory, near Reate,
the modern Rieti, famous for the rearing of horses. VII, 937.

Ru'frae: a city in Campania. VII, 975.

Ru'mor: Fama; personification of rumor. IV, 229.

Rutu'lians: an Italian people whose ruler was Turnus. VII,
623.

Sabae'an: of Saba, or Sheba, in Arabia, famous for its per-
fumes. I, 594.

Sa'bines: an ancient people of Italy. When Romulus needed
women for his settlement, he invited the Sabines to a
festival; when all were at the theater, his men, at a given
signal, carried off the Sabine women. Also see TATIUS. VII,
932.

Sabi'nus: fabled ancestor of the Sabines. VII, 237.

Sa'ces: a Latin. XII, 864.

Sacra'nians: a people of Latium that fought under Turnus.
VII, 1046.

Sacra'tor: an Etruscan. X, 1025.

Sa'garis: servant of Aeneas. V, 346.

Sagun'tine: pike, from Saguntum (Livy XXI, 8). A large,
heavy iron-tipped spear bearing lighted tow or pitch and
hurled by a catapult or similar machine. In the *Aeneid*
Turnus throws one by hand. The Latin text has *phalarica*,
but with the text of Livy and Conington's notes at hand,
I have used "Saguntine pike." IX, 943.

Sa'lamis: the kingdom ruled by Telamon, husband of Priam's
sister Hesione. VIII, 206.

Sa'lian priests: variant used in this translation for SALII. VIII, 860.

Sa'lii: "leapers"; members of an old Roman priesthood whose ritual included singing and dancing. Though they are chiefly known as priests of Mars, there is ancient authority supporting Virgil's depiction of them as participating in the rites of Hercules. VIII, 374.

Sa'lius:
    1.   a companion of Aeneas. He is a contestant in the foot race. V, 393.
    2.   a Rutulian. X, 1034.

Sallenti'ni: a people of coastal Calabria. III, 521.

Salmo'neus: king of Elis, punished in Tartarus for his impious counterfeiting of Jupiter's might when he imitated lightning with burning torches. VI, 774.

Sa'më: an island near Ithaca. III, 350.

Sa'mos:
    1.   an Aegean island off the coast of Asia Minor. One of Juno's favored places, it was the site of a temple to her that was famous throughout the ancient world. Now Samo. I, 25.
    2.   another name for SAMOTHRACE. VII, 276.

Sa'mothrace or Samothra'cia: an island in the Aegean Sea, west of Troy and south of Thrace; now Samothraki. VII, 276.

Sar'nus: a river in Campania. VII, 974.

Sarpe'don: son of Jupiter, leader of the Lycians, ally of Troy. He fell in the Trojan war (*Iliad,* XVI, 419). I, 141.

Sarras'tes: a people of Campania who lived near the river Sarnus. VII, 973.

Sati'culans: people of Saticula, a town in Campania, north of Capua. VII, 961.

Sa'tura: a swamp supposed to be part of the Pontine marshes. VII, 1052.

Sa'turn: identified with the Greek god Cronos; father of Jupiter, Juno, Pluto, and Neptune; after Jupiter dethroned and drove Saturn from Olympus, he settled in Italy, for which reason it is sometimes called Saturnian land. His reign there was a golden age. I, 35.

Satur'nia:
    1.   a city built by Saturn. It is traditionally located on the Capitoline Hill. VIII, 469.
    2.   another name for Juno, daughter of Saturn. XII, 239.

Satur'nian: see SATURNIA (2). V, 798.

Scae'an: "left-hand"; the strongest and best-known gates of Troy. They faced the Grecian camp. II, 827.

Sci'piö:

1. Publius Cornelius, Africanus the Elder (236/5–183 B.C.). Conqueror of Hannibal at Zama in 202 B.C. VI, 1121.
2. Publius Scipio Aemilianus (ca. 185–129 B.C.), son of AEMILIUS PAULUS and adopted by the son of Scipio (1); after his destruction of Carthage in 146 B.C., he was called Africanus the Younger. VI, 1121.

Scylace'um: city of southern Italy, on a coast dangerous to ships. III, 721.

Scyl'la: a sea monster—one of the two personifying the dangers of the Straits of Messina—who ravaged passing ships. I, 280.

Scy'ros: an Aegean island, birthplace of PYRRHUS. II, 639.

Sebe'this: a nymph, daughter of the river and god Sebethus, near Naples. VII, 968.

Seli'nus: a coastal town of western Italy. III, 912.

Seres'tus: a Trojan, comrade of Aeneas. I, 857.

Serges'tus: a Trojan, comrade of Aeneas, feared lost in the storm: he is seen by Aeneas and Achates at Dido's temple. Founder of the Sergian house, he is commander of the "Centaur" in the boat race in Book V. I, 720.

Ser'gian: see SERGESTUS. V, 165.

Serra'nus:

1. name for C. Atilius Regulus, consul in 257 B.C. He received the news of his consulship while he was plowing and sowing. Serere means "to sow." VI, 1124.
2. a Rutulian killed by Nisus. IX, 446.

Seve'rus: a mountain in Sabine territory, to the east of Nursia. VII, 938.

Shades: spirits of the dead, I, 771.

Si'byl: a prophetic priestess. V, 970.

Sica'nian: Sicilian; from the name of a race of early inhabitants who apparently emigrated to Sicily from Italy. VII, 1045.

Sici'lian: of SICILY. I, 774.

Si'cily: modern Sicily. Also see TRINACRIA. I, 51.

Si'dicine: of the Sidicines, a people of Campania whose capital was Teanum, modern Teano. VII, 957.

Si'don: a Phoenician city near Tyre. Tyre was an offshoot of Sidon. I, 869.

Sido'nian: of SIDON. I, 632.

Sige'an: of SIGEUM. VII, 387.

Sige'um: a promontory near Troy. II, 426.

Si'la: a mountain forest in Bruttium, now Calabria. XII, 950.

Silva'nus: Italian woodland god. VIII, 781.

Sil'via: daughter of TYRRHUS. When Ascanius unknowingly

kills her pet deer, she calls upon the Latins nearby to fight the Trojans. VII, 643.

Sil'vius: foreordained son of Aeneas and Lavinia. VI, 1008.

Sil'vius Aene'as: an Alban king who, according to the accepted story, was long kept from the throne. VI, 1015.

Si'moïs: one of the rivers of Troy. I, 141.

Si'non: Greek infiltrator who gained asylum in Troy with his story of having fled because Ulysses was plotting to have him offered up as a human sacrifice. He released the Greek soldiers from the wooden horse. II, 110.

Si'rens: beautiful maidens, or creatures with women's faces and the bodies of birds. Their sweet singing lured sailors to destruction on the rocks which they inhabited. See *Odyssey*, XII. V, 1153.

Sorac'të: a mountain, not far to the north of, and visible from, Rome. On it was a temple to Apollo. VII, 916.

Spa'nish: same as the modern word. VII, 876.

Spar'ta: a city-state of Greece, the home of Menelaus and his wife Helen. In historic times a small military caste exercised ruthless control there over a much larger enslaved population; both boys and girls of this upper class received rigorous physical training. I, 447.

Spi'o: a Nereid. V, 1092.

Star of Morning: Lucifer, the son of Aurora and father of Ceyx. II, 1078.

Ste'ropes: see CYCLOPS. VIII, 556.

Sthe'nelus:
1. a Greek warrior (in the *Iliad* he is Diomedes' charioteer) concealed in the wooden horse. II, 361.
2. a Trojan. XII, 460.

Sthe'nius: a Rutulian, adversary of PALLAS (3). X, 536.

Stro'phades: islands of the Ionian Sea, supposed dwelling of the Harpies. III, 275.

Strymo'nian: of the Strymon, a river in Thrace, home of the cranes. X, 369.

Strymo'nius: a soldier of Aeneas. X, 575.

Sty'gian: of the STYX. III, 284.

Styx: the flood of deadly hate, a river in the lower world. Those dead who had the right to passage were ferried across the Styx by Charon and took up residence in the lower world. The others are displaced persons who crowded its nearer bank. An oath sworn by the Styx was unbreakable, even for the gods. VI, 187.

Su'cro: a Rutulian. XII, 681.

Sul'mo:
1. a Rutulian in the troop of Volcens. IX, 550.
2. an Italian whose sons fought for Turnus. X, 714.

Sy'baris: a Trojan. XII, 491.

Sychae'us: Dido's husband, murdered by her brother, Pygmalion. I, 484.

Symae'thus: a river of eastern Sicily, near Mount Etna. IX, 778.

Syr'tes: a sandbank, and especially the treacherous sandbanks of two wide gulfs off the shores of northern Africa, the Greater Syrtis off Tripoli and the Lesser Syrtis off Tunis. In plural: Syrtes. Also used of the coastal regions facing the Syrtes. VI, 85.

Syr'tis: see SYRTES. IV, 54.

Tabur'nus: range of mountains in Campania. XII, 950.

Ta'gus: one of the men of Volcens. IX, 559.

Ta'lon: a Rutulian. XII, 693.

Ta'naïs: a Rutulian. XII, 694.

Tar'chon: an Etruscan, chief of Agylla (CAERE), ally of Aeneas. VIII, 656.

Taren'tum: famous port city and bay of southern Italy, modern Taranto. See HERCULES. III, 717.

Tarpe'ia (trisyllable; the "i" counts as a consonantal "y"): a comrade of Camilla. Not the Tarpeia of the Tarpeian rock. XI, 863.

Tarpe'ian house: see TARPEIAN ROCK. VIII, 454.

Tarpe'ian rock: located on the Capitoline hill, it was a place of execution from which criminals were hurled to their deaths. It was named after a Roman, Tarpeia, who betrayed Rome out of her love for the Sabine king Titus Tatius. VIII, 846.

Tar'quin: Etruscan name borne by two kings of Rome; one of them was Tarquin the Proud, whose expulsion by Lucius Junius BRUTUS in 510 B.C. ended the kingship at Rome. VI, 1083.

Tar'quitus: an Italian, son of Faunus and Dryope, a warrior of Turnus. X, 760.

Tarta'reän: of TARTARUS. VI, 391.

Tar'tarus: the region of the lower world where punishment was inflicted on the shades of the guilty. IV, 325.

Ta'tius: King of the SABINES, ruling at CURES. Following the rape of the Sabine women, he led a punitive expedition against the Romans but was finally reconciled with them through the intervention of the women themselves. He then shared the kingship of the two peoples, now united, with Romulus. VIII, 827.

Te'geän: of Tegea, a town in ARCADIA. V, 395.

Tele'boäns: a people whom Homer describes as pirates in the Ionian islands. Later they, or some of them, occupied Capri. VII, 970.

Te'lon: ruler of the Teleboans on Capri; he was the father of OEBALUS by the nymph Sebethis. VII, 967.

Te'nedos: a small island in the Aegean Sea near Troy. II, 30.

Te'reus: a Trojan, killed by Camilla. XI, 889.

Te'trica: a mountain of Italy, in Sabine territory. VII, 938.

Teu'cer:

1. an ancient king of Troy, after whom the domain is sometimes called Teucria and the people Teucrians. I, 330.

2. a Greek, half-brother of the Telamonian Ajax. (This is the Ajax who, vanquished by Ulysses in the contest for the arms left by Achilles, went mad and committed suicide.) Teucer was banished by his father for having failed to bring his brother safely home from the wars. Migrating to Cyprus, he founded the city of Salamis. I, 868.

Teu'crians: see TEUCER (1). I, 346.

Teuth'ras: an ally of Aeneas. X, 559.

Teu'tons: the German peoples. Some invaded Italy with the Cimbri and were routed by Caius Marius in 102 and 101 B.C. VII, 977.

Thae'mon: brother of SARPEDON. X, 180.

Thali'a: a sea nymph. V, 1092.

Tha'myris: a Trojan. XII, 461.

Thap'sus: coastal city of eastern Sicily. III, 891.

Thau'mas: father of IRIS. IX, 6.

Theä'no: mother of MIMAS by AMYCUS (4). X, 964.

Thebes: capital of Boeotia, scene of Euripides' *Bacchae*. See PENTHEUS. IV, 649.

Themil'las: a Trojan. IX, 768.

Thermo'don: a river in Asia Minor, flowing into the Black Sea in Amazon country. XI, 869.

The'ron: an Italian, adversary of Aeneas. X, 430.

Thersi'lochus:

1. a warrior, son of Antenor; a Trojan whose shade Aeneas meets in the lower world. VI, 636.

2. a Trojan. XII, 491.

The'seus: son of the Athenian king Aegeus; he killed the Minotaur and carried off Ariadne, but then deserted her. Later he undertook to help his friend PIRITHOUS to carry off Proserpina from the lower world. VI, 43.

Thessan'drus: a Greek, concealed in the wooden horse. II, 361.

The'tis: a sea goddess, daughter of Nereus, wife of Peleus, and mother of Achilles. V, 1090.

Tho'as:

1. a Greek in the wooden horse. II, 363.

2. a soldier of Aeneas. X, 577.

Thrace: a region in northwestern Greece, favorite home of Mars. I, 448.

Thra'cia: THRACE. XII, 452.

Thra'cians: the people of THRACE. III, 20.

Thro'nius: a Trojan. X, 1034.

Thy'bris: an ancient Italian king, reputedly a brigand. From his death in battle along its banks, the river TIBER is supposed to derive its name. VIII, 431.

Thym'ber: a Rutulian, son of Daucus and twin brother of Larides. He is with the army of Turnus. X, 540.

Thym'bra: a city in the Troad, a center of Apollo's worship. III, 112.

Thymbrae'us: a Trojan. XII, 615.

Thym'bris: an old soldier of Aeneas. He appears in the front line of defense at the Trojans' camp. X, 178.

Thymoe'tes:
1. a Trojan. II, 47.
2. son of Hicetaon; he is shown in the front line of defense at the Trojans' camp. X, 177.
3. a Trojan, perhaps the same as Thymoetes (2). XII, 492.

Ti'ber: river in Italy. Rome was founded on the Tiber's left bank, some fourteen miles from its mouth at Ostia. I, 22.

Tiberi'nus: god of the river Tiber. VIII, 38.

Ti'bur: ancient town of Italy not far from Rome on the river Anio; its founders were emigrants from Greece. VII, 832.

Ti'burtines (following the OED accent for the adjective Ti'-burtine) or **Tibur'tines** (the line allows both): people of TIBUR. XI, 1005.

Tibur'tus: one of the three brothers—grandsons of Amphiaraus, a king of Argos—who founded Tibur, to which he gave his name. VII, 886.

Tima'vus: a river in northern Italy; it flows into the Adriatic with a very swift current. I, 341.

Tiryn'thius: an epithet of Hercules, from Tiryns, a city near Argos in the Peloponnesus. The mother of Hercules was a daughter of the king of Tiryns. VII, 873.

Tisi'phonë: one of the Furies. VI, 755.

Ti'tan: one of the Titans, pre-Olympian deities. One of them, Hyperion ("Going-on-High"), was lord of the sun. IV, 769.

Titho'nus: consort of AURORA. She won for him the gift of eternal life but forgot to ask for that of eternal youth as well. IV, 806.

Ti'työs: a giant. He was killed by Apollo and Diana and punished in Tartarus for his attempt to violate their mother, Latona. VI, 789.

Tma'rian: of Epirus; from Tmarus, a mountain there. V, 818.

Tma'rus: a Rutulian participating in the attack on Aeneas' camp. IX, 915.

Tolum'nius: an Italian augur who fights on the side of Turnus. XI, 567.

Torqua'tus, Ti'tus Man'lius: his cognomen supposedly came from a collar (*torques*) taken as spoil from a giant Celt he killed in single combat; a consul who put to death his own son, in 340 B.C., for disobeying orders. See BRUTUS for another early consul who put his own sons to death. VI, 1094.

Trina'criä (appears only as four syllables in this translation): Sicily, so called because it was "three-cornered," with three capes—PELORUS, PACHYNUS, LILYBAEUM. III, 499.

Tri'ton: a sea divinity, the son of NEPTUNE (Poseidon) and Amphitrite. He was famous as a musician for blowing his conch horn. I, 203.

Trito'nian: an epithet of Minerva (Pallas Athena), from Lake Tritonis in Libya, near which she was supposed to have been born. II, 830.

Tri'via: see DIANA and HECATE. This translation uses Diana for Trivia in its nine occurrences.

Tro'ilus: son of Priam, slain by Achilles. I, 671.

Tro'jan: adj. and noun for the people of TROY. As a noun, usually a soldier from Troy. I, 46.

Troy: city located on the northwest coast of Asia Minor, in the region called the Troad, at the southern entrance to the Hellespont (Dardanelles). The traditional date for its destruction is 1180 B.C. I, 3.

Tul'la: a comrade of Camilla. XI, 863.

Tullus (Hostilius): third king of Rome, according to tradition; he was the conqueror and destroyer of ALBA LONGA. VI, 1078.

Tur'nus: king of the Rutulians and Aeneas' rival for the hand of Lavinia. VII, 69.

Tus'can: Etruscan, relating to the people who may have come originally from Asia Minor and who settled the district of Etruria to the north of Latium. Their civilization—showing in its artifacts some Greek influence—had much influence on the civilization of the Romans. Synonyms are Etrurian, Lydian, Maeonian, Tyrrhenian. VII, 53.

Tus'cany: ETRURIA. See TUSCAN. VIII, 660.

Ty'deus: a Greek, father of Diomedes. II, 232.

Tynda'reös: Leda's mortal husband, sometimes spoken of as the father of Helen. II, 763.

Typho'eän (Milton and, thus, the OED syllabify and accent as "Typhoe'an"): from Typhoeus, one of the rebellious giants whom Jupiter slew with his thunderbolts. I, 930.

Typho'eus: see TYPHOEAN. VIII, 393.

Tyre: commercial, maritime city of Phoenicia. It was famous for its purple dye. I, 20.

Ty'res: an Arcadian ally of Aeneas. X, 559.

Ty'rian: of TYRE. I, 553.

Ty'rians: people of TYRE. I, 624.

Tyrrhe'nian: an arm of the Mediterranean between the western coast of Italy and the eastern coasts of Sicily, Sardinia, and Corsica. Sometimes used synonymously with TUSCAN. I, 98.

Tyrrhe'nus: an Etruscan. XI, 806.

Tyr'rhus: keeper of the herds, or "chief ranger," for Latinus. He is the father of SILVIA. VII, 641.

Uca'legon: a Trojan. II, 425.

U'fens:
1. a "highlander," ally of Turnus, chief of the Aequi. VII, 982.
2. a river in Latium. VII, 1053.

Ulys'ses: one of the greatest of the Greek chieftains besieging Troy. He was renowned for his sagacity; Virgil, from the Trojan side, depicts him as a wily schemer. From his home in Ithaca, he is sometimes called "the Ithacan." He is the central figure of the *Odyssey*. II, 10.

Um'brian: from Umbria, a region of north-central Italy, well known for its hunting dogs. XII, 998.

Um'bro: Marsian warrior-priest, magician, and snake charmer. VII, 989.

Va'lerus: an Etruscan. X, 1032.

Ve'lia: a bay and then an Italian coastal city south of Salerno. VI, 481.

Veli'nus: name of an Italian lake and river. The river is a tributary to the Nar, which meets it in a waterfall. The Velinus' waters are sulphurous. VII, 682.

Veni'lia: an Italian nymph, mother of Turnus. X, 105.

Ve'nulus: an Italian, messenger of Turnus to Diomedes. VIII, 10.

Ve'nus: Greek Aphrodite, goddess of love and beauty; daughter of Jupiter by Dione; mother by Anchises of Aeneas. She is especially devoted to the Trojans; on Olympus her husband is Vulcan; she is the mother of Cupid. Later, she is the tutelary goddess of the house of the Caesars. I, 318.

Ves'ta: goddess of the hearth and hearth fire. I, 410.

Ve'sulus: mountain of the Italian Alps in Liguria, modern Mt. Viso; the river Po has its source there. X, 971.

Vir′bius:
1. a name given to HIPPOLYTUS when, after his resurrection, he lived in Italy (supposedly from *vir bis,* because he lived twice as a man). VII, 999.
2. son of HIPPOLYTUS and Aricia. He is an ally of Turnus. VII, 1021.

Vol′cens: a Latin, leader of cavalry sent as reinforcements to Turnus. IX, 494.

Vol′scian: (adj.) of the VOLSCIANS. XI, 615.

Vol′scians: a people inhabiting Latium, south of Rome, near the river Liris. VII, 1055.

Voltur′nus: a river of Campania. VII, 960.

Vo′lusus: a warrior on the "general staff" of Turnus. XI, 614.

Vul′can: Greek Hephaestus, god of fire and of the forge; his name gives us the word volcano. Vulcan fashions the thunderbolts of Jupiter with the help of the CYCLOPS (2). His home is on the island of VULCANIA. II, 424.

Vulca′nia: home of VULCAN, an island off northeastern Sicily. VIII, 554.

Xan′thus:
1. a river of Troy. I, 670.
2. a river in Lycia, near a town of the same name; modern Essenide. IV, 192.

Zacyn′thus: an island in the Ionian Sea near Ithaca. III, 350.

Ze′phyrs: in general, winds. The Zephyr is the personification of a mild, warm, westerly Italian wind, coinciding with the melting of snows and the beginning of spring. IV, 298.

A
BIBLIOGRAPHICAL
NOTE

The following list of works is meant to serve three purposes. It is a partial record of the many indebtednesses incurred as I worked on this translation; it offers suggestions for further reading to readers of this translation; it will help less experienced librarians with convenient indications for a basic and a beyond-the-basic Virgil shelf. The third purpose is always at peace with the first two; the first and second purpose most often coincide, but at times they do not.

Commentaries

The basic commentary always before me as I worked was the three-volume edition by John Conington and Henry Nettleship, *P. Vergili Maronis opera. The Works of Virgil with a Commentary*. Vol. 1 has introductory material, the *Eclogues*, and the *Georgics;* Vol. 2, the *Aeneid* 1–6; Vol. 3, the *Aeneid* 7–12. (Vol. 1, 5th ed. further revised by F. Haverfield, London 1898; Vol. 2, 4th ed. London 1884; Vol. 3, 3rd ed. London 1883. All three vols. repr. Hildesheim 1963.) Other commentaries consulted were: J. W. Mackail, *The Aeneid* (Oxford 1930); T. E. Page, *The Aeneid of Virgil* (2 vols. 1900; latest repr. London and New York 1964); Chr. Gottl. Heyne, *P. Virgilii Maronis opera* (5 vols. 4th ed. edited by G. P. E. Wagner, Leipzig and London 1830–1841; repr. Hildesheim 1968), with the *Aeneid* commentary in Vols. 2 and 3. Servius and Servius Danielis were consulted in Vols. 1 and 2 of G. Thilo's edition, *Servii Grammatici qui feruntur in Vergilii carmina commentarii* (3 vols., the last in

two parts, with the second part edited by G. Hagen, 1881–
1902; repr. Leipzig and Berlin, 1923; repr. Hildesheim 1961)
and in the two volumes that have appeared so far of *Servia-
norum in Vergilii carmina commentatorium editionis Harvardi-
anae* (Vol. 2, with seven editors, covering *Aeneid* 1–2, Lancas-
ter, Pa. 1946; Vol. 3, edited by A. F. Stocker and A. H. Travis,
covering *Aeneid* 3–5, Oxford 1965). For a brief, clear discussion
of the Servius and Servius Danielis question see Arthur F.
Stocker, "Servius servus magistrorum," *Vergilius* 9 (1963) 7–
14. Also used: James Henry, *Aeneidea* (4 vols. plus an Appendix
volume, London-Dublin-Meissen 1873–1892).

Editions and commentaries on individual books of the *Aeneid*
which I used: Book 1, R. S. Conway (Cambridge 1935); Book
2, R. G. Austin (Oxford 1964); Book 3, R. D. Williams (Oxford
1962); Book 4, Corso Buscaroli (*Il libro di Didone*, Milan
1932), A. S. Pease (Cambridge, Mass. 1935), Ettore Paratore
(Rome 1947), R. G. Austin (Oxford 1955), and Alfred Schmitz
(*Infelix Dido*, Gembloux 1960); Book 5, R. D. Williams (Ox-
ford 1960); Book 6, Eduard Norden (3rd ed. 1927 but with
preface dated 1928; 4th ed. Darmstadt 1957), the finest edition
we have of any of the books of the *Aeneid*, with supplementary
material that is invaluable; Book 7, W. Warde Fowler (*Virgil's
Gathering of the Clans*, Oxford 1916); Book 8, W. Warde
Fowler (*Aeneas at the Site of Rome*, Oxford 1917); Book 12,
W. Warde Fowler (*The Death of Turnus*, Oxford 1919) and
W. S. Maguiness (London 1953).

Texts

Editions of the *Aeneid*—alone or as part of the complete works
—primarily useful for their texts were: F. A. Hirtzel, *P. Vergili
Maronis opera* (Oxford 1900; often reprinted); Remigio Sab-
badini (3rd ed. edited by L. Castiglioni, Turin and elsewhere
1945); H. R. Fairclough, *Virgil* (2 vols. 2nd ed. London and
Cambridge, Mass. 1934; often reprinted), the Loeb Classics
edition with facing English translation in prose. Hirtzel's Ox-
ford Classical Texts edition has now been "replaced" by R. A. B.
Mynor's *P. Vergili Maronis opera* (Oxford 1969), which ap-
peared too late for my use. I have *usually* followed Fairclough's
text.

Concordance and dictionaries

The concordance used was M. N. Wetmore, *Index verborum
Vergilianus* (New Haven 1911; repr. 1930; repr. Darmstadt
1961). Dictionaries consulted: H. Merguet, *Lexicon zu Vergilius*
(1912; repr. Hildesheim 1960); the larger G. A. Koch, *Voll-
ständiges Wörterbuch zu den Gedichten des P. Vergilius Maro*
(5th ed. Hannover 1875); the smaller G. A. Koch, *Schulwörter-*

buch zur Aeneide, ed. V. H. Koch (2nd ed. revised by H. Georges, Hannover 1890); and the standard C. T. Lewis and C. Short, *A Latin Dictionary* (Oxford 1879; often reprinted). The first fascicle of the Oxford Latin Dictionary, now in progress, appeared in 1968, too late for much use.

Early lives of Virgil
For the texts of the early lives of Virgil, see the edition by Colin Hardie, *Vitae Vergilianae antiquae* (latest ed. Oxford 1966).

Secondary works
The following selection of secondary works covers Virgil's art, life, and times. (I have not had space here to note works on Virgil's after-life on earth, his influence, and on the translations of Virgil.) Books are listed in chronological order (following the dates of the first edition), but where more than one work of a man is listed, all his titles follow immediately. Starred items are those most useful for the beginning student of Virgil: C.-A. Sainte-Beuve, *Etude sur Virgile* (1857; 3rd ed. Paris 1878); W. Y. Sellar, *The Roman Poets of the Augustan Age: Virgil* (1877; 3rd ed. Oxford 1897); T. R. Glover, *Virgil* (London and New York 1912; revised ed. of *Studies in Virgil,* London 1904); Richard Heinze, *Virgils epische Technik* 1903; 3rd. ed. Leipzig 1915; repr. with the sole addition of a paragraph noting that no changes have been made, Leipzig 1928; repr. Darmstadt 1957); A. Bellesort, *Virgile, son oeuvre et son temps* (Paris 1920); Tenney Frank, *Vergil: A Biography* (1922; repr. New York 1965); A. Cartault, *L'art de Virgile dans l'Enéide* (2 vols. Paris 1926); D. L. Drew, *The Allegory of the Aeneid* (Oxford 1927); Henry W. Prescott, *The Development of Virgil's Art* (Chicago 1927) using Heinze's work freely, and therefore very useful for those without German; John Sparrow, *Half-lines and Repetitions in Virgil* (Oxford 1931); W. F. Jackson Knight, *Vergil: Epic and Anthropology,* ed. John Christie (London 1967) reprints, with corrections, his *Vergil's Troy: Essays on the Second Book of the Aeneid* (1932), *Cumaëan Gates: A Reference of the Sixth Aeneid to the Initiation Pattern* (1936), and "The Holy City of the East," which first appeared in *Vergilius 2* (January 1939); also W. F. Jackson Knight's *Accentual Symmetry in Vergil* (1939; repr. Oxford 1950) and his richest work on Virgil's style, * *Roman Vergil* (1944; revised ed. London 1966); Cyril Bailey, **Religion in Virgil* (Oxford 1935); L.-A. Constans, *L'Enéide de Virgile* (Paris 1938); André Cordier, *Etudes sur le vocabulaire épique dans l'Enéide* (Paris 1939); Ronald Syme, * *The Roman Revolution* (1939; latest repr. London-Oxford-New York 1968); C. M. Bowra, *From Virgil to Milton* (London 1945) 1–85; Ettore Paratore, *Virgilio*

(1945; 3rd ed. Florence 1961); Robert W. Cruttwell, *Virgil's Mind at Work* (Oxford 1946); Viktor Pöschl, *Die Dichtkunst Virgils: Bild und Symbol in der Aeneis* (1950; 2nd ed. Vienna 1964), Eng. tr. by Gerda Seligson from the first edition as * *The Art of Vergil: Image and Symbol in the Aeneid* (Ann Arbor 1962); A. M. Guillemin, *Virgile* (Paris 1951); Jacques Perret, *Virgile, l'homme et l'oeuvre* (Paris 1952); Karl Büchner, *P. Vergilius Maro, der Dichter der Römer* (1955, as article on Virgil in Pauly-Wissowa, *Realencyclopädie der classischen Alter-tumwissenschaft;* repr. separately Stuttgart 1960), a blessing; George E. Duckworth, *Structural Patterns and Proportions in Vergil's Aeneid* (Ann Arbor 1962), a work that will at some points seem maniacal to many and, to use the Russian Formal-ists' term, insufficiently "motivated" even to those who—like my-self—are very bound to structure; more consistently "motivated" are Duckworth's "Vergil's Subjective Style and Its Relation to Meter," *Vergilius* 12 (1966) 1–9, with useful extensions of the considerations on symmetry in the hexameter line in C. G. Cooper's *An Introduction to the Latin Hexameter* (Melbourne 1952), and Duckworth's recent *Vergil and Classical Hexameter Poetry: A Study in Metrical Variety* (Ann Arbor, 1969); Kenneth Quinn, * *Latin Explorations* (London 1963), for Chapter 2 on Dido and especially Chapter 4 on "The Tempo of Virgilian Epic," and his * *Virgil's "Aeneid": A Critical De-scription* (Ann Arbor 1968); Thomas Halter, *Form und Gehalt in Vergils Aeneis* (München 1963); Pierre Boyancé, *La religion de Virgile* (Paris 1963); Franz Josef Worstbrock, *Elemente einer Poetik der Aeneis* (Münster, Westf. 1963); Brooks Otis, * *Virgil, A Study in Civilized Poetry* (Oxford 1963 on title page, 1964 on copyright page); Georg Nicolaus Knauer, *Die Aeneis und Homer* (Göttingen 1964); Armando Salvatore, *In-troduzione alla lettura di Virgilio* (Naples 1965); Michael C. J. Putnam, * *The Poetry of the Aeneid* (Cambridge, Mass. 1966), on Books 2, 5, 8, 12; Steele Commager, ed., * *Virgil: A Collec-tion of Critical Essays* (Englewood Cliffs, N.J. 1966), extremely convenient for the essays it reprints by C. M. Bowra, C. S. Lewis, Wendell Clausen, Brooks Otis, Adam Parry, Bernard Knox, R. A. Brooks, and Viktor Pöschl—and, therefore a fine starting place for the general reader; Jean-Paul Brisson, *Virgile* (Paris 1966); Georges Dumézil, *Mythe et epopée: l'idéologie des trois fonc-tions dans les épopées des peuples indo-européens* (Paris 1968), especially pp. 337–447 on the last six books of the *Aeneid;* Wil-liam S. Anderson, * *The Art of the Aeneid* (Englewood Cliffs, N.J. 1969), a brief, modest, clear work for students, but with some indications in the last chapter, on "Translation and Ver-gilian Style," that were—with Quinn on Virgilian tempo—the outside words closest to my aims in this translation; Donald R. Dudley, ed., * *Virgil* (New York 1969), a collection of essays especially useful for the contributions by Brooks Otis, A. J. Gossage, J. H. Whitfield, R. D. Williams, and W. F. Jackson Knight, supplementing the Commager collection noted above.

Bibliographies

For further bibliographical indications on works on Virgil in this century, see the following sources: G. Mambelli, *Gli studi virgiliani nel secolo XX: contributo ad una bibliografia generale* (2 vols. Florence 1940); continuing where Mambelli left off, George E. Duckworth, *Recent Work on Vergil: A Bibliographical Survey, 1940–56*, reprinted from *The Classical World* 51 (1958), and *Recent Work on Vergil* (*1957–1963*), reprinted from *The Classical World* 57 (1964), with both reprints available very cheaply from *The Classical World* or the Vergilian Society, Exeter, N.H. For work past 1963 see the annual volumes of *L'année philologique*, with the most recent volume (Vol. 38, Paris 1969) covering 1967; and the annual bibliographies by Alexander G. McKay in *Vergilius*, the Vergilian Society journal. For the period covered by Mambelli and Duckworth also consult: S. Lambrino, *Bibliographie classique des années 1896–1914. Première partie: auteurs et textes* (Paris 1951); J. Marouzeau, *Dix années de bibliographie classique: 1914–1924* (2 vols. Paris 1927–1928; repr. Paris 1969); and the issues of *L'année philologique* covering the years from 1924 on. R. D. Williams has done a pamphlet survey of recent Virgilian scholarship, *Virgil*, Greece and Rome, New Surveys in the Classics, No. 1, 1967; and Jane Ellen Heffner with Mason Hammond and M. C. J. Putnam has compiled "A Bibliographical Handlist on Vergil's *Aeneid* for Teachers and Students in Secondary Schools," *The Classical World* 60 (May 1967) 377–388. Still useful, too, the annotated bibliography in Jacques Perret, *Virgile, l'homme et l'oeuvre* (Paris 1952) 168–188, a volume already cited above.

At the end of any book list on Virgil, one should remember these words of Heyne: "*difficile est Virgilium et sine interprete recte legere, et cum interprete*"; "it is hard to read Virgil right without an interpreter—and with one."